To my father, who taught me to think, and my mother, who gave me the courage to dream.

To my wife, Sue, who always brings out the best in me.

To my daughter Ava, who kept me on the right track by asking, "Are you finished with the book yet?"

To my daughter Lili, who brings joy to our lives with her smiles.

OBJECT ORIENTED SYSTEMS DEVELOPMENT

OBJECT ORIENTED SYSTEMS DEVELOPMENT

Ali Bahrami

Boeing Applied Research & Technology

Irwin McGraw-Hill

Boston   Burr Ridge, IL   Dubuque, IA   Madison, WI New York   San Francisco   St. Louis
Bangkok   Bogotá   Caracas   Lisbon   London   Madrid   Mexico City
Milan   New Delhi   Seoul   Singapore   Sydney   Taipei   Toronto

Irwin/McGraw-Hill

A Division of The McGraw·Hill Companies

Vice president/Editor-in-chief: *Michael W. Junior*
Senior sponsoring editor: *Rick Williamson*
Developmental editor: *Christine Wright*
Marketing manager: *Jodi McPherson*
Project managers: *Christine Parker/Alisa Watson*
Production supervisor: *Michael R. McCormick*
Cover designer: *Steven Vena/SrV Unlimited Design*
Supplemental coordinator: *Carol Loreth*
Compositor: *York Graphic Services, Inc.*
Typeface: *10.5/12 Times Roman*
Printer: *R. R. Donnelley & Sons Company*

OBJECT ORIENTED SYSTEMS DEVELOPMENT

This book is printed on acid-free paper.

2 3 4 5 6 7 8 9 0 DOC/DOC 3 2 1 0

ISBN 0-256-25348-X

Library of Congress Cataloging-in-Publication Data

Bahrami, Ali.
    Object oriented systems development / Ali Bahrami.
      p. cm.
    Includes index.
    ISBN 0-256-25348-X
    1. System design.   2. Object-oriented programming (Computer science) I. Title.
QA76.9.S88B33 1999
005.1'2—dc21   98-43126

http://www.mhhe.com

CONTENTS

PART TWO

Methodology, Modeling, and Unified Modeling Language

PART FOUR

Object-Oriented Design

PREFACE

Over the last 20 years, software has become increasingly complex. Today's applications are much more sophisticated and developed to more demanding requirements than in the past. Software development techniques, tools, and technologies are changing rapidly. The software development methods we will use in the next millennium will differ significantly from current methods, and we have no crystal ball to tell us what methods or approaches will be used 20 years (or even 10 years) from now. However, it is apparent that object-oriented development and its core concepts are here to stay. Many schools have recognized this and made the object-oriented systems development course an essential part of the computer information systems or computer science programs. This book is intended for an introductory course in object-oriented systems development at the junior, senior, or first-year graduate level. The main goal of this book is to provide a clear description of the concepts underlying object-oriented systems development.

This book is not centered around any particular programming language or CASE tools. Instead, it discusses fundamental concepts that are applicable to a variety of systems. However, the approach used in this book is based on the best practices that have proven successful in system development and more specifically the work done by Booch, Rumbaugh, and Jacobson. Furthermore, the book uses the Object Management Group's unified modeling language (UML) for modeling, describing, analyzing, and designing an application.

This book has a number of unique features:

- Use of the unified modeling language.
- A comprehensive treatment of the entire system life cycle using object-oriented techniques (with the exception of implementation).
- Inclusion of the Popkin System Architect CASE tool (as a software packaging option).

- Coverage of introductory and essential topics as well as advanced subjects in object-oriented systems development.
- Use of a use-case-driven approach.
- Use of a running case study for applying the lessons learned.
- Appendix providing a documentation template.

STRUCTURE OF THE BOOK

The book contains 14 chapters with a running case study for applying the concepts learned. Each chapter concludes with a summary, a list of the key terms discussed in the chapter, review questions, and problems that require students to apply their knowledge based on the chapter material. The chapters are grouped into five parts.

Part One

The first part provides an overview of object-oriented systems development and discusses why we should study it. In this part, we also look at object basics and the systems development life cycle. Part One consists of Chapter 1, "Overview of Object-Oriented Systems Development"; Chapter 2, "Object Basics"; and Chapter 3, "Object-Oriented Systems Development Life Cycle."

Part Two

The second part introduces various object-oriented methodologies, including the unified approach, which will be used in this text, and an introduction to unified modeling language (UML). This part consists of Chapter 4, "Object-Oriented Methodologies," and Chapter 5, "Unified Modeling Language."

Part Three

The third part introduces object-oriented analysis, which is the process of extracting the needs of a system and what the system must do to satisfy the users' requirements. The goal of object-oriented analysis first is to understand the domain of the problem and the system's responsibilities by understanding how the users use or will use the system. Next, the classes that make up the system must be identified, as well as their behaviors, the relationships among them, and their structure. This part consists of Chapter 6, "Object-Oriented Analysis Process: Identifying Use Cases"; Chapter 7, "Object Analysis: Classification"; and Chapter 8, "Identifying Object Relationships, Attributes, and Methods."

Part Four

The fourth part covers object-oriented design. In this part, we will learn that the classes identified during analysis provide us a framework for the design phase. This part consists of Chapter 9, "The Object-Oriented Design Process and Design Axioms"; Chapter 10, "Designing Classes"; Chapter 11, "Access Layer: Object Storage and Object Interoperability"; and Chapter 12, "View Layer: Designing Interface Objects."

Part Five

In this part, different dimensions of software quality and testing are discussed. Testing may be conducted for different reasons. *Quality assurance* testing looks for potential problems in a proposed design. *Usability testing*, on the other hand, tests how well the interface fits user needs and expectations. To ensure *user satisfaction*, we must measure user satisfaction along the way as the design takes form. Part Five consists of Chapter 13, "Software Quality Assurance," and Chapter 14, "System Usability and Measuring User Satisfaction."

Appendices

The book includes two appendices. Appendix A provides a template for documenting a system requirement. The template can be to create an effective system document. Finally, Appendix B provides an overview of Windows and graphical user interface (GUI) basics.

INSTRUCTIONAL SUPPORT MATERIAL

The text is accompanied by an Instructor's CD-ROM. The CD-ROM contains files for an Instructor's Manual consisting of a lecture outline, teaching suggestions, comprehensive Power Point classroom presentation files, the user satisfaction test spreadsheet (see Chapter 14), answers to selected problems and questions, and test bank and computerized testing software with multiple-choice and short-answer questions.

SOFTWARE PACKAGING OPTIONS

Popkin's System Architect CASE tool is available as a packaging option with this text.

ACKNOWLEDGMENTS

No textbook can be published without the involvement of many people, and I would like to acknowledge those who have helped bring this book to fruition. I am grateful, first, to my wife Sue and my older daughter Ava, who have put up with me for the past four years. The publication of this book would not have been possible without the vision and foresight of my editor, Rick Williamson, and the expertise of developmental editor Christine Wright. I am grateful for their support in this project. My special thanks go to Christine Parker and Alisa Watson, the project managers who kept everything on time.

This book has taken four years to complete. It was reviewed by a number of reviewers at different stages of its development and rewritten three times based on the reviewers' comments and suggestions. I thank the reviewers for their constructive comments and encouragement. Their comments have materially enhanced the final copy of this book. These reviewers include

Joseph H. Austin, Jr., Ambassador University

Chris Basso, Signex Corporation

John Carson, George Washington University

Kevin C. Dittman, Purdue University

Jane Fedorowicz, Bentley College

Bill C. Hardgrave, University of Arkansas–Fayetteville

Christopher G. Jones, Utah Valley State College

Jinwoo Kim, Yonsei University, Korea

Michael V. Mannino, University of Colorado–Denver

Stevan Mrdalj, Eastern Michigan University

Richard G. Ramirez, Iowa State University

Elmer G. Swartzmeyer, Georgia State University

Jos Von Hillegersberg, Erasmus University, the Netherlands

Janet Wesson, University of Port Elizabeth, South Africa

David F. Wood, Robert Morris College

This book has been tested for three semesters in my object-oriented software development course at Rhode Island College. I would like to thank all the students who provided me with excellent feedback. Friends and colleagues, who have given me support, ideas, and comments, were invaluable. The friends who have materially contributed to this project include Dr. Crist Costa and Professor Jules Cohen.

Although my father, who encouraged me to write this book, could not see its finish, his spirit was with me throughout the project and kept me going. Last but not least, my youngest daughter was born during the final stages of the book. Her unconditional love energized me to finish this book.

Ali Bahrami
Boeing Applied Research & Technology

PART ONE

INTRODUCTION

The objective of Part I is to provide an overview of object-oriented systems development and why we should study it. In this part, we also look at object basics and the systems development life cycle. Part I consists of Chapters 1, 2, and 3.

CHAPTER 1

An Overview of Object-Oriented Systems Development

Chapter Objectives

You should be able to define and understand

- The object-oriented philosophy and why we need to study it.
- The unified approach.

1.1 INTRODUCTION

Software development is dynamic and always undergoing major change. The methods we will use in the future no doubt will differ significantly from those currently in practice. We can anticipate which methods and tools are going to succeed, but we cannot predict the future. Factors other than just technical superiority will likely determine which concepts prevail.

Today a vast number of tools and methodologies are available for systems development. *Systems development* refers to all activities that go into producing an information systems solution. Systems development activities consist of systems analysis, modeling, design, implementation, testing, and maintenance. A *software development methodology* is a series of processes that, if followed, can lead to the development of an application. The software processes describe how the work is to be carried out to achieve the original goal based on the system requirements. Furthermore, each process consists of a number of steps and rules that should be performed during development. The software development process will continue to exist as long as the development system is in operation.

This chapter provides an overview of object-oriented systems development and discusses why we should study it. Furthermore, we study the unified approach, which is the methodology used in this book for learning about object-oriented systems development.

1.2 TWO ORTHOGONAL VIEWS OF THE SOFTWARE

Object-oriented systems development methods differ from traditional development techniques in that the traditional techniques view software as a collection of programs (or functions) and isolated data. What is a program? Niklaus Wirth [8], the inventor of Pascal, sums it up eloquently in his book entitled, interestingly enough, *Algorithms + Data Structures = Programs*: "A software system is a set of mechanisms for performing certain action on certain data."

This means that there are two different, yet complementary ways to view software construction: We can focus primarily on the functions or primarily on the data. The heart of the distinction between traditional system development methodologies and newer object-oriented methodologies lies in their primary focus, where the traditional approach focuses on the functions of the system—What is it doing?—object-oriented systems development centers on the object, which combines data and functionality. As we will see, this seemingly simple shift in focus radically changes the process of software development.

1.3 OBJECT-ORIENTED SYSTEMS DEVELOPMENT METHODOLOGY

Object-oriented development offers a different model from the traditional software development approach, which is based on functions and procedures. In simplified terms, object-oriented systems development is a way to develop software by building self-contained modules or objects that can be easily replaced, modified, and reused. Furthermore, it encourages a view of the world as a system of cooperative and collaborating objects. In an object-oriented environment, software is a collection of discrete objects that encapsulate their data as well as the functionality to model real-world "objects." An object orientation yields important benefits to the practice of software construction. Each object has attributes (data) and methods (functions). Objects are grouped into classes; in object-oriented terms, we discover and describe the classes involved in the problem domain.

In an object-oriented system, everything is an object and each object is responsible for itself. For example, every Windows application needs Windows objects that can open themselves on screen and either display something or accept input. A Windows object is responsible for things like opening, sizing, and closing itself. Frequently, when a window displays something, that something also is an object (a chart, for example). A chart object is responsible for things like maintaining its data and labels and even for drawing itself.

The object-oriented environment emphasizes its cooperative philosophy by allocating tasks among the objects of the applications. In other words, rather than writing a lot of code to do all the things that have to be done, you tend to create a lot of helpers that take on an active role, a spirit, and that form a community whose interactions become the application. Instead of saying, "System, compute the payroll of this employee," you tell the employee object, "compute your payroll." This has a powerful effect on the way we approach software development.

1.4 WHY AN OBJECT ORIENTATION?

Object-oriented methods enable us to create sets of objects that work together synergistically to produce software that better model their problem domains than similar systems produced by traditional techniques. The systems are easier to adapt to changing requirements, easier to maintain, more robust, and promote greater design and code reuse. Object-oriented development allows us to create modules of functionality. Once objects are defined, it can be taken for granted that they will perform their desired functions and you can seal them off in your mind like black boxes. Your attention as a programmer shifts to what they do rather than how they do it. Here are some reasons why object orientation works [3–7]:

- *Higher level of abstraction*. The top-down approach supports abstraction at the function level. The object-oriented approach supports abstraction at the object level. Since objects encapsulate both data (attributes) and functions (methods), they work at a higher level of abstraction. The development can proceed at the object level and ignore the rest of the system for as long as necessary. This makes designing, coding, testing, and maintaining the system much simpler.
- *Seamless transition among different phases of software development*. The traditional approach to software development requires different styles and methodologies for each step of the process. Moving from one phase to another requires a complex transition of perspective between models that almost can be in different worlds. This transition not only can slow the development process but also increases the size of the project and the chance for errors introduced in moving from one language to another. The object-oriented approach, on the other hand, essentially uses the same language to talk about analysis, design, programming, and database design. This seamless approach reduces the level of complexity and redundancy and makes for clearer, more robust system development.
- *Encouragement of good programming techniques*. A class in an object-oriented system carefully delineates between its interface (specifications of *what* the class can do) and the implementation of that interface (*how* the class does what it does). The routines and attributes within a class are held together tightly. In a properly designed system, the classes will be grouped into subsystems but remain independent; therefore, changing one class has no impact on other classes, and so, the impact is minimized. However, the object-oriented approach is not a panacea; nothing is magical here that will promote perfect design or perfect code. But, by raising the level of abstraction from the function level to the object level and by focusing on the real-world aspects of the system, the object-oriented method tends to promote clearer designs, which are easier to implement, and provides for better overall communication. Using object-oriented language is not strictly necessary to achieve the benefits of an object orientation. However, an object-oriented language such as C++, Smalltalk, or Java adds support for object-oriented design and makes it easier to produce more modular and reusable code via the concept of class and inheritance [5].
- *Promotion of reusability*. Objects are reusable because they are modeled directly out of a real-world problem domain. Each object stands by itself or within a small circle of peers (other objects). Within this framework, the class does not

concern itself with the rest of the system or how it is going to be used within a particular system. This means that classes are designed generically, with reuse as a constant background goal. Furthermore, the object orientation adds inheritance, which is a powerful technique that allows classes to be built from each other, and therefore, only differences and enhancements between the classes need to be designed and coded. All the previous functionality remains and can be reused without change.

1.5 OVERVIEW OF THE UNIFIED APPROACH

This book is organized around the unified approach for a better understanding of object-oriented concepts and system development. The *unified approach* (UA) is a methodology for software development that is proposed by the author, and used in this book. The UA, based on methodologies by Booch, Rumbaugh, and Jacobson, tries to combine the best practices, processes, and guidelines along with the Object Management Group's unified modeling language. The *unified modeling language* (UML) is a set of notations and conventions used to describe and model an application. However, the UML does not specify a methodology or what steps to follow to develop an application; that would be the task of the UA. Figure 1–1 depicts the essence of the unified approach. The heart of the UA is Jacobson's use case. The use case represents a typical interaction between a user and a computer system to capture the users' goals and needs. In its simplest usage, you capture a use case by talking to typical users and discussing the various ways they might want to use the system. The use cases are entered into all other activities of the UA.

The main advantage of an object-oriented system is that the class tree is dynamic and can grow. Your function as a developer in an object-oriented environment is to foster the growth of the class tree by defining new, more specialized classes to perform the tasks your applications require. After your first few projects, you will accumulate a repository or class library of your own, one that performs the operations your applications most often require. At that point, creating additional applications will require no more than assembling classes from the class library. Additionally, applying lessons learned from past developmental efforts to future projects will improve the quality of the product and reduce the cost and development time.

This book uses a layered architecture to develop applications. *Layered architecture* is an approach to software development that allows us to create objects that represent tangible elements of the business independent of how they are represented to the user through an interface or physically stored in a database. The layered approach consists of view or user interface, business, and access layers. This approach reduces the interdependence of the user interface, database access, and business control; therefore, it allows for a more robust and flexible system.

1.6 ORGANIZATION OF THIS BOOK

Chapter 2 introduces the basics of the object-oriented approach and why we should study it. Furthermore, we learn that the main thrust of the object-oriented approach

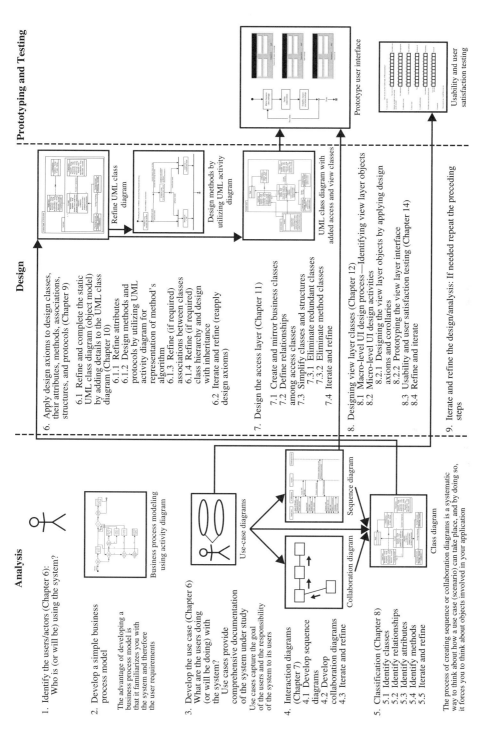

FIGURE 1-1

The unified approach road map.

is to provide a set of objects that closely reflects the underlying application. For example, the user who needs to develop a financial application could develop it in a financial language with considerably less difficulty. An object-oriented approach allows the base concepts of the language to be extended to include ideas closer to those of its application. You can define a new data type (object) in terms of an existing data type until it appears that the language directly supports the primitives of the application. The real advantage of using an object-oriented approach is that you can build on what you already have.

Chapter 3 explains the object-oriented system development life cycle (SDLC). The essence of the software process is the transformation of users' needs in the application domain into a software solution that is executed in the implementation domain. The concept of use case or set of scenarios can be a valuable tool for understanding the users' needs. We will learn that an object-oriented approach requires a more rigorous process up front to do things right. We need to spend more time gathering requirements, developing a requirements model, developing an analysis model, then turning that into the design model. This chapter concludes Part I (Introduction) of the book.

Chapter 4 is the first chapter of Part II (Methodology, Modeling, and Unified Modeling Language). Chapter 4 looks at the current trend in object-oriented methodologies, which is toward combining the best aspects of today's most popular methods. We also take a closer look at the unified approach.

Chapter 5 describes the unified modeling language in detail. The UML merges the best of the notations developed by the so-called three amigos—Booch, Rumbaugh, and Jacobson—in their attempt to unify their modeling efforts. The unified modeling language originally was called the *unified method* (UM). However, the methodologies that were an integral part of the Booch, Rumbaugh, and Jacobson methods were separated from the notation; and the unification efforts of Booch, Jacobson, and Rumbaugh eventually focused more on the graphical modeling language and its semantics and less on the underlying process and methodology. They sum up the reason for the name as follows:

The UML is intended to be a universal language for modeling systems, meaning that it can express models of many different kinds and purposes, just as a programming language or a natural language can be used in many different ways. Thus, a single universal process for all styles of development did not seem possible or even desirable: what works for a shrink-wrapped software project is probably wrong for a one-of-a-kind globally distributed, human-critical family of systems. However, the UML can be used to express the artifacts of all of these different processes, namely, the models that are produced. Our move to the UML does not mean that we are ignoring the issues of process. Indeed, the UML assumes a process that is use case driven, architecture-centered, iterative and incremental. It is our observation that the details of this general development process must be adapted to the particular development culture or application domain of a specific organization. We are also working on process issues, but we have chosen to separate the modeling language from the process. By making the modeling language and its process nearly independent, we therefore give users and other methodologists considerable degrees of freedom to craft a specific process yet still use a common language of expression. This is not unlike blueprints for buildings: there is a commonly understood language for blueprints, but there are a number of different ways to build, depending upon the nature of what is being built and who is doing the building. This is why we say that the UML is essentially the language of blueprints for software. [2, p. 5]

The UML has become the standard notation for object-oriented modeling systems. It is an evolving notation that is still under development. Chapter 5 concludes this part of the book.

Chapter 6 is the first chapter of Part III (Object-Oriented Analysis: Use-Case Driven). The goal of object-oriented analysis is to first understand the domain of the problem and the system's responsibilities by understanding how the users use or will use the system. The main task of the analysis is to capture a complete, unambiguous, and consistent picture of the requirements of the system. This is accomplished by constructing several models of the system. These models concentrate on describing what the system does rather than how it does it. Separating the behavior of a system from the way it is implemented requires viewing the system from the users' perspective rather than that of the machine. This analysis is focused on the domain of the problem and concerned with externally visible behavior [1]. Other activities of object-oriented analysis are to identify the objects that make up the system, their behaviors, and their relationships. Chapter 6 explains the object-oriented analysis process and provides a detailed discussion of use-case driven object-oriented analysis. The use case is a typical interaction between a user and a computer system utilized to capture users' goals and needs. The use-case model represents the users' view of the system or the users' needs. In its simplest usage, you capture a use case by talking to typical users and discussing the various things they might want to do with the system. The heart of the UA is the Jacobson's use case. The use cases are a part of all other activities of the UA (see Figure 1–1).

The main activities of the object-oriented analysis are to identify classes in the system. Finding classes is one of the hardest activities in the analysis. There is no such a thing as the *perfect* class structure or the *right* set of objects. Nevertheless, several techniques, such as the use-case driven approach or the noun phrase and other classification methods, can offer us guidelines and general rules for identifying the classes in the given problem domain. Furthermore, identifying classes is an iterative process, and as you gain more experience, you will get better at identifying classes. In Chapter 7, we study four approaches to identifying classes: the noun phrase, class categorization, use-case driven, and class responsibilities collaboration approaches.

In an object-oriented environment, objects take on an active role in a system. These objects do not exist in isolation but interact with each other. Indeed, their interactions and relationships become the application. Chapter 8 describes the guidelines for identifying object relationships, attributes, and methods. Chapter 8 concludes the object-oriented analysis part of the book.

Chapter 9 is the first chapter of Part IV (Object-Oriented Design). In this part of the book, we learn how to elevate the analysis model into actual objects that can perform the required task. Emphasis is shifted from the application domain to implementation. The classes identified during analysis provide a framework for the design phase. Object-oriented design and object-oriented analysis are distinct disciplines, but they are intertwined as well. Object-oriented development is highly incremental; in other words, you start with object-oriented analysis, model it, create an object-oriented design, then some more of each, again and again, gradually refining and completing the models of the system. Part IV describes object-oriented design. Other activities of object-oriented design are the user interface design and prototype and the design of the database access. Chapter 9 explains the object-oriented design process and design axioms. The main objective of the axiomatic approach is to formalize the design process and assist in establishing a scientific foundation for the object-oriented design process, so as to provide a fundamental basis of the creation of systems. These guidelines, with incremental and evolutionary styles of software development, will provide you a powerful way for designing systems.

In Chapter 10, we look at guidelines and approaches that you can use to design objects and their methods. Although the design concepts to be discussed in this chapter are general, we concentrate on designing the business objects. Chapter 10 describes the first step of the object-oriented design process, which consists of applying design axioms to design objects and their attributes, methods, associations, structures, and protocols.

Chapter 11 introduces issues regarding object storage, relational and object-oriented database management systems, and object interoperability. We then look at current trends to combine object and relational systems to provide a very practical solution to the problem of object storage. We conclude the chapter with how to design the access layer objects. The main idea behind the access layer is to create a set of classes that know how to communicate with the data source, regardless of their format, whether it is a file, relational database, mainframe, or Internet. The access classes must be able to translate any data-related requests from the business layer into the appropriate protocol for data access. Access layer classes provide easy migration to emerging distributed object technology, such as CORBA and DCOM. Furthermore, they should be able to address the (relatively) modest needs of two-tier client-server architectures as well as the difficult demands of fine-grained, peer-to-peer distributed-object architectures.

The main goals of view layer objects are to display and obtain the information needed in an accessible, efficient manner. The design of your user interface and view layer objects, more than anything else, affects how a user interacts and therefore experiences the application. A well-designed user interface has visual appeal that motivates users to use the application. In Chapter 12, we learn how to design the view layer by mapping the user interface objects to the view layer objects; we look at user interface design rules, which are based on several design axioms, and finally at the guidelines for developing a graphical user interface. This chapter concludes the object-oriented design part of the book.

Chapter 13 is the first chapter of Part V (Software Quality), which discusses different aspects of software quality and testing. In Chapter 13, we look at testing strategies, the impact of object orientation on software quality, and guidelines for developing comprehensive test cases and plans that can detect and identify potential problems before delivering the software to the users.

Usability testing is different from quality assurance testing in that, rather than finding programming defects, you assess how well the interface or the software fits users' needs and expectations. Furthermore, to ensure usability of the system, we must measure user satisfaction throughout the system development. Chapter 14 describes usability and user satisfaction tests. We study how to develop user satisfaction and usability tests based on the use cases identified during the analysis phase.

Appendix A contains a template for documenting a system requirement. The template in this appendix is not to replace the documentation capability of a CASE tool but to be used as an example for issues or modeling elements that are needed for creating an effective system document. Finally, Appendix B provides a review of Windows and graphical user interface basics.

1.7 SUMMARY

In an object-oriented environment, software is a collection of discrete objects that encapsulate their data and the functionality to model real-world "objects." Once objects are defined, you can take it for granted that they will perform their desired functions and so seal them off in your mind like black boxes. Your attention as a programmer shifts to what they do rather than how they do it. The object-oriented life cycle encourages a view of the world as a system of cooperative and collaborating agents.

An object orientation produces systems that are easier to evolve, more flexible, more robust, and more reusable than a top-down structure approach. An object orientation

- Allows working at a higher level of abstraction.
- Provides a seamless transition among different phases of software development.
- Encourages good development practices.
- Promotes reusability.

The unified approach (UA) is the methodology for software development proposed and used in this book. Based on the Booch, Rumbaugh, and Jacobson methodologies, the UA consists of the following concepts:

- Use-case driven development.
- Utilizing the unified modeling language for modeling.
- Object-oriented analysis (utilizing use cases and object modeling).
- Object-oriented design.
- Repositories of reusable classes and maximum reuse.
- The layered approach.
- Incremental development and prototyping.
- Continuous testing.

KEY TERMS

Layered architecture (p. 6)
Software development methodology (p. 3)

Unified approach (UA) (p. 6)
Unified modeling language (UML) (p. 6)

REVIEW QUESTIONS

1. What is system development methodology?
2. What are orthogonal views of software?
3. What is the object-oriented systems development methodology?
4. How does the object-oriented approach differ from the traditional top-down approach?
5. What are the advantages of object-oriented development?
6. Describe the components of the unified approach.

PROBLEMS

1. Object-oriented development already is big in industry and will grow bigger in the years to come. More and more companies will use an object-oriented approach to build their complex (multimedia, workflow, database, artificial intelligence, real-time, and client-server) systems. Research the library or WWW to obtain an article about a major company that has used object-oriented technology to build its future information system.
2. Consult the WWW or library to obtain an article on a real-world application that has incorporated object-oriented tools. Write a summary report of your findings.
3. Consult the WWW or library to obtain an article on an object-oriented methodology. Write a summary of your findings.
4. Consult the WWW or library to obtain an article that describes a large software system that was behind schedule, over budget, and failed to achieve the expected functionality. What factors were blamed, and how could the failure have been avoided?
5. Consult the WWW or library to obtain an article on visual and object-oriented programming. Write a paper based on your findings.

REFERENCES

1. Anderson, Michael; and Bergstrand, John. "Formalizing Use Cases with Message Sequence Charts." Master's thesis, Department of Communication Systems at Lund Institute of Technology, 1995.
2. Booch, Grady; Jacobson, Ivar; and Rumbaugh, James. *The Unified Modeling Language, Notation Guide Version 1.1.* http://www.rational.com/uml/html/notation (September 1997).
3. Edwards, John. "Lessons Learned in Practical Application of the OO Paradigm." Object-Oriented Systems Symposium, Washington, DC, January 1990.
4. Graham, Ian. *Object Oriented Methods*, 2d ed. Reading MA: Addison-Wesley Publishing Company, 1994.
5. King, Gary Warren. "Object-Oriented Really Is Better Than Structured." http://www.oz.net/~gking/whyoop.htm (September 20, 1995).
6. Lassesen, Kenneth M. "Leveraging the Mainframe in Business Solutions with Microsoft Access and Visual Basic." *TechEd* (1995).
7. Burnett, Margaret; Goldberg, Adele; and Lewis, Ted, eds. *Visual Object-Oriented Programming: Concepts and Environments.* Englewood Cliffs, NJ: Prentice-Hall/Manning Publications, 1995.
8. Wirth, Niklaus. *Algorithms + Data Structure = Programs.* Englewood Cliffs, NJ: Prentice-Hall, 1975.

CHAPTER 2

Object Basics

Chapter Objectives

You should be able to define and understand
- Why we need to study object-oriented concepts.
- Objects and classes—and their differences.
- Class attributes and methods.
- The concept of messages.
- Class hierarchy inheritance and multiple inheritance.
- Object relationships and associations.
- Encapsulation and information hiding.
- Polymorphism.
- Advantage of the object-oriented approach.
- Aggregations.
- Static and dynamic binding.
- Object persistence.
- Meta-classes.

2.1 INTRODUCTION

If there is a single motivating factor behind object-oriented system development, it is the desire to make software development easier and more natural by raising the level of abstraction to the point where applications can be implemented in the same terms in which they are described by users. Indeed, the name *object* was chosen because "everyone knows what an object is." The real question, then, is not so much "What is an object?" but "What do objects have to do with system development?"

Let us develop the notion of an object through an example. A car is an *object:* a real-world entity, identifiably separate from its surroundings. A car has a well-defined set of attributes in relation to other objects—such as color, manufacturer, cost, and owner—and a well-defined set of things you normally do with it—drive it, lock it, tow it, and carry passengers in it. In an object model, we call the former *properties* or *attributes* and the latter *procedures* or *methods*. **Properties** (or **attributes**) describe the state (data) of an object. **Methods** (procedures) define its behavior. Stocks and bonds might be objects for a financial investment application. Parts and assemblies might be objects of a bill of materials application. Therefore, we can conclude that an object is whatever an application wants to "talk" about.

2.2 AN OBJECT-ORIENTED PHILOSOPHY

Most programming languages provide programmers with a way of describing processes. Although most programming languages are computationally equivalent (a process describable in one is describable in another), the ease of description, reusability, extensibility, readability, computational efficiency, and ability to maintain the description can vary widely depending on the language used. It has been said that, "One should speak English for business, French for seduction, German for engineering, and Persian for poetry." A similar quip could be made about programming languages.

A language, natural or programming, provides its users a base set of constructs. Many programming languages derive their base ideas from the underlying machine. The machine may "understand" or recognize data types such as integers, floating point numbers, and characters; and the programming language will represent precisely these types as structures. The machine may understand indirect addressing modes or base plus offset addressing; and the programming language correspondingly will represent the concepts of pointers and vectors. Nothing is terribly wrong with this, but these concepts are pretty far removed from those of a typical application. In practical terms, it means that a user or programmer is implementing, say, a financial investment (risk, returns, growth, and the various investment instruments) into the much lower-level primitives of the programming language, like vectors or integers.

It would be marvelous if we could build a machine whose underlying primitives were precisely those of an application. The user who needs to develop a financial application could develop a financial investment machine directly in financial investment machine language with no mental translation at all. Clearly, it is too expensive to design new hardware on a per-application basis. But, it really is not necessary to go this far, because programming languages can bridge the semantic gap between the concepts of the application and those of the underlying machine.

A fundamental characteristic of **object-oriented programming** is that it allows the base concepts of the language to be extended to include ideas and terms closer to those of its applications. New data types can be defined in terms of existing data types until it appears that the language directly supports the primitives of the application. In our financial investment example, a bond (data type) may be defined that has the same understanding within the language as a character data type. A buy operation on a bond can be defined that has the same understanding as the familiar plus (+) operation on a number. Using this data abstraction mechanism, it is possible to create new, higher-level, and more specialized data abstractions. You can work directly in the language, manipulating the kinds of "objects" required by you or your application, without having to constantly struggle to bridge the gap between how to conceive of these objects and how to write the code to represent them.

The fundamental difference between the object-oriented systems and their traditional counterparts is the way in which you approach problems. Most traditional development methodologies are either algorithm centric or data centric. In an *algorithm-centric methodology,* you think of an algorithm that can accomplish the task, then build data structures for that algorithm to use. In a ***data-centric methodology,*** you think how to structure the data, then build the algorithm around that structure.

In an object-oriented system, however, the algorithm and the data structures are packaged together as an object, which has a set of attributes or properties. The state of these attributes is reflected in the values stored in its data structures. In addition, the object has a collection of procedures or methods—things it can do—as reflected in its package of methods. The attributes and methods are equal and inseparable parts of the object; one cannot ignore one for the sake of the other. For example, a car has certain attributes, such as *color, year, model,* and *price,* and can perform a number of operations, such as *go, stop, turn left*, and *turn right*.

The traditional approach to software development tends toward writing a lot of code to do all the things that have to be done. The code is the plans, bricks, and mortar that you use to build structures. You are the only active entity; the code, basically, is just a lot of building materials. The object-oriented approach is more like employing a lot of helpers that take on an active role and form a community whose interactions become the application. Instead of saying, "System, write the value of this number to the screen," we tell the number object, "Write yourself." This has a powerful effect on the way we approach software development.

In summary, object-oriented programming languages bridge the semantic gap between the ideas of the application and those of the underlying machine, and objects represent the application data in a way that is not forced by hardware architecture.

2.3 OBJECTS

The term *object* was first formally utilized in the Simula language, and objects typically existed in Simula programs to simulate some aspect of reality [5]. The term ***object*** means a combination of data and logic that represents some real-world entity. For example, consider a Saab automobile. The Saab can be represented in a computer program as an object. The "data" part of this object would be the car's name, color, number of doors, price, and so forth. The "logic" part of the object could be a collection of programs (show mileage, change mileage, stop, go).

In an object-oriented system, everything is an object: A spreadsheet, a cell in a spreadsheet, a bar chart, a title in a bar chart, a report, a number or telephone number, a file, a folder, a printer, a word or sentence, even a single character all are examples of an object. Each of us deals with objects daily. Some objects, such as a telephone, are so common that we find them in many places. Other objects, like the folders in a file cabinet or the tools we use for home repair, may be located in a certain place [7].

When developing an object-oriented application, two basic questions always arise:

• What objects does the application need?
• What functionality should those objects have?

For example, every Windows application needs Windows objects that can either display something or accept input. Frequently, when a window displays something, that something is an object as well.

Conceptually, each object is responsible for itself. For example, a Windows object is responsible for things like opening, sizing, and closing itself. A chart object is responsible for maintaining its data and labels and even for drawing itself.

Programming in an object-oriented system consists of adding new kinds of objects to the system and defining how they behave. Frequently, these new object classes can be built from the objects supplied by the object-oriented system.

2.4 OBJECTS ARE GROUPED IN CLASSES

Many of us find it fairly natural to partition the world into objects, properties (states), and procedures (behavior). This is a common and useful partitioning or classification. Also, we routinely divide the world along a second dimension: We distinguish classes from instances. When an eagle flies over us, we have no trouble identifying it as an eagle and not an airplane. What is occurring here? Even though we might never have seen this particular bird before, we can immediately identify it as an eagle. Clearly, we have some general idea of what eagles look like, sound like, what they do, and what they are good for—a generic notion of eagles, or what we call the *class* eagle.

Classes are used to distinguish one type of object from another. In the context of object-oriented systems, a *class* is a set of objects that share a common structure and a common behavior; a single object is simply an *instance* of a class [3]. A class is a specification of structure (instance variables), behavior (methods), and inheritance for objects. (Inheritance is discussed later in this chapter.)

Classes are an important mechanism for classifying objects. The chief role of a class is to define the properties and procedures (the state and behavior) and applicability of its instances. The class car, for example, defines the *property* color. Each individual car (formally, each instance of the class car) will have a value for this property, such as maroon, yellow, or white.

In an object-oriented system, a *method* or behavior of an object is defined by its class. Each object is an instance of a class. There may be many different classes.

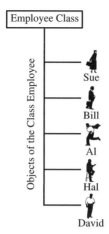

FIGURE 2-1
Sue, Bill, Al, Hal, and David are instances or objects of the class Employee.

Think of a class as an object template (see Figure 2–1). Every object of a given class has the same data format and responds to the same instructions. For example, employees, such as Sue, Bill, Al, Hal, and David all are instances of the class Employee. You can create unlimited instances of a given class. The instructions responded to by each of those instances of employee are managed by the class. The data associated with a particular object is managed by the object itself. For example, you might have two employee objects, one called Al and the other Bill. Each employee object is responsible for its own data, such as social security number, address, and salary. In short, the objects you use in your programs are instances of classes. You can use any of the predefined classes that are part of an object-oriented system or you can create your own.

2.5 ATTRIBUTES: OBJECT STATE AND PROPERTIES

Properties represent the state of an object. Often, we want to refer to the description of these properties rather than how they are represented in a particular programming language. In our example, the properties of a car, such as color, manufacturer, and cost, are abstract descriptions (see Figure 2–2). We could represent

FIGURE 2-2
The attributes of a car object.

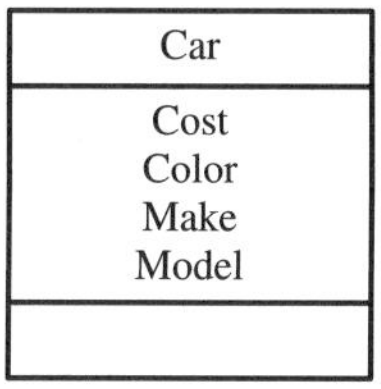

Car
Cost
Color
Make
Model

each property in several ways in a programming language. For color, we could choose to use a sequence of characters such as *red,* or the (stock) number for red paint, or a reference to a full-color video image that paints a red swatch on the screen when displayed. Manufacturer could be denoted by a name, a reference to a manufacturer object, or a corporate tax identification number. Cost could be a floating point number, a fixed point number, or an integer in units of pennies or even lira. The importance of this distinction is that an object's abstract state can be independent of its physical representation.

2.6 OBJECT BEHAVIOR AND METHODS

When we talk about an elephant or a car, we usually can describe the set of things we normally do with it or that it can do on its own. We can drive a car, we can ride an elephant, or the elephant can eat a peanut. Each of these statements is a description of the object's behavior. In the object model, object behavior is described in methods or procedures. A method implements the behavior of an object. Basically, a method is a function or procedure that is defined for a class and typically can access the internal state of an object of that class to perform some operation. *Behavior* denotes the collection of methods that abstractly describes what an object is capable of doing. Each procedure defines and describes a particular behavior of an object. The object, called the *receiver,* is that on which the method operates. Methods encapsulate the behavior of the object, provide interfaces to the object, and hide any of the internal structures and states maintained by the object. Consequently, procedures provide us the means to communicate with an object and access its properties. The use of methods to exclusively access or update properties is considered good programming style, since it limits the impact of any later changes to the representation of the properties.

Objects take responsibility for their own behavior. In an object-oriented system, one does not have to write complicated code or utilize extensive conditional checks through the use of case statements for deciding what function to call based on a data type or class. For example, an employee object knows how to compute its salary. Therefore, to compute an employee salary, all that is required is to send the *computePayroll* "message" to the employee object. This simplification of code simplifies application development and maintenance.

2.7 OBJECTS RESPOND TO MESSAGES

An object's capabilities are determined by the methods defined for it. Methods conceptually are equivalent to the function definitions used in procedural languages. For example, a draw method would tell a chart how to draw itself. However, to do an operation, a message is sent to an object. Objects perform operations in response to messages. For example, when you press on the brake pedal of a car, you send a *stop* message to the car object. The car object knows how to respond to the *stop* message, since brakes have been designed with specialized parts such as brake pads and drums precisely to respond to that message. Sending the same *stop* message to a different object, such as a tree, however, would be meaningless and could result in an unanticipated (if any) response. Following a set of conventions, or protocols, protects the developer or user from unauthorized data manipulation.

Messages essentially are nonspecific function calls: We would send a *draw* message to a chart when we want the chart to draw itself. A message is different from a subroutine call, since different objects can respond to the same message in different ways. For example, cars, motorcycles, and bicycles will all respond to a *stop* message, but the actual operations performed are object specific.

In the top example, depicted in Figure 2–3, we send a *Brake* message to the *Car* object. In the middle example, we send a *multiplication* message to *5* object followed by the number by which we want to multiply 5. In the bottom example, a *Compute Payroll* message is sent to the *Employee* object, where the employee object knows how to respond to the *Payroll* message. Note that the message makes no assumptions about the class of the receiver or the arguments; they are simply objects. It is the receiver's responsibility to respond to a message in an appropriate manner. This gives you a great deal of flexibility, since different objects can respond to the same message in different ways. This is known as *polymorphism* (more on polymorphism later in this chapter), meaning "many shapes (behaviors)." Polymorphism is the main difference between a message and a subroutine call.

Methods are similar to functions, procedures, or subroutines in more traditional programming languages, such as COBOL, Basic, or C. The area where methods and functions differ, however, is in how they are invoked. In a Basic program, you call the subroutine (e.g., GOSUB 1000); in a C program, you call the function by name (e.g., draw chart). In an object-oriented system, you invoke a method of an object by sending an object a message. A message is much more general than a function call. To draw a chart, you would send a *draw* message to the chart object. Notice that *draw* is a more general instruction than, say, *draw a chart*. That is because the *draw* message can be sent to many other objects, such as a line or circle, and each object could act differently.

It is important to understand the difference between methods and messages. Say you want to tell someone to make you French onion soup. Your instruction is the

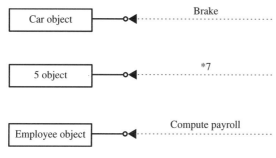

FIGURE 2–3
Objects respond to messages according to methods defined in its class.

message, the way the French onion soup is prepared is the method, and the French onion soup is the object. In other words, the message is the instruction and the method is the implementation. An object or an instance of a class understands messages. A message has a name, just like a method, such as cost, set cost, cooking time. An object understands a message when it can match the message to a method that has a same name as the message. To match up the message, an object first searches the methods defined by its class. If found, that method is called up. If not found, the object searches the superclass of its class. If it is found in a superclass, then that method is called up. Otherwise, it continues the search upward. An error occurs only if none of the superclasses contains the method.

A message differs from a function in that a function says how to do something and a message says what to do. Because a message is so general, it can be used over and over again in many different contexts. The result is a system more resilient to change and more reusable, both within an application and from one application to another.

2.8 ENCAPSULATION AND INFORMATION HIDING

Information hiding is the principle of concealing the internal data and procedures of an object and providing an interface to each object in such a way as to reveal as little as possible about its inner workings. As in conventional programming, some languages permit arbitrary access to objects and allow methods to be defined outside of a class. For example, Simula provides no protection, or information hiding, for objects, meaning that an object's data, or *instance variables*, may be accessed wherever visible. However, most object-oriented languages provide a well-defined interface to their objects through classes. For example, C++ has a very general *encapsulation* protection mechanism with public, private, and protected members. Public members (member data and member functions) may be accessed from anywhere. For instance, the *computePayroll* method of an employee object will be public. Private members are accessible only from within a class. An object data representation, such as a list or an array, usually will be private. Protected members can be accessed only from subclasses.

Often, an object is said to *encapsulate* the data and a program. This means that the user cannot see the inside of the object "capsule," but can use the object by calling the object's methods [8]. Encapsulation or information hiding is a design goal of an object-oriented system. Rather than allowing an object direct access to another object's data, a message is sent to the target object requesting information. This ensures not only that instructions are operating on the proper data but also that no object can operate directly on another object's data. Using this technique, an object's internal format is insulated from other objects.

Another issue is per-object or per-class protection. In *per-class protection*, the most common form (e.g., Ada, C++, Eiffel), class methods can access any object of that class and not just the receiver. In *per-object protection*, methods can access only the receiver.

An important factor in achieving encapsulation is the design of different classes of objects that operate using a common *protocol*, or object's user interface. This means that many objects will respond to the same message, but each will perform the message using operations tailored to its class. In this way, a program can send a generic message and leave the implementation up to the receiving object, which reduces interdependencies and increases the amount of interchangeable and reusable code.

A car engine is an example of encapsulation. Although engines may differ in implementation, the interface between the driver and the car is through a common protocol: Step on the gas to increase power and let up on the gas to decrease power. Since all drivers know this protocol, all drivers can use this method in all cars, no matter what engine is in the car. That detail is insulated from the rest of the car and from the driver. This simplifies the manipulation of car objects and the maintenance of code.

Data abstraction is a benefit of the object-oriented concept that incorporates encapsulation and polymorphism. Data are abstracted when they are shielded by a full set of methods and only those methods can access the data portion of an object.

2.9 CLASS HIERARCHY

An object-oriented system organizes classes into a subclass-superclass hierarchy. Different properties and behaviors are used as the basis for making distinctions between classes and subclasses. At the top of the *class hierarchy* are the most general classes and at the bottom are the most specific. The family car in Figure 2–4 is a subclass of car. A *subclass* inherits all of the properties and methods (procedures) defined in its *superclass*. In this case, we can drive a family car just as we can drive any car or, indeed, almost any motor vehicle. Subclasses generally add new methods and properties specific to that class. Subclasses may refine or constrain the state and behavior inherited from its superclass. In our example, race cars

FIGURE 2–4
Superclass/subclass hierarchy.

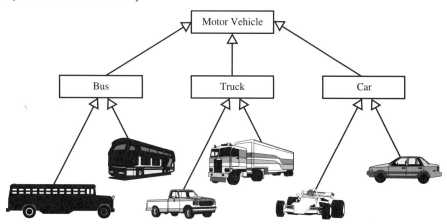

only have one occupant, the driver. In this manner, subclasses modify the attribute (number of passengers) of its superclass, Car.

By contrast, superclasses generalize behavior. It follows that a more general state and behavior is modeled as one moves up the superclass-subclass hierarchy (or simply class hierarchy) and a more specific state is modeled as one moves down.

It is evident from our example that the notion of subclasses and superclasses is relative. A class may simultaneously be the subclass to some class and a superclass to another class(es). Truck is a subclass of a motor vehicle and a superclass of both 18-wheeler and pickup. For example, Ford is a class that defines Ford car objects (see Figure 2–5). However, more specific classes of Ford car objects are Mustang, Taurus, Escort, and Thunderbird. These classes define Fords in a much more specialized manner than the Ford car class itself. Since the Taurus, Escort, Mustang, and Thunderbird classes are more specific classes of Ford cars, they are considered subclasses of class Ford and the Ford class is their superclass. However, the Ford class may not be the most general in our hierarchy. For instance, the Ford class is the subclass of the Car class, which is the subclass of the Vehicle class. Object-oriented notation will be covered in Chapter 5, the chapter on object-oriented modeling.

The car class defines how a car behaves. The Ford class defines the behavior of Ford cars (in addition to cars in general), and the Mustang class defines the behavior of Mustangs (in addition to Ford cars in general). Of course, if all you

FIGURE 2–5
Class hierarchy for Ford class.

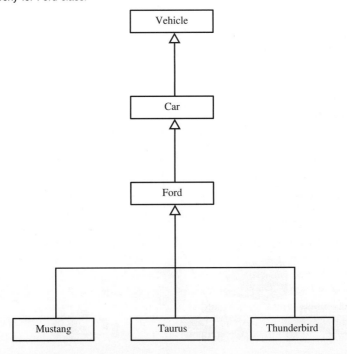

wanted was a Ford Mustang object, you would write only one class, Mustang. The class would define exactly how a Ford Mustang car operates. This methodology is limiting because, if you decide later to create a Ford Taurus object, you will have to duplicate most of the code that describes not only how a vehicle behaves but also how a car, and specifically a Ford, behaves.

This duplication occurs when using a procedural language, since there is no concept of hierarchy and inheriting behavior. An object-oriented system eliminates duplicated effort by allowing classes to share and reuse behaviors.

You might find it strange to define a Car class. After all, what is an instance of the Car class? There is no such thing as a generic car. All cars must be of some make and model. In the same way, there are no instances of Ford class. All Fords must belong to one of the subclasses: Mustang, Escort, Taurus, or Thunderbird. The Car class is a formal class, also called an abstract class. *Formal* or *abstract classes* have no instances but define the common behaviors that can be inherited by more specific classes.

In some object-oriented languages, the terms *superclass* and *subclass* are used instead of *base* and *derived*. In this book, the terms *superclass* and *subclass* are used consistently.

2.9.1 Inheritance

Inheritance is the property of object-oriented systems that allows objects to be built from other objects. Inheritance allows explicitly taking advantage of the commonality of objects when constructing new classes. Inheritance is a relationship between classes where one class is the parent class of another (derived) class. The parent class also is known as the *base class* or *superclass*. Inheritance provides programming by extension as opposed to programming by reinvention [10]. The real advantage of using this technique is that we can build on what we already have and, more important, reuse what we already have. Inheritance allows classes to share and reuse behaviors and attributes. Where the behavior of a class instance is defined in that class's methods, a class also inherits the behaviors and attributes of all of its superclasses.

For example, the Car class defines the general behavior of cars. The Ford class inherits the general behavior from the Car class and adds behavior specific to Fords. It is not necessary to redefine the behavior of the car class; this is inherited. Another level down, the Mustang class inherits the behavior of cars from the Car class and the even more specific behavior of Fords from the Ford class. The Mustang class then adds behavior unique to Mustangs.

Assume that all Fords use the same braking system. In that case, the *stop* method would be defined in class Ford (and not in Mustang class), since it is a behavior shared by all objects of class Ford. When you step on the brake pedal of a Mustang, you send a *stop* message to the Mustang object. However, the *stop* method is not defined in the Mustang class, so the hierarchy is searched until a *stop* method is found. The *stop* method is found in the Ford class, a superclass of the Mustang class, and it is invoked (see Figure 2–6).

In a similar way, the Mustang class can inherit behaviors from the Car and the Vehicle classes. The behaviors of any given class really are behaviors of its su-

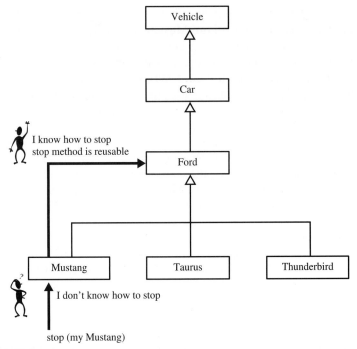

FIGURE 2–6
Inheritance allows reusability.

perclass or a collection of classes. This straightforward process of inheritance prevents you from having to redefine every behavior into every level or reinvent the wheel, or brakes, for that matter.

Suppose that most Ford cars use the same braking system, but the Thunderbird has its own antilock braking system. In this case, the Thunderbird class would redefine the *stop* method. Therefore, the *stop* method of the Ford class would never be invoked by a Thunderbird object. However, its existence higher up in the class hierarchy causes no conflict, and other Ford cars will continue to use the standard braking system.

Dynamic inheritance allows objects to change and evolve over time. Since base classes provide properties and attributes for objects, changing base classes changes the properties and attributes of a class. A previous example was a Windows object changing into an icon and then back again, which involves changing a base class between a Windows class and an Icon class. More specifically, *dynamic inheritance* refers to the ability to add, delete, or change parents from objects (or classes) at run time.

In object-oriented programming languages, variables can be declared to hold or reference objects of a particular class. For example, a variable declared to reference a motor vehicle is capable of referencing a car or a truck or any subclass of motor vehicle.

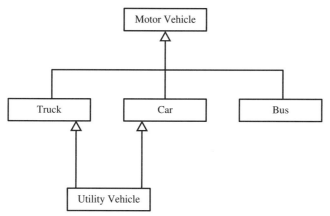

FIGURE 2-7
Utility vehicle inherits from both the Car and Truck classes.

2.9.2 Multiple Inheritance

Some object-oriented systems permit a class to inherit its state (attributes) and be-haviors from more than one superclass. This kind of inheritance is referred to as *multiple inheritance*. For example, a utility vehicle inherits attributes from both the Car and Truck classes (see Figure 2–7).

Multiple inheritance can pose some difficulties. For example, several distinct parent classes can declare a member within a multiple inheritance hierarchy. This then can become an issue of choice, particularly when several superclasses define the same method. It also is more difficult to understand programs written in mul-tiple inheritance systems.

One way of achieving the benefits of multiple inheritance in a language with single inheritance is to inherit from the most appropriate class and then add an ob-ject of another class as an attribute.

2.10 POLYMORPHISM

Poly means "many" and *morph* means "form." In the context of object-oriented systems, it means objects that can take on or assume many different forms. *Poly-morphism* means that the same operation may behave differently on different classes [11]. Booch [1–3] defines *polymorphism* as the relationship of objects of many different classes by some common superclass; thus, any of the objects des-ignated by this name is able to respond to some common set of operations in a dif-ferent way. For example, consider how driving an automobile with a manual trans-mission is different from driving a car with an automatic transmission. The manual transmission requires you to operate the clutch and the shift, so in addition to all other mechanical controls, you also need information on when to shift gears. Therefore, although driving is a behavior we perform with all cars (and all motor vehicles), the specific behavior can be different, depending on the kind of car we are driving. A car with an automatic transmission might implement its *drive* method to use information such as current speed, engine RPM, and current gear. Another car might implement the *drive* method to use the same information but require additional information, such as "the clutch is depressed." The method is the same for both cars, but the implementation invoked depends on the type of car (or the class of object). This concept, termed *polymorphism*, is a fundamental concept of any object-oriented system.

Polymorphism allows us to write generic, reusable code more easily, because we can specify general instructions and delegate the implementation details to the objects involved. Since no assumption is made about the class of an object that receives a message, fewer dependencies are needed in the code and, therefore, maintenance is easier. For example, in a payroll system, manager, office worker, and production worker objects all will respond to the *compute payroll* message, but the actual operations performed are object specific.

2.11 OBJECT RELATIONSHIPS AND ASSOCIATIONS

Association represents the relationships between objects and classes. For example, in the statement "a pilot *can fly* planes" (see Figure 2–8), the italicized term is an association.

Associations are bidirectional; that means they can be traversed in both directions, perhaps with different connotations. The direction implied by the name is the forward direction; the opposite direction is the inverse direction. For example, *can fly* connects a pilot to certain airplanes. The inverse of *can fly* could be called *is flown by*.

An important issue in association is **cardinality**, which specifies how many instances of one class may relate to a single instance of an associated class [12]. Cardinality constrains the number of related objects and often is described as being "one" or "many." Generally, the multiplicity value is a single interval, but it may be a set of disconnected intervals. For example, the number of cylinders in an engine is four, six, or eight. Consider a client-account relationship where one client can have one or more accounts and vice versa (in case of joint accounts); here the cardinality of the client-account association is many to many.

2.11.1 Consumer-Producer Association

A special form of association is a consumer-producer relationship, also known as a **client-server association** or a **use relationship**. The **consumer-producer relationship** can be viewed as one-way interaction: One object requests the service of another object. The object that makes the request is the consumer or client, and the object that receives the request and provides the service is the producer or

FIGURE 2–8
Association represents the relationship among objects, which is bidirectional.

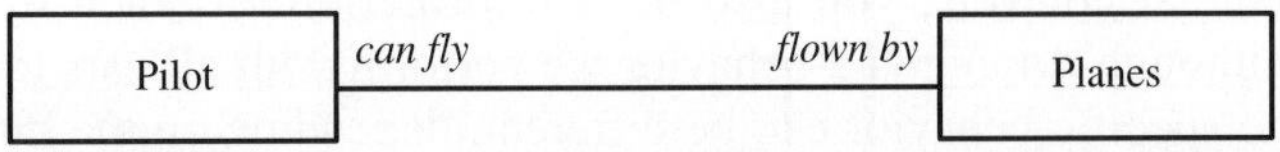

FIGURE 2–9
The consumer/producer association.

server. For example, we have a print object that prints the consumer object. The print producer provides the ability to print other objects. Figure 2–9 depicts the consumer-producer association.

2.12 AGGREGATIONS AND OBJECT CONTAINMENT

All objects, except the most basic ones, are composed of and may contain other objects. For example, a spreadsheet is an object composed of cells, and cells are objects that may contain text, mathematical formulas, video, and so forth. Breaking down objects into the objects from which they are composed is decomposition. This is possible because an object's attributes need not be simple data fields; attributes can reference other objects. Since each object has an identity, one object can refer to other objects. This is known as **_aggregation_**, where an attribute can be an object itself. For instance, a car object is an aggregation of engine, seat, wheels, and other objects (see Figure 2–10).

FIGURE 2–10
A Car object is an aggregation of other objects such as engine, seat, and wheel objects.

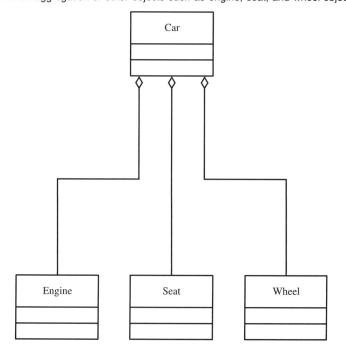

2.13 CASE STUDY: A PAYROLL PROGRAM

Consider a payroll program that processes employee records at a small manufacturing firm. The company has several classes of employees with particular payroll requirements and rules for processing each. This company has three types of employees:

1. *Managers* receive a regular salary.
2. *Office Workers* receive an hourly wage and are eligible for overtime after 40 hours.
3. *Production Workers* are paid according to a piece rate.

We will walk through traditional and object-oriented system development approaches to highlight their similarities and differences with an eye on object-oriented concepts.[1] The main focus of this exercise is to better understand the object-oriented approach. To keep the discussion simple, many issues (such as data flow diagrams, entity-relationship diagrams, feasibility analysis, and documentation) will not be addressed here.

2.13.1. Structured Approach

The traditional structured analysis/structured design (SA/SD) approach relies on modeling the processes that manipulate the given input data to produce the desired output. The first few steps in SA/SD involve creation of preliminary data flow diagrams and data modeling. Data modeling is a systems development methodology concerned with the system's entities, their associations, and their activities. Data modeling is accomplished through the use of entity-relationship diagrams. The SA/SD approach encourages the top-down design (also known as *top-down decomposition* or *stepwise refinement),* characterized by moving from a general statement about the process involved in solving a problem down toward more and more detailed statements about each specific task in the process. Top-down design works well because it lets us focus on fewer details at once. It is a logical technique that encourages orderly system development and reduces the level of complexity at each stage of the design. For obvious reasons, top-down design works best when applied to problems that clearly have a hierarchical nature. Unfortunately, many real-world problems are not hierarchical. Top-down function-based design has other limitations that become apparent when developing and maintaining large systems.

Top-down design works by continually refining a problem into simpler and simpler chunks. Each chunk is analyzed and specified by itself, with little regard (if any) for the rest of the system. This, after all, is one reason why top-down design is so effective at analyzing a problem. The method works well for the initial design of a system and helps ensure that the specifications for the problem are met and solved. However, each program element is designed with only a limited set of requirements in mind. Since it is unlikely that this exact set of requirements will

---

[1]Structured approach is a valid approach. It is estimated that 25 percent of firms use structured development approaches. Therefore, it will continue to play a role in systems development.

return in the next problem, the program's design and code are not general and reusable. Top-down design does not preclude the creation of general routines that are shared among many programs, but it does not encourage it. Indeed, the idea of combining reusable programs into a system is a bottom-up approach, quite the opposite of the top-down style [9].

Once the system modeling and analysis have been completed, we can proceed to design. During the design phase, many issues must be studied. These include user interface design (input and output), hardware and software issues such as system platform and operating systems, and data or database management issues. In addition, people and procedural issues, such as training and documentation, must be addressed.

Finally, we proceed to implementing the system using a procedural language. Most current programming languages, such as FORTRAN, COBOL, and C, are based on procedural programming. That is, the programmer tells the computer exactly how to process each piece of data, presents selections from which the user can choose, and codes an appropriate response for each choice. Today's applications are much more sophisticated and developed with more demanding requirements than in the past, which makes systems development using these tools much more difficult.

In a procedural approach such as C or COBOL, the payroll program would include conditional logic to check the employee code and compute the payroll accordingly:

```
FOR EVERY EMPLOYEE DO
     BEGIN
          IF   employee = manager      THEN
                  CALL   computeManagerSalary
          IF   employee = office worker   THEN
                  CALL   computeOfficeWorkerSalary
          IF   employee = production worker   THEN
                  CALL   computeProductionWorkerSalary
     END
```

If new classes of employees are added, such as temporary office workers ineligible for overtime or junior production workers who receive an hourly wage plus a lower piece rate, then the main logic of the application must be modified to accommodate these requirements:

```
FOR EVERY EMPLOYEE DO
     BEGIN
          IF   employee = manager   THEN
                  CALL   computeManagerSalary
          IF   employee = office worker   THEN
                  CALL   computeOfficeWorkerSalary
          IF   employee = production worker   THEN
                  CALL   computeProductionWorkerSalary
```

```
IF   employee = temporary office worker   THEN
         CALL   computeTemporaryOfficeWorkerSalary
IF   employee = junior production worker   THEN
         CALL   computeJuniorProductionWorkerSalary
END
```

Similarly, other areas of the program that pertain to data entry or reporting might have to be modified to take into account new kinds of employees. A procedural language does not lend itself easily to writing code in a generic and reusable way. Therefore you must provide detailed processing steps for each type (class) of employee. The main problem with this traditional way of programming is the following:

> The introduction of new classes of data with different needs requires changing the main logic of the program. It also may require the addition of new code in many different areas of the application.

This problem limits a programmer's ability to reuse code, since each function or procedure is tied to the data on which it operates. On the other hand, object-oriented programming allows the programmer to solve problems by creating logical objects that incorporate both data and functionality in a unit. You can create fully tested and debugged classes of objects that can be reused in other programs and this, in turn, can reduce the amount of code that must be written for successive applications.

2.13.2 The Object-Oriented Approach

Object-oriented systems development consists of

- Object-oriented analysis.
- Object-oriented information modeling.
- Object-oriented design.
- Prototyping and implementation.
- Testing, iteration, and documentation.

Object-oriented software development encourages you to view the problem as a system of cooperative objects. Object-oriented analysis shares certain aspects with the structured approach, such as determining the system requirements. However, one major difference is that we do not think of data and procedures separately, because objects incorporate both. When developing an object-oriented application, two basic questions always arise:

- What objects does the application need?
- What functionality should those objects have?

Each object is entirely responsible for itself. For example, an employee object is responsible for things (operations) like computing payrolls, printing paychecks, and storing data about itself, such as its name, address, and social security number. The first task in object-oriented analysis is to find the class of objects that will compose the system. At the first level of analysis, we can look at the physical entities in the system. That is, who are the players and how do they cooperate to do the work of the system? These entities (objects) could be individuals, organizations, machines, units of information, molecules, pictures, or whatever else makes sense in the context of the real-world system. This usually is a very good starting point for deciding what *classes* to design. At this level, you must look at the physical entities in the system. In the process of developing the model, the objects that emerge can help us establish a workable system. However, Coad and Yourdon [4] have listed the following clues for finding the candidate classes and objects:

- *Persons.* What role does a person play in the system? For example, customers, employees of which the system needs to keep track.
- *Places.* These are physical locations, buildings, stores, sites or offices about which the system keeps information.
- *Things or events.* These are events, points in time that must be recorded. For example, the system might need to remember when a customer makes an order; therefore, an order is an object. Associated with things remembered are attributes (after all, things to remember are objects) such as who, what, when, where, how, or why. For example, some of the data or attributes of *order object* are customer-ID (who), date-of-order (when), soup-ID (what), and so on.

Next, we need to identify the hierarchical relation between superclasses and subclasses. Another task in object-oriented analysis is to identify the attributes (properties) of objects, such as color, cost, and manufacturer. Identifying behavior (methods) is next. The main question to ask is What services must a class provide? The answer to the question allows us to identify the methods a class must contain. Once you identify the overall system's responsibilities and the information it needs to remember, you can assign each responsibility to the class to which it logically belongs.

As in the structured approach, we need to model the system's objects and their relationships. For example, the objects in our payroll system are Employee, Manager, Production Worker, and Temporary Office Worker.

Other objects (things) are part of the system, such as the paycheck or the product being made and the process being used to make the product. However, here we focus on the class of Employees. The payroll program would have different classes of Employees corresponding to the different types of employees in the company (see Figure 2–11). Every employee object would know how to calculate its payroll according to its own requirements.

The goal of object-oriented analysis is to identify objects and classes that support the problem domain and system's requirements. Object-oriented design identifies and defines additional objects and classes that support an implementation of the requirements [4]. For example, during design you might need to add objects for the user interface for the systems; that is, data entry windows, browse windows, and the like.

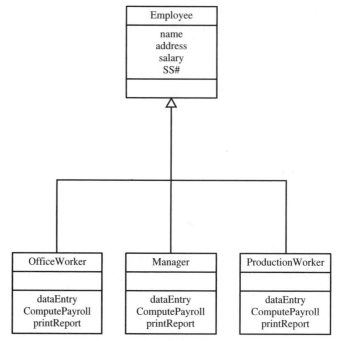

FIGURE 2–11
Class hierarchy for the payroll application.

The main program would be written in a general way that looped through all of the employees and sent a message to each employee to calculate its payroll:

```
FOR EVERY EMPLOYEE DO
    BEGIN
            employee computePayroll
    END
```

If a new class of employee were added, a class for that type of employee would have to be created (see Figure 2–12). This class would know how to calculate its payroll. Unlike the procedural approach, the main program and other related parts of the program would not have to be modified; changes would be limited to the addition of a new class.

2.14 ADVANCED TOPICS

2.14.1 Object and Identity

A special feature of object-oriented systems is that every object has its own unique and immutable identity. An object's identity comes into being when the object is created and continues to represent that object from then on. This identity never is confused with another object, even if the original object has been deleted. The identity name never changes even if all the properties of the object change—it is

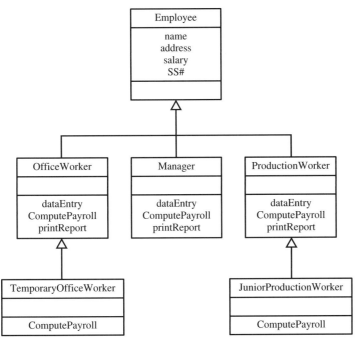

FIGURE 2–12
The hierarchy for the payroll application.

independent of the object's state. In particular, the identity does not depend on the object's name, or its key, or its location. All these can change with no effect on being able to recognize the object as the "same one."

In an object system, object identity often is implemented through some kind of **object identifier** (OID) or unique identifier (UID). An OID is dispensed by a part of the object-oriented programming system that is responsible for guaranteeing the uniqueness of every identifier. OIDs are never reused.

As another example (see Figure 2–13), cars may have an "owner" property of class Person. A particular instance of a car, a black Saab 900S, is owned by person instance named Hal. In an object system, the relationship between the car and Hal can be implemented and maintained by a reference. A reference in an object-oriented system is similar to a pointer in other programming languages. Pointers refer directly to the address of the thing they point to in the physical memory. **Object references** directly denote the object to which they refer. References often are implemented by using the UID of the object as the reference, since the UID guarantees object identity over time. Fortunately, we need not be concerned with or manage the UID. Most object-oriented systems will perform that transparently.

In Figure 2–13, the owner property of a car contains a reference to the person instance named Hal. In addition, an object may refer back to an object that refers to it. In this example, a person has an *owns* property that contains a reference to the car instance. References may or may not carry class information with them.

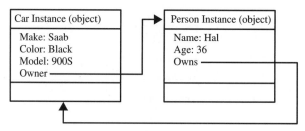

FIGURE 2–13
The owner property of a car contains a reference to the person instance named Hal.

2.14.2 Static and Dynamic Binding

The process of determining (dynamically) at run time which function to invoke is termed *dynamic binding*. Making this determination earlier, at compile time, is called *static binding*. Static binding optimizes the calls; dynamic binding occurs when polymorphic calls are issued. Not all function invocations require dynamic binding.

Dynamic binding allows some method invocation decisions to be deferred until the information is known. A run-time selection of methods often is desired, and even required, in many applications, including databases and user interaction (e.g., GUIs). For example, a cut operation in an Edit submenu may pass the cut operation (along with parameters) to any object on the Desktop, each of which handles the message in its own way. If an (application) object can cut many kinds of objects, such as text and graphic objects, many overloaded cut methods, one per type of object to be cut, are available in the receiving object; the particular method being selected is based on the actual type of object being cut (which in the GUI case is not available until run time) [6].

2.14.3 Object Persistence

Objects have a lifetime. They are explicitly created and can exist for a period of time that, traditionally, has been the duration of the process in which they were created. A file or a database can provide support for objects having a longer lifeline— longer than the duration of the process for which they were created. From a language perspective, this characteristic is called *object persistence*. An object can persist beyond application session boundaries, during which the object is stored in a file or a database, in some file or database form. The object can be retrieved in another application session and will have the same state and relationship to other objects as at the time it was saved. The lifetime of an object can be explicitly terminated. After an object is deleted, its state is inaccessible and its persistent storage is reclaimed. Its identity, however, is never reused, not even after the object is deleted. Object storage and its access from the database will be covered in Chapter 11.

2.14.4 Meta-Classes

Earlier, we said that, in an object-oriented system, everything is an object: numbers, arrays, records, fields, files, forms, and so forth. How about a class? Is a class an object? Yes, a class is an object. So, if it is an object, it must belong to a class (in classical object-oriented systems, anyway). Indeed, such a class belongs to a class called a *meta-class*, or a class of classes. For example, classes must be implemented in some way; perhaps with dictionaries for methods, instances, and parents and methods to perform all the work of being a class. This can be declared in a class named *meta-class*. The meta-class also can provide services to application programs, such as returning a set of all methods, instances, or parents for review (or even modification). Therefore, we can say that all objects are instances of a class and all classes are instances of a meta-class. The meta-class is a class and therefore an instance of itself.

Generally speaking, meta-classes are used by the compiler. For example, the meta-classes handle messages to classes, such as constructors, "new," and "class variables" (a term from Smalltalk), which are variables shared between all instances of a class (static member data in C++).

2.15 SUMMARY

The goal of object-oriented programming is to make development easier, quicker, and more natural by raising the level of abstraction to the point where applications can be implemented in the same terms in which they are described by the application domain. The main thrust of object-oriented programming is to provide the user with a set of objects that closely reflects the underlying application. The user who needs to develop a financial application could develop it in a financial language with considerably less difficulty. Object-oriented programming allows the base concepts of the language to be extended to include ideas closer to those of its application. You can define a new data type (object) in terms of an existing data type until it appears that the language directly supports the primitives of the application. The real advantage of using the object-oriented approach is that you can build on what you already have.

Object-oriented software development is a significant departure from the traditional structured approach. The main advantage of the object-oriented approach is the ability to reuse code and develop more maintainable systems in a shorter amount of time. Additionally, object-oriented systems are better designed, more resilient to change, and more reliable, since they are built from completely tested and debugged classes.

Rather than treat data and procedures separately, object-oriented systems link both closely into objects. Events occur when objects respond to messages. The objects themselves determine the response to the messages, allowing the same message to be sent to many objects.

Each object is an instance of a class. Classes are organized hierarchically in a class tree, and subclasses inherit the behavior of their superclasses. Good object-oriented programming uses encapsulation and polymorphism, which, when used in the definition of classes, result in completely reusable abstract data classes. Objects have a lifetime. They are explicitly created and can exist for a period of time that, traditionally, has been the duration of the process for which they were created. A file or a database can provide support for objects having a longer lifeline—longer than the duration of the process for which they were created.

KEY TERMS

Abstract classes (p. 23)
Aggregation (p. 27)
Algorithm-centric methodology (p. 15)
Association (p. 26)
Attribute (p. 14)
Base classes (p. 23)
Cardinality (p. 26)
Class hierarchy (p. 21)
Class (p. 16)
Client-server association (p. 26)
Consumer-producer relationship (p. 26)
Data-centric methodology (p. 15)
Derived classes (p. 23)
Dynamic binding (p. 34)
Dynamic inheritance (p. 24)
Encapsulation (p. 20)
Formal classes (p. 23)
Inheritance (p. 23)
Instance (p. 16)
Instance variable (p. 20)
Message (p. 19)
Meta-class (p. 35)
Method (p. 14)
Multiple inheritance (p. 25)
Object (p. 15)
Object identifier (OID) (p. 33)
Object-oriented programming (p. 14)
Object persistence (p. 34)
Object reference (p. 33)
Per-class protection (p. 20)
Per-object protection (p. 20)
Polymorphism (p. 25)
Property (p. 14)
Protocol (p. 20)
Static binding (p. 34)
Subclass (p. 21)
Superclass (p. 21)
Use relationship (p. 26)

REVIEW QUESTIONS

1. What is an object?
2. What is the main advantage of object-oriented development?
3. What is polymorphism?

4. What is the difference between an object's methods and an object's attributes?

5. How are classes organized in an object-oriented environment?

6. How does object-oriented development eliminate duplication?

7. What is inheritance?

8. What is data abstraction?

9. Why is encapsulation important?

10. What is a protocol?

11. What is the difference between a method and a message?

12. Why is polymorphism useful?

13. How are objects identified in an object-oriented system?

14. What is the lifetime of an object and how can you extend the lifetime of an object?

15. What is association?

16. What is a consumer-producer relationship?

17. What is a formal class?

18. What is an instance?

For questions 19–25 match the term to the definition:

a. object

b. class

c. method

d. class hierarchy

e. inheritance

f. message

g. polymorphism

19. _____ An object template.

20. _____ A unit of functionality.

21. _____ The scheme for representing the relationships between classes.

22. _____ The generic message-sending scheme that allows flexibility in design.

23. _____ The scheme for sharing operations and data between related classes.

24. _____ A high-level instruction to perform an operation on an object.

25. _____ The implementation of a high-level operation for a specific class of objects.

PROBLEMS

1. Identify the attributes and methods of a dishwasher object.

2. Identify all the attributes and methods of the checkbook object. Write a short description of services that each method will provide.

3. If you are in market to buy a car, which attributes or services are relevant to you.

4. Identify objects in a payroll system.

5. Create a class hierarchy to organize the following drink classes: alcoholic, nonalcoholic, grape juice, mineral water, lemonade, beer, and wine. (Hint: At the top of the hierarchy are the most general classes and at the bottom are the most specific. Classes should be related to one another in superclass-subclass hierarchies.)

6. Assume the drinks in problem 6 have the following characteristics:

- Alcoholic drinks are not for drivers or children.
- Nonalcoholic drinks are thirst quenching.
- Wine is made of grapes and for adults only.
- Grape juice is made from grapes and has the taste of a fruit.

- Mineral water is bubbling and does not taste like fruit.
- Lemonade is bubbling and tastes like a fruit.

How would you define the class hierarchy? (Hint: Utilize the inheritance capability of an object-oriented system.)

REFERENCES

1. Booch, Grady. *Software Engineering with Ada*, 2d ed. Menlo Park, CA: Benjamin-Cummings, 1987.
2. Booch, Grady. *Software Components with Ada, Structures, Tools, and Subsystems.* Menlo Park, CA: Benjamin-Cummings, 1987.
3. Booch, Grady. *Object-Oriented Design with Applications*, 2d ed. Menlo Park, CA: Benjamin-Cummings, 1994.
4. Coad, P.; and Yourdon, E. *Object-Oriented Design.* Englewood Cliffs, NJ: Yourdon Press Computing Series, 1991.
5. Dahl, O. J.; and Nygaard, K. "SIMULA—An Agol Based Simulation Language." *Communications of the ACM* 9, no. 9 (1966), pp. 671–78.
6. Garfinkel, Simson L.; and Michael K. Mahoney. *NeXTSTEP Programming Step One: Object-Oriented Applications.* New York: Springer-Verlag, 1993.
7. IBM. "Human-User Interaction, Object-Oriented User Interface." http://www.ibm.com/ibm/hci, 1997.
8. Kim, Won. *Introduction to Object-Oriented Databases.* Cambridge, MA: The MIT Press, 1990.
9. King, Gary Warren. "Object-Oriented Really Is Better Than Structured." 1996, http://www.oz.net/~gking/whyoop.htm.
10. LaLonde, Wilf R.; and Pugh, John R. *Inside Smalltalk*, vol.1. Englewood Cliffs, NJ: Prentice-Hall Engineering, Science, and Math, 1990.
11. Rumbaugh, James; Blaha, Michael; Permerlani, William; Eddy, Frederick; and Lorensen, William. *Object-Oriented Modeling and Design.* Englewood Cliffs, NJ: Prentice-Hall, 1991.

CHAPTER 3

Object-Oriented Systems Development Life Cycle

He who does not lay his foundations beforehand may by great abilities do so afterwards, although with great trouble to the architect and danger to the building.

—Niccolo Machiavelli
The Prince

Chapter Objectives

You should be able to define and understand

- The software development process.
- Building high-quality software.
- Object-oriented systems development.
- Use-case driven systems development.
- Prototyping.
- Component-based development.
- Rapid application development.

3.1 INTRODUCTION

The essence of the *software development process* that consists of analysis, design, implementation, testing, and refinement is to transform users' needs into a software solution that satisfies those needs. However, some people view the software development process as interesting but feel it has little importance in developing software. It is tempting to ignore the process and plunge into the implementation and programming phases of software development, much like the builder who would bypass the architect. Some programmers have been able to ignore the counsel of systems development in building a system; but, in general, the dynamics of software development provide little room for such shortcuts, and bypasses have been less than successful. Furthermore, the object-oriented approach requires a more rigorous process to do things right. This way, you need not see code until after about 25 percent of the development time, because you need to spend more time gathering requirements, developing a requirements model and an analysis model, then turning them into the design model. Now, you can develop code quickly—you have a recipe for doing it. However, you should construct a prototype of some of the key system components shortly after the products are selected, to understand how easy or difficult it will be to implement some of the features of the system. The prototype also can give users a chance to comment on the usability and usefulness of the design and let you assess the fit between the software tools selected, the functional specification, and the users' needs.

This chapter introduces you to the systems development life cycle in general and, more specifically, to an object-oriented approach to software development. The main point of this chapter is the idea of building software by placing emphasis on the analysis and design aspects of the software life cycle. The emphasis is intended to promote the building of high-quality software (meeting specifications and being adaptable for change). The software industry previously suffered from the lack of focus on the early stages of the life cycle [5].

3.2 THE SOFTWARE DEVELOPMENT PROCESS

System development can be viewed as a process. Furthermore, the development itself, in essence, is a process of change, refinement, transformation, or addition to the existing product. Within the process, it is possible to replace one subprocess with a new one, as long as the new subprocess has the same interface as the old one, to allow it to fit into the process as a whole. With this method of change, it is possible to adapt the new process. For example, the object-oriented approach provides us a set of rules for describing inheritance and specialization in a consistent way when a subprocess changes the behavior of its parent process.

The process can be divided into small, interacting phases—subprocesses. The subprocesses must be defined in such a way that they are clearly spelled out, to allow each activity to be performed as independently of other subprocesses as possible. Each subprocess must have the following [1]:

- A description in terms of how it works
- Specification of the input required for the process
- Specification of the output to be produced

The software development process also can be divided into smaller, interacting subprocesses. Generally, the software development process can be viewed as a series of transformations, where the output of one transformation becomes the input of the subsequent transformation (see Figure 3–1):

- *Transformation 1 (analysis)* translates the users' needs into system requirements and responsibilities. The way they use the system can provide insight into the users' requirements. For example, one use of the system might be analyzing an incentive payroll system, which will tell us that this capacity must be included in the system requirements.
- *Transformation 2 (design)* begins with a problem statement and ends with a detailed design that can be transformed into an operational system. This transformation includes the bulk of the software development activity, including the

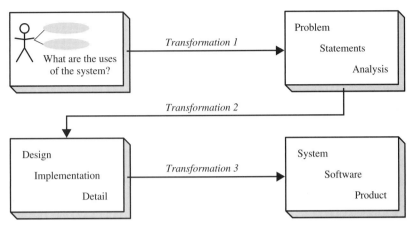

FIGURE 3–1
Software process reflecting transformation from needs to a software product that satisfies those needs.

definition of how to build the software, its development, and its testing. It also includes the design descriptions, the program, and the testing materials.

- *Transformation 3 (implementation)* refines the detailed design into the system deployment that will satisfy the users' needs. This takes into account the equipment, procedures, people, and the like. It represents embedding the software product within its operational environment. For example, the new compensation method is programmed, new forms are put to use, and new reports now can be printed. Here, we try to answer the following question: What procedures and resources are needed to compensate the employees under the new accounting system?

An example of the software development process is the ***waterfall approach***,[1] which starts with deciding *what* is to be done (what is the problem). Once the requirements have been determined, we next must decide *how* to accomplish them. This is followed by a step in which we *do it*, whatever "it" has required us to do. We then must *test* the result to see if we have satisfied the users' requirements. Finally, we *use* what we have done (see Figure 3–2).

In the real world, the problems are not always well-defined and that is why the waterfall model has limited utility. For example, if a company has experience in building accounting systems, then building another such product based on the existing design is best managed with the waterfall model, as it has been described. Where there is uncertainty regarding what is required or how it can be built, the waterfall model fails. This model assumes that the requirements are known before the design begins, but one may need experience with the product before the re-

---

[1]Many in the software development community feel that the waterfall model has been discarded, whereas others believe it offers a high-level representation of the software process.

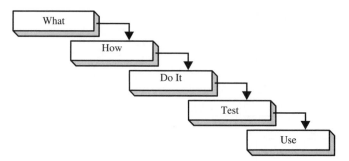

FIGURE 3–2
The waterfall software development process.

quirements can be fully understood. It also assumes that the requirements will remain static over the development cycle and that a product delivered months after it was specified will meet the delivery-time needs.

Finally, even when there is a clear specification, it assumes that sufficient design knowledge will be available to build the product. The waterfall model is the best way to manage a project with a well-understood product, especially very large projects. Clearly, it is based on well-established engineering principles. However, its failures can be traced to its inability to accommodate software's special properties and its inappropriateness for resolving partially understood issues; furthermore, it neither emphasizes nor encourages software reusability.

After the system is installed in the real world, the environment frequently changes, altering the accuracy of the original problem statement and, consequently, generating revised software requirements. This can complicate the software development process even more. For example, a new class of employees or another shift of workers may be added or the standard workweek or the piece rate changed. By definition, any such changes also change the environment, requiring changes in the programs. As each such request is processed, system and programming changes make the process increasingly complex, since each request must be considered in regard to the original statement of needs as modified by other requests.

3.3 BUILDING HIGH-QUALITY SOFTWARE

The software process transforms the users' needs via the application domain to a software solution that satisfies those needs. Once the system (programs) exists, we must test it to see if it is free of bugs. High-quality products must meet users' needs and expectations. Furthermore, the products should attain this with minimal or no defects, the focus being on improving products (or services) prior to delivery rather than correcting them after delivery. The ultimate goal of building high-quality software is user satisfaction. To achieve high quality in software we need to be able to answer the following questions:

- How do we determine when the system is ready for delivery?
- Is it now an operational system that satisfies users' needs?

- Is it correct and operating as we thought it should?
- Does it pass an evaluation process?

There are two basic approaches to systems testing. We can test a system according to how it has been built or, alternatively, what it should do. Blum [3] describes a means of system evaluation in terms of four quality measures: correspondence, correctness, verification, and validation. *Correspondence* measures how well the delivered system matches the needs of the operational environment, as described in the original requirements statement. *Validation* is the task of predicting correspondence. True correspondence cannot be determined until the system is in place (see Figure 3–3). *Correctness* measures the consistency of the product requirements with respect to the design specification. Blum argues that *verification* is the exercise of determining correctness. However, correctness always is objective. Given a specification and a product, it should be possible to determine if the product precisely satisfies the requirements of the specification. For example, does the payroll system accurately compute the amount of compensation? Does it report productivity accurately and to the satisfaction of the workers, and does it handle information as originally planned?

Validation, however, is always subjective, and it addresses a different issue— the appropriateness of the specification. This may be considered 20/20 hindsight: Did we uncover the true users' needs and therefore establish the proper design? If the evaluation criteria could be detailed, they would have been included in the specification. Boehm [4] observes that these quality measures, verification and validation, answer the following questions:

- *Verification*. Am I building the product right?
- *Validation*. Am I building the right product?

Validation begins as soon as the project starts, but verification can begin only after a specification has been accepted. Verification and validation are independent

FIGURE 3–3
Four quality measures (correspondence, correctness, validation, and verification) for software evaluation.

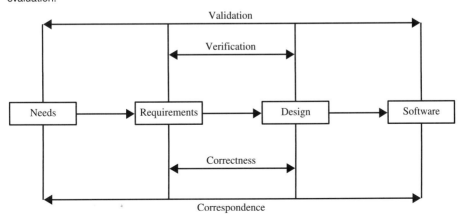

of each other. It is possible to have a product that corresponds to the specification, but if the specification proves to be incorrect, we do not have the right product; for example, say a necessary report is missing from the delivered product, since it was not included in the original specification. A product also may be correct but not correspond to the users' needs; for example, after years of waiting, a system is delivered that satisfies the initial design statement but no longer reflects current operating practices. Blum argues that, when the specification is informal, it is difficult to separate verification from validation. Chapter 13 looks at the issue of software validation and correspondence by proposing a way to measure user satisfaction and software usability. The next section looks at an object-oriented software development approach that eliminates many of the shortcomings of traditional software development, such as the waterfall approach.

3.4 OBJECT-ORIENTED SYSTEMS DEVELOPMENT: A USE-CASE DRIVEN APPROACH

The object-oriented *software development life cycle* (SDLC) consists of three macro processes: object-oriented analysis, object-oriented design, and object-oriented implementation (see Figure 3–4).

The use-case model can be employed throughout most activities of software development. Furthermore, by following the life cycle model of Jacobson, Ericsson,

FIGURE 3–4

The object-oriented systems development approach. Object-oriented analysis corresponds to transformation 1; design to transformation 2, and implementation to transformation 3 of Figure 3–1.

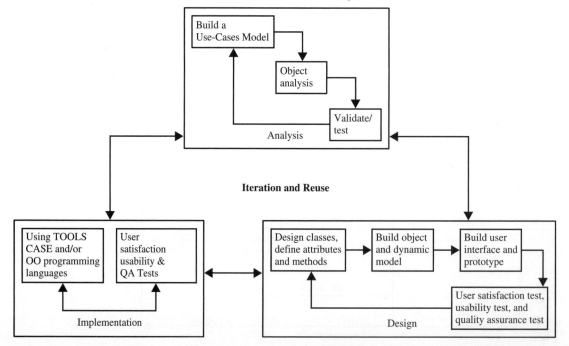

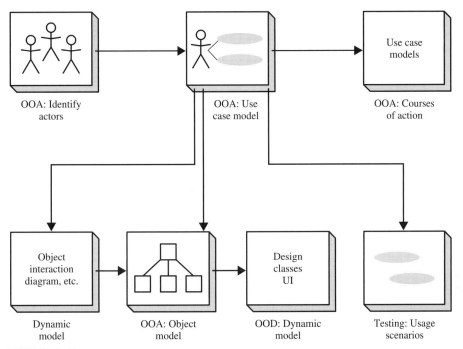

FIGURE 3–5

By following the life cycle model of Jacobson et al., we produce designs that are traceable across requirements, analysis, implementation, and testing.

and Jacobson [11], one can produce designs that are traceable across requirements, analysis, design, implementation, and testing (as shown in Figure 3–5). The main advantage is that all design decisions can be traced back directly to user requirements. Usage scenarios can become test scenarios.

Object-oriented system development includes these activities:

• Object-oriented analysis—use case driven
• Object-oriented design
• Prototyping
• Component-based development
• Incremental testing

Object-oriented software development encourages you to view the problem as a system of cooperative objects. Furthermore, it advocates incremental development. Although object-oriented software development skills come only with practice, by following the guidelines listed in this book you will be on the right track for building sound applications. We look at these activities in detail in subsequent chapters.

3.4.1 Object-Oriented Analysis—Use-Case Driven

The object-oriented analysis phase of software development is concerned with determining the system requirements and identifying classes and their relationship to other classes in the problem domain. To understand the system requirements, we need to identify the users or the actors. Who are the actors and how do they use the system? In object-oriented as well as traditional development, scenarios are used to help analysts understand requirements. However, these scenarios may be treated informally or not fully documented. Ivar Jacobson [10] came up with the concept of the *use case,* his name for a scenario to describe the user–computer system interaction. The concept worked so well that it became a primary element in system development. The object-oriented programming community has adopted use cases to a remarkable degree. Scenarios are a great way of examining who does what in the interactions among objects and what *role* they play; that is, their interrelationships. This intersection among objects' roles to achieve a given goal is called *collaboration*. The scenarios represent only one possible example of the collaboration. To understand all aspects of the collaboration and all potential actions, several different scenarios may be required, some showing usual behaviors, others showing situations involving unusual behavior or exceptions.

In essence, a use case is a typical interaction between a user and a system that captures users' goals and needs. In its simplest usage, you capture a use case by talking to typical users, discussing the various things they might want to do with the system.

Expressing these high-level processes and interactions with customers in a scenario and analyzing it is referred to as *use-case modeling*. The use-case model represents the users' view of the system or users' needs. For example, consider a word processor, where a user may want to be able to replace a word with its synonym or create a hyperlink. These are some uses of the system, or a system responsibility.

This process of developing uses cases, like other object-oriented activities, is iterative—once your use-case model is better understood and developed you should start to identify classes and create their relationships.

Looking at the physical objects in the system also provides us important information on objects in the systems. The objects could be individuals, organizations, machines, units of information, pictures, or whatever else makes up the application and makes sense in the context of the real-world system. While developing the model, objects emerge that help us establish a workable system. It is necessary to work iteratively between use-case and object models. For example, the objects in the incentive payroll system might include the following examples:

The employee, worker, supervisor, office administrator.

The paycheck.

The product being made.

The process used to make the product.

Of course, some problems have no basis in the real world. In this case, it can be useful to pose the problem in terms of analogous physical objects, kind of a mental simulation. It always is possible to think of a problem in terms of some kinds of objects, although in some cases, the objects may be synthetic or esoteric, with no direct physical counterparts. The objects need to have meaning only within the context of the application's domain. For example, the application domain might be a payroll system; and the tangible objects might be the paycheck, employee, worker, supervisor, office administrator; and the intangible objects might be tables, data entry screen, data structures, and so forth.

Documentation is another important activity, which does not end with object-oriented analysis but should be carried out throughout the system development. However, make the documentation as short as possible. The 80–20 rule generally applies for documentation: 80 percent of the work can be done with 20 percent of the documentation. The trick is to make sure that the 20 percent is easily accessible and the rest (80 percent) is available to those (few) who need to know. Remember that documentation and modeling are not separate activities, and good modeling implies good documentation.

3.4.2 Object-Oriented Design

The goal of *object-oriented design* (OOD) is to design the classes identified during the analysis phase and the user interface. During this phase, we identify and define additional objects and classes that support implementation of the requirements [8]. For example, during the design phase, you might need to add objects for the user interface to the system (e.g., data entry windows, browse windows).

Object-oriented design and object-oriented analysis are distinct disciplines, but they can be intertwined. Object-oriented development is highly incremental; in other words, you start with object-oriented analysis, model it, create an object-oriented design, then do some more of each, again and again, gradually refining and completing models of the system. The activities and focus of object-oriented analysis and object-oriented design are intertwined—grown, not built (see Figure 3–4).

First, build the object model based on objects and their relationships, then iterate and refine the model:

- Design and refine classes.
- Design and refine attributes.
- Design and refine methods.
- Design and refine structures.
- Design and refine associations.

Here are a few guidelines to use in your object-oriented design:

- Reuse, rather than build, a new class. Know the existing classes.
- Design a large number of simple classes, rather than a small number of complex classes.
- Design methods.
- Critique what you have proposed. If possible, go back and refine the classes.

3.4.3 Prototyping

Although the object-oriented analysis and design describe the system features, it is important to construct a prototype of some of the key system components shortly after the products are selected. It has been said "a picture may be worth a thousand words, but a prototype is worth a thousand pictures"[author unknown]. Not only is this true, it is an understatement of the value of software prototyping. Essentially, a prototype is a version of a software product developed in the early stages of the product's life cycle for specific, experimental purposes. A prototype enables you to fully understand how easy or difficult it will be to implement some of the features of the system. It also can give users a chance to comment on the usability and usefulness of the user interface design and lets you assess the fit between the software tools selected, the functional specification, and the user needs. Additionally, prototyping can further define the use cases, and it actually makes use-case modeling much easier. Building a prototype that the users are happy with, along with documentation of what you did, can define the basic courses of action for those use cases covered by the prototype. The main idea here is to build a prototype with uses-case modeling to design systems that users like and need.

Traditionally, prototyping was used as a "quick and dirty" way to test the design, user interface, and so forth, something to be thrown away when the "industrial strength" version was developed. However, the new trend, such as using rapid application development, is to refine the prototype into the final product. Prototyping provides the developer a means to test and refine the user interface and increase the usability of the system. As the underlying prototype design begins to become more consistent with the application requirements, more details can be added to the application, again with further testing, evaluation, and rebuilding, until all the application components work properly within the prototype framework.

Prototypes have been categorized in various ways. The following categories are some of the commonly accepted prototypes and represent very distinct ways of viewing a prototype, each having its own strengths:

- A *horizontal prototype* is a simulation of the interface (that is, it has the entire user interface that will be in the full-featured system) but contains no functionality. This has the advantages of being very quick to implement, providing a good overall feel of the system, and allowing users to evaluate the interface on the basis of their normal, expected perception of the system.
- A *vertical prototype* is a subset of the system features with complete functionality. The principal advantage of this method is that the few implemented functions can be tested in great depth. In practice, prototypes are a hybrid between horizontal and vertical: The major portions of the interface are established so the user can get the feel of the system, and features having a high degree of risk are prototyped with much more functionality [7].
- An *analysis prototype* is an aid for exploring the problem domain. This class of prototype is used to inform the user and demonstrate the proof of a concept. It is not used as the basis of development, however, and is discarded when it has served its purpose. The final product will use the concepts exposed by the prototype, not its code.
- A *domain prototype* is an aid for the incremental development of the ultimate

software solution. It often is used as a tool for the staged delivery of subsystems to the users or other members of the development team. It demonstrates the feasibility of the implementation and eventually will evolve into a deliverable product [9].

The typical time required to produce a prototype is anywhere from a few days to several weeks, depending on the type and function of prototype. Prototyping should involve representation from all user groups that will be affected by the project, especially the end users and management members to ascertain that the general structure of the prototype meets the requirements established for the overall design. The purpose of this review is threefold:

1. To demonstrate that the prototype has been developed according to the specification and that the final specification is appropriate.
2. To collect information about errors or other problems in the system, such as user interface problems that need to be addressed in the intermediate prototype stage.
3. To give management and everyone connected with the project the first (or it could be second or third . . .) glimpse of what the technology can provide.

The evaluation can be performed easily if the necessary supporting data is readily available. Testing considerations must be incorporated into the design and subsequent implementation of the system.

Prototyping is a useful exercise at almost any stage of the development. In fact, prototyping should be done in parallel with the preparation of the functional specification. As key features are specified, prototyping those features usually results in modifications to the specification and even can reveal additional features or problems that were not obvious until the prototype was built.

3.4.4 Implementation: Component-Based Development

Manufacturers long ago learned the benefits of moving from custom development to assembly from prefabricated components. Component-based manufacturing makes many products available to the marketplace that otherwise would be prohibitively expensive. If products, from automobiles to plumbing fittings to PCs, were custom-designed and built for each customer, the way business applications are, then large markets for these products would not exist. Low-cost, high-quality products would not be available. Modern manufacturing has evolved to exploit two crucial factors underlying today's market requirements: reduce cost and time to market by building from prebuilt, ready-tested components, but add value and differentiation by rapid customization to targeted customers [13].

Today, software components are built and tested in-house, using a wide range of technologies. For example, computer-aided software engineering (CASE) tools allow their users to rapidly develop information systems. The main goal of CASE technology is the automation of the entire information system's development life cycle process using a set of integrated software tools, such as modeling, methodology, and automatic code generation. However, most often, the code generated by

CASE tools is only the skeleton of an application and a lot needs to be filled in by programming by hand. A new generation of CASE tools is beginning to support component-based development.

Component-based development (CBD) is an industrialized approach to the software development process. Application development moves from custom development to assembly of prebuilt, pretested, reusable software components that operate with each other. Two basic ideas underlie component-based development. First, the application development can be improved significantly if applications can be assembled quickly from prefabricated software components. Second, an increasingly large collection of interpretable software components could be made available to developers in both general and specialist catalogs. Put together, these two ideas move application development from a craft activity to an industrial process fit to meet the needs of modern, highly dynamic, competitive, global businesses. The industrialization of application development is akin to similar transformations that occurred in other human endeavors.

A CBD developer can assemble components to construct a complete software system. Components themselves may be constructed from other components and so on down to the level of prebuilt components or old-fashioned code written in a language such as C, assembler, or COBOL. Visual tools or actual code can be used to "glue" together components. Although it is practical to do simple applications using only "visual glue" (e.g., by "wiring" components together as in Digitalk's Smalltalk PARTS, or IBM's VisualAge), putting together a practical application still poses some challenges. Of course, all these are "under the hood" and should be invisible to end users. The impact to users will come from faster product development cycles, increased flexibility, and improved customization features. CBD will allow independently developed applications to work together and do so more efficiently and with less development effort [13].

Existing (legacy) applications support critical services within an organization and therefore cannot be thrown away. Massive rewriting from scratch is not a viable option, as most legacy applications are complex, massive, and often poorly documented. The CBD approach to legacy integration involves application wrapping, in particular component wrapping, technology. An application wrapper surrounds a complete system, both code and data. This wrapper then provides an interface that can interact with both the legacy and the new software systems (see Figure 3–6). Off-the-shelf application wrappers are not widely available. At present, most application wrappers are homegrown within organizations. However, with component-based development technology emerging rapidly, component wrapper technology will be used more widely.

The *software components* are the functional units of a program, building blocks offering a collection of reusable services. A software component can request a service from another component or deliver its own services on request. The delivery of services is independent, which means that components work together to accomplish a task. Of course, components may depend on one another without interfering with each other. Each component is unaware of the context or inner workings of the other components. In short, the object-oriented concept addresses analysis, design, and programming, whereas component-based development is

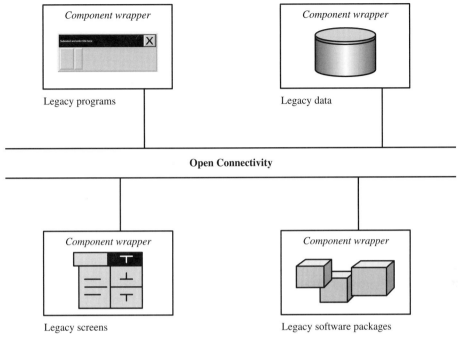

FIGURE 3–6
Reusing legacy system via component wrapping technology.

concerned with the implementation and system integration aspects of software development.

Rapid application development (RAD) is a set of tools and techniques that can be used to build an application faster than typically possible with traditional methods. The term often is used in conjuction with software prototyping. It is widely held that, to achieve RAD, the developer sacrifices the quality of the product for a quicker delivery. This is not necessarily the case. RAD is concerned primarily with reducing the "time to market," not exclusively the software development time. In fact, one successful RAD application achieved a substantial reduction in time to market but realized no significant reduction in the individual software cycles [12].

RAD does not replace the system development life cycle (see the Real-World case) but complements it, since it focuses more on process description and can be combined perfectly with the object-oriented approach. The task of RAD is to build the application quickly and incrementally implement the design and user requirements, through tools such as Delphi, VisualAge, Visual Basic, or PowerBuilder.

After the overall design for an application has been completed, RAD begins. The main objective of RAD is to build a version of an application rapidly to see whether we actually have understood the problem (analysis). Further, it determines whether the system does what it is supposed to do (design). RAD involves a number of iterations. Through each iteration we might understand the problem a little

BOX 3.1

Real-World Issues on the Agenda

THERE'S NEVER ENOUGH UP-FRONT PLANNING WITH RAD

By Clair Tristram

What's the single largest reason that RAD [rapid application development] projects fail? Poor up-front planning, according to the experts. "Planning is a bad word these days, but I happen to think it's a good idea," says Carma McClure, vice president of research at Extended Intelligence Inc., a Chicago-based consulting firm. "You've got to have control over the process." Runaway requirements are a dangerous problem with RAD.

If you choose RAD methodologies to develop your application, you're vulnerable. You won't have a hefty set of requirements to protect you from users. Instead, the same users who are critical to the RAD equation are the very same people who can be counted on to change their minds about what they want. So how do you keep your RAD project on track and on time? Here are some suggestions.

WRITE THINGS DOWN

Sure, you've gotten rid of the onerous task of creating a hefty requirement document by choosing RAD over the waterfall approach. But don't make the mistake of neglecting to write down your business objective at the beginning of the project, and make sure your clients agree on what the core requirements should be.

"A lot of people get stuck in what we call 'proto cycling'," says Richard Hunter, research director at Gartner Group Inc., in Stamford, CT. "They don't know what the business problem is that they're trying to solve, and in that case it can take a long time to find out what you're doing."

AVOID "SHALLOW" PROTOTYPING

RAD tools make great demos, but can you deliver?

Make sure that your team understands the underlying architecture of the prototypes they develop and that they can develop prototype features under a deadline that actually works, rather than just look pretty. "RAD helps you build a model quickly," notes McClure. "Users can make suggestions and virtually see the results. But you need to control your team."

INVOLVE USERS IN COST-BENEFIT DECISIONS

Your users see a prototype interface that seems to change effortlessly from iteration to iteration and they may not understand the amount of effort it will take to actually get those changes implemented. Make sure they do.

"We've eliminated the problem by being very specific about the impact of any changes and involving the user team in setting priorities," says Rick Irving, director of worldwide sales systems at American Express Stored Value Group, in Salt Lake City.

DON'T DEVELOP APPLICATIONS IN ISOLATION

"RAD makes it easy to come up quickly with something good for a single group, but that doesn't satisfy the needs of additional groups," McClure says. "Will you throw it away and start over?"

To avoid clusters of applications with limited utility, McClure recommends honing an understanding of how your RAD project fits into your company's strategic system plan before you begin. That, and always build with reuse in mind.

Source: Clair Tristram, "There's never enough up-front planning with RAD," *PC Week* 13, no. 12 (March 25, 1995).

---

better and make an improvement. RAD encourages the incremental development approach of "grow, do not build" software.

Prototyping and RAD do not replace the object-oriented software development model. Instead, in a RAD application, you go through those stages in rapid (or incomplete) fashion, completing a little more in the next iteration of the prototype. One thing that you should remember is that RAD tools make great demos. However, make sure that you can develop prototype features within a deadline that actually works, rather than just looks good.

3.4.5 Incremental Testing

If you wait until after development to test an application for bugs and performance, you could be wasting thousands of dollars and hours of time. That's what happened at Bankers Trust in 1992: "Our testing was very complete and good, but it was costing a lot of money and would add months onto a project," says Glenn Shimamoto, vice president of technology and strategic planning at the New York bank [6]. In one case, testing added nearly six months to the development of a funds transfer application. The problem was that developers would turn over applications to a quality assurance (QA) group for testing only after development was completed. Since the QA group wasn't included in the initial plan, it had no clear picture of the system characteristics until it came time to test.

3.5 REUSABILITY

A major benefit of object-oriented system development is reusability, and this is the most difficult promise to deliver on. For an object to be really reusable, much more effort must be spent designing it. To deliver a reusable object, the development team must have the up-front time to design reusability into the object. The potential benefits of reuse are clear: increased reliability, reduced time and cost for development, and improved consistency. You must effectively evaluate existing software components for reuse by asking the following questions as they apply to the intended applications [2]:

- Has my problem already been solved?
- Has my problem been partially solved?
- What has been done before to solve a problem similar to this one?

To answer these questions, we need detailed summary information about existing software components. In addition to the availability of the information, we need some kind of search mechanism that allows us to define the candidate object simply and then generate broadly or narrowly defined queries. Thus, the ideal system for reuse would function like a skilled reference librarian. If you have a question about a subject area, all potential sources could be identified and the subject area could be narrowed by prompting. Some form of browsing with the capability to provide detailed information would be required, one where specific subjects could be looked up directly.

The reuse strategy can be based on the following:

- Information hiding (encapsulation).
- Conformance to naming standards.
- Creation and administration of an object repository.
- Encouragement by strategic management of reuse as opposed to constant redevelopment.
- Establishing targets for a percentage of the objects in the project to be reused (i.e., 50 percent reuse of objects).

3.6 SUMMARY

This chapter introduces the system development life cycle (SDLC) in general and object-oriented and use-case driven SDLC specifically. The essence of the software process is the transformation of users' needs through the application domain into a software solution that is executed in the implementation domain. The concept of the use case, or a set of scenarios, can be a valuable tool for understanding the users' needs. The emphasis on the analysis and design aspects of the software life cycle is intended to promote building high-quality software (meeting the specifications and being adaptable for change).

High-quality software provides users with an application that meets their needs and expectations. Four quality measures have been described: correspondence, correctness, verification, and validation. Correspondence measures how well the delivered system corresponds to the needs of the problem. Correctness determines whether or not the system correctly computes the results based on the rules created during the system analysis and design, measuring the consistency of product requirements with respect to the design specification. Verification is the task of determining correctness (am I building the *product right?*). Validation is the task of predicting correspondence (am I building the *right product?*).

Object-oriented design requires more rigor up front to do things right. You need to spend more time gathering requirements, developing a requirements model and an analysis model, then turning them into the design model. Now, you can develop code quickly—you have a recipe for doing it. Object-oriented systems development consists of three macro processes: object-oriented analysis, object-oriented design, and object-oriented implementation. Object-oriented analysis requires building a use-case model and interaction diagrams to identify users' needs and the system's classes and their responsibility, then validating and testing the model, documenting each step along the way. Object-oriented design centers on establishing design classes and their protocol; building class diagrams, user interfaces, and prototypes; testing user satisfaction and usability based on usage and use cases. The use-case concept can be employed through most of the activities of software development. Furthermore, by following Jacobson's life cycle model, one can produce designs that are traceable across requirements, analysis, design, implementation, and testing.

Component-based development (CBD) is an industrialized approach to software development. Software components are functional units, or building blocks offering a collection of reusable services. A CBD developer can assemble components to construct a complete software system. Components themselves may be constructed from other components and so on down to the level of prebuilt components or old-fashioned code written in a language such as C, assembler, or COBOL. The object-oriented concept addresses analysis, design, and programming; whereas component-based development is concerned with the implementation and system integration aspects of software development.

The rapid application development (RAD) approach to systems development rapidly develops software to quickly and incrementally implement the design by using tools such as CASE.

Reusability is a major benefit of object-oriented system development. It is also the most difficult promise to deliver. To develop reusable objects, you must spend time up front to design reusability in the objects.

KEY TERMS

Analysis prototype (p. 48)
Collaboration (p. 46)
Component-based development (CBD) (p. 50)
Correctness (p. 43)
Correspondence (p. 43)
Domain prototype (p. 48)
Horizontal prototype (p. 48)
Object-oriented analysis (p. 45)
Object-oriented design (OOD) (p. 47)
Rapid application development (RAD) (p. 51)
Role (p. 46)
Software components (p. 50)
Software development life cycle (SDLC) (p. 44)
Software development process (p. 39)
Use case (p. 46)
Validation (p. 43)
Vertical prototype (p. 48)
Verification (p. 43)
Waterfall approach (p. 41)

REVIEW QUESTIONS

1. What is the waterfall SDLC?
2. What are some of the advantages and disadvantages of the waterfall process?
3. What is the software development process?
4. What is software correspondence?
5. What is software correctness?
6. What is software validation?
7. What is software verification?
8. How is software verification different from validation?
9. What is prototyping and why is it useful?
10. What are some of the advantages and disadvantages of prototyping?
11. If you have to choose between prototyping and the waterfall approach, which one would you select and why?
12. Describe the macro processes of the object-oriented system development approach.
13. What is the object-oriented SDLC? Compare it with traditional approaches.
14. What are some of the object-oriented analysis processes?
15. What are the object-oriented design processes?
16. What is use-case modeling?
17. What is object modeling?

18. Why can users get involved more easily in prototyping than the traditional software development process such as the waterfall approach?

19. What is RAD?

20. Why is CBD important?

21. Why is reusability important? How does object-oriented software development promote reusability?

PROBLEMS

1. Take a look at the Web site of Popkin software (www.popkin.com). Find out if SA (System Architect) has repository of objects. Write a report on your findings.

2. What are some of the classes of your university system? (Do not worry if you are not sure how to identify objects yet, it will be covered in later chapters. For example, a possible class might be Professor. Think about other objects based on your own personal experience.)

3. You have been hired as a system analyst for the Matrix Corporation. Your first assignment is to propose a new system for communication among employees. Assuming that you would like to apply the waterfall approach, what would you do at the "what" phase? How would you accomplish it? Should you develop several alternatives or just one, and why? Come up with several alternatives.

4. Most of the Comnet Bank data processing systems were developed in the late 1960s. Although the systems are working properly at this time and they meet management's information needs, an increasing percentage of the systems' development efforts are spent on maintaining existing programs. In addition, in the past several years, the internal audit department has hired two EDP auditors who specialize in auditing computer code in these programs. They have found it almost impossible to follow the code's logic, since most of the coding is not documented, is poorly designed and coded, and has been modified many times (spaghetti code). As a result, they have abandoned direct review of program code as an audit technique. Do you think that Comnet Bank has a problem? If so, what is the nature and cause of the problem? What do you recommend to correct it? Should the bank abandon the old system and start from scratch or should it reuse the legacy system by applying component-based development. Do some research on CBD and write a report on your findings.

REFERENCES

1. Anderson, Michael; and Bergstrand, John. "Formalizing Use Cases with Message Sequence Charts." Masters thesis, Department of Communication Systems at Lund Institute of Technology, 1995.

2. Binder, Robert. "Software Process Improvement: A Case Study." *Software Development* 2, no. 1 (January 1994).

3. Blum, Bruce I. *Software Engineering, a Holistic View.* New York: Oxford University Press, 1992.

4. Boehm, Barry W. "Verifying and Validating Software Requirements and Design Specifications." *Software* (January 1984), pp. 75–88.

5. Booch, Grady. *Object Oriented Design with Applications.* Menlo Park, CA: Benjamin-Cummings, 1991.

6. Callaway, Erin. "Continuous Testing Cures the Last-Minute Crunch." *PC Week* 13, no. 12 (March 25, 1995).

7. Card, D. "The RAD Fad: Is Timing Really Everything?" *IEEE Software Engineering* 12, no. 5 (September 1995), pp. 19–22.

8. Coad, Peter; and Yourdon, Edward. *Object-Oriented Analysis*, 2d ed. Englewood Cliffs, NJ: Yourdon Press, Prentice-Hall, 1991.

9. Dollas, A. "Reducing the Time to Market Through Rapid Prototyping." *IEEE Computer* 28, no. 2 (February 1995), pp. 14–15.

10. Jacobson, Ivar. *Object-Oriented Software Engineering: A Use Case Driven Approach.* Reading, MA: Addison-Wesley, Object Technology Series, 1994.

11. Jacobson, Ivar; Ericsson, Maria; and Jacobson, Agneta. *The Object Advantage Business Process Reengineering with Object Technology.* Reading, MA: Addison-Wesley Publishing Company, 1995.

12. Rafii, F.; and Perkins, S. "Internationalizing Software with Concurrent Engineering." *IEEE Software Engineering* 12, no. 5 (September 1995), pp. 39–46.

13. Short, Keith. *Component Based Development and Object Modeling.* Texas Instruments Software, February 1997.

PART TWO

METHODOLOGY, MODELING, AND UNIFIED MODELING LANGUAGE

Object-oriented methodology is a set of methods, models, and rules for developing systems. Modeling is the process of describing an existing or proposed system. It can be used during any phase of the software life cycle. A model is an abstraction of a phenomenon for the purpose of understanding it. Since a model excludes unnecessary details; it is easier to manipulate than the real object. Modeling provides a means for communicating ideas in an easy to understand and unambiguous form while also accommodating a system's complexity. In this part we will look at Object-Oriented Methodologies in Chapter 4, and Unified Modeling Language in Chapter 5.

CHAPTER 4

Object-Oriented Methodologies

*Anyone who observes software develop-
ment cannot but be impressed by its
repetitive nature. Over and over again,
programmers weave a number of basic
patterns: sorting, searching, reading,
writing, comparing, traversing, allocating, synchronizing, and so forth. Experienced programmers know the feeling
of deja vu so characteristic of their
trade [18].*

Chapter Objectives

You should be able to define and understand

- Object-oriented methodologies.
  - The Rumbaugh et al. OMT.
  - The Booch methodology.
  - Jacobson's methodologies.
- Patterns.
- Frameworks.
- Unified approach (UA).

This chapter studies some of the well-known object-oriented methodologies and emerging techniques such as use of patterns and frameworks. The chapter concludes with the unified approach (UA), which is a combination of the best practices and methodologies described in this chapter. The UA is a conceptual model used in this book for studying object-oriented concepts and system development.

4.1 INTRODUCTION: TOWARD UNIFICATION—TOO MANY METHODOLOGIES

In the 1980s, many methodologists were wondering how analysis and design methods and processes would fit into an object-oriented world. Object-oriented methods suddenly had become very popular, and it was apparent that the techniques to help people execute good analysis and design were just as important as the object-oriented concept itself.

To get a feel for object-oriented methodologies, let us look at some of the methods developed in the 1980s and 1990s. This list by no means is complete [14].

- 1986. Booch [6] developed the object-oriented design concept, the Booch method.
- 1987. Sally Shlaer and Steve Mellor [21] created the concept of the recursive design approach.
- 1989. Beck and Cunningham produced class-responsibility-collaboration cards.
- 1990. Wirfs-Brock, Wilkerson, and Wiener [23] came up with responsibility-driven design.
- 1991. Jim Rumbaugh led a team at the research labs of General Electric to develop the object modeling technique (OMT) [19].
- 1991. Peter Coad and Ed Yourdon [11] developed the Coad lightweight and prototype-oriented approach to methods.
- 1994. Ivar Jacobson [16] introduced the concept of the use case and object-oriented software engineering (OOSE).

These methodologies and many other forms of notational language provided system designers and architects many choices but created a very split, competitive, and confusing environment. Most of the methods were very similar but contained a number of often annoying minor differences, and each had a group of practitioners that liked its ideas. The same basic concepts appeared in very different notations, which caused confusion among the users [14].

The trend in object-oriented methodologies, sometimes called *second-generation object-oriented methods*, has been toward combining the best aspects of the most popular methods instead of coming out with new methodologies, which was the tendency in first-generation object-oriented methods. In the next section, to give you a taste of object-oriented methodologies, we will look at some of the most popular ones.

4.2 SURVEY OF SOME OF THE OBJECT-ORIENTED METHODOLOGIES

Many methodologies are available to choose from for system development. Each methodology is based on modeling the business problem and implementing the application in an object-oriented fashion; the differences lie primarily in the documentation of information and modeling notations and language. An application can be implemented in many ways to meet the same requirements and provide the same functionality. The largest noticeable differences will be in the trade-offs and detailed design decisions made. Two people using the same methodology may produce application designs that look radically different. This does not necessarily mean that one is right and one is wrong, just that they are different. In the following sections, we look at the methodologies and their modeling notations developed by Rumbaugh et al., Booch, and Jacobson which are the origins of the Unified Modeling Language (UML).

Each method has its strengths. The Rumbaugh et al. method is well-suited for describing the object model or the static structure of the system. The Jacobson et al. method is good for producing user-driven analysis models. The Booch method produces detailed object-oriented design models.

4.3 RUMBAUGH ET AL.'S OBJECT MODELING TECHNIQUE

The object modeling technique (OMT) presented by Jim Rumbaugh and his co-workers describes a method for the analysis, design, and implementation of a system using an object-oriented technique. OMT is a fast, intuitive approach for identifying and modeling all the objects making up a system. Details such as class attributes, method, inheritance, and association also can be expressed easily. The dynamic behavior of objects within a system can be described using the OMT dynamic model. This model lets you specify detailed state transitions and their descriptions within a system. Finally, a process description and consumer-producer relationships can be expressed using OMT's functional model. OMT consists of four phases, which can be performed iteratively:

1. *Analysis.* The results are objects and dynamic and functional models.
2. *System design.* The results are a structure of the basic architecture of the system along with high-level strategy decisions.
3. *Object design.* This phase produces a design document, consisting of detailed objects static, dynamic, and functional models.
4. *Implementation.* This activity produces reusable, extendible, and robust code.

OMT separates modeling into three different parts:

1. An *object model*, presented by the object model and the data dictionary.
2. A *dynamic model*, presented by the state diagrams and event flow diagrams.
3. A *functional model*, presented by data flow and constraints.

4.3.1 The Object Model

The object model describes the structure of objects in a system: their identity, relationships to other objects, attributes, and operations. The object model is represented graphically with an object diagram (see Figure 4–1). The object diagram contains classes interconnected by association lines. Each class represents a set of individual objects. The association lines establish relationships among the classes. Each association line represents a set of links from the objects of one class to the objects of another class.

4.3.2 The OMT Dynamic Model

OMT provides a detailed and comprehensive dynamic model, in addition to letting you depict states, transitions, events, and actions. The OMT state transition diagram is a network of states and events (see Figure 4–2). Each state receives one or more events, at which time it makes the transition to the next state. The next state depends on the current state as well as the events.

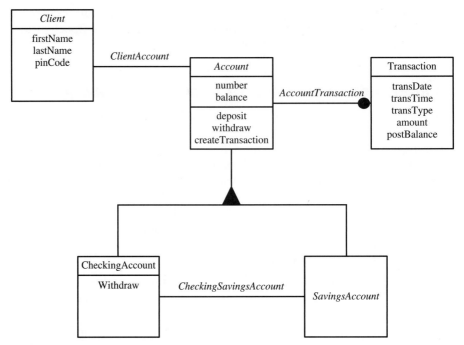

FIGURE 4–1

The OMT object model of a bank system. The boxes represent classes and the filled triangle represents specialization. Association between Account and transaction is one too many; since one account can have many transactions, the filled circle represents many (zero or more). The relationship betwen Client and Account classes is one to one: A client can have only one account and account can belong to only one person (in this model joint accounts are not allowed).

4.3.3 The OMT Functional Model

The OMT data flow diagram (DFD) shows the flow of data between different processes in a business. An OMT DFD provides a simple and intuitive method for describing business processes without focusing on the details of computer systems [3].

Data flow diagrams use four primary symbols:

1. The *process* is any function being performed; for example, verify Password or PIN in the ATM system (see Figure 4–3).
2. The *data flow* shows the direction of data element movement; for example, PIN code.
3. The *data store* is a location where data are stored; for example, account is a data store in the ATM example.
4. An *external entity* is a source or destination of a data element; for example, the ATM card reader.

Overall, the Rumbaugh et al. OMT methodology provides one of the strongest tool sets for the analysis and design of object-oriented systems.

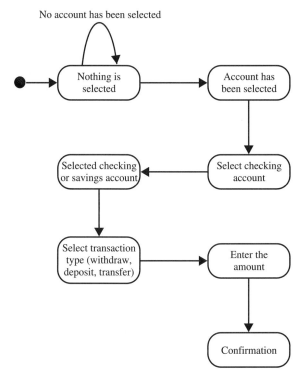

FIGURE 4–2
State transition diagram for the bank application user interface. The round boxes represent states and the arrows represent transitions.

4.4 THE BOOCH METHODOLOGY

The Booch methodology is a widely used object-oriented method that helps you design your system using the object paradigm. It covers the analysis and design phases of an object-oriented system. Booch sometimes is criticized for his large set of symbols. Even though Booch defines a lot of symbols to document almost every design decision, if you work with his method, you will notice that you never use all these symbols and diagrams. You start with class and object diagrams (see Figures 4–4 and 4–5) in the analysis phase and refine these diagrams in various steps. Only when you are ready to generate code, do you add design symbols—and this is where the Booch method shines, you can document your object-oriented code. The Booch method consists of the following diagrams:

Class diagrams
Object diagrams
State transition diagrams
Module diagrams
Process diagrams
Interaction diagrams

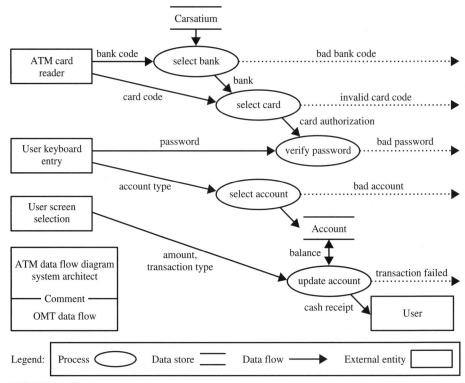

FIGURE 4–3

OMT DFD of the ATM system. The data flow lines include arrows to show the direction of data element movement. The circles represent processes. The boxes represent external entities. A data store reveals the storage of data.

The Booch methodology prescribes a macro development process and a micro development process.

4.4.1 The Macro Development Process

The macro process serves as a controlling framework for the micro process and can take weeks or even months. The primary concern of the macro process is technical management of the system. Such management is interested less in the actual object-oriented design than in how well the project corresponds to the requirements set for it and whether it is produced on time. In the macro process, the traditional phases of analysis and design to a large extent are preserved [4].

The macro development process consists of the following steps:

1. *Conceptualization*. During conceptualization, you establish the core requirements of the system. You establish a set of goals and develop a prototype to prove the concept.

2. *Analysis and development of the model*. In this step, you use the class diagram to describe the roles and responsibilities objects are to carry out in performing

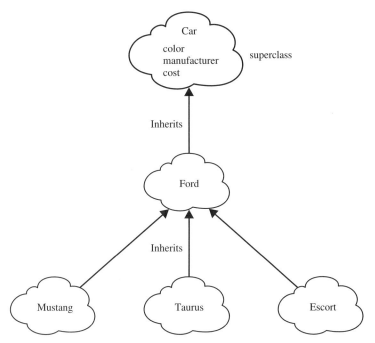

FIGURE 4–4

Object modeling using Booch notation. The arrows represent specialization; for example, the class Taurus is subclass of the class Ford.

the desired behavior of the system. Then, you use the object diagram to describe the desired behavior of the system in terms of scenarios or, alternatively, use the interaction diagram to describe behavior of the system in terms of scenarios.

3. *Design or create the system architecture.* In the design phase, you use the class diagram to decide what classes exist and how they relate to each other. Next, you use the object diagram to decide what mechanisms are used to regulate how objects collaborate. Then, you use the module diagram to map out where each class and object should be declared. Finally, you use the process diagram to determine to which processor to allocate a process. Also, determine the schedules for multiple processes on each relevant processor.

4. *Evolution or implementation.* Successively refine the system through many iterations. Produce a stream of software implementations (or executable releases), each of which is a refinement of the prior one.

5. *Maintenance.* Make localized changes to the system to add new requirements and eliminate bugs.

4.4.2 The Micro Development Process

Each macro development process has its own micro development processes. The micro process is a description of the day-to-day activities by a single or small group of software developers, which could look blurry to an outside viewer, since the analysis and design phases are not clearly defined.

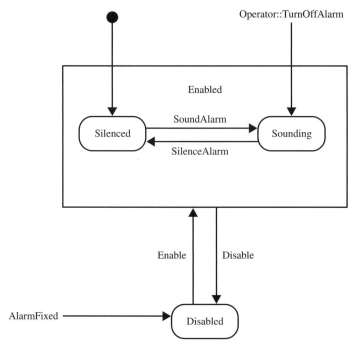

FIGURE 4–5

An alarm class state transition diagram with Booch notation. This diagram can capture the state of a class based on a stimulus. For example, a stimulus causes the class to perform some processing, followed by a transition to another state. In this case, the alarm silenced state can be changed to alarm sounding state and vice versa.

The micro development process consists of the following steps:

1. *Identify classes and objects.*
2. *Identify class and object semantics.*
3. *Identify class and object relationships.*
4. *Identify class and object interfaces and implementation.*

4.5 THE JACOBSON ET AL. METHODOLOGIES

The Jacobson et al. methodologies (e.g., object-oriented Business Engineering (OOBE), object-oriented Software Engineering (OOSE), and Objectory) cover the entire life cycle and stress traceability between the different phases, both forward and backward. This traceability enables reuse of analysis and design work, possibly much bigger factors in the reduction of development time than reuse of code. At the heart of their methodologies is the use-case concept, which evolved with Objectory (Object Factory for Software Development).

4.5.1 Use Cases

Use cases are scenarios for understanding system requirements. A use case is an interaction between users and a system. The use-case model captures the goal of the user and the responsibility of the system to its users (see Figure 4–6). In the requirements analysis, the use cases are described as one of the following [4]:

- Nonformal text with no clear flow of events.
- Text, easy to read but with a clear flow of events to follow (this is a recommended style).
- Formal style using pseudo code.

The use case description must contain

- *How* and *when* the use case begins and ends.
- The interaction between the use case and its actors, including *when* the interaction occurs and *what* is exchanged.
- *How* and *when* the use case will need data stored in the system or will store data in the system.
- *Exceptions* to the flow of events.
- *How* and *when* concepts of the problem domain are handled.

Every single use case should describe one main flow of events. An exceptional or additional flow of events could be added. The exceptional use case extends another use case to include the additional one. The use-case model employs extends and uses relationships. The extends relationship is used when you have one use case that is similar to another use case but does a bit more. In essence, it extends the functionality of the original use case (like a subclass). The uses relationship reuses common behavior in different use cases.

Use cases could be viewed as concrete or abstract. An ***abstract use case*** is not complete and has no actors that initiate it but is used by another use case. This inheritance could be used in several levels. Abstract use cases also are the ones that have uses or extends relationships.

FIGURE 4–6
Some uses of a library. As you can see, these are external views of the library system from an actor such as a member. The simpler the use case, the more effective it will be. It is unwise to capture all of the details right at the start; you can do that later.

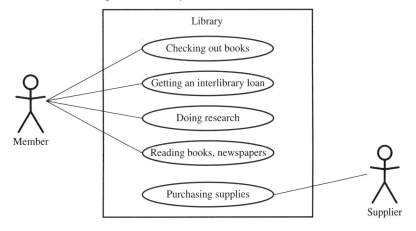

4.5.2 Object-Oriented Software Engineering: Objectory

Object-oriented software engineering (OOSE), also called *Objectory*, is a method of object-oriented development with the specific aim to fit the development of large, real-time systems. The development process, called *use-case driven development*, stresses that use cases are involved in several phases of the development (see Figure 4–7), including analysis, design, validation, and testing. The use-case scenario begins with a user of the system initiating a sequence of interrelated events.

The system development method based on OOSE, Objectory, is a disciplined process for the industrialized development of software, based on a use-case driven design. It is an approach to object-oriented analysis and design that centers on understanding the ways in which a system actually is used. By organizing the analysis and design models around sequences of user interaction and actual usage scenarios, the method produces systems that are both more usable and more robust, adapting more easily to changing usage. Jacobson et al.'s Objectory has been developed and applied to numerous application areas and embodied in the CASE tool systems.

Objectory is built around several different models:

- *Use case-model*. The use-case model defines the outside (actors) and inside (use case) of the system's behavior.
- *Domain object model*. The objects of the "real" world are mapped into the domain object model.
- *Analysis object model*. The analysis object model presents how the source code (implementation) should be carried out and written.
- *Implementation model*. The implementation model represents the implementation of the system.
- *Test model*. The test model constitutes the test plans, specifications, and reports.

FIGURE 4–7
The use-case model is considered in every model and phase.

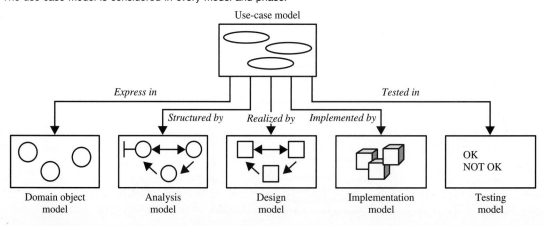

| Domain object model | Analysis model | Design model | Implementation model | Testing model |

The maintenance of each model is specified in its associated process. A process is created when the first development project starts and is terminated when the developed system is taken out of service.

4.5.3 Object-Oriented Business Engineering

Object-oriented business engineering (OOBE) is object modeling at the enterprise level. Use cases again are the central vehicle for modeling, providing traceability throughout the software engineering processes.

- *Analysis phase*. The analysis phase defines the system to be built in terms of the problem-domain object model, the requirements model, and the analysis model. The analysis process should not take into account the actual implementation environment. This reduces complexity and promotes maintainability over the life of the system, since the description of the system will be independent of hardware and software requirements. Jacobson [16] does not dwell on the development of the problem-domain object model, but refers the developer to Coad and Yourdon's [11] or Booch's [6] discussion of the topic, who suggest that the customer draw a picture of his view of the system to promote discussions. In their view, a full development of the domain model will not localize changes and therefore will not result in the most "robust and extensible structure." This model should be developed just enough to form a base of understanding for the requirements model. The analysis process is iterative but the requirements and analysis models should be stable before moving on to subsequent models. Jacobson et al. suggest that prototyping with a tool might be useful during this phase to help specify user interfaces.
- *Design and implementation phases*. The implementation environment must be identified for the design model. This includes factors such as Database Management System (DBMS), distribution of process, constraints due to the programming language, available component libraries, and incorporation of graphical user interface tools. It may be possible to identify the implementation environment concurrently with analysis. The analysis objects are translated into design objects that fit the current implementation environment.
- *Testing phase*. Finally, Jacobson describes several testing levels and techniques. The levels include unit testing, integration testing, and system testing.

4.6 PATTERNS

An emerging idea in systems development is that the process can be improved significantly if a system can be analyzed, designed, and built from prefabricated and predefined system components. One of the first things that any science or engineering discipline must have is a vocabulary for expressing its concepts and a language for relating them to each other. Therefore, we need a body of literature to help software developers resolve commonly encountered, difficult problems and a vocabulary for communicating insight and experience about these problems and their solutions. The primary focus here is not so much on technology as on creating a culture to document and support sound engineering architecture and design [5].

In this section, we look at the concept of patterns; and in the next section, we look at another emerging method, frameworks.

The use of design patterns originates in the work done by a building architect named Christopher Alexander during the late 1970s. Alexander wrote two books, *A Pattern Language* [1] and *A Timeless Way of Building* [2], that, in addition to giving examples, described his rationale for documenting patterns. Alexander's articulation on pattern work was soon employed by object-oriented thinkers looking for ways to describe commonly occurring design solutions and programming paradigms. As described in their seminal work in cataloging program design concepts, Gamma, Helm, Johnson, and Vlissides [15] say that the design pattern

> identifies the key aspects of a common design structure that make it useful for creating a reusable object-oriented design. [Furthermore, it] identifies the participating classes and instances, their roles and collaborations, and the distribution of responsibilities. It describes when it applies, whether it can be applied in view of other design constraints, and the consequences and trade-offs of its use.

Another book that helped popularize the use of patterns is *Pattern-Oriented Software Architecture—A System* by Frank Buschmann, Regine Meunier, Hans Rohnert, Peter Sommerlad, and Michael Stal [10]. Currently, patterns are being used largely for software architecture and design and, more recently, for organizations, specification models, and many other aspects of software development processes.

The main idea behind using patterns is to provide documentation to help categorize and communicate about solutions to recurring problems. The pattern has a name to facilitate discussion and the information it represents. A definition that more closely reflects its use within the patterns community is by Riehle and Züllighoven [20]:

> A *pattern* is [an] instructive information that captures the essential structure and insight of a successful family of proven solutions to a recurring problem that arises within a certain context and system of forces.

The documentation of a pattern, in essence, provides the contexts under which it is suitable and the constraints and forces that may affect a solution or its consequences. Communication about patterns is enabled by a vocabulary that describes the pattern and its related components such as name, context, motivation, and solution. By classifying these components and their nature (such as the structural or behavioral nature of the solution), we can categorize patterns.

A pattern involves a general description of a solution to a recurring problem bundle with various goals and constraints. But a pattern does more than just identify a solution, it also explains why the solution is needed. For better or for worse, however, the meteoric rise in popularity of software patterns frequently has caused them to be overhyped. Patterns have achieved buzzword status: It is immensely popular to use the word *pattern* to garner an audience. However, not every solution, algorithm, best practice, maxim, or heuristic constitutes a pattern (one or more key pattern ingredients may be absent). Even if something appears to have all the requisite pattern components, it should not be considered a pattern until it has been verified to be a recurring phenomenon (preferably found in at least three existing systems; this often is called the *rule of three*). A "pattern in waiting," which is not yet known to recur, sometimes is called a ***proto-pattern***. Many also feel it is inappropriate to decisively call something a *pattern* until it has undergone some degree of peer scrutiny or review [5]. Coplien [12] explains that a good pattern will do the following:

- *It solves a problem.* Patterns capture solutions, not just abstract principles or strategies.
- *It is a proven concept.* Patterns capture solutions with a track record, not theories or speculation.
- *The solution is not obvious.* The best patterns generate a solution to a problem indirectly—a necessary approach for the most difficult problems of design.
- *It describes a relationship.* Patterns do not just describe modules, but describe deeper system structures and mechanisms.
- *The pattern has a significant human component.* All software serves human comfort or quality of life; the best patterns explicitly appeal to aesthetics and utility.

The majority of the initial patterns developed focus on design problems and still design patterns represent most solutions. However, more recent patterns encompass all aspects of software engineering, including development organization, the software development process, project planning, requirements engineering, and software configuration management.

4.6.1 Generative and Nongenerative Patterns

Generative patterns are patterns that not only describe a recurring problem, they can tell us how to generate something and can be observed in the resulting system architectures they helped shape. Nongenerative patterns are static and passive: They describe recurring phenomena without necessarily saying how to reproduce them. We should strive to document generative patterns because they not only show us the characteristics of good systems, they teach us how to build them. Alexander explains that the most useful patterns are generative:

> These patterns in our minds are, more or less, mental images of the patterns in the world: they are abstract representations of the very morphological rules which define the patterns in the world. However, in one respect they are very different. The patterns in the world merely exist. But the same patterns in our minds are dynamic. They have force. They are generative. They tell us what to do; they tell us how we shall, or may, generate them; and they tell us too, that under certain circumstances, we must create them. Each pattern is a rule which describes what you have to do to generate the entity which it defines. [2, pp. 181–82]

Alexander wants patterns, and especially pattern languages, to be capable of generating whole, living structures. Part of the desire to create architectures that emulate life lies in the unique ability of living things to evolve and adapt to their ever-changing environments (not only for the sake of individual survival but also for survival of the species). Alexander wants to impart these same qualities into his architecture. Similarly, in software, good software architecture is all about being adaptable and resilient to change. So another aspect of generativity is about striving to create "living" architecture capable of dynamically adapting to fulfill changing needs and demands.

The successive application of several patterns, each encapsulating its own problem and forces, unfolds a larger solution, which emerges indirectly as a result of the smaller solutions. It is the generation of such emergent behavior that appears to be what is meant by *generativity*. In this fashion, a pattern language should guide its users to generate whole architectures that possess the quality. This particular aspect of Alexander's paradigm seems a bit too mystical for some people's tastes [5].

4.6.2 Patterns Template

Every pattern must be expressed "in the form of a rule [template] which establishes a relationship between a context, a system of forces which arises in that context, and a configuration, which allows these forces to resolve themselves in that context" [2].

Currently, several different pattern templates have been defined that eventually will represent a pattern. Despite this, it is generally agreed that a pattern should contain certain essential components. The following essential components should be clearly recognizable on reading a pattern [5]:

- *Name*. A meaningful name. This allows us to use a single word or short phrase to refer to the pattern and the knowledge and structure it describes. Good pattern names form a vocabulary for discussing conceptual abstractions. Sometimes, a pattern may have more than one commonly used or recognizable name in the literature. In this case, it is common practice to document these nicknames or synonyms under the heading of aliases or also known as. Some pattern forms also provide a classification of the pattern in addition to its name.
- *Problem*. A statement of the problem that describes its intent: the goals and objectives it wants to reach within the given context and forces. Often the forces oppose these objectives as well as each other.
- *Context*. The *preconditions* under which the problem and its solution seem to recur and for which the solution is desirable. This tells us the pattern's applicability. It can be thought of as the initial configuration of the system before the pattern is applied to it.
- *Forces*. A description of the relevant *forces* and constraints and how they interact or conflict with one another and with the goals we wish to achieve (perhaps with some indication of their priorities). A concrete scenario that serves as the *motivation* for the pattern frequently is employed (see also Examples). Forces reveal the intricacies of a problem and define the kinds of *trade-offs* that must be considered in the presence of the tension or dissonance they create. A good pattern description should fully encapsulate all the forces that have an impact on it.

- *Solution*. Static relationships and dynamic rules describing how to realize the desired outcome. This often is equivalent to giving instructions that describe how to construct the necessary products. The description may encompass pictures, diagrams, and prose that identify the pattern's structure, its participants, and their collaborations, to show how the problem is solved. The solution should describe not only the *static structure* but also *dynamic behavior*. The static structure tells us the form and organization of the pattern, but often the behavioral dynamics is what makes the pattern "come alive." The description of the pattern's solution may indicate guidelines to keep in mind (as well as pitfalls to avoid) when attempting a concrete implementation of the solution. Sometimes, possible variants or specializations of the solution are described as well.
- *Examples*. One or more sample applications of the pattern that illustrate a specific initial context; how the pattern is applied to and transforms that context; and the resulting context left in its wake. Examples help the reader understand the pattern's use and applicability. Visual examples and analogies often can be very useful. An example may be supplemented by a *sample implementation* to show one way the solution might be realized. Easy-to-comprehend examples from known systems usually are preferred.
- *Resulting context*. The state or configuration of the system after the pattern has been applied, including the consequences (both good and bad) of applying the pattern, and other problems and patterns that may arise from the new context. It describes the *postconditions* and *side effects* of the pattern. This is sometimes called a *resolution of forces* because it describes which forces have been resolved, which ones remain unresolved, and which patterns may now be applicable. Documenting the resulting context produced by one pattern helps you correlate it with the initial context of other patterns (a single pattern often is just one step toward accomplishing some larger task or project).
- *Rationale*. A justifying explanation of steps or rules in the pattern and also of the pattern as a whole in terms of how and why it resolves its forces in a particular way to be in alignment with desired goals, principles, and philosophies. It explains how the forces and constraints are orchestrated in concert to achieve a resonant harmony. This tells us how the pattern actually works, why it works, and why it is "good." The solution component of a pattern may describe the outwardly visible structure and behavior of the pattern, but the rationale is what provides insight into the *deep structures* and *key mechanisms* going on beneath the surface of the system.
- *Related patterns*. The static and dynamic relationships between this pattern and others within the same pattern language or system. Related patterns often share common forces. They also frequently have an initial or resulting context that is compatible with the resulting or initial context of another pattern. Such patterns might be predecessor patterns whose application leads to this pattern, successor patterns whose application follows from this pattern, alternative patterns that describe a different solution to the same problem but under different forces and constraints, and codependent patterns that may (or must) be applied simultaneously with this pattern.
- *Known uses*. The known occurrences of the pattern and its application within existing systems. This helps validate a pattern by verifying that it indeed is a

proven solution to a *recurring problem*. Known uses of the pattern often can serve as instructional examples (see also Examples).

Although it is not strictly required, good patterns often begin with an abstract that provides a short summary or overview. This gives readers a clear picture of the pattern and quickly informs them of its relevance to any problems they may wish to solve (sometimes such a description is called a *thumbnail sketch* of the pattern, or a **pattern thumbnail**). A pattern should identify its target audience and make clear what it assumes of the reader.

4.6.3 Antipatterns

A pattern represents a "best practice," whereas an antipattern represents "worst practice" or a "lesson learned." Antipatterns come in two varieties:

- Those describing a bad solution to a problem that resulted in a bad situation.
- Those describing how to get out of a bad situation and how to proceed from there to a good solution.

Antipatterns are valuable because often it is just as important to see and understand bad solutions as to see and understand good ones. Coplien explains that

> The study of anti-patterns is an important research activity. The presence of "good" patterns in a successful system is not enough; you also must show that those patterns are absent in unsuccessful systems. Likewise, it is useful to show the presence of certain patterns (anti-patterns) in unsuccessful systems, and their absence in successful systems. [12]

4.6.4 Capturing Patterns

Writing good patterns is *very* difficult, explains Appleton [5]. Patterns should provide not only facts (like a reference manual or users' guide) but also tell a story that captures the experience they are trying to convey. A pattern should help its users comprehend existing systems, customize systems to fit user needs, and construct new systems. The process of looking for patterns to document is called **pattern mining** (or sometimes *reverse architecting*). An interesting initiative started within the software community is to share experience with patterns and develop an ever-growing repository of patterns. People can contribute new solutions, lessons learned (or antipatterns), and more examples within a variety of contexts.

How do you know a pattern when you come across one? The answer is you do not always know. You may jot down the beginning of some things you think are patterns, but it may turn out that these are not patterns at all, or they are only pieces of patterns, simply good principles, or general rules that may form part of the rationale for a particular pattern. It is important to remember that a solution in which no forces are present is *not* a pattern [5].

These guidelines are summarized from Buschmann et al. [10]:

- *Focus on practicability*. Patterns should describe *proven solutions* to recurring problems rather than the latest scientific results.

- *Aggressive disregard of originality.* Pattern writers do *not* need to be the original inventor or discoverer of the solutions that they document.
- *Nonanonymous review.* Pattern submissions are *shepherded* rather than reviewed. The shepherd contacts the pattern author(s) and discusses with him or her how the patterns might be clarified or improved on.
- *Writers' workshops instead of presentations.* Rather than being presented by the individual authors, the patterns are discussed in writers' workshops, open forums where all attending seek to improve the patterns presented by discussing what they like about them and the areas in which they are lacking.
- *Careful editing.* The pattern authors should have the opportunity to incorporate all the comments and insights during the shepherding and writers' workshops before presenting the patterns in their finished form.

4.7 FRAMEWORKS

Frameworks are a way of delivering application development patterns to support best practice sharing during application development—not just within one company, but across many companies—through an emerging framework market. This is not an entirely new idea. Consider the following [22]:

- An experienced programmer almost never codes a new program from scratch—she'll use macros, copy libraries, and templatelike code fragments from earlier programs to make a start on a new one. Work on the new program begins by filling in new domain-specific code inside the older structures.
- A seasoned business consultant who has worked on many consulting projects performing data modeling almost never builds a new data model from scratch—he'll have a selection of model fragments that have been developed over time to help new modeling projects hit the ground running. New domain-specific terms will be substituted for those in his library models.

A *framework* is a way of presenting a generic solution to a problem that can be applied to all levels in a development [22]. However, design and software frameworks are the most popular. A definition of an object-oriented software framework is given by Gamma et al. [15]:

> A framework is a set of cooperating classes that make up a reusable design for a specific class of software. A framework provides architectural guidance by partitioning the design into abstract classes and defining their responsibilities and collaborations. A developer customizes a framework to a particular application by subclassing and composing instances of framework classes. The framework captures the design decisions that are common to its application domain. Frameworks thus emphasize design reuse over code reuse, though a framework will usually include concrete subclasses you can put to work immediately.

A single framework typically encompasses several design patterns. In fact, a framework can be viewed as the implementation of a system of design patterns.

Even though they are related in this manner, it is important to recognize that frameworks and design patterns are two distinctly separate beasts: A framework is executable software, whereas design patterns represent knowledge and experience about software. In this respect, frameworks are of a physical nature, while patterns are of a logical nature: Frameworks are the physical realization of one or more software pattern solutions; patterns are the instructions for how to implement those solutions [5].

Gamma et al. describe the major differences between design patterns and frameworks as follows [15]:

- *Design patterns are more abstract than frameworks*. Frameworks can be embodied in code, but only examples of patterns can be embodied in code. A strength of frameworks is that they can be written down in programming languages and not only studied but executed and reused directly. In contrast, design patterns have to be implemented each time they are used. Design patterns also explain the intent, trade-offs, and consequences of a design.
- *Design patterns are smaller architectural elements than frameworks*. A typical framework contains several design patterns but the reverse is never true.
- *Design patterns are less specialized than frameworks*. Frameworks always have a particular application domain. In contrast, design patterns can be used in nearly any kind of application. While more specialized design patterns are certainly possible, even these would not dictate an application architecture.

4.8 THE UNIFIED APPROACH

The approach promoted in this book is based on the best practices that have proven successful in system development and, more specifically, the work done by Booch, Rumbaugh, and Jacobson in their attempt to unify their modeling efforts. The unified approach (UA) (see Figure 1-1) establishes a unifying and unitary framework around their works by utilizing the unified modeling language (UML) to describe, model, and document the software development process. The idea behind the UA is not to introduce yet another methodology. The main motivation here is to combine the best practices, processes, methodologies, and *guidelines* along with UML notations and diagrams for better understanding object-oriented concepts and system development.

The unified approach to software development revolves around (but is not limited to) the following processes and concepts (see Figure 4–8). The processes are:

Use-case driven development
Object-oriented analysis
Object-oriented design
Incremental development and prototyping
Continuous testing

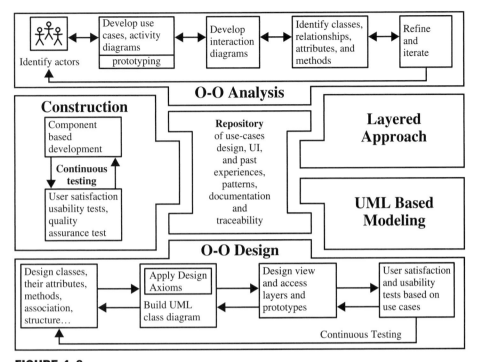

FIGURE 4–8
The processes and components of the unified approach.

The methods and technology employed include

Unified modeling language used for modeling.

Layered approach.

Repository for object-oriented system development patterns and frameworks.

Component-based development (Although, UA promote component-based development, the treatment of the subject is beyond the scope of the book.)

The UA allows iterative development by allowing you to go back and forth between the design and the modeling or analysis phases. It makes backtracking very easy and departs from the linear waterfall process, which allows no form of backtracking.

4.8.1 Object-Oriented Analysis

Analysis is the process of extracting the needs of a system and what the system must do to satisfy the users' requirements. The goal of object-oriented analysis is to first understand the domain of the problem and the system's responsibilities by understanding how the users use or will use the system. This is accomplished by constructing several models of the system. These models concentrate on describing what the system does rather than how it does it. Separating the behavior of a system from the way it is implemented requires viewing the system from the user's perspective rather than that of the machine. OOA Process consists of the following Steps:

1. Identify the Actors.
2. Develop a simple business process model using UML Activity diagram.
3. Develop the Use Case.
4. Develop interaction diagrams.
5. Identify classes.

4.8.2 Object-Oriented Design

Booch [9] provides the most comprehensive object-oriented design method. Ironically, since it is so comprehensive, the method can be somewhat imposing to learn and especially tricky to figure out where to start. Rumbaugh et al.'s and Jacobson et al.'s high-level models provide good avenues for getting started. UA combines these by utilizing Jacobson et al.'s analysis and interaction diagrams, Booch's object diagrams, and Rumbaugh et al.'s domain models. Furthermore, by following Jacobson et al.'s life cycle model, we can produce designs that are traceable across requirements, analysis, design, coding, and testing. OOD Process consists of:

- Designing classes, their attributes, methods, associations, structures and protocols, apply design axioms
- Design the Access Layer
- Design and prototype User interface
- User Satisfaction and Usability Tests based on the Usage/Use Cases
- Iterate and refine the design

4.8.3 Iterative Development and Continuous Testing

You must iterate and reiterate until, eventually, you are satisfied with the system. Since testing often uncovers design weaknesses or at least provides additional information you will want to use, repeat the entire process, taking what you have learned and reworking your design or moving on to reprototyping and retesting. Continue this refining cycle through the development process until you are satisfied with the results. During this iterative process, your prototypes will be incrementally transformed into the actual application. The UA encourages the integration of testing plans from day 1 of the project. Usage scenarios can become test scenarios; therefore, use cases will drive the usability testing. Usability testing is the process in which the functionality of software is measured. Chapter 13 will cover usability testing.

4.8.4 Modeling Based on the Unified Modeling Language

The unified modeling language was developed by the joint efforts of the leading object technologists Grady Booch, Ivar Jacobson, and James Rumbaugh with contributions from many others. The UML merges the best of the notations used by the three most popular analysis and design methodologies: Booch's methodology, Jacobson et al.'s use case, and Rumbaugh et al.'s object modeling technique. The

UML is becoming the universal language for modeling systems; it is intended to be used to express models of many different kinds and purposes, just as a programming language or a natural language can be used in many different ways. The UML has become the standard notation for object-oriented modeling systems. It is an evolving notation that still is under development. The UA uses the UML to describe and model the analysis and design phases of system development (UML notations will be covered in Chapter 5).

4.8.5 The UA Proposed Repository

In modern businesses, best practice sharing is a way to ensure that solutions to process and organization problems in one part of the business are communicated to other parts where similar problems occur. Best practice sharing eliminates duplication of problem solving. For many companies, best practice sharing is institutionalized as part of their constant goal of quality improvement. Best practice sharing must be applied to application development if quality and productivity are to be added to component reuse benefits. Such sharing extends the idea of software reusability to include all phases of software development such as analysis, design, and testing [22].

The idea promoted here is to create a repository that allows the maximum reuse of previous experience and previously defined objects, patterns, frameworks, and user interfaces in an easily accessible manner with a completely available and easily utilized format. As we saw previously, central to the discussion on developing this best practice sharing is the concept of a pattern. Everything from the original user request to maintenance of the project as it goes to production should be kept in the repository. The advantage of repositories is that, if your organization has done projects in the past, objects in the repositories from those projects might be useful. You can select any piece from a repository—from the definition of one data element, to a diagram, all its symbols, and all their dependent definitions, to entries—for reuse.

The UA's underlying assumption is that, if we design and develop applications based on previous experience, creating additional applications will require no more than assembling components from the library. Additionally, applying lessons learned from past developmental mistakes to future projects will increase the quality of the product and reduce the cost and development time. Some basic capability is available in most object-oriented environments, such as Microsoft repository, VisualAge, PowerBuilder, Visual C++, and Delphi. These repositories contain all objects that have been previously defined and can be reused for putting together a new software system for a new application. If a new requirement surfaces, new objects will be designed and stored in the main repository for future use.

The same arguments can be made about patterns and frameworks. Specifications of the software components, describing the behavior of the component and how it should be used, are registered in the repository for future reuse by teams of developers.

The repository should be accessible to many people. Furthermore, it should be relatively easy to search the repository for classes based on their attributes, methods,

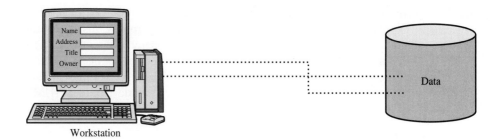

FIGURE 4–9
Two-layered architecture: interface and data.

or other characteristics. For example, application developers could select prebuilt components from the central component repository that match their business needs and assemble these components into a single application, customizing where needed.

Tools to fully support a comprehensive repository are not accessible yet, but this will change quickly and, in the near future, we will see more readily available tools to capture all phases of software development into a repository for use and reuse.

4.8.6 The Layered Approach to Software Development

Most systems developed with today's CASE tools or client-server application development environments tend to lean toward what is known as *two-layered architecture*: interface and data (see Figure 4–9).

In a two-layered system, user interface screens are tied to the data through routines that sit directly behind the screens; for example, a routine that executes when you click on a button. With every interface you create, you must re-create the business logic needed to run the screen. The routines required to access the data must exist within every screen. Any change to the business logic must be accomplished in every screen that deals with that portion of the business. This approach results in objects that are very specialized and cannot be reused easily in other projects.

A better approach to systems architecture is one that isolates the functions of the interface from the functions of the business. This approach also isolates the business from the details of the data access (see Figure 4–10). Using the three-

FIGURE 4–10
Objects are completely independent of how they are represented or stored.

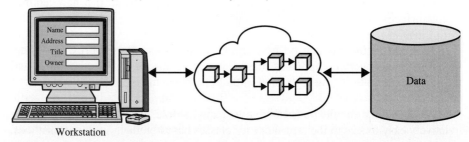

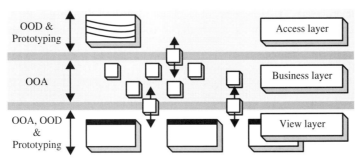

FIGURE 4–11
Business objects represent tangible elements of the application. They should be completely independent of how they are represented to the user or how they are physically stored.

layered approach, you are able to create objects that represent tangible elements of your business yet are completely independent of how they are represented to the user (through an interface) or how they are physically stored (in a database). The three-layered approach consists of a view or user interface layer, a business layer, and an access layer (see Figure 4–11).

4.8.6.1 The Business Layer   The business layer contains all the objects that represent the business (both data and behavior). This is where the real objects such as Order, Customer, Line item, Inventory, and Invoice exist. Most modern object-oriented analysis and design methodologies are generated toward identifying these kinds of objects.

The responsibilities of the business layer are very straightforward: Model the objects of the business and how they interact to accomplish the business processes. When creating the business layer, however, it is important to keep in mind a couple of things. These objects should not be responsible for the following:

• *Displaying details*. Business objects should have no special knowledge of how they are being displayed and by whom. They are designed to be independent of any particular interface, so the details of how to display an object should exist in the interface (view) layer of the object displaying it.
• *Data access details*. Business objects also should have no special knowledge of "where they come from." It does not matter to the business model whether the data are stored and retrieved via SQL or file I/O. The business objects need to know only to whom to talk about being stored or retrieved. The business objects are modeled during the object-oriented analysis.

A business model captures the static and dynamic relationships among a collection of business objects. Static relationships include object associations and aggregations. For example, a customer could have more than one account or an order could be aggregated from one or more line items. Dynamic relationships show how the business objects interact to perform tasks. For example, an order interacts with inventory to determine product availability. An individual business object can appear in different business models. Business models also incorporate control objects that direct their processes. The business objects are identified during the object-oriented analysis. Use cases can provide a wonderful tool to capture business objects.

4.8.6.2 The User Interface (View) Layer The user interface layer consists of objects with which the user interacts as well as the objects needed to manage or control the interface. The user interface layer also is called the *view layer*.

This layer typically is responsible for two major aspects of the applications:

- *Responding to user interaction*. The user interface layer objects must be designed to translate actions by the user, such as clicking on a button or selecting from a menu, into an appropriate response. That response may be to open or close another interface or to send a message down into the business layer to start some business process; remember, the business logic does not exist here, just the knowledge of which message to send to which business object.
- *Displaying business objects*. This layer must paint the best possible picture of the business objects for the user. In one interface, this may mean entry fields and list boxes to display an order and its items. In another, it may be a graph of the total price of a customer's orders.

The user interface layer's objects are identified during the object-oriented design phase. However, the requirement for a user interface or how a user will use the system is the responsibility of object-oriented analysis. Use cases can provide a very useful tool for understanding user interface requirements.

4.8.6.3 The Access Layer The access layer contains objects that know how to communicate with the place where the data actually reside, whether it be a relational database, mainframe, Internet, or file. Regardless of where the data actually reside, the access layer has two major responsibilities:

- *Translate request*. The access layer must be able to translate any data-related requests from the business layer into the appropriate protocol for data access. (For example, if Customer number 55552 needs to be retrieved, the access layer must be able to create the correct SQL statement and execute it.)
- *Translate results*. The access layer also must be able to translate the data retrieved back into the appropriate business objects and pass those objects back up into the business layer.

Access objects are identified during object-oriented design.

4.9 SUMMARY

In this chapter, we looked at current trends in object-oriented methodologies, sometimes known as *second-generation object-oriented methods*, which have been toward combining the best aspects of today's most popular methods.

Each method has its strengths. Rumbaugh et al. have a strong method for producing object models (sometimes known as *domain object models*). Jacobson et al. have a strong method for producing user-driven requirement and object-oriented analysis models. Booch has a strong method for producing detailed object-oriented design models.

Each method has a weakness, too. While Rumbaugh et al.'s OMT has strong methods for modeling the problem domain, OMT models cannot fully express the requirements. Jacobson et al. deemphasize object modeling and, although they cover a fairly wide range of the life cycle, they do not treat object-oriented design to the same level as Booch, who focuses almost entirely on design, not analysis.

Booch and Rumbaugh et al. are object centered in their approaches and focus more on figuring out what are the objects of a system, how are they related, and how do they collaborate with each other. Jacobson et al. are more user centered, in that everything in their approach derives from use cases or usage scenarios.

The main idea behind a pattern is the documentation to help categorize, communicate about, and locate solutions to recurring problems. Frameworks are a way of delivering application development patterns to support best practice sharing during application development. A single framework typically encompasses several design patterns. In fact, a framework can be viewed as the implementation of a system of design patterns. Writing good patterns is very difficult, since it should not only provide facts but also tell a story that captures the experience the pattern is trying to convey.

The UA is an attempt to combine the best practices, processes, and guidelines along with UML notations and diagrams for better understanding object-oriented concepts and object-oriented system development. The UA consists of the following processes:

- Use-case driven development
- Object-oriented analysis
- Object-oriented design
- Incremental development and prototyping
- Continuous testing

Futhermore, it utilizes the methods and technologies such as, unified modeling language, layered approach and promotes repository for all phases of software development.

KEY TERMS

Abstract use case (p. 69)
Framework (p. 77)
Pattern (p. 72)
Pattern mining (p. 76)
Pattern thumbnail (p. 76)
Proto-pattern (p. 73)

REVIEW QUESTIONS

1. What is a method?
2. What is a methodology?
3. What is process?

4. Describe the difference between a method and a process?

5. What are the phases of OMT? Briefly describe each phase.

6. What is an object model? What are the other OMT models?

7. What is the main advantage of DFD?

8. What is the strength of OMT?

9. Name five Booch diagrams.

10. Briefly describe the Booch system development processes.

11. What is the strength of Booch methodology?

12. What is Objectory?

13. Name the models in Objectory.

14. What is a use case?

15. What is the reason for having abstract use cases?

16. What are some of the ways that use cases can be described?

17. What must a use case contain?

18. What is the strength of the Jacobson et al. methodology?

19. Describe the difference between patterns and frameworks.

PROBLEMS

1. Consult the World Wide Web or a library to obtain an article on a real-world application that has incorporated a use-case model. Write a summary report of your finding.

2. Consult the Web or the library to obtain an article on future trends in object-oriented software development. Write a summary of your findings.

3. The best way to learn how to recognize and document useful patterns is by learning from others who have done it well. Consult the Web or the library to obtain articles that describe patterns (do not choose just one) and try to see if you can recognize all the necessary pattern components and desirable qualities mentioned in this chapter. When you see one that appeals to you, ask yourself why it is good. If you see one you dislike, try to figure out exactly what about the pattern leaves you unsatisfied. Read as much as you can, and try to learn from the masters. For an excellent source on patterns, obtain the paper written by Appleton [5]; it provides numerous resources for learning more about patterns. Examine how it is meaningful to you and how it will help you accomplish future goals. Write a summary of your findings.

4. Imagine that you are a methodologist and would like to develop your own object-oriented methodology by combining many different object-oriented methodologies. Use the materials in this chapter, Chapter 3, and the Web to create your own object-oriented methodology system development life cycle.

5. Consult the Web or the library to obtain an article that compares different methodologies.

6. This chapter did not cover all the methodologies listed earlier. Consult the Web or your friendly school library and write a short paper on one of the following methodologies:

a. Shlaer and Mellor's concept of the recursive design approach.

b. Beck and Cunningham's Classes, Responsibilities, and Collaborators (CRC) cards.

c. Wirfs-Brock et al.'s responsibility-driven design.

d. Coad and Yourdon's lightweight and prototype-oriented approach to methods.

REFERENCES

1. Alexander, Christopher; Ishikawa, Sara; and Silverstein, Murray. *A Pattern Language: Towns, Building, Construction.* Oxford University Press, 1977.

2. Alexander, Christopher. *Timeless Way of Building.* Oxford University Press, 1979.

3. Alter, Steven. *Information Systems: A Management Perspective*, 2d ed. Menlo Park, CA: Benjamin-Cummings, 1996.

4. Anderson, Michael; and Bergstrand, John. "Formalizing Use Cases with Message Sequence Charts." Master thesis, Department of Communication Systems at Lund Institute of Technology, 1995.

5. Brad Appleton. "Patterns and Software: Essential Concepts and Terminology." http://www.enteract.com/~bradapp/docs/patterns-intro.html, 1997.

6. Booch, Grady. *Software Engineering with Ada*, 2d ed. Menlo Park, CA: Benjamin-Cummings, 1987.

7. Booch, Grady. *Software Components with Ada, Structures, Tools, and Subsystems.* Menlo Park, CA: Benjamin-Cummings, 1987.

8. Booch, Grady. *Object-Oriented Design with Applications.* Menlo Park, CA: Benjamin-Cummings, 1991.

9. Booch, Grady; Jacobson, Ivar; and Rumbaugh, James. *The Unified Modeling Language, Notation Guide Version 1.0.* January 1997.

10. Buschmann, Frank; Meunier, Regine; Rohnert, Hans; Sommerlad, Peter; and Stal, Michael. *Pattern-Oriented Software Architecture—A System of Patterns.* Chichester, UK: Wiley and Sons Ltd., 1996.

11. Coad, Peter; and Yourdon, Edward. *Object-Oriented Design.* Englewood Cliffs, NJ: Yourdon Press Computing Series, 1991.

12. Coplien, James O. *Advanced C++ Programming Styles and Idioms.* Reading, MA: Addison-Wesley, 1992.

13. Coplien, James O. "A Development Process Generative Pattern Language." Proceedings of Pattern Languages of Program Design 1992, Monticello, August 1994. James O. Coplien. *A Development Process Generative Pattern Language.* In James O. Coplien and Douglas C. Schmidt, editors, *Pattern Languages of Program Design,* Chapter 13, 183–237. Addison-Wesley, Reading, MA, 1995.

14. Fowler, Martin; and Scott, Kendall. *UML Distilled: Applying the Standard Object Modeling Language.* Reading, MA: Addison-Wesley, 1997.

15. Gamma, E.; Helm, R.; Johnson, R.; and Vlissides, J. *Design Patterns.* Reading, MA: Addison-Wesley, 1995.

16. Jacobson, Ivar. *Object-Oriented Software Engineering: A Use Case Driven Approach.* Reading, MA: Addison-Wesley, Object Technology Series, 1994.

17. Jacobson, Ivar; Ericsson, Maria; and Jacobson, Agneta. *The Object Advantage Business Process Reengineering with Object Technology.* Reading, MA: Addison-Wesley, 1995.

18. Meyer, Bertrand. *Object-Oriented Software Construction.* Hertfordshire, England: Prentice-Hall International, 1988.

19. Rumbaugh, James; Blaha, Michael; Premerlani, William; Eddy, Frederick; and Lorensen, William. *Object-Oriented Modeling and Design.* Englewood Cliffs, NJ: Prentice-Hall, 1991.

20. Riehle, D.; and Züllighoven, H. "Understanding and Using Patterns in Software Development." *Theory and Practice of Object Systems* 2, no. 1 (1996).

21. Shlaer, Sally; and Mellor, Stephen J. *Object Lifecycles, Modeling the World in States.* Englewood Cliffs, NJ: Prentice-Hall, 1992.

22. Short, Keith. Component Based Development and Object Modeling. Texas Instruments Software, February 1997.

23. Wirfs-Brock, Rebecca; Wilkerson, Brian; and Wiener, Lauren. *Designing Object-Oriented Software.* Englewood Cliffs, NJ: Prentice-Hall, 1990.

CHAPTER 5

Unified Modeling Language

Model is a simplified representation of reality.

—Efraim Turban [9]

Chapter Objectives

You should be able to define and understand

- Modeling and its benefit.
- Different types of models.
- Basics of Unified Modeling Language (UML) and its modeling diagrams.
  - UML Class diagram.
  - UML Use case diagram.
  - UML Sequence diagram.
  - UML Collaboration diagram.
  - UML Statechart diagram.
  - UML Activity diagram.
  - UML Component diagram.
  - UML Deployment diagram.

5.1 INTRODUCTION

A *model* is an abstract representation of a system, constructed to understand the system prior to building or modifying it. The term *system* is used here in a broad sense to include any process or structure. For example, the organizational structure of a corporation, health services, computer software, instruction of any sort (including computers), the national economy, and so forth all would be termed *systems*.

Efraim Turban [9] describes a model as a simplified representation of reality. A model is simplified because reality is too complex or large and much of the complexity actually is irrelevant to the problem we are trying to describe or solve. A model provides a means for conceptualization and communication of ideas in a precise and unambiguous form. The characteristics of simplification and representation are difficult to achieve in the real world, since they frequently contradict each other. Thus, modeling enables us to cope with the complexity of a system.

Most modeling techniques used for analysis and design involve graphic languages. These graphic languages are sets of symbols. The symbols are used according to certain rules of the methodology for communicating the complex relationships of information more clearly than descriptive text. The main goal of most CASE tools is to aid us in using these graphic languages, along with their associated methodologies.

Modeling frequently is used during many of the phases of the software life cycle, such as analysis, design, and implementation. For example, Objectory is built around several different models:

- *Use-case model.* The use-case model defines the outside (actors) and inside (use case) of the system's behavior.
- *Domain object model.* Objects of the "real" world are mapped into the domain object model.
- *Analysis object model.* The analysis object model presents how the source code (i.e., the implementation) should be carried out and written.
- *Implementation model.* The implementation model represents the implementation of the system.
- *Test model.* The test model constitutes the test plans, specifications, and reports.

Modeling, like any other object-oriented development, is an iterative process. As the model progresses from analysis to implementation, more detail is added, but it remains essentially the same.

In this chapter, we look at unified modeling language (UML) notations and diagrams. The main idea here is to gain exposure to the UML syntax, semantics, and modeling constructs. Many new concepts will be introduced here from a modeling standpoint. We apply these concepts in system analysis and design contexts in later chapters.

5.2 STATIC AND DYNAMIC MODELS

Models can represent static or dynamic situations. Each representation has different implications for how the knowledge about the model might be organized and represented [7].

5.2.1 Static Model

A *static model* can be viewed as a snapshot of a system's parameters at rest or at a specific point in time. Static models are needed to represent the structural or static aspect of a system. For example, a customer could have more than one account or an order could be aggregated from one or more line items. Static models assume stability and an absence of change in data over time. The unified modeling language class diagram is an example of a static model.

5.2.2 Dynamic Model

A *dynamic model*, in contrast to a static model, can be viewed as a collection of procedures or behaviors that, taken together, reflect the behavior of a system over time. Dynamic relationships show how the business objects interact to perform tasks. For example, an order interacts with inventory to determine product availability.

A system can be described by first developing its static model, which is the structure of its objects and their relationships to each other frozen in time, a baseline. Then, we can examine changes to the objects and their relationships over time. Dynamic modeling is most useful during the design and implementation phases of the system development. The UML interaction diagrams and activity models are examples of UML dynamic models.

5.3 WHY MODELING?

Building a model for a software system prior to its construction is as essential as having a blueprint for building a large building. Good models are essential for communication among project teams. As the complexity of systems increases, so does the importance of good modeling techniques. Many other factors add to a project's success, but having a rigorous modeling language is essential. A modeling language must include [2]

- Model elements—fundamental modeling concepts and semantics.
- Notation—visual rendering of model elements.
- Guidelines—expression of usage within the trade.

In the face of increasingly complex systems, visualization and modeling become essential, since we cannot comprehend any such system in its entirety. The use of visual notation to represent or model a problem can provide us several benefits relating to clarity, familiarity, maintenance, and simplification.

- *Clarity*. We are much better at picking out errors and omissions from a graphical or visual representation than from listings of code or tables of numbers. We very easily can understand the system being modeled because visual examination of the whole is possible.
- *Familiarity*. The representation form for the model may turn out to be similar to the way in which the information actually is represented and used by the employees currently working in the problem domain. We, too, may find it more comfortable to work with this type of representation.
- *Maintenance*. Visual notation can improve the maintainability of a system. The visual identification of locations to be changed and the visual confirmation of

those changes will reduce errors. Thus, you can make changes faster, and fewer errors are likely to be introduced in the process of making those changes.

• *Simplification*. Use of a higher level representation generally results in the use of fewer but more general constructs, contributing to simplicity and conceptual understanding.

Turban cites the following advantages of modeling [9]:

1. Models make it easier to express complex ideas. For example, an architect builds a model to communicate ideas more easily to clients.
2. The main reason for modeling is the reduction of complexity. Models reduce complexity by separating those aspects that are unimportant from those that are important. Therefore, it makes complex situations easier to understand.
3. Models enhance and reinforce learning and training.
4. The cost of the modeling analysis is much lower than the cost of similar experimentation conducted with a real system.
5. Manipulation of the model (changing variables) is much easier than manipulating a real system.

To summarize, here are a few key ideas regarding modeling:

• A model is rarely correct on the first try.
• Always seek the advice and criticism of others. You can improve a model by reconciling different perspectives.
• Avoid excess model revisions, as they can distort the essence of your model. Let simplicity and elegance guide you through the process.

5.4 INTRODUCTION TO THE UNIFIED MODELING LANGUAGE

The unified modeling language is a language for specifying, constructing, visualizing, and documenting the software system and its components. The UML is a graphical language with sets of rules and semantics. The rules and semantics of a model are expressed in English, in a form known as *object constraint language* (OCL). OCL is a specification language that uses simple logic for specifying the properties of a system. The UML is not intended to be a visual programming language in the sense of having all the necessary visual and semantic support to replace programming languages. However, the UML does have a tight mapping to a family of object-oriented languages, so that you can get the best of both worlds.

The goals of the unification efforts were to keep it simple; to cast away elements of existing Booch, OMT, and OOSE methods that did not work in practice; to add elements from other methods that were more effective; and to invent new methods only when an existing solution was unavailable. Because the UML authors, in effect, were designing a language (albeit a graphical one), they had to strike a proper balance between minimalism (everything is text and boxes) and overengineering (having a symbol or figure for every conceivable modeling element). To that end, they were very careful about adding new things: They did not want to make the UML unnecessarily complex. A similar situation exists with the problem of UML not supporting other diagrams. Booch et al. explain that other diagrams, such as the data flow diagram (DFD), were not included in the UML because they do not fit as cleanly into a consistent object-oriented paradigm. For example, activity diagrams accomplish much of what people want from DFDs and then some; activity diagrams also are useful for modeling work flow. The authors of the UML clearly are promoting the UML diagrams over all others for object-oriented projects but do not condemn all other diagrams. Along the way, however, some things were found that were advantageous to add because they had proven useful in other modeling practice.

The primary goals in the design of the UML were as follows [2, p. 3]:

1. Provide users a ready-to-use, expressive visual modeling language so they can develop and exchange meaningful models.
2. Provide extensibility and specialization mechanisms to extend the core concepts.
3. Be independent of particular programming languages and development processes.
4. Provide a formal basis for understanding the modeling language.
5. Encourage the growth of the OO tools market.
6. Support higher-level development concepts.
7. Integrate best practices and methodologies.

This section of the chapter is based on the *The Unified Modeling Language, Notation Guide Version 1.1* written by Grady Booch, Ivar Jacobson, and James Rumbaugh [2].

5.5 UML DIAGRAMS

Every complex system is best approached through a small set of nearly independent views of a model; no single view is sufficient. Every model may be expressed at different levels of fidelity. The best models are connected to reality. The UML defines nine graphical diagrams:

1. Class diagram (static)
2. Use-case diagram
3. Behavior diagram (dynamic):
    3.1. Interaction diagram:
        3.1.1. Sequence diagram
        3.1.2. Collaboration diagram
    3.2. Statechart diagram
    3.3. Activity diagram
4. Implementation diagram:
    4.1. Component diagram
    4.2. Deployment diagram

The choice of what models and diagrams one creates has a great influence on how a problem is encountered and how a corresponding solution is shaped. We will study applications of different diagrams throughout the book. However, in this chapter we concentrate on the UML notations and its semantics.

5.6 UML CLASS DIAGRAM

The UML *class diagram*, also referred to as *object modeling*, is the main static analysis diagram. These diagrams show the static structure of the model. A class diagram is a collection of static modeling elements, such as classes and their relationships, connected as a graph to each other and to their contents; for example, the things that exist (such as classes), their internal structures, and their relationships to other classes. Class diagrams do not show temporal information, which is required in dynamic modeling.

Object modeling is the process by which the logical objects in the real world (problem space) are represented (mapped) by the actual objects in the program (logical or a mini world). This visual representation of the objects, their relationships, and their structures is for ease of understanding. To effectively develop a model of the real world and to determine the objects required in the system, you first must ask what objects are needed to model the system. Answering the following questions will help you to stay focused on the problem at hand and determine what is inside the problem domain and what is outside it:

• What are the goals of the system?
• What must the system accomplish?

You need to know what objects will form the system because, in the object-oriented viewpoint, objects are the primary abstraction. The main task of object modeling is to graphically show what each object will do in the problem domain, describe the structure (such as class hierarchy or part-whole) and the relationships among objects (such as associations) by visual notation, and determine what behaviors fall within and outside the problem domain.

5.6.1 Class Notation: Static Structure

A class is drawn as a rectangle with three components separated by horizontal lines. The top name compartment holds the class name, other general properties of the class, such as attributes, are in the middle compartment, and the bottom compartment holds a list of operations (see Figure 5–1).

Either or both the attribute and operation compartments may be suppressed. A separator line is not drawn for a missing compartment if a compartment is suppressed; no inference can be drawn about the presence or absence of elements in it. The class name and other properties should be displayed in up to three sections. A stylistic convention of UML is to use an italic font for abstract classes and a normal (roman) font for concrete classes.

5.6.2 Object Diagram

A static object diagram is an instance of a class diagram. It shows a snapshot of the detailed state of the system at a point in time. Notation is the same for an object diagram and a class diagram. Class diagrams can contain objects, so a class diagram with objects and no classes is an object diagram.

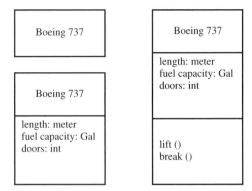

FIGURE 5-1
In class notation, either or both the attributes and operation compartments may be suppressed.

5.6.3 Class Interface Notation

Class interface notation is used to describe the externally visible behavior of a class; for example, an operation with public visibility. Identifying class interfaces is a design activity of object-oriented system development. The UML notation for an interface is a small circle with the name of the interface connected to the class. A class that requires the operations in the interface may be attached to the circle by a dashed arrow. The dependent class is not required to actually use all of the operations. For example, a Person object may need to interact with the BankAccount object to get the Balance; this relationship is depicted in Figure 5–2 with UML class interface notation.

5.6.4 Binary Association Notation

A binary association is drawn as a solid path connecting two classes, or both ends may be connected to the same class. An association may have an association name. Furthermore, the association name may have an optional black triangle in it, the point of the triangle indicating the direction in which to read the name. The end of an association, where it connects to a class, is called the *association role* (see Figure 5–3).

5.6.5 Association Role

A simple association—the technical term for it is *binary association*—is drawn as a solid line connecting two class symbols. The end of an association, where it connects to a class, shows the association role. The role is part of the association, not

FIGURE 5-2
Interface notation of a class.

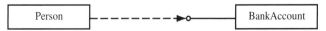

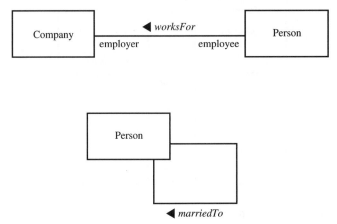

FIGURE 5–3
Association notation.

part of the class. Each association has two or more roles to which it is connected. In Figure 5–3, the association worksFor connects two roles, employee and employer. A Person is an employee of a Company and a Company is an employer of a Person.

The UML uses the term a*ssociation navigation* or *navigability* to specify a role affiliated with each end of an association relationship. An arrow may be attached to the end of the path to indicate that navigation is supported in the direction of the class pointed to. An arrow may be attached to neither, one, or both ends of the path. In particular, arrows could be shown whenever navigation is supported in a given direction. In the UML, association is represented by an open arrow, as represented in Figure 5–4. Navigability is visually distinguished from inheritance, which is denoted by an unfilled arrowhead symbol near the superclass.

In Figure 5–4, the association is navigable in only one direction, from the BankAccount to Person, but not the reverse. This might indicate a design decision, but it also might indicate an analysis decision, that the Person class is frozen and cannot be extended to know about the BankAccount class, but the BankAccount class can know about the Person class.

5.6.6 Qualifier

A *qualifier* is an association attribute. For example, a person object may be associated to a Bank object. An attribute of this association is the account#. The account# is the qualifier of this association (see Figure 5–5).

FIGURE 5–4
Association notation.

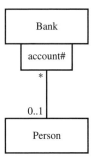

FIGURE 5–5
The figure depicts association qualifier and its multiplicity.

A qualifier is shown as a small rectangle attached to the end of an association path, between the final path segment and the symbol of the class to which it connects. The qualifier rectangle is part of the association path, not part of the class. The qualifier rectangle usually is smaller than the attached class rectangle (see Figure 5–5).

5.6.7 Multiplicity

Multiplicity specifies the range of allowable associated classes. It is given for roles within associations, parts within compositions, repetitions, and other purposes. A multiplicity specification is shown as a text string comprising a period-separated sequence of integer intervals, where an interval represents a range of integers in this format (see Figure 5–5):

lower bound .. upper bound.

The terms *lower bound* and *upper bound* are integer values, specifying the range of integers including the lower bound to the upper bound. The star character (*) may be used for the upper bound, denoting an unlimited upper bound. If a single integer value is specified, then the integer range contains the single values. For example,

0..1
0..*
1..3, 7..10, 15, 19..*

5.6.8 OR Association

An *OR association* indicates a situation in which only one of several potential associations may be instantiated at one time for any single object. This is shown as a dashed line connecting two or more associations, all of which must have a class in common, with the constraint string {or} labeling the dashed line (see Figure 5–6). In other words, any instance of the class may participate in, at most, one of the associations at one time.

5.6.9 Association Class

An *association class* is an association that also has class properties. An association class is shown as a class symbol attached by a dashed line to an association

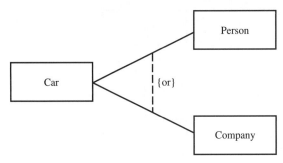

FIGURE 5–6
An OR association notation. A car may associate with a person or a company.

path. The name in the class symbol and the name string attached to the association path are the same (see Figure 5–7). The name can be shown on the path or the class symbol or both. If an association class has attributes but no operations or other associations, then the name may be displayed on the association path and omitted from the association class to emphasize its "association nature." If it has operations and attributes, then the name may be omitted from the path and placed in the class rectangle to emphasize its "class nature."

5.6.10 N-Ary Association

An *n-ary association* is an association among more than two classes. Since n-ary association is more difficult to understand, it is better to convert an n-ary association to binary association. However, here, for the sake of completeness, we cover the notation of n-ary association. An n-ary association is shown as a large diamond with a path from the diamond to each participant class. The name of the association (if any) is shown near the diamond. The role attachment may appear on each path as with a binary association. Multiplicity may be indicated; however, qualifiers and aggregation are not permitted. An association class symbol may be at-

FIGURE 5–7
Association class.

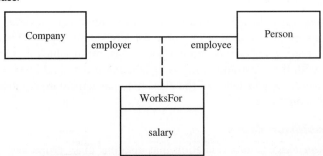

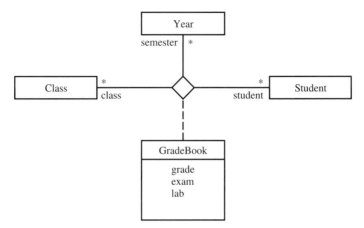

FIGURE 5–8

An n-ary (ternary) association that shows association among class, year, and student classes. The association class GradeBook which contains the attributes of the associations such as grade, exam, and lab.

tached to the diamond by a dashed line, indicating an n-ary association that has attributes, operation, or associations. The example depicted in Figure 5–8 shows the grade book of a class in each semester.

5.6.11 Aggregation and Composition (a-part-of)

Aggregation is a form of association. A hollow diamond is attached to the end of the path to indicate aggregation. However, the diamond may not be attached to both ends of a line, and it need not be presented at all (see Figure 5–9).

Composition, also known as the *a-part-of*, is a form of aggregation with strong ownership to represent the component of a complex object. Composition also is referred to as a *part-whole relationship*. The UML notation for composition is a solid diamond at the end of a path. Alternatively, the UML provides a graphically nested form that, in many cases, is more convenient for showing composition (see Figure 5–10).

Parts with multiplicity greater than one may be created after the aggregate itself but, once created, they live and die with it. Such parts can also be explicitly removed before the death of the aggregate.

5.6.12 Generalization

Generalization is the relationship between a more general class and a more specific class. Generalization is displayed as a directed line with a closed, hollow arrowhead

FIGURE 5–9

Association path.

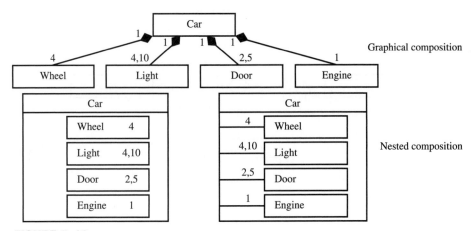

FIGURE 5–10
Different ways to show composition.

at the superclass end (see Figure 5–11). The UML allows a *discriminator* label to be attached to a generalization of the superclass. For example, the class Boeing-Airplane has instances of the classes Boeing 737, Boeing 747, Boeing 757, and Boeing 767, which are subclasses of the class BoeingAirplane. Ellipses (...) indicate that the generalization is incomplete and more subclasses exist that are not shown (see Figure 5–12). The constructor complete indicates that the generalization is complete and no more subclasses are needed.

If a text label is placed on the hollow triangle shared by several generalization paths to subclasses, the label applies to all of the paths. In other words, all subclasses share the given properties.

FIGURE 5–11
Generalization notation.

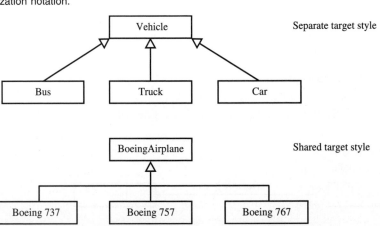

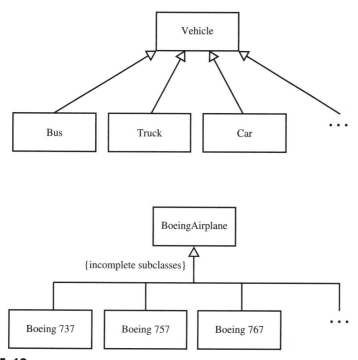

FIGURE 5–12
Ellipses (. . .) indicate that additional classes exist and are not shown.

5.7 USE-CASE DIAGRAM

The use-case concept was introduced by Ivar Jacobson in the object-oriented software engineering (OOSE) method [5]. The functionality of a system is described in a number of different use cases, each of which represents a specific flow of events in the system.

A use case corresponds to a sequence of transactions, in which each transaction is invoked from outside the system (actors) and engages internal objects to interact with one another and with the system's surroundings.

The description of a use case defines what happens in the system when the use case is performed. In essence, the use-case model defines the outside (actors) and inside (use case) of the system's behavior. Use cases represent specific flows of events in the system. The use cases are initiated by actors and describe the flow of events that these actors set off. An actor is anything that interacts with a use case: It could be a human user, external hardware, or another system. An actor represents a category of user rather than a physical user. Several physical users can play the same role. For example, in terms of a Member actor, many people can be members of a library, which can be represented by one actor called *Member*.

A *use-case diagram* is a graph of actors, a set of use cases enclosed by a system boundary, communication (participation) associations between the actors and the use cases, and generalization among the use cases.

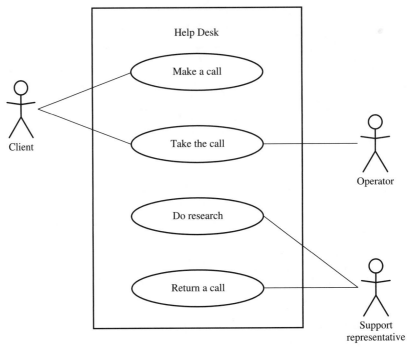

FIGURE 5–13
A use-case diagram shows the relationship among actors and use cases within a system.

Figure 5–13 diagrams use cases for a Help Desk. A use-case diagram shows the relationship among the actors and use cases within a system. A client makes a call that is taken by an operator, who determines the nature of the problem. Some calls can be answered immediately; other calls require research and a return call.

A use case is shown as an ellipse containing the name of the use case. The name of the use case can be placed below or inside the ellipse. Actors' names and use case names should follow the capitalization and punctuation guidelines of the model.

An actor is shown as a class rectangle with the label <<actor>>, or the label and a stick figure, or just the stick figure with the name of the actor below the figure (see Figure 5–14).

FIGURE 5–14
The three representations of an actor are equivalent.

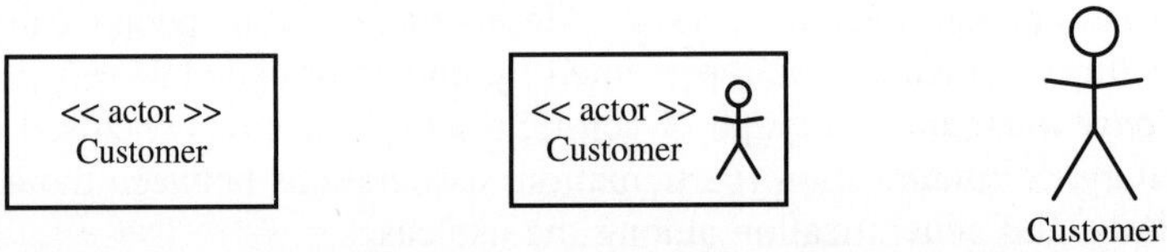

These relationships are shown in a use-case diagram:

1. *Communication.* The communication relationship of an actor in a use case is shown by connecting the actor symbol to the use-case symbol with a solid path. The actor is said to "communicate" with the use case.
2. *Uses.* A uses relationship between use cases is shown by a generalization arrow from the use case.
3. *Extends.* The extends relationship is used when you have one use case that is similar to another use case but does a bit more. In essence, it is like a subclass.

5.8 UML DYNAMIC MODELING (BEHAVIOR DIAGRAMS)

It is impossible to capture all details of a complex system in just one model or view. Kleyan and Gingrich explain:

> One must understand both the structure and the function of the objects involved. One must understand the taxonomic structure of class objects, the inheritance and mechanisms used, the individual behaviors of objects, and the dynamic behavior of the system as a whole. The problem is somewhat analogous to that of viewing a sports event such as tennis or a football game. Many different camera angles are required to provide an understanding of the action taking place. Each camera reveals particular aspects of the action that could not be conveyed by one camera alone. [6]

The diagrams we have looked at so far largely are static. However, events happen dynamically in all systems: Objects are created and destroyed, objects send messages to one another in an orderly fashion, and in some systems, external events trigger operations on certain objects. Furthermore, objects have states. The state of an object would be difficult to capture in a static model.

> The state of an object is the result of its behavior. Booch provides us an excellent example: "When a telephone is first installed, it is in idle state, meaning that no previous behavior is of great interest and that the phone is ready to initiate and receive calls. When someone picks up the handset, we say that the phone is now off-hook and in the dialing state; in this state, we do not expect the phone to ring: we expect to be able to initiate a conversation with a party or parties on another telephone. When the phone is on-hook, if it rings and then we pick up the handset, the phone is now in the receiving state, and we expect to be able to converse with the party that initiated the conversation [1]."

Booch explains that describing a systematic event in a static medium such as on a sheet of paper is difficult, but the problem confronts almost every discipline. In object-oriented development, you can express the dynamic semantics of a problem with the following diagrams:

Behavior diagrams (dynamic):
- Interaction diagrams:
  - Sequence diagrams
  - Collaboration diagrams
- Statechart diagrams
- Activity diagrams

Each class may have an associated activity diagram that indicates the behavior of the class's instance (its object). In conjunction with the use-case model, we may provide a scripts or an interaction diagram to show the time or event ordering of messages as they are evaluated [1].

5.8.1 UML Interaction Diagrams

Interaction diagrams are diagrams that describe how groups of objects collaborate to get the job done. *Interaction diagrams* capture the behavior of a single use case, showing the pattern of interaction among objects. The diagram shows a number of example objects and the messages passed between those objects within the use case [3]. There are two kinds of interaction models: sequence diagrams and collaboration diagrams.

5.8.1.1 UML Sequence Diagram *Sequence diagrams* are an easy and intuitive way of describing the behavior of a system by viewing the interaction between the system and its environment. A sequence diagram shows an interaction arranged in a time sequence. It shows the objects participating in the interaction by their lifelines and the messages they exchange, arranged in a time sequence.

A sequence diagram has two dimensions: the vertical dimension represents time, the horizontal dimension represents different objects. The vertical line is called the object's *lifeline*. The *lifeline* represents the object's existence during the interaction. This form was first popularized by Jacobson. An object is shown as a box at the top of a dashed vertical line (see Figure 5–15). A role is a slot for an object within a collaboration that describes the type of object that may play the role and its relationships to other roles. However, a sequence diagram does not show the relationships among the roles or the association among the objects. An object role is shown as a vertical dashed line, the lifeline.

FIGURE 5–15

An example of a sequence diagram.

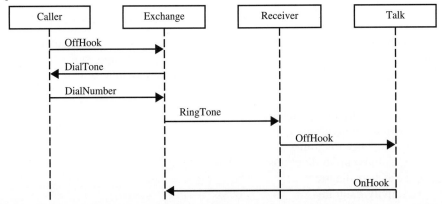

Each message is represented by an arrow between the lifelines of two objects. The order in which these messages occur is shown top to bottom on the page. Each message is labeled with the message name. The label also can include the argument and some control information and show self-delegation, a message that an object sends to itself, by sending the message arrow back to the same lifeline. The horizontal ordering of the lifelines is arbitrary. Often, call arrows are arranged to proceed in one direction across the page, but this is not always possible and the order conveys no information.

The sequence diagram is very simple and has immediate visual appeal—this is its great strength. A sequence diagram is an alternative way to understand the overall flow of the control of a program. Instead of looking at the code and trying to find out the overall sequence of behavior, you can use the sequence diagram to quickly understand that sequence [3].

5.8.1.2 UML Collaboration Diagram Another type of interaction diagram is the collaboration diagram. A *collaboration diagram* represents a collaboration, which is a set of objects related in a particular context, and interaction, which is a set of messages exchanged among the objects within the collaboration to achieve a desired outcome. In a collaboration diagram, objects are shown as figures. As in a sequence diagram, arrows indicate the message sent within the given use case. In a collaboration diagram, the sequence is indicated by numbering the messages. Some people argue that numbering the messages makes it more difficult to see the sequence than drawing the lines on the page. However, since the collaboration diagram is more compressed, other things can be shown more easily—for example, how the objects are linked together—and the layout can be overlaid with packages or other information.

A collaboration diagram provides several numbering schemes. The simplest is illustrated in Figure 5–16. You can also use a decimal numbering scheme (see Fig-

FIGURE 5–16
A collaboration diagram with simple numbering.

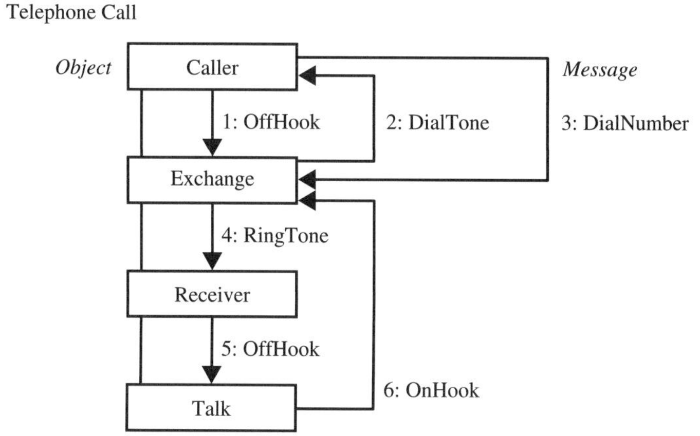

Telephone Call

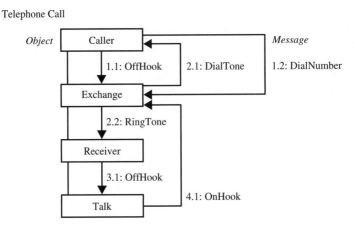

FIGURE 5–17
A collaboration diagram with decimal numbering.

ure 5–17), where 1.2: DialNumber means that the Caller (1) is calling the Exchange (2); hence, the number 1.2. The UML uses the decimal scheme because it makes it clear which operation is calling which other operation, although it can be hard to see the overall sequence [3].

Different people have different preferences when it comes to deciding whether to use sequence or collaboration diagrams. Fowler and Scott suggest that a sequence diagram is easier to read. Others prefer a collaboration diagram, because they can use the layout to indicate how objects are statically connected [3]. Fowler and Scott argue that the main advantage of interaction diagrams (both collaboration and sequence) is simplicity. You easily can see the message by looking at the diagram. The disadvantage of interaction diagrams is that they are great only for representing a single sequential process; they begin to break down when you want to represent conditional looping behavior. However, conditional behavior can be represented in sequence or collaboration diagrams through two methods. The preferred method is to use separate diagrams for each scenario. Another way is to use conditions on messages to indicate the behavior. The main guideline in developing interaction diagrams is simplicity. The interaction diagram loses its clarity with more complex conditional behavior. If you want to capture complex behavior in a single diagram, use an activity diagram, which will be described in a later section.

An interaction diagram basically is used to examine the behavior of objects within a single use case. It is good at showing collaboration among the objects but not so good at precise definition of the behavior [3].

5.8.2 UML Statechart Diagram

A *statechart diagram* (also called a *state diagram*) shows the sequence of states that an object goes through during its life in response to outside stimuli and messages. The state is the set of values that describes an object at a specific point in time and is represented by state symbols and the transitions are represented by arrows connecting the state symbols. A statechart diagram may contain subdiagrams.

A state diagram represents the state of the method execution (that is, the state of the object executing the method), and the activities in the diagram represent the activities of the object that performs the method. The purpose of the state diagram is to understand the algorithm involved in performing a method. To complete an object-oriented design, the activities within the diagram must be assigned to objects and the control flows assigned to links in the object diagram.

A statechart diagram is similar to a Petri net diagram, where a token (shown by a solid black dot) represents an activity symbol. When an activity symbol appears within a state symbol, it indicates the execution of an operation. Executing a particular step within the diagram represents a state within the execution of the overall method. The same operation name may appear more than once in a state diagram, indicating the invocation of the same operation in a different phase. An outgoing solid arrow attached to a statechart symbol indicates a transition triggered by the completion of the activity. The name of this implicit event need not be written, but conditions that depend on the result of the activity or other values may be included. An event occurs at the instant in time when the value is changed. A message is data passed from one object to another. At a minimum, a message is a name that will trigger an operation associated with the target object; for example, an Employee object that contains the name of an employee. If the Employee object received a message (*getEmployeeName*) asking for the name of the employee, an operation contained in the Employee class (e.g., returnEmployeeName) would be invoked. That operation would check the attribute Employee and then assign the value associated with that attribute back to the object that sent the message in the first place. In this case, the state of the Employee object would not have been changed. Now, consider a situation where the same Employee object received a message (*updateEmployeeAddress*) that contained a parameter (2000 21st Street, Seattle, WA):

updateEmployeeAddress (2000 21st Street, Seattle, WA)

In this case the object would invoke an operation from its class that would modify the value associated with the attribute Employee, changing it from the old address to the new address; therefore, the state of the employee object has been changed.

A state is represented as a rounded box, which may contain one or more compartments. The compartments are all optional. The name compartment and the internal transition compartment are two such compartments:

- The *name compartment* holds the optional name of the state. States without names are "anonymous" and all are distinct. Do not show the same named state twice in the same diagram, since it will be very confusing.
- The *internal transition compartment* holds a list of internal actions or activities performed in response to events received while the object is in the state, without changing states.

The syntax used is this: event-name argument-list / action-expression; for example, help / display help.

Two special events are *entry* and *exit*, which are reserved words and cannot be used for event names. These terms are used in the following ways: entry / action-expression (the action is to be performed on entry to the state) and exit / action-expressed (the action is to be performed on exit from the state).

The statechart supports nested state machines; to activate a substate machine use the keyword *do*: do / machine-name (argument-list). If this state is entered, after the entry action is completed, the nested (sub)state machine will be executed with its initial state. When the nested state machine reaches its final state, it will exit the action of the current state, and the current state will be considered completed. An initial state is shown as a small dot, and the transition from the initial state may be labeled with the event that creates the objects; otherwise, it is unlabeled. If unlabeled, it represents any transition to the enclosing state. A final state is shown as a circle surrounding a small dot, a bull's-eye. This represents the completion of activity in the enclosing state and triggers a transition on the enclosing state labeled by the implicit activity completion event, usually displayed as an unlabeled transition (see Figure 5–18).

The transition can be simple or complex. A simple transition is a relationship between two states indicating that an object in the first state will enter the second state and perform certain actions when a specific event occurs; if the specified con-

FIGURE 5–18

A simple state Idle and a nested state. The dialing state contains substates, which consist of start and dial states.

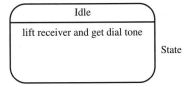

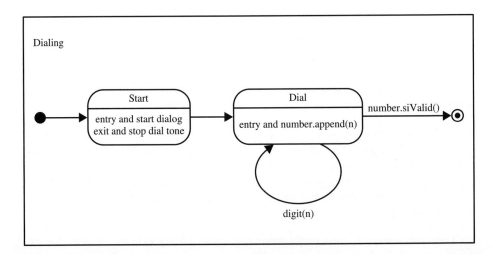

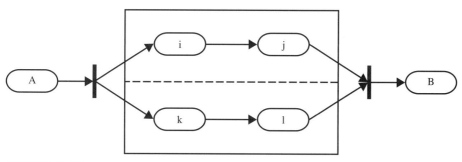

FIGURE 5–19
A complex transition.

ditions are satisfied, the transition is said to "fire." Events are processed one at a time. An event that triggers no transition is simply ignored.

A complex transition may have multiple source and target states. It represents a synchronization or a splitting of control into concurrent threads. A complex transition is enabled when all the source states are changed, after a complex transition "fires" all its destination states. A complex transition is shown as a short heavy bar.[1] The bar may have one or more solid arrows from states to the bar (these are source states); the bar also may have one or more solid arrows from the bar to states (these are the destination states). A transition string may be shown near the bar. Individual arrows do not have their own transition strings (see Figure 5–19).

There certainly is no reason to prepare a state diagram for each class in your system. Indeed, many developers create rather large systems without bothering to create any state diagrams. However, state diagrams are useful when you have a class that is very dynamic. In that situation, it often is helpful to prepare a state diagram to be sure you understand each of the possible states an object of the class could take and what event (message) would trigger each transition from one state to another. In effect, state diagrams emphasize the use of events and states to determine the overall activity of the system.

5.8.3 UML Activity Diagram

An *activity diagram* is a variation or special case of a state machine, in which the states are activities representing the performance of operations and the transitions are triggered by the completion of the operations. Unlike state diagrams that focus on the events occurring to a single object as it responds to messages, an activity diagram can be used to model an entire business process. The purpose of an activity diagram is to provide a view of flows and what is going on inside a use case or among several classes. However, activity diagram can also be used to represent a class's method implementation as we will see throughout the book.

---

[1]A synchronization bar, which can represent synchronization, forking, or both.

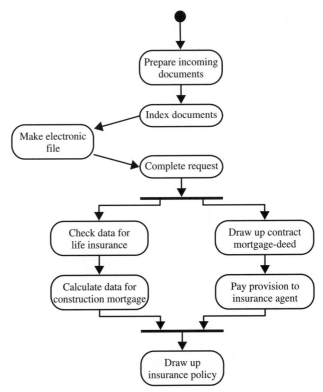

FIGURE 5-20
An activity diagram for processing mortgage requests (Loan: Processing Mortgage Request).

An activity model is similar to a statechart diagram, where a token (shown by a black dot) represents an operation. An activity is shown as a round box, containing the name of the operation. When an operation symbol appears within an activity diagram or other state diagram, it indicates the execution of the operation. Executing a particular step within the diagram represents a state within the execution of the overall method. The same operation name may appear more than once in a state diagram, indicating the invocation of the same operation in different phases. An outgoing solid arrow attached to an activity symbol indicates a transition triggered by the completion of the activity. The name of this implicit event need not be written, but the conditions that depend on the result of the activity or other values may be included (see Figure 5–20). Several transitions with different conditions imply a branching off of control. If conditions are not disjoint, then the branch is nondeterministic. The concurrent control is represented by multiple arrows leaving a synchronization bar, which is represented by a short thick bar with incoming and outgoing arrows. Joining concurrent control is expressed by multiple arrows entering the synchronization bar. The activity diagram depicted in Figure 5–20, "Process Mortgage Request," is a multistep operation, all of which are completed before the single operation Draw up insurance policy.

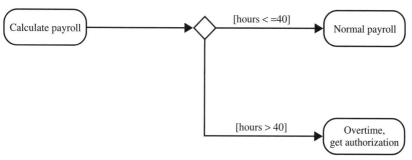

FIGURE 5–21
A decision.

An activity diagram is used mostly to show the internal state of an object, but external events may appear in them. An external event appears when the object is in a "wait state," a state during which there is no internal activity by the object and the object is waiting for some external event to occur as the result of an activity by another object (such as a user input or some other signal). The two states are wait state and activity state. More than one possible event might take the object out of the wait state; the first one that occurs triggers the transition. A wait state is the "normal" state.

Activity and state diagrams express a decision when conditions (the UML calls them *guard conditions*) are used to indicate different possible transitions that depend on Boolean conditions of container object. The figure provided for a decision is the traditional diamond shape, with one or more incoming arrows and two or more outgoing arrows, each labeled by a distinct guard condition. All possible outcomes should appear on one of the outgoing transitions (see Figure 5–21).

Actions may be organized into swimlanes, each separated from neighboring swimlanes by vertical solid lines on both sides. Each **swimlane** represents responsibility for part of the overall activity and may be implemented by one or more objects. The relative ordering of the swimlanes has no semantic significance but might indicate some affinity. Each action is assigned to one swimlane. A transition may cross lanes; there is no significance to the routing of the transition path (see Figure 5–22).

5.8.4 Implementation Diagrams

Implementation diagrams show the implementation phase of systems development, such as the source code structure and the run-time implementation structure. There are two types of implementation diagrams: Component diagrams show the structure of the code itself, and deployment diagrams show the structure of the run-time system. These are relatively simple, high-level diagrams compared with the diagrams we have considered so far. Although we look at component-based development later in this book, a full discussion of implementation is beyond the scope of this book. This section is included to show the place of implementation in the UML.

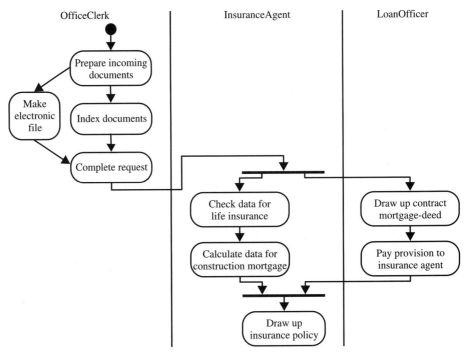

FIGURE 5–22
Swimlanes in an activity diagram.

5.8.4.1 Component Diagram *Component diagrams* model the physical components (such as source code, executable program, user interface) in a design. These high-level physical components may or may not be equivalent to the many smaller components you use in the creation of your application. For example, a user interface may contain many other off-the-shelf components purchased to put together a graphical user interface.

Another way of looking at components is the concept of packages. A package is used to show how you can group together classes, which in essence are smaller scale components. Packages will be covered in the next section, but a point worth mentioning here is that a package usually will be used to group logical components of the application, such as classes, and not necessarily physical components. However, the package could be a first approximation of what eventually will turn into physical grouping. In that case, the package will become a component [4].

A component diagram is a graph of the design's components connected by dependency relationships. A component is represented by the boxed figure shown in Figure 5–23. Dependency is shown as a dashed arrow.

5.8.4.2 Deployment Diagram *Deployment diagrams* show the configuration of run-time processing elements and the software components, processes, and objects that live in them. Software component instances represent run-time manifestations

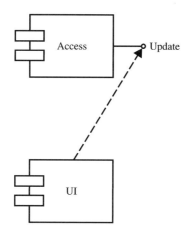

FIGURE 5–23
A component diagram.

of code units. In most cases, component diagrams are used in conjunction with deployment diagrams to show how physical modules of code are distributed on various hardware platforms. In many cases, component and deployment diagrams can be combined [4].

A deployment diagram is a graph of nodes connected by communication association. Nodes may contain component instances, which means that the component lives or runs at that node. Components may contain objects; this indicates that the object is part of the component. Components are connected to other components by dashed-arrow dependencies, usually through interfaces, which indicate one component uses the services of another. Each node or processing element in the

FIGURE 5–24
The basic UML notation for a deployment diagram.

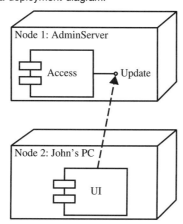

system is represented by a three-dimensional box. Connections between the nodes (or platforms) themselves are shown by solid lines (see Figure 5–24).

5.9 MODEL MANAGEMENT: PACKAGES AND MODEL ORGANIZATION

A *package* is a grouping of model elements. Packages themselves may contain other packages. A package may contain both subordinate packages and ordinary model elements. The entire system can be thought of as a single high-level package with everything else in it. All UML model elements and diagrams can be organized into packages.

A package is represented as a folder, shown as a large rectangle with a tab attached to its upper left corner. If contents of the package are not shown, then the name of the package is placed within the large rectangle. If contents of the package are shown, then the name of the package may be placed on the tab (see Figure 5–25). The contents of the package are shown within the large rectangle.

Figure 5–26 shows an example of several packages. This figure shows three packages (Clients, Bank, and Customer) and three classes (Account class, Savings class, and Checking class) inside the Business Model package. A real model would have many more classes in each package. The contents might be shown if they

FIGURE 5–25
A package and its contents.

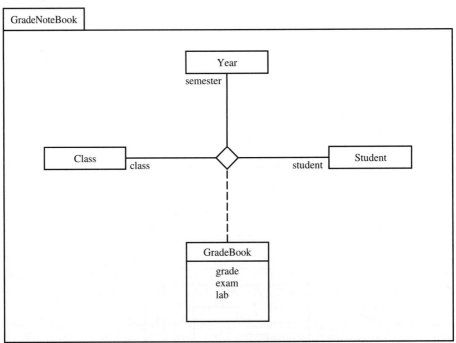

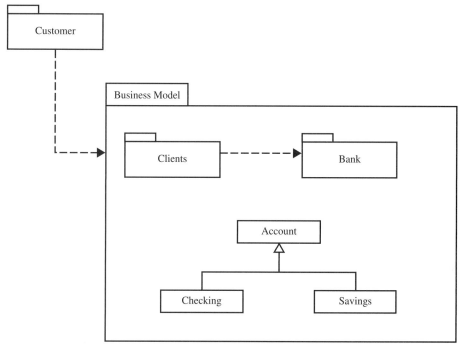

FIGURE 5–26
A package and its dependencies.

are small, or they might be suppressed from higher levels. The entire system is a package.

Figure 5–26 also shows the hierarchical structure, with one package dependent on other packages. For example, the Customer depends on the package Business Model, meaning that one or more elements within Customer depend on one or more elements within the other packages. The package Business Model is shown partially expanded. In this case, we see that the package Business Model owns the classes Bank, Checking, and Savings as well as the packages Clients and Bank. Ownership may be shown by a graphic nesting of the figures or by the expansion of a package in a separate drawing.

Packages can be used to designate not only logical and physical groupings but also use-case groups. A use-case group, as the name suggests, is a package of use cases.

Model dependency represents a situation in which a change to the target element may require a change to the source element in the dependency, thus indicating the relationship between two or more model elements. It relates the model elements themselves and does not require a set of instances for its meaning. A dependency is shown as a dashed arrow from one model element to another on which the first element is dependent (see Figure 5–27).

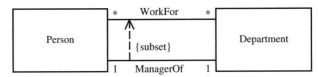

FIGURE 5–27
An example of constraints. A person is a manager of people who work for the accounting department.

5.10 UML EXTENSIBILITY

In this section, we look at general purpose mechanisms, which may be applied to any modeling element, and at the extensibility of the UML.

5.10.1 Model Constraints and Comments

Constraints are assumptions or relationships among model elements specifying conditions and propositions that must be maintained as true; otherwise the system described by the model would be invalid. Some constraints, such as association OR constraints, are predefined in the UML; others may be defined by users.

Constraints are shown as text in braces, {} (see Figure 5–27). The UML also provides language for writing constraints in the OCL. However, the constraint may be written in a natural language. A constraint may be a "comment," in which case it is written in text. For an element whose notation is a text string such as an attribute, the constraint string may follow the element text string. For a list of elements whose notation is a list of text strings, such as the attributes within class, the constraint string may appear as an element in the list. The constraint applies to

FIGURE 5–28
Note.

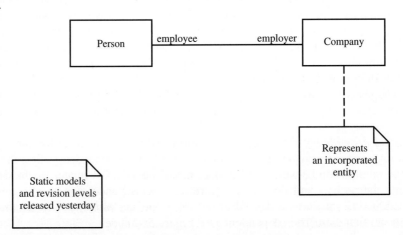

all succeeding elements of the list until reaching another constraint string list element or the end of the list. A constraint attached to an individual list element does not supersede the general constraints but may modify individual constraints within the constraint's string. For a class or association path, the constraints string may be placed near the symbol name.

The example depicted in Figure 5–27 shows two classes and two associations. The constraint is shown as a dashed arrow from one element to the other, labeled by the constraints string in braces. The direction of the arrow is relevant information within the constraint.

5.10.2 Note

A *note* is a graphic symbol containing textual information; it also could contain embedded images. It is attached to the diagram rather than to a model element. A note is shown as a rectangle with a "bent corner" in the upper right corner. It can contains any length text (see Figure 5–28).

5.10.3 Stereotype

Stereotypes represent a built-in extensibility mechanism of the UML. User-defined extensions of the UML are enabled through the use of stereotypes and constraints. A stereotype, in effect, is a new class of modeling element introduced during modeling. It represents a subclass of an existing modeling element with the same form (attributes and relationships) but a different intent. UML stereotypes extend and tailor the UML for a specific domain or process.

The general presentation of a stereotype is to use a figure for the base element but place a keyword string above the name of the element (if used, the keyword string is the name of a stereotype within matched guillemets, "<<", ">>", such as <<flow>>. Note that a guillemet looks like a double angle-bracket, but it is a single character in most fonts. The stereotype allows extension of UML notation as well as a graphic figure, texture, and color. The figure can be used in one of two ways: (1) instead of or in addition to the stereotype keyword string as part of the symbol for the base model element or (2) as the entire base model element (see Figure 5–29). Other information contained by the base model element symbol is suppressed.

The main shortcoming of extensive use of stereotypes is that it makes the model less universal and not easily interchangeable with other tools or software systems.

5.11 UML META-MODEL

The UML defines notations as well as a meta-model. UML graphic notations can be used not only to describe the system's components but also to describe a model itself. This is known as a *meta-model*. In other words, a *meta-model* is a model of modeling elements. The purpose of the UML meta-model is to provide a single,

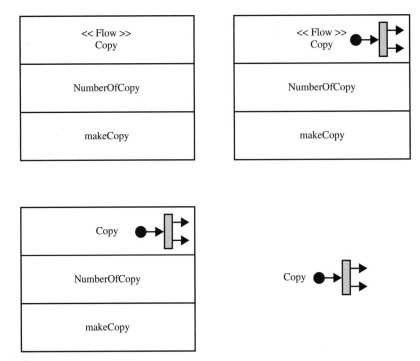

FIGURE 5–29
Various forms of stereotype notation.

common, and definitive statement of the syntax and semantics of the elements of the UML.

The meta-model provides us a means to connect different UML diagrams. The connection between the different diagrams is very important, and the UML attempts to make these couplings more explicit through defining the underlying model (meta-model) while imposing no methodology.

The presence of this meta-model has made it possible for its developers to agree on semantics and how those semantics would be best rendered. This is an important step forward, since it can assure consistency among diagrams. The meta-model also (in the future) can serve as a means to exchange data between different CASE tools. Additionally, the meta-model has made it possible for a team to explore ways to make the modeling language much simpler by, in a sense, unifying the elements of the unified modeling language. Figure 5–30 is an example of the UML meta-model that describes *relationship* with association and generalization; similarly *association* is depicted as a composition of association roles. Here we have used UML modeling elements (such as generalization and composition) to describe the model itself; hence, the term *meta-model*.

Most users of methods do not need such a deep understanding to get some value out of UML notation. However, it does help define what constitutes a well-formed model, that is, one that is syntactically correct.

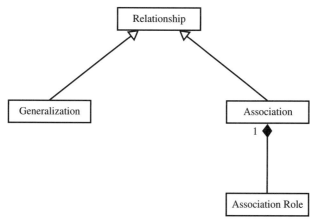

FIGURE 5–30
The UML meta-model describing the relationship between association and generalization.
Association is depicted as a composition of association roles. Here, we use UML modeling elements (such as generalization and composition) to describe the model itself, hence, the term
meta-model.

5.12 SUMMARY

A model is a simplified representation of reality, simplified because reality is too complex or large and much of the complexity actually is irrelevant to the problem being described or solved.

The unified modeling language was developed by Booch, Jacobson, and Rumbaugh. The UML encompasses the unification of their modeling notations.

The UML class diagram is the main static structure analysis diagram for the system. It represents the class structure of a system with relationships between classes and inheritance structure. The class diagram is developed through use-case, sequence, and collaboration diagrams.

The use-case diagram captures information on how the system or business works or how you wish it to work. It is a scenario-building approach in which you model the processes of the system. It is an excellent way to lead into object-oriented analysis of the system.

In the UML sequence diagram is for dynamic modeling, where objects are represented by vertical lines and messages passed back and forth between the objects are modeled by horizontal vectors between the objects.

The UML collaboration diagram is an alternative view of the sequence diagram, showing in a scenario how objects interrelate with one another.

Statechart diagrams, another form of dynamic modeling, focus on the events occurring within a single object as it responds to messages; an activity diagram is used to model an entire business process. Thus, an activity model can represent several different classes.

Implementation diagrams show the implementation phase of systems development, such as the source code and run-time implementation structures. The two types of implementation diagrams are component diagrams, which show the structure of the code itself, and deployment diagrams, which show the structure of the run-time system.

Stereotypes represent a built-in extensibility mechanism of the UML. User-defined extensions of the UML are enabled through the use of stereotypes and constraints.

UML graphical notations can be used not only to describe the system's components but also to describe a model itself; this is known as a *meta-model*. It is a model of modeling elements. The purpose of the UML meta-model is to provide a single, common, and definitive statement of the syntax and semantics of the elements of the UML.

KEY TERMS

Activity diagram (p. 109)
Association class (p. 97)
Class diagram (p. 94)
Collaboration diagram (p. 105)
Component diagram (p. 112)
Deployment diagram (p. 112)
Dynamic model (p. 91)
Generalization (p. 99)
Implementation diagram (p. 111)
Interaction diagram (p. 104)
Lifeline (p. 104)
Meta-model (p. 117)
Model dependency (p. 115)
Model (p. 89)
Multiplicity (p. 97)
N-ary association (p. 98)
Note (p. 117)
OR association (p. 97)
Package (p. 114)
Qualifier (p. 96)
Sequence diagram (p. 104)
Statechart diagram (p. 106)
Static model (p. 90)
Stereotype (p. 117)
Swimlane (p. 111)
Use-case diagram (p. 101)

REVIEW QUESTIONS

1. What is a model?
2. Why do we need to model a problem?

3. What is data modeling?

4. What are the different types of modeling? Briefly describe each.

5. What is UML? What is the importance of UML?

6. Describe the class diagram.

7. How would you represent or model extremely visible behavior of a class?

8. What is an association role?

9. What is multiplicity?

10. What is a qualifier?

11. What are some of the forms of associations? Draw their UML representations.

12. How would you show complete and incomplete generalizations?

13. What are model constraints, and how are they represented in the UML?

14. How does the UML group model elements?

15. Name and describe the relationships in a use case diagram.

16. What are some of the UML dynamic diagrams?

17. When would you use interaction diagrams?

18. What is the difference between sequence diagrams and collaboration diagrams?

19. What is the purpose of an activity model?

20. What is a meta-model? Is understanding a meta-model important?

PROBLEMS

1. Run through Quick Start of the Popkin's Object Architecture.

Problems 2–4 are based on the Rhode Island Video Entertainment Library (RIVEL) case. The Rhode Island Video Entertainment Library (RIVEL) is a group organized to encourage and administer the free exchange of videotapes in Rhode Island. RIVEL's membership has gotten larger than can be administered efficiently by Tony Costa, its only paid employee. Accordingly, the RIVEL members unanimously have hammered out a resolution to automate their currently manual videotape operation.

Tony is very enthusiastic about the object-oriented stuff. Your task is to develop an object model of RIVEL to better understand the RIVEL requirements. You are to develop an object information model: the hierarchy of objects and their relationships with no specific implementation plan. The implementing contractor will worry about that.

The following classes have been identified:

- *People class.* The people is a formal class. It has no direct instance but provides us with general class for the members as well as the employee class.
- *Member class.* A member is an individual or group that has contributed one or more media to the library.
- *Employee class.* An employee is an individual who uses the system, such as a librarian.
- *Media class.* A formal class (another generalization), this provides a general class for disc and tape classes.
- *Tape class.* A tape is one of the physical media on which programs might be recorded.
- *Disc class.* A disc is one of the physical media on which programs might be recorded.
- *Loan class.* Loan associates members to media they wish to borrow.
- *Contribution class.* Contribution associates members to media they have contributed.

2. Use SA/Object Architect to model the generalization of the RIVEL.

3. Use Object Architect to model the association of the RIVEL.

4. Use Object Architect to model the aggregation/a-part-of of the RIVEL.

REFERENCES

1. Booch, Grady. *Object-Oriented Design with Applications*, 2d ed. Menlo Park, CA: Benjamin-Cummings, 1994.
2. Booch, Grady; Jacobson, Ivar; and Rumbaugh, James. *The Unified Modeling Language, Notation Guide Version 1.1*. September 1997.
3. Fowler, Martin; and Scott, Kendall. *UML Distilled: Applying the Standard Object Modeling Language*. Reading, MA: Addison-Wesley, 1997.
4. Harmon, Paul; and Watson, Mark. *Understanding UML: The Developer's Guide with a Web-Based Application in Java*. San Francisco: Morgan Kaufmann, 1997.
5. Jacobson, Ivar. *Object-Oriented Software Engineering: A Use Case Driven Approach*. Addison-Wesley, 1994.
6. Kleyan, M.; and Gingrich, P. "GraphTree—Understanding Object-Oriented Systems Using Concurrently Animated Views." *SIGPLAN Notices* 23, no. 11 (1988), p.192.
7. Martin, James; and Odell, James. *Object-Oriented Analysis and Design*. New York: Prentice Hall, 1992.
8. Shlaer, Sally; and Mellor, Stephen J. *Object Lifecycles, Modeling the World in States*. Englewood Cliffs, NJ: Prentice-Hall, 1992.
9. Turban, Efraim. *Decision Support and Expert Management System's Management Support Systems*, 3d ed. New York: Macmillan Publishing Company, 1993.

PART III

OBJECT-ORIENTED ANALYSIS: USE-CASE DRIVEN

Analysis is the process of extracting the needs of a system and what the system must do to satisfy the users' requirements. The goal of object-oriented analysis is to understand the domain of the problem and the system's responsibilities by understanding how the users use or will use the system. This part consists of Chapters 6, 7, and 8.

CHAPTER 6

Object-Oriented Analysis Process: Identifying Use Cases

. . . just think of all the Christmas presents that are never removed from their boxes before being returned.
—Gause and Weinberg [6]

Chapter Objectives

You should be able to define and understand

- The object-oriented analysis process.
- The use-case modeling and analysis.
- Identifying actors.
- Identifying use cases.
- Developing effective documentation.

6.1 INTRODUCTION

The first step in finding an appropriate solution to a given problem is to understand the problem and its domain. The main objective of the analysis is to capture a complete, unambiguous, and consistent picture of the requirements of the system and what the system must do to satisfy the users' requirements and needs. This is accomplished by constructing several models of the system that concentrate on describing what the system does rather than how it does it. Separating the behavior of a system from the way that behavior is implemented requires viewing the system from the perspective of the user rather than that of the machine.

Analysis is the process of transforming a problem definition from a fuzzy set of facts and myths into a coherent statement of a system's requirements. In Chapter 3, we looked at the software development process as three basic transformations. The objective of this chapter is to describe Transformation 1, which is the transformation of the users' needs into a set of problem statements and requirements (also known as *requirement determination*). In this phase of the software process, you must analyze how the users will use the system and what is needed to accomplish the system's operational requirements. Analysis involves a great deal of interaction with the people who will be affected by the system, including the actual users and anyone else on whom its creation will have an impact. The analyst has four major tools at his or her disposal for extracting information about a system:

1. Examination of existing system documentation
2. Interviews
3. Questionnaire
4. Observation

In addition, there are minor methods, such as literature review. However, these activities must be directed by a use-case model that can capture the user requirements. The inputs to this phase are the users' requirements, both written and oral, which will be reduced to the model of the required operational capability of the system.

An object-oriented environment allows the same set of models to be used for analysis, design, and implementation. The analyst is concerned with the uses of the system, identifying the objects and inheritance, and thinks about the events that change the state of objects. The designer adds detail to this model, perhaps designing screens, user interaction, and database access. The thought process flows so naturally from analyst to designer that it may be difficult to tell where analysis ends and design begins [8].

6.2 WHY ANALYSIS IS A DIFFICULT ACTIVITY

Analysis is a creative activity that involves understanding the problem, its associated constraints, and methods of overcoming those constraints. This is an iterative process that goes on until the problem is well understood [11].

Norman [9] explains the three most common sources of requirement difficulties:

1. Fuzzy descriptions
2. Incomplete requirements
3. Unnecessary features

A common problem that leads to requirement ambiguity is a fuzzy and ambiguous description, such as "fast response time" or "very easy and very secure updating mechanisms." A requirement such as fast response time is open to interpretation, which might lead to user dissatisfaction if the user's interpretation of a fast response is different from the systems analyst's interpretation [9].

Incomplete requirements mean that certain requirements necessary for successful system development are not included for a variety of reasons. These reasons could include the users' forgetting to identify them, high cost, politics within the business, or oversight by the system developer. However, because of the iterative nature of object-oriented analysis and the unified approach (see Chapter 4), most of the incomplete requirements can be identified in subsequent tries.

When addressing features of the system, keep in mind that every additional feature could affect the performance, complexity, stability, maintenance, and support costs of an application. Features implemented by a small extension to the application code do not necessarily have a proportionally small effect on a user interface. For example, if the primary task is selecting a single object, extending it to support selection of multiple objects could make the frequent, simple task more difficult to carry out. A number of other factors also may affect the design of an application. For example, deadlines may require delivering a product to market with a minimal design process, or comparative evaluations may force considering additional features. Remember that additional features and shortcuts can affect the product. There is no simple equation to determine when a design trade-off is appropriate.

Analysis is a difficult activity. You must understand the problem in some application domain and then define a solution that can be implemented with software. Experience often is the best teacher. If the first try reflects the errors of an incomplete understanding of the problems, refine the application and try another run.

6.3 BUSINESS OBJECT ANALYSIS: UNDERSTANDING THE BUSINESS LAYER

Business object analysis is a process of understanding the system's requirements and establishing the goals of an application. The main intent of this activity is to understand users' requirements. The outcome of the business object analysis is to identify classes that make up the business layer and the relationships that play a role in achieving system goals.

To understand the users' requirements, we need to find out how they "use" the system. This can be accomplish by developing use cases. Use cases are scenarios for understanding system requirements.

In addition to developing use cases, which will be described in the next section, the uses and the objectives of the application must be discussed with those who are going to use it or be affected by the system. Usually, domain users or experts are the best authorities. Try to understand the expected inputs and desired responses. Defer unimportant details until later. State *what* must be done, not *how* it should be done. This, of course, is easier said than done. Yet another tool that can be very useful for understanding users' requirements is preparing a prototype of the user interface. Preparation of a prototype usually can help you better understand how the system will be used, and therefore it is a valuable tool during business object analysis. (We defer the discussion of prototyping a user interface to Chapter 12.)

Having established what users want by developing use cases then documenting and modeling the application, we can proceed to the design and implementation. The unified approach (UA) steps can overlap each other. The process is iterative, and you may have to backtrack to previously completed steps for another try. Separating the *what* from the *how* is no simple process. Fully understanding a problem and defining how to implement it may require several tries or iterations. In this chapter, we see how a use-case model can assist us in capturing an application's requirements.

6.4 USE-CASE DRIVEN OBJECT-ORIENTED ANALYSIS: THE UNIFIED APPROACH

The object-oriented analysis (OOA) phase of the unified approach uses actors and use cases to describe the system from the users' perspective. The *actors* are external factors that interact with the system; *use cases* are scenarios that describe how actors use the system. The use cases identified here will be involved throughout the development process.

The OOA process consists of the following steps (see Figure 6–1):

1. Identify the actors:
  - Who is using the system?
  - Or, in the case of a new system, who will be using the system?

2. Develop a simple business process model using UML activity diagram.

3. Develop the use case:
  - What are the users doing with the system?
  - Or, in case of the new system, what will users be doing with the system?
  - Use cases provide us with comprehensive documentation of the system under study.

4. Prepare interaction diagrams:
  - Determine the sequence.
  - Develop collaboration diagrams.

5. Classification—develop a static UML class diagram:
  - Identify classes.
  - Identify relationships.
  - Identify attributes.
  - Identify methods.

6. Iterate and refine: If needed, repeat the preceding steps.

This chapter focuses on steps 1 to 3.

FIGURE 6–1

The object-oriented analysis process in the Unified Approach (UA).

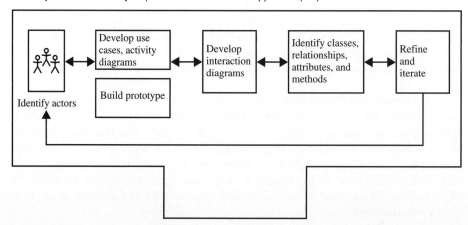

6.5 BUSINESS PROCESS MODELING

This is not necessarily the start of every project, but when required, business processes and user requirements may be modeled and recorded to any level of detail. This may include modeling as-is processes and the applications that support them and any number of phased, would-be models of reengineered processes or implementation of the system. These activities would be enhanced and supported by using an activity diagram. Business process modeling can be very time consuming, so the main idea should be to get a basic model without spending too much time on the process. The advantage of developing a business process model is that it makes you more familiar with the system and therefore the user requirements and also aids in developing use cases. For example, let us define the steps or activities involved in using your school library. These activities can be represented with an activity diagram (see Figure 6–2).

Developing an activity diagram of the business process can give us a better understanding of what sort of activities are performed in a library by a library member.

6.6 USE-CASE MODEL

Use cases are scenarios for understanding system requirements. A use-case model can be instrumental in project development, planning, and documentation of systems

FIGURE 6–2
This activity diagram (AD) shows some activities that can be performed by a library member.

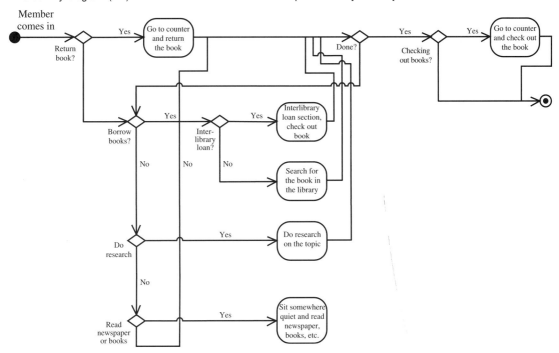

requirements. A use case is an interaction between users and a system; it captures the goal of the users and the responsibility of the system to its users. For example, take a car; typical uses of a car include "take you different places" or "haul your stuff" or a user may want to use it "off the road." The **use-case model** describes the uses of the system and shows the courses of events that can be performed. In other words, it shows a system in terms of its users and how it is being used from a user point of view. Furthermore, it defines what happens in the system when the use case is performed. In essence, the use-case model tries to systematically identify uses of the system and therefore the system's responsibilities. A use-case model also can discover classes and the relationships among subsystems of the systems.

A use-case model can be developed by talking to typical users and discussing the various things they might want to do with the application being prepared. Each use or scenario represents what the user wants to do. Each use case must have a name and short textual description, no more than a few paragraphs [5] (see Chapter 4).

Since the use-case model provides an external view of a system or application, it is directed primarily toward the users or the "actors" of the systems, not its implementers (see Figure 6–3). The use-case model expresses *what* the business or application will do and not *how*; that is the responsibility of the UML class dia-

FIGURE 6–3
Some uses of a library. As you can see, these are uses of external views of the library system by an actor such as a member, circulation clerk, or supplier instead of a developer of the library system. The simpler the use-case model, the more effective it will be. It is not wise to capture all the details right at the start; you can do that later.

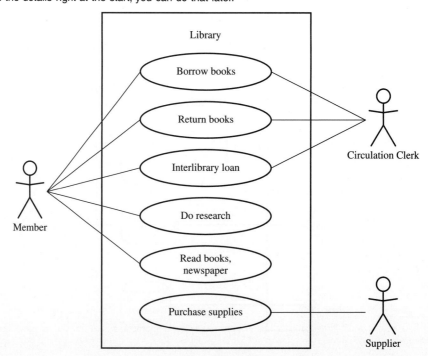

gram [7]. The UML class diagram, also called an *object model*, represents the static relationships between objects, inheritance, association, and the like. The object model represents an internal view of the system, as opposed to the use-case model, which represents the external view of the system. The object model shows how the business is run. Jacobson, Ericsson, and Jacobson call the use-case model a "what model," in contrast to the object model, which is a "how model."[1]

6.6.1 Use Cases under the Microscope

An important issue that can assist us in building correct use cases is the differentiation between user goals and system interactions [5]. Use cases represent the things that the user is doing with the system, which can be different from the users' goals. However, by focusing on users' goals first, we can come up with use cases to satisfy them. Let us take a closer look at the definition of *use case* by Jacobson et al. [7, italics added to highlight the words that are discussed next]: "A *Use Case* is a sequence of *transactions in a system* whose task is to yield results of *measurable value* to an individual *actor* of the system."

Now let us take a look at the key words of this definition:

- *Use case*. Use case is a special flow of events through the system. By definition, many courses of events are possible and many of these are very similar. It is suggested that, to make a use-case model meaningful, we must group the courses of events and call each group a use-case class. For example, how you would borrow a book from the library depends on whether the book is located in the library, whether you are the member of the library, and so on. All these alternatives often are best grouped into one or two use cases, called Borrow books and Get an interlibrary loan (we will look at the relationships of these two use cases in the next section). By grouping the uses cases, we can manage complexities and reduce the number of use cases in a package.
- *Actors*. An actor is a user playing a role with respect to the system. When dealing with actors, it is important to think about roles rather than just people and their job titles [5]. For instance, a first-class passenger may play the role of business-class passenger. The actor is the key to finding the correct use cases. Actors carry out the use cases. A single actor may perform many use cases; furthermore, a use case may have several actors performing it. An actor also can be an external system that needs some information from the current system. Actors can be the ones that get value from the use case, or they can just participate in the use case [5].
- *In a system*. This simply means that the actors communicate with the system's use case.
- *A measurable value*. A use case must help the actor to perform a task that has some identifiable value; for example, the performance of a use case in terms of price or cost. For example, borrowing books is something of value for a member of the library.

---

[1]The *how model* here does not mean how the system can be implemented but how the scenarios can be handled internally.

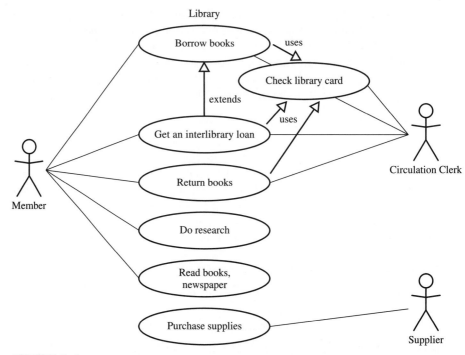

FIGURE 6–4
The use-case diagram depicts the extends and uses relationships, where the interlibrary loan is a special case of checking out books. Entering into the system is common to get an interlibrary loan, borrow books, and return books use cases, so it is being "used" by all these use cases.

- *Transaction.* A transaction is an atomic set of activities that are performed either fully or not at all. A transaction is triggered by a stimulus from an actor to the system or by a point in time being reached in the system.

The following are some examples of use cases for the library (see Figure 6–4). Three actors appear in Figure 6–4: a member, a circulation clerk, and a supplier.

- Use-case name: *Borrow books.* A member takes books from the library to read at home, registering them at the checkout desk so the library can keep track of its books. Depending on the member's record, different courses of events will follow.
- Use-case name: *Get an interlibrary loan.* A member requests a book that the library does not have. The book is located at another library and ordered through an interlibrary loan.
- Use-case name: *Return books.* A member brings borrowed books back to the library.
- Use-case name: *Check library card.* A member submits his or her library card to the clerk, who checks the borrower's record.
- Use-case name: *Do research.* A member comes to the library to do research. The member can search in a variety of ways (such as through books, journals, CD-ROM, WWW) to find information on the subjects of that research.

- Use-case name: *Read books, newspaper.* A member comes to the library for a quiet place to study or read a newspaper, journal, or book.
- Use-case name: *Purchase supplies.* The supplier provides the books, journals, and newspapers purchased by the library.

In Figure 6–4, the library has an environment with three types of actors (member, circulation clerk, and supplier) and seven use cases (borrow books, return books, get an interlibrary loan, do research, read books or newspaper, and purchase supplies).

6.6.2 Uses and Extends Associations

A use-case description can be difficult to understand if it contains too many alternatives or exceptional flows of events that are performed only if certain conditions are met as the use-case instance is carried out [7]. A way to simplify the description is to take advantage of extends and uses associations. The extends and uses associations often are sources of confusion, so let us take a look at these relationships.

The *extends association* is used when you have one use case that is similar to another use case but does a bit more or is more specialized; in essence, it is like a subclass. In our example, *checking out a book* is the basic use case. This is the case that will represent what happens when all goes smoothly. However, many things can affect the flow of events. For example, the book already might be checked out or the library might not have the requested book. Therefore, we cannot always perform the usual behavior associated with the given use case and need to create other use cases to handle the new situations. Of course, one option is to put this variation within the use case. However, the use case quickly would become cluttered with lots of special logic, which would obscure the normal flow [5].

To remedy this problem, we can use the extends association. Here, you put the base or normal behavior in one use case and the unusual behaviors somewhere else; but instead of cutting and pasting the shared behavior between the base (common) and more specialized use cases, you utilize an extends association to expand the common behavior to fit the special circumstances. Figure 6–4 "extends" Figure 6–3 to include extends and uses associations.

The *uses association* occurs when you are describing your use cases and notice that some of them have subflows in common. To avoid describing a subflow more than once in several use cases, you can extract the common subflow and make it a use case of its own. This new use case then can be used by other use cases. The relationships among the other use cases and this new extracted use case is called a *uses association.* The uses association helps us avoid redundancy by allowing a use case to be shared. For example, checking a library card is common among the borrow books, return books, and interlibrary loan use cases (see Figure 6–4).

The similarity between extends and uses associations is that both can be viewed as a kind of inheritance. When you want to share common sequences in several use cases, utilize the *uses association* by extracting common sequences into a new, shared use case. The *extends association* is found when you add a bit more specialized, new use case that extends some of the use cases that you have.

Use cases could be viewed as concrete or abstract. An *abstract use case* is not complete and has no initiation actors but is used by a *concrete use case*, which does interact with actors. This inheritance could be used at several levels. Abstract use cases also are the use cases that have uses or extends associations. All the use cases depicted in Figure 6–4 are concrete, since they all have initiation actors.

Fowler and Scott provide us excellent guidelines for addressing variations in use-case modeling [5]:

1. Capture the simple and normal use case first.
2. For every step in that use case, ask
   • What could go wrong here?
   • How might this work out differently?
3. Extract common sequences into a new, shared use case with the uses association. If you are adding more specialized or exceptional uses cases, take advantage of use cases you already have with the extends association.

6.6.3 Identifying the Actors

Identifying the actors is (at least) as important as identifying classes, structures, associations, attributes, and behavior. The term *actor* represents the role a user plays with respect to the system. When dealing with actors, it is important to think about roles rather than people or job titles [5]. A user may play more than one role. For instance, a member of a public library also may play the role of volunteer at the help desk in the library. However, an actor should represent a single user; in the library example, the member can perform tasks some of which can be done by others and others that are unique. However, try to isolate the roles that the users can play [1]. (See Figure 6–5.)

You have to identify the actors and understand how they will use and interact with the system. In a thought-provoking book on requirement analysis, Gause and Weinberg [6, pp. 69–70] explain what is known as the *railroad paradox*:

FIGURE 6–5
The difference between users and actors.

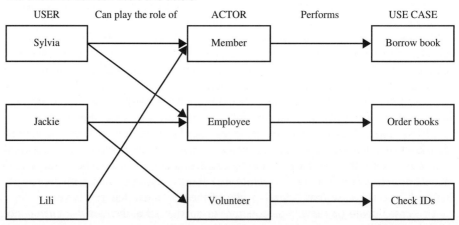

When trying to find all users, we need to beware of the *Railroad Paradox*. When railroads were asked to establish new stops on the schedule, they "studied the requirements," by sending someone to the station at the designated time to see if anyone was waiting for a train. Of course, nobody was there because no stop was scheduled, so the railroad turned down the request because there was no demand.

Gause and Weinberg concluded that the railroad paradox appears everywhere there are products and goes like this (which should be avoided):

1. The product is not satisfying the users.
2. Since the product is not satisfactory, potential users will not use it.
3. Potential users ask for a better product.
4. Because the potential users do not use the product, the request is denied.

Therefore, since the product does not meet the needs of some users, they are not identified as potential users of a better product. They are not consulted and the product stays bad [6]. The railroad paradox suggests that a new product actually can create users where none existed before. Candidates for actors can be found through the answers to the following questions:

- Who is using the system? Or, who is affected by the system? Or, which groups need help from the system to perform a task?
- Who affects the system? Or, which user groups are needed by the system to perform its functions? These functions can be both main functions and secondary functions, such as administration.
- Which external hardware or other systems (if any) use the system to perform tasks?
- What problems does this application solve (that is, for whom)?
- And, finally, how do users use the system (use case)? What are they doing with the system.

When requirements for new applications are modeled and designed by a group that excludes the targeted users, not only will the application not meet the users' needs, but potential users will feel no involvement in the process and not be committed to giving the application a good try. Always remember Veblen's principle: "There's no change, no matter how awful, that won't benefit some people; and no change, no matter how good, that won't hurt some."

Another issue worth mentioning is that actors need not be human, although actors are represented as stick figures within a use-case diagram. An actor also can be an external system. For example, an accounting system that needs information from a system to update its accounts is an actor in that system [5].

Jacobson et al. provide us with what I call the *two–three rule* for identifying actors: Start with naming at least two, preferably three, people who could serve as the actors in the system. Other actors can be identified in the subsequent iterations. Remember this, like any other software development process, is an iterative process. For example, assume we are modeling a company that specializes in marketing jewelry. The first actor that comes to mind is the final customer; actually three different regular customers would buy the product. Another type of actor is the jewelry buyers for exclusive stores; they know all about quality and nothing else. A third type of customer is boutique owners, who know what designs are in fashion. Each of these individuals requires his or her own use case, since they represent different roles that can be played in the system. Still other actors might be identified through subsequent iterations.

6.6.4 Guidelines for Finding Use Cases

When you have defined a set of actors, it is time to describe the way they interact with the system. This should be carried out sequentially, but an iterated approach may be necessary. Here are the steps for finding use cases [1]:

1. For each actor, find the tasks and functions that the actor should be able to perform or that the system needs the actor to perform. The use case should represent a course of events that leads to a clear goal (or, in some cases, several distinct goals that could be alternatives for the actor or for the system).
2. Name the use cases (see Section 6.6.8).
3. Describe the use cases briefly by applying terms with which the user is familiar. This makes the description less ambiguous.

Once you have identified the use-cases candidates, it may not be apparent that all of these use cases need to be described separately; some may be modeled as variants of others. Consider what the actors want to do.

It is important to separate actors from users. The actors each represent a role that one or several users can play. Therefore, it is not necessary to model different actors that can perform the same use case in the same way. The approach should allow different users to be different actors and play one role when performing a particular actor's use case. Thus, each use case has only one main actor. To achieve this, you have to

- Isolate users from actors.
- Isolate actors from other actors (separate the responsibilities of each actor).
- Isolate use cases that have different initiating actors and slightly different behavior (if the actor had been the same, this would be modeled by a use-case alternative behavior) [1].

While finding use cases, you might have to make changes to your set of actors. All actor changes should be updated in the textual description of actors and use cases. The change should be carried out with care, since changes to the set of actors affect the use cases as well.

When specifying use cases, you might discover that some of them are variants of each other. If so, try to see how you can reuse the use case through extends or uses associations [1].

6.6.5 How Detailed Must a Use Case Be? When to Stop Decomposing and When to Continue

A use case, as already explained, describes the courses of events that will be carried out by the system. Jacobson et al. believe that, in most cases, too much detail may not be very useful.

During analysis of a business system, you can develop one use-case diagram as the system use case and draw packages on this use case to represent the various business domains of the system. For each package, you may create a child use-case diagram (see the case in Section 6.7 for an example). On each child use-case diagram, you can draw all of the use cases of the domain, with actions and inter-actions. You can further refine the way the use cases are categorized. The extends and uses relationships can be used to eliminate redundant modeling of scenarios.

When should use cases be employed? Use cases are an essential tool in capturing requirements and planning and controlling any software development project. Capturing use cases is a primary task of the analysis phase. Although most use cases are captured at the beginning of the project, you will uncover more as you proceed.

How many use cases do you need? Ivar Jacobson believes that, for a 10-person-year project, he would expect 20 use cases (not counting the uses and extends associations). Other researchers, such as Fowler and Scott, would come up with 100 use cases for a project of the same magnitude. Some prefer smaller grained, more detailed use cases. There is no magic formula; you need to be flexible and work with whatever magnitude you find comfortable [5]. The UML specification recommends that at least one scenario be prepared for each significantly different kind of use case instance. Each scenario shows a different sequence of interactions between actors and the system, with all decisions definite. When you have arrived at the lowest use-case level, which cannot be broken down any further, you may create a sequence diagram and an accompanying collaboration diagram for the use case. With the sequence and collaboration diagrams, you can model the implementation of the scenario [10].

6.6.6 Dividing Use Cases into Packages

Each use case represents a particular scenario in the system. You may model either how the system currently works or how you want it to work. Typically, a design is broken down into packages. You must narrow the focus of the scenarios in your system. For example, in a library system, the various scenarios involve a supplier providing books or a member doing research or borrowing books. In this case, there should be three separate packages, one each for Borrow books, Do research, and Purchase books. Many applications may be associated with the library system and one or more databases used to store the information (see Figure 6–6).

6.6.7 Naming a Use Case

Use-case names should provide a general description of the use-case function. The name should express what happens when an instance of the use case is performed. Jacobson et al. recommend that the name should be active, often expressed in the form of a verb (Borrow) or verb and noun (Borrow books). The naming should be done with care; the description of the use case should be descriptive and consistent. For example, the use case that describes what happens when a person deposits money into an ATM machine could be named either *receive money* or *deposit money*.

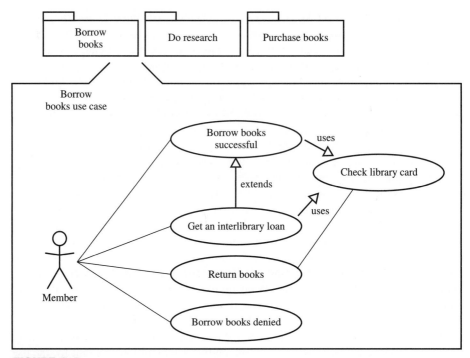

FIGURE 6–6
A library system can be divided into many packages, each of which encompasses multiple use cases.

6.7 DEVELOPING EFFECTIVE DOCUMENTATION

Documenting your project not only provides a valuable reference point and form of communication but often helps reveal issues and gaps in the analysis and design. A document can serve as a communication vehicle among the project's team members, or it can serve as an initial understanding of the requirements. Blum [3] concludes that management has responsibility for resources such as software, hardware, and operational expenses. In many projects, documentation can be an important factor in making a decision about committing resources. Application software is expected to provide a solution to a problem. It is very difficult, if not impossible, to document a poorly understood problem. The main issue in documentation during the analysis phase is to determine what the system must do. Decisions about how the system works are delayed to the design phase. Blum raises the following questions for determining the importance of documentation: How will a document be used? (If it will not be used, it is not necessary.) What is the objective of the document? What is the management view of the document? Who are the readers of the document?

6.7.1 Organization Conventions for Documentation

The documentation depends on the organization's rules and regulations. Most organizations have established standards or conventions for developing documentation. However, in many organizations, the standards border on the nonexistent. In other cases, the standards may be excessive. Too little documentation invites disaster; too much documentation, as Blum put it, transfers energy from the problem-solving tasks to a mechanical and unrewarding activity. Each organization determines what is best for it, and you must respond to that definition and refinement [3]. Bell and Evans [2] provide us with guidelines and a template for preparing a document that has been adapted for documenting the unified approach's systems development (see Appendix A). Remember that your modeling effort becomes the analysis, design, and testing documentation. However this template which is based on the unified approach life cycle (see Figure 1–1) assists you in organizing and composing your models into an effective documentation.

6.7.2 Guidelines for Developing Effective Documentation

Bell and Evans [2] provide us the following guidelines for making documents fit the needs and expectations of your audience:

- *Common cover*. All documents should share a common cover sheet that identifies the document, the current version, and the individual responsible for the content. As the document proceeds through the life cycle phases, the responsible individual may change. That change must be reflected in the cover sheet [2]. Figure 6–7 depicts a cover sheet template.
- *80–20 rule*. As for many applications, the 80–20 rule generally applies for documentation: 80 percent of the work can be done with 20 percent of the documentation. The trick is to make sure that the 20 percent is easily accessible and the rest (80 percent) is available to those (few) who need to know.
- *Familiar vocabulary*. The formality of a document will depend on how it is used and who will read it. When developing a documentation use a vocabulary that your readers understand and are comfortable with. The main objective here is to communicate with readers and not impress them with buzz words.
- *Make the document as short as possible*. Assume that you are developing a manual. The key in developing an effective manual is to eliminate all repetition; present summaries, reviews, organization chapters in less than three pages; and make chapter headings task oriented so that the table of contents also could serve as an index [4].
- *Organize the document*. Use the rules of good organization (such as the organization's standards, college handbooks, Strunk and White's *Elements of Style*, or the University of Chicago *Manual of Style*) within each section. Appendix A provides a template for developing documentation for a project. Most CASE tools provide documentation capability by providing customizable reports. The purpose of these guidelines is to assist you in creating an effective documentation.

```
┌─────────────────────────────┐
│                             │
│      (Document Name)        │
│           for               │
│        (Product)            │
│      (Version Number)       │
│                             │
│                             │
│    Responsible Individual   │
│           Name:             │
│           Title:            │
│                             │
│                             │
└─────────────────────────────┘
```

FIGURE 6–7
Cover sheet template.

6.8 CASE STUDY: ANALYZING THE VIANET BANK ATM—THE USE-CASE DRIVEN PROCESS

6.8.1 Background

Much of the work that must be done in the early stages of the system development process involves gathering requirements and other related information. These activities focus on gaining a better understanding of the business problem to be solved and the requirements and restrictions related to the application being developed. As explained in the previous section, use cases are employed to capture information on how a system or business currently works or how you wish it to work. Once you have a good understanding of the requirements, you can analyze it further and begin to design your application. Using a CASE tool, such as the Popkin Object Architect or a similar tool, enables you to systematically capture requirements, identify classes, design, and finally implement the application.

Let us review object-oriented analysis, which is divided into the following activities:

1. Identify the actors: Who is using the system?
2. Develop a business process model using a UML activity diagram.
3. Develop the use case: What are the users doing with the system?
4. Develop interaction diagrams.
5. Develop a static UML class diagram.
6. If needed, repeat the preceding steps.

The following section provides a description of the ViaNet bank ATM system's requirements.

- The bank client must be able to deposit an amount to and withdraw an amount from his or her accounts using the touch screen at the ViaNet bank ATM kiosk. Each transaction must be recorded, and the client must be able to review all transactions performed against a given account. Recorded transactions must include the date, time, transaction type, amount, and account balance after the transaction.

- A ViaNet bank client can have two types of accounts: a checking account and savings account. For each checking account, one related savings account can exist.
- Access to the ViaNet bank accounts is provided by a PIN code consisting of four integer digits between 0 and 9.
- One PIN code allows access to all accounts held by a bank client.
- No receipts will be provided for any account transactions.
- The bank application operates for a single banking institution only.
- Neither a checking nor a savings account can have a negative balance. The system should automatically withdraw money from a related savings account if the requested withdrawal amount on the checking account is more than its current balance. If the balance on a savings account is less than the withdrawal amount requested, the transaction will stop and the bank client will be notified.

In this chapter, we identify the actors and use cases of the ViaNet bank ATM system that will be used by subsequent chapters.

6.8.2 Identifying Actors and Use Cases for the ViaNet Bank ATM System

The bank application will be used by one category of users: bank clients. Notice that identifying the actors of the system is an iterative process and can be modified as you learn more about the system. The actor of the bank system is the bank client. The bank client must be able to deposit an amount to and withdraw an amount from his or her accounts using the bank application.

The following scenarios show use-case interactions between the actor (bank client) and the bank. In real life application these use cases are created by system requirements, examination of existing system documentation, interviews, questionnaire, observation, etc.

- Use-case name: *Bank ATM transaction*. The bank clients interact with the bank system by going through the approval process. After the approval process, the bank client can perform the transaction. Here are the steps in the ATM transaction use case:
  1. Insert ATM card.
  2. Perform the approval process.
  3. Ask type of transaction.
  4. Enter type of transaction.
  5. Perform transaction.
  6. Eject card.
  7. Request take card.
  8. Take card.
  These steps are shown in the Figure 6–8 activity diagram.
- Use-case name: *Approval process*. The client enters a PIN code that consists of four digits. If the PIN code is valid, the client's accounts become available. (See Figure 6–9.) Here are the steps:
  1. Request password.

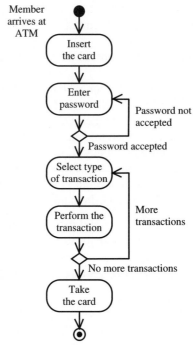

FIGURE 6–8
Activities involved in an ATM transaction.

2. Enter password.
3. Verify password.
- Use-case name: *Invalid PIN*. If the PIN code is not valid, an appropriate message is displayed to the client. This use case extends the approval process. (See Figure 6–9.)
- Use-case name: *Deposit amount*. The bank clients interact with the bank system after the approval process by requesting to deposit money to an account. The client selects the account for which a deposit is going to be made and enters an amount in dollar currency. The system creates a record of the transaction. (See Figure 6–10.) This use case extends the bank ATM transaction use case. Here are the steps:
1. Request account type.
2. Request deposit amount.
3. Enter deposit amount.
4. Put the check or cash in the envelope and insert it into ATM.
- Use-case name: *Deposit savings*. The client selects the savings account for which a deposit is going to be made. All other steps are similar to the deposit amount use case. The system creates a record of the transaction. This use case extends the deposit amount use case. (See Figure 6–11.)

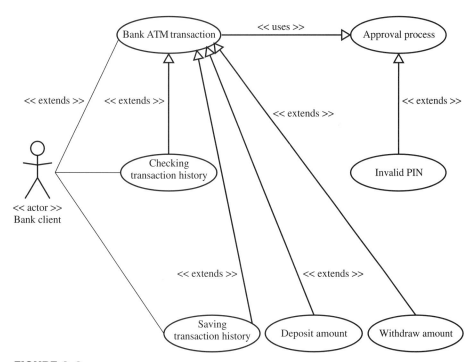

FIGURE 6–9
Transaction use cases.

- Use-case name: *Deposit checking*. The client selects the checking account for which a deposit is going to be made. All other steps are similar to the deposit amount use case. The system creates a record of the transaction. This use case extends the deposit amount use case. (See Figure 6–10.)
- Use-case name: *Withdraw amount*. The bank clients interact with the bank system (after the approval process) by requesting to withdraw money from an account. The client tries to withdraw an amount from a checking account. After verifying that the funds are sufficient, the transaction is performed. The system creates a record of the transaction. This use case extends the bank ATM transaction use case. (See Figure 6–10.) Here are the steps:
  1. Request account type.
  2. Request withdrawal amount.
  3. Enter withdrawal amount.
  4. Verify sufficient funds.
  5. Eject cash.
- Use-case name: *Withdraw checking*. The client tries to withdraw an amount from his or her checking account. The amount is less than or equal to the checking account's balance, and the transaction is performed. The system creates a record of the transaction. This use case extends the withdraw amount use case. (See Figure 6–10.)

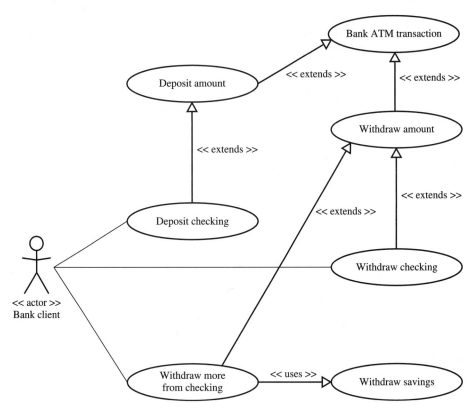

FIGURE 6–10
The checking account use-cases.

- Use-case name: *Withdraw more from checking*. The client tries to withdraw an amount from his or her checking account. If the amount is more than the checking account's balance, the insufficient amount is withdrawn from the related savings account. The system creates a record of the transaction and the withdrawal is successful. This use case extends the withdraw checking use case and uses the withdraw savings use case. (See Figure 6–10.)
- Use-case name: *Withdraw savings*. The client tries to withdraw an amount from a savings account. The amount is less than or equal to the balance and the transaction is performed on the savings account. The system creates a record of the transaction since the withdrawal is successful. This use case extends the withdraw amount use case. (See Figure 6–11.)
- Use-case name: *Withdraw savings denied*. The client withdraws an amount from a savings account. If the amount is more than the balance, the transaction is halted and a message is displayed. This use case extends the withdraw savings use case. (See Figure 6–11.)
- Use-case name: *Checking transaction history*. The bank client requests a history of transactions for a checking account. The system displays the transaction his-

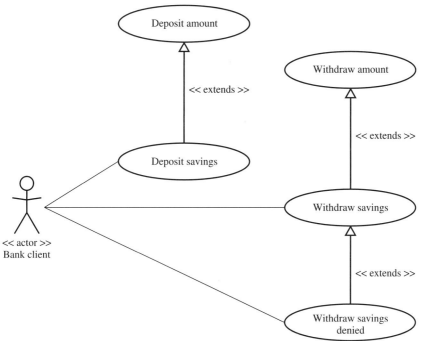

FIGURE 6–11
The savings account use-cases package.

tory for the checking account. This use case extends the bank transaction use case. (See Figure 6–9.)

• Use-case name: *Savings transaction history*. The bank client requests a history of transactions for a savings account. The system displays the transaction history for the savings account. This use case extends the bank transaction use case. (See Figure 6–9.)

The use-case list contains at least one scenario of each significantly different kind of use-case instance. Each scenario shows a different sequence of interactions between actors and the system, with all decisions definite. If the scenario consists of an *if* statement, for each condition create one scenario.

Note that the *extends* association is used when you have a use case that is similar to another use case but does a bit more. In essence, it is a subclass. In the example, the Checking withdraw use case extends the Withdraw amount use case. The Withdraw amount use case represents the case when all goes smoothly. However, many things can affect the flow of events, such as when the withdrawal is for more than the amount of money in the checking account. Withdraw more from checking is the use case that extends the Checking withdraw. You can put this variation within the Checking withdraw use case, too. However, this would clutter the use case with lots of special logic, which would obscure the normal flow. To review, the uses association occurs when a behavior is common to more than one use case and you want to avoid copying the description of that behavior. The Approval process is such a use case that is used by Bank transaction use case.

As you can see, use cases are an essential tool for identifying requirements. Developing use cases is an iterative process. Although most use cases are generated at this phase of system development, you will uncover more as you proceed. Fowler and Scott advise us to keep an eye out for them at all times. Every use case represents a potential requirement.

6.8.3 The ViaNet Bank ATM Systems' Packages

Each use case represents a particular scenario in the system. As explained earlier, it is better to break down the use cases into packages. Narrow the focus of the scenarios in the system. In the bank system, the various scenarios involve checking account, savings account, and general bank transactions. (See Figure 6–12.)

Remember, use case is a method for capturing the way a system or business works. Use cases are used to model the scenarios. The scenarios are described textually or through a sequence of steps. Modeling with use cases is a recommended tool in finding the objects of a system. In the next chapter, we look at identifying classes based on the use cases identified here.

6.9 SUMMARY

This chapter provides a detailed discussion of use-case driven object-oriented analysis process and how to develop use cases. The main objective of the analysis is to capture a complete, unambiguous, and consistent picture of the requirements of the system. This is accomplished by constructing several models of the system. These models concentrate on describing what the system does rather than how the system does it. Separating the behavior of a system from the way it is implemented requires viewing the system from the perspective of the users rather than that of the machine. Analysis is a creative activity that involves understanding the prob-

FIGURE 6–12
The ViaNet bank business system can be divided into three packages.

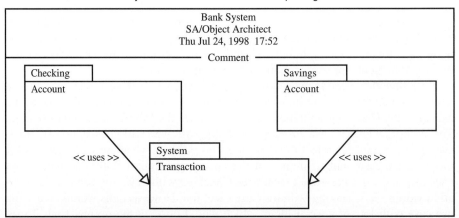

lem, its associated constraints, and methods of overcoming those constraints. This is an iterative process that goes on until the problem is well understood. The main objective of object-oriented analysis is to find out *what* the problem is by developing a use-case model, which Jacobson et al. call the "what model."

We saw that use cases are an essential tool in capturing requirements. Capturing use cases is one of the first things to do in coming up with requirements. Every use case is a potential requirement. A use-case model can be developed by talking to typical users and discussing the various things they might want to do with the application. Each use case or scenario represents what the user wants to do. Each use case must have a name and short textual description, no more than a few paragraphs.

Requirements must be traceable across analysis, design, coding, and testing. The unified approach follows Jacobson et al.'s life cycle to produce systems that can be traced across all phases of the developments.

The key in developing effective documentation is to eliminate all repetition; present summaries, reviews, organization chapters in less than three pages; and make chapter headings task oriented so that the table of contents also could serve as an index.

Use the 80–20 rule: 80 percent of the work can be done with 20 percent of the documentation. Make sure that the 20 percent is easily accessible and the rest (80 percent) is available to those few who need to know.

Appendix A provides a template for documentation. However, for the most part, the modeling activity is the main source of documenting the OOA.

KEY TERMS

Abstract use case (p. 133)
Actor (p. 128)
Concrete use case (p. 133)
Extends association (p. 133)
Two–three rule (p. 135)
Use cases (p. 128)
Use-case model (p. 130)
Uses association (p. 133)

REVIEW QUESTIONS

1. What is the purpose of analysis? Why do we need analysis?
2. Why is analysis a difficult task?
3. What approach is proposed in this chapter to manage complexity in the analysis phase?
4. What is the what model?
5. What is a use-case model?
6. What is involved in the analysis process? Where should we start?
7. Describe the basic activities in object-oriented analysis.
8. Why is use-case modeling useful in analysis?
9. Who are the actors?
10. Why are uses and extends associations useful in use-case modeling?
11. How would you identify actors?

12. What is the 80–20 rule?

13. Why is documentation an important part of analysis?

14. The criterion for something to be an actor is that it lies outside the part of the business being modeled; yet it interacts with that part in some way. Why must the actor be someone or something outside the part of the business being modeled?

15. What is the difference between users and actors?

PROBLEMS

1. Lee Turner is director of information systems (IS) for the city of Providence. The IS department's customers are the public library, the fire department, the police department, the finance department, the sanitation department, and the water department. Lee believes close communication with these customers is the key to meeting their needs. Currently, the police and fire departments need fast access to a map of the city for dispatching the city's ambulance and fire trucks to accident sites.

a. Who are the actors?

b. How would you incorporate the users' needs into the system development process?

c. Develop a simple use-case model.

2. The Book Store sells textbooks but also many other items, ranging from Rhode Island College (RIC) sweatshirts to computers. The text purchasing department has unique characteristics, including advance notice from faculty members and issues dealing with unsold copies. Purchasing the other items is as for any retail store. An extension of both areas is the checkout (or sales) process. This process should include the cash registers, scanners, and sales slips. In fact, this process often is unduly slow. Develop an activity diagram to show the business process of the book store.

3. All students must provide information about inoculations and other health information when entering RIC. A physical exam may be necessary at the Health Services office. This health information is recorded on a health card, which often is hard to file and retrieve when needed, due to the number of cards. Delays in filling and retrieving cause problems for other functions on campus. For example, a student may not be enrolled unless the card is filed. What if the card is filed but not retrieved or otherwise recorded? A student needs the data recorded to participate in organized athletics. Again, the difficulty in retrieving the card can produce difficulties for the Athletics department. How would you go about creating use cases? Come up with one or two use-cases for health services.

4. Grandma, the owner of Grandma's Soup Unlimited, cans her soup and sells it by mail order. She wants to redo her ordering and shipping and, down the road, she would also like to have a new payroll system in place. Your job is to design a system to handle ordering and shipping with an eye on the payroll system.

She, along with most of her employees (majority of them are college students), likes the idea of the Graphical User interface interfaces and down the road utilizing e-commerce (electronic commerce) or doing business on the Internet. Grandma states that she would like this new system to be visual and easy to use and assumes it will be able to do all the things her spreadsheet program did.

During the interview, Grandma mentioned that she wants her system to be "expandable." In other words, she wants it to be able to grow with her needs. By grow, she was also referring to her store because she plans on opening a few more stores in the near future. She wants the flexibility of adding new/different types of services, such as new soups, cans, and even hiring different types of employees. Grandma is not sure what these different employees will do yet, but she assures us there will be some changes in the future. She would also like to have better reports made from her data.

Some other aspects of Grandma's payroll system were also discussed during the interview. There are many different kinds of employees, such as clerk, telephone operator, cook, manager, even owner of future stores. Some of these employees are full-time, others are part-time, and some are even salaried. All of the employees have some commonalties, but there are also many differences among them.

Grandma makes a variety of soups, including Beef-Barley Soup, Beef Stew, Cheese Soup, Cheesy Chicken-Corn Chowder, Chicken Vegetable-Noodle Soup, Cream of Broccoli Soup, Cream of Chicken Soup, Cream of Potato Soup, Cream of Onion Soup, Cream of Pea Soup, Fish Chowder, French Onion Soup, New England Clam Chowder, and Old Fashioned Vegetable-Beef Soup. Each uses different ingredients. For instance, French Onion Soup contains onion, butter, flour, French bread, cheddar cheese, wine, and vegetables.

Here are some more requirements:
- Grandma's philosophy about customer service is "first come, first served."
- Grandma needs a list of pending orders. (Keep in mind that sometimes the orders really pile up.)

   a. Develop some of the use cases of the Grandma Soup Unlimited system.

REFERENCES

1. Anderson, Michael; and John Bergstrand. "Formalizing Use Cases with Message Sequence Charts." Master thesis, Department of Communication Systems, Lund Institute of Technology, 1995.
2. Bell, Paula; and Evans, Charlotte. *Mastering Documentation with Document Masters for Systems Development, Control and Delivery.* New York: John Wiley & Sons, 1989.
3. Blum, Bruce I. *Software Engineering: A Holistic View.* New York: Oxford University Press, 1992.
4. Carroll, John M. "Minimalist Training." *Datamation* (November 1, 1984), pp.125–36.
5. Fowler, Martin; and Kendall Scott. *UML Distilled.* Reading, MA: Addison-Wesley, 1997.
6. Gause, Donald G.; and G. M. Weinberg. *Exploring Requirements: Quality Before Design.* New York: Dorset House Publishing, 1989.
7. Jacobson, Ivar; Maria Ericsson; and Agneta Jacobson. *The Object Advantage Business Process Reengineering with Object Technology.* Reading, MA: Addison-Wesley, 1995.
8. Martin, James; and James Odell. *Object-Oriented Analysis and Design.* Englewood Cliffs, NJ: Prentice-Hall, 1992.
9. Norman, Ronald. *Object-Oriented Systems Analysis and Design.* Englewood Cliffs, NJ: Prentice-Hall, 1996.
10. *Object Modeling Quick Start.* Popkin Software & Systems, 1997.
11. Shumate, Ken; and Marilyn Keller. *Software Specification and Design: A Disciplined Approach for Real-Time Systems.* New York: John Wiley & Sons, 1992.

CHAPTER 7

Object Analysis: Classification

Chapter Objectives

You should be able to define and understand

- The concept of classification.
- How to identify classes with the noun phrase approach.
- How to identify classes with the common class patterns approach.
- How to identify classes and object behavior analyzed by sequence/collaboration modeling.
- How to identify classes with the classes, responsibilities, and collaborators (CRC) approach.

7.1 INTRODUCTION

Object-oriented analysis is a process by which we can identify classes that play a role in achieving system goals and requirements. Unfortunately, classes rarely just are there for the picking [3]. Identification of classes is the hardest part of object-oriented analysis and design. Booch [2, p. 145] argues that, "There is no such a thing as the *perfect* class structure, nor the *right* set of objects. As in any engineering discipline, our design choice is compromisingly shaped by many competing factors." Gabriel, White, and Bobrow, the three designers of the object-oriented language CLOS, respond to the issue of how to identify classes: "That's a fundamental question for which there is no easy answer. I try things" [4].

In this chapter, we look at four approaches for identifying classes and their behaviors in the problem domain. Discovering classes is one of the hardest activities in object-oriented analysis. However, the process is incremental and iterative and, furthermore, as you gain experience it will become easier to identify the classes.

7.2 CLASSIFICATIONS THEORY

Classification, the process of checking to see if an object belongs to a category or a class, is regarded as a basic attribute of human nature.

Booch [2, p. 146] explains that,

> intelligent classification is part of all good science. . . . Classification guides us in making decisions about modularization. We may choose to place certain classes and objects together in the same module or in different modules, depending upon the sameness we find among these declarations; coupling and cohesion are simply measures of this sameness. Classification also plays a role in allocating processes to procedures. We place certain processes together in the same processor or different processors, depending upon packaging, performance, or reliability concerns.

Human beings classify information every instant of their waking lives. We recognize the objects around us, and we move and act in relation to them. A human being is a very sophisticated information system, partly because he or she possesses a superior classification capability [11]. For example, when you see a new model of a car, you have no trouble identifying it as a car. What has occurred here, even though you may never have seen this particular car before, is that you not only can immediately identify it as a car, but you also can guess the manufacturer and model. Clearly, you have some general idea of what cars look like, sound like, do, and are good for—you have a notion of car-kind or, in object-oriented terms, the class car.

Classes are an important mechanism for classifying objects. The chief role of a class is to define the attributes, methods, and applicability of its instances. The class car, for example, defines the property color. Each individual car (formally, each instance of the class car) will have a value for this property, such as maroon, yellow, or white.

It is fairly natural to partition the world into objects that have properties (attributes) and methods (behaviors). It is common and useful partitioning or classification, but we also routinely divide the world along a second dimension: We distinguish classes from instances. A class is a specification of structure, behavior, and the description of an object. Classification is concerned more with identifying the class of an object than the individual objects within a system. Martin and Odell explain that classes are important because they create conceptual building blocks for designing systems:

> In object-oriented programming, these building blocks guide the designer in defining the classes and their data structures. In addition, object types (classes) provide an index

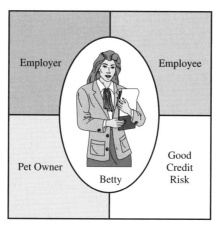

FIGURE 7–1
The same object, Betty, can be classified in many ways.

for system process. For instance, operations such as Hire, Promote, Retire, and Fire are intimately tied to the object type (class) Employee, because they change the state of an employee. In other words, an object should only be manipulated via the operations associated with its type. Without object types (classes), then, operations cannot be defined properly. [6, p. 76]

Tou and Gonzalez describe the recognition of concrete patterns or classes by humans as a psychophysiological problem that involves a relationship between a person and a physical stimulus [11]. When you perceive a real-world object, you make an inductive inference and associate this perception with some general concepts or clues that you have derived from your past experience. Human recognition, in reality, is a question of estimating the relative odds that the input data can be associated with a class from a set of known classes, which depend on our past experiences and clues for recognition. Intelligent classification is intellectually hard work and may seem rather arbitrary. That is how our minds work [6]. Martin and Odell have observed in object-oriented analysis and design that, "In fact, an object can be categorized in more than one way. For example, in Figure 7–1 one person may regard the object Betty as a *Woman*. Her boss regards her as an *Employee*. The person who mows her lawn classifies her as an *Employer*. The local animal control agency licenses her as a *Pet Owner*. The credit bureau reports that Betty is an instance of the object types called *Good Credit Risk*—and so on." [6, p. 77]

The problem of classification may be regarded as one of discriminating *things*, not between the individual objects but between classes, via the search for features or invariant attributes or behaviors among members of a class. Classification can be defined as the categorization of input data (things) into identifiable classes via the extraction of significant features of attributes of the data from a background of irrelevant detail. Another issue in relationships among classes is studied in Chapter 8.

7.3 APPROACHES FOR IDENTIFYING CLASSES

In the following sections, we look at four alternative approaches for identifying classes: the noun phrase approach; the common class patterns approach; the use-case driven, sequence/collaboration modeling approach; and the Classes, Responsibilities, and Collaborators (CRC) approach.

The first two approaches have been included to increase your understanding of the subject; the unified approach uses the use-case driven approach for identifying classes and understanding the behavior of objects. However, you always can combine these approaches to identify classes for a given problem.

Another approach that can be used for identifying classes is Classes, Responsibilities, and Collaborators (CRC) developed by Cunningham, Wilkerson, and Beck. Classes, Responsibilities, and Collaborators, more technique than method, is used for identifying classes responsibilities and therefore their attributes and methods.

7.4 NOUN PHRASE APPROACH

The noun phrase approach was proposed by Rebecca Wirfs-Brock, Brian Wilkerson, and Lauren Wiener [12]. In this method, you read through the requirements or use cases looking for noun phrases. Nouns in the textual description are considered to be classes and verbs to be methods of the classes (identifying methods will be covered in Chapter 8). All plurals are changed to singular, the nouns are listed, and the list divided into three categories (see Figure 7–2): relevant classes, fuzzy classes (the "fuzzy area," classes we are not sure about), and irrelevant classes.

It is safe to scrap the irrelevant classes, which either have no purpose or will be unnecessary. Candidate classes then are selected from the other two categories. Keep in mind that identifying classes and developing a UML class diagram just like other activities is an iterative process. Depending on whether such object modeling is for the analysis or design phase of development, some classes may need to be added or removed from the model and, remember, flexibility is a virtue. You must be able to formulate a statement of purpose for each candidate class; if not, simply eliminate it.

7.4.1 Identifying Tentative Classes

The following are guidelines for selecting classes in an application:

- Look for nouns and noun phrases in the use cases.
- Some classes are implicit or taken from general knowledge.
- All classes must make sense in the application domain; avoid computer implementation classes—defer them to the design stage.
- Carefully choose and define class names.

As explained before, finding classes is not easy. The more practice you have, the better you get at identifying classes. Finding classes is an incremental and iterative process. Booch [2, p. 149] explains this point elegantly: "Intelligent classification is intellectually hard work, and it best comes about through an incremental and iterative process. This incremental and iterative nature is evident in the development of such diverse software technologies as graphical user interfaces,

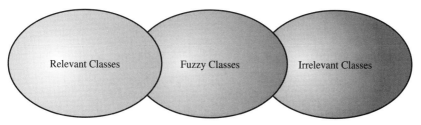

FIGURE 7–2
Using the noun phrase strategy, candidate classes can be divided into three categories: Relevant Classes, Fuzzy Area or Fuzzy Classes (those classes that we are not sure about), and Irrelevant Classes.

database standards, and even fourth-generation languages." As Shaw observed [9, p. 143], in software engineering,

> the development of individual abstractions often follows a common pattern. First the problems are solved ad hoc. As experience accumulates, some solutions turn out to work better than others, and a sort of folklore is passed informally from person to person. Eventually, the useful solutions are understood more systematically, and they are codified and analyzed. This enables the development of models that support automatic implementation and theories that allow the generalization of the solution. This in turn enables a more sophisticated level of practice and allows us to tackle harder problems—which we often approach ad hoc, starting the cycle over again.

7.4.2 Selecting Classes from the Relevant and Fuzzy Categories

The following guidelines help in selecting candidate classes from the relevant and fuzzy categories of classes in the problem domain.

- *Redundant classes*. Do not keep two classes that express the same information. If more than one word is being used to describe the same idea, select the one that is the most meaningful in the context of the system. This is part of building a common vocabulary for the system as a whole [12]. Choose your vocabulary carefully; use the word that is being used by the user of the system.
- *Adjectives classes*. Wirfs-Brock, Wilkerson, and Wiener warn us about adjectives: "Be wary of the use of adjectives. Adjectives can be used in many ways. An adjective can suggest a different kind of object, different use of the same object, or it could be utterly irrelevant. Does the object represented by the noun behave differently when the adjective is applied to it? If the use of the adjective signals that the behavior of the object is different, then make a new class" [12, p. 38]. For example, Adult Members behave differently than Youth Members, so the two should be classified as different classes.
- *Attribute classes*. Tentative objects that are used only as values should be defined or restated as attributes and not as a class. For example, Client Status and Demographic of Client are not classes but attributes of the Client class.
- *Irrelevant classes*. Each class must have a purpose and every class should be clearly defined and necessary. You must formulate a statement of purpose for each candidate class. If you cannot come up with a statement of purpose, simply eliminate the candidate class.

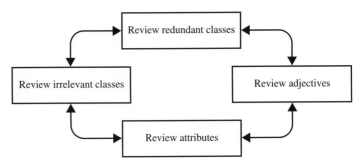

FIGURE 7–3

The process of eliminating the redundant classes and refining the remaining classes is not sequential. You can move back and forth among these steps as often as you like.

Remember that this is an incremental process. Some classes will be missing, others will be eliminated or refined later. Unless you are starting with a lot of domain knowledge, you probably are missing more classes than you will eliminate. Although some classes ultimately may become superclasses, at this stage simply identify them as individual, specific classes. Your design will go through many stages on its way to completion, and you will have adequate opportunity to revise it [12].

Like any other activity of software development, the process of identifying relevant classes and eliminating irrelevant classes is an incremental process. Each iteration often uncovers some classes that have been overlooked. The repetition of the entire process, combined with what you already have learned and the reworking of your candidate classes will enable you to gain a better understanding of the system and the classes that make up your application. Classification is the essence of good object-oriented analysis and design. You must continue this refining cycle through the development process until you are satisfied with the results. Remember that this process (of eliminating redundant classes, classes containing adjectives, possible attributes, and irrelevant classes) is not sequential. You can move back and forth among these steps as often as you like (see Figure 7–3).

7.4.3 The ViaNet Bank ATM System: Identifying Classes by Using Noun Phrase Approach

To better understand the noun phrase method, we will go through a case and apply the noun phrase strategy for identifying the classes. We must start by reading the use cases and applying the principles discussed in this chapter for identifying classes (see Chapter 6 for the description and use cases of the bank system).

7.4.4 Initial List of Noun Phrases: Candidate Classes

The initial study of the use cases of the bank system produces the following noun phrases (candidate classes—maybe).

Account

Account Balance

Amount
Approval Process
ATM Card
ATM Machine
Bank
Bank Client
Card
Cash
Check
Checking
Checking Account
Client
Client's Account
Currency
Dollar
Envelope
Four Digits
Fund
Invalid PIN
Message
Money
Password
PIN
PIN Code
Record
Savings
Savings Account
Step
System
Transaction
Transaction History

It is safe to eliminate the irrelevant classes. The candidate classes must be selected from relevant and fuzzy classes. The following irrelevant classes can be eliminated because they do not belong to the problem statement: Envelope, Four Digits, and Step. Strikeouts indicate eliminated classes.

Account
Account Balance
Amount
Approval Process
ATM Card

ATM Machine

Bank

BankClient

Card

Cash

Check

Checking

Checking Account

Client

Client's Account

Currency

Dollar

~~Envelope~~

~~Four Digits~~

Fund

Invalid PIN

Message

Money

Password

PIN

PIN Code

Record

Savings

Savings Account

~~Step~~

System

Transaction

Transaction History

7.4.5 Reviewing the Redundant Classes and Building a Common Vocabulary

We need to review the candidate list to see which classes are redundant. If different words are being used to describe the same idea, we must select the one that is the most meaningful in the context of the system and eliminate the others.

The following are the different class names that are being used to refer to the same concept:

Client, BankClient	= BankClient (the term chosen)
Account, Client's Account	= Account
PIN, PIN Code	= PIN
Checking, Checking Account	= Checking Account

Savings, Savings Account	= Savings Account
Fund, Money	= Fund
ATM Card, Card	= ATM Card

Here is the revised list of candidate classes:

Account

Account Balance

Amount

Approval Process

ATM Card

Bank

BankClient

~~Card~~

Cash

Check

~~Checking~~

Checking Account

~~Client~~

~~Client's Account~~

Currency

Dollar

~~Envelope~~

~~Four Digits~~

Fund

Invalid PIN

Message

~~Money~~

Password

PIN

~~PIN Code~~

Record

~~Savings~~

Savings Account

~~Step~~

System

Transaction

Transaction History

7.4.6 Reviewing the Classes Containing Adjectives

We again review the remaining list, now with an eye on classes with adjectives. The main question is this: Does the object represented by the noun behave differently when the adjective is applied to it? If an adjective suggests a different kind of class or the class represented by the noun behaves differently when the adjective is applied to it, then we need to make a new class. However, if it is a different use of the same object or the class is irrelevant, we must eliminate it.

In this example, we have no classes containing adjectives that we can eliminate.

7.4.7 Reviewing the Possible Attributes

The next review focuses on identifying the noun phrases that are attributes, not classes. The noun phrases used only as values should be restated as attributes. This process also will help us identify the attributes of the classes in the system.

Amount: A value, not a class.

Account Balance: An attribute of the Account class.

Invalid PIN: It is only a value, not a class.

Password: An attribute, possibly of the BankClient class.

Transaction History: An attribute, possibly of the Transaction class.

PIN: An attribute, possibly of the BankClient class.

Here is the revised list of candidate classes. Notice that the eliminated classes are strikeouts (they have a line through them).

Account

~~Account Balance~~

~~Amount~~

Approval Process

ATM Card

Bank

BankClient

~~Card~~

Cash

Check

~~Checking~~

Checking Account

~~Client~~

~~Client's Account~~

Currency

Dollar

~~Envelope~~

~~Four Digits~~

Fund

~~Invalid PIN~~

Message

~~Money~~

~~Password~~

~~PIN~~

~~PIN Code~~

Record

~~Savings~~

Savings Account

~~Step~~

System

Transaction

~~Transaction History~~

7.4.8 Reviewing the Class Purpose

Identifying the classes that play a role in achieving system goals and requirements is a major activity of object-oriented analysis. Each class must have a purpose. Every class should be clearly defined and necessary in the context of achieving the system's goals. If you cannot formulate a statement of purpose for a class, simply eliminate it. The classes that add no purpose to the system have been deleted from the list. The candidate classes are these:

ATM Machine class: Provides an interface to the ViaNet bank.

ATMCard class: Provides a client with a key to an account.

BankClient class: A client is an individual that has a checking account and, possibly, a savings account.

Bank class: Bank clients belong to the Bank. It is a repository of accounts and processes the accounts' transactions.

Account class: An Account class is a *formal* (or *abstract)* class, it defines the common behaviors that can be inherited by more specific classes such as CheckingAccount and SavingsAccount.

CheckingAccount class: It models a client's checking account and provides more specialized withdrawal service.

SavingsAccount class: It models a client's savings account.

Transaction class: Keeps track of transaction, time, date, type, amount, and balance.

No doubt, some classes are missing from the list and others will be eliminated or refined later. Unless you are starting with a lot of domain knowledge, you probably will miss more classes than you will eliminate. After all, this is an incremental process; as you learn more about the problem, your design will go through many stages on its way to completion. Remember, there is no such thing as the "right" set of classes. However, the process of identifying classes can improve gradually through this incremental process.

The major problem with the noun phrase approach is that it depends on the completeness and correctness of the available document, which is rare in real life. On the other hand, large volumes of text on system documentation might lead to too many candidate classes. Even so, the noun phrase exercise can be very educational and useful if combined with other approaches, especially with use cases as we did here.

7.5 COMMON CLASS PATTERNS APPROACH

The second method for identifying classes is using *common class patterns*, which is based on a knowledge base of the common classes that have been proposed by various researchers, such as Shlaer and Mellor [10], Ross [8], and Coad and Yourdon [3]. They have compiled and listed the following patterns for finding the candidate class and object:

- *Name. **Concept class***
  Context. A concept is a particular idea or understanding that we have of our world. The concept class encompasses principles that are not tangible but used to organize or keep track of business activities or communications. Martin and Odell [6, p. 236] describe concepts elegantly, "Privately held ideas or notions are called conceptions. When an understanding is shared by another, it becomes a concept. To communicate with others, we must share our individually held conceptions and arrive at agreed concepts." Furthermore, Martin and Odell explain that, without concepts, mental life would be total chaos since every item we encountered would be different.
  Example. Performance is an example of concept class object.
- *Name. **Events class***
  Context. Events classes are points in time that must be recorded. Things happen, usually to something else at a given date and time or as a step in an ordered sequence. Associated with things remembered are attributes (after all, the things to remember are objects) such as who, what, when, where, how, or why.
  Example. Landing, interrupt, request, and order are possible events.
- *Name. **Organization class***
  Context. An organization class is a collection of people, resources, facilities, or groups to which the users belong; their capabilities have a defined mission, whose existence is largely independent of the individuals.
  Example. An accounting department might be considered a potential class.
- *Name. **People class*** (also known as person, roles, and roles played class)
  Context. The people class represents the different roles users play in interacting with the application. People carry out some function. What role does a person play in the system? Coad and Yourdon [3] explain that a class which is represented by a person can be divided into two types: those representing users of the system, such as an operator or clerk who interacts with the system; and those representing people who do not use the system but about whom information is kept by the system.
  Example. Employee, client, teacher, and manager are examples of people.
- *Name. **Places class***
  Context. Places are physical locations that the system must keep information about.

Example. Buildings, stores, sites, and offices are examples of places.

≭ • *Name.* ***Tangible things and devices class***

Context. This class includes physical objects or groups of objects that are tangible and devices with which the application interacts.

Example. Cars are an example of tangible things, and pressure sensors are an example of devices.

7.5.1 The ViaNet Bank ATM System: Identifying Classes by Using Common Class Patterns

To better understand the common class patterns approach, we once again will try to identify classes in the bank system by applying common class patterns. The common class patterns are concepts, events, organization, people, places, and tangible things and devices.

Events classes are points in time that must be recorded. Associated with things remembered are attributes (after all, the things to remember are objects) such as who, what, when, where, how, or why. The bank system events classes follow.

Account class: An Account class is a *formal* (or *abstract)* class; it defines the common behaviors that can be inherited by more specific classes such as CheckingAccount and SavingsAccount.

CheckingAccount class: It models a client's checking account and provides more specialized withdrawal service.

SavingsAccount class: It models a client's savings account.

Transaction class: It keeps track of transaction, time, date, type, amount, and balance.

Organization classes specify collections of people, resources, facilities, or groups to which the users belong, and their capabilities have a defined mission, whose existence is largely independent of individuals. The bank system's organization class follows.

Bank class: Bank clients belong to the Bank. It is a repository of accounts and processes the accounts' transactions.

People and person classes answer this question: What role does a person play in the system? Coad and Yourdon [3] explain that a class being represented by a person can be divided into two types: those representing the users of the system, such as an operator or a clerk who interacts with systems, and those people who do not use the system but about whom information is kept by the system. The following is the bank system people and person class.

BankClient class: A client is an individual that has a checking account and, possibly, a savings account.

Place classes represent physical locations, buildings, stores, sites, or offices about which the system needs to keep track. Place classes are not applicable to this bank system.

The *tangible things and devices* classes represent physical objects or groups of objects that are tangible and devices with which the application interacts. In the banking system, tangible and device classes include these items.

ATMMachine class: It allows access to all accounts held by a bank client.

7.6 USE-CASE DRIVEN APPROACH: IDENTIFYING CLASSES AND THEIR BEHAVIORS THROUGH SEQUENCE/COLLABORATION MODELING

The use-case driven approach is the third approach that we examine in this chapter and the one that is recommended. From the previous chapter, we learned that use cases are employed to model the scenarios in the system and specify what external actors interact with the scenarios. The scenarios are described in text or through a sequence of steps. Use-case modeling is considered a problem-driven approach to object-oriented analysis, in that the designer first considers the problem at hand and not the relationship between objects, as in a data-driven approach.

Modeling with use cases is a recommended aid in finding the objects of a system and is the technique used by the unified approach. Once the system has been described in terms of its scenarios, the modeler can examine the textual description or steps of each scenario to determine what objects are needed for the scenario to occur. However, this is not a magical process in which you start with use cases, develop a sequence diagram, and voilà, classes appear before your eyes. The process of creating sequence or collaboration diagrams is a systematic way to think about how a use case (scenario) can take place; and by doing so, it forces you to think about objects involved in your application.

When building a new system, designers model the scenarios of the way the system of business should work. When redesigning an existing system, many modelers choose to first model the scenarios of the current system, and then model the scenarios of the way the system should work. Developing scenarios also requires us to think about class methods, which will be studied in Chapter 8.

7.6.1 Implementation of Scenarios

The UML specification recommends that at least one scenario be prepared for each significantly different use-case instance. Each scenario shows a different sequence of interaction between actors and the system, with all decisions definite. In essence, this process helps us to understand the behavior of the system's objects.

When you have arrived at the lowest use-case level, you may create a child sequence diagram or accompanying collaboration diagram for the use case. With the sequence and collaboration diagrams, you can model the implementation of the scenario [7].

Like use-case diagrams, sequence diagrams are used to model scenarios in the systems. Whereas use cases and the steps or textual descriptions that define them offer a high-level view of a system, the sequence diagram enables you to model a more specific analysis and also assists in the design of the system by modeling the interactions between objects in the system.

As explained in Chapter 5, in a sequence diagram, the objects involved are drawn on the diagram as a vertical dashed line, with the name of the objects at the top. Horizontal lines corresponding to the events that occur between objects are drawn between the vertical object lines. The event lines are drawn in sequential order, from the top of the diagram to the bottom. They do not necessarily correspond to the steps defined for a use-case scenario.

7.6.2 The ViaNet Bank ATM System: Decomposing a Use-Case Scenario with a Sequence Diagram: Object Behavior Analysis

A sequence diagram represents the sequence and interactions of a given use case or scenario. Sequence diagrams are among the most popular UML diagrams and, if used with an object model or class diagram, can capture most of the information about a system [5]. Most object-to-object interactions and operations are considered events, and events include signals, inputs, decisions, interrupts, transitions, and actions to or from users or external devices. An event also is considered to be any action by an object that sends information. The event line represents a message sent from one object to another, in which the "from" object is requesting an operation be performed by the "to" object. The "to" object performs the operation using a method that its class contains. Developing sequence or collaboration diagrams requires us to think about objects that generate these events and therefore will help us in identifying classes.

To identify objects of a system, we further analyze the lowest level use cases with a sequence and collaboration diagram pair (actually, most CASE tools such as SA/Object allow you to create only one, either a sequence or a collaboration diagram, and the system generates the other one). Sequence and collaboration diagrams represent the order in which things occur and how the objects in the system send messages to one another. These diagrams provide a macro-level analysis of the dynamics of a system. Once you start creating these diagrams, you may find that objects may need to be added to satisfy the particular sequence of events for the given use case.

You can draw sequence diagrams to model each scenario that exists when a BankClient withdraws, deposits, or needs information on an account. By walking through the steps, you can determine what objects are necessary for those steps to take place. Therefore, the process of creating sequence or collaboration diagrams can assist you in identifying classes or objects of the system. This approach can be combined with noun phrase and class categorization for the best results.

In Chapter 6, we identified the use cases for the bank system. The following are the low level (executable) use cases:

Deposit Checking
Deposit Savings
Invalid PIN
Withdraw Checking
Withdraw More from Checking
Withdraw Savings
Withdraw Savings Denied

Checking Transaction History
Savings Transaction History

Let us create a sequence/collaboration diagram for the following use cases:

- Invalid PIN use case
- Withdraw Checking use case
- Withdraw More from Checking use case

Sequence/collaboration diagrams are associated with a use case. For example, to model the sequence/collaboration diagrams in SA/Object, you must first select a use case, such as the Invalid PIN use case, then associate a sequence or collaboration child process.

To create a sequence you must think about the classes that probably will be involved in a use-case scenario. Keep in mind that *use case* refers to a process, not a class. However, a use case can contain many classes, and the same class can occur in many different use cases. Point of caution: you should defer the interfaces classes to the design phase and concentrate on the identifying business classes here.

Consider how we would prepare a sequence diagram for the Invalid PIN use case. Here, we need to think about the sequence of activities that the actor BankClient performs:

- Insert ATM Card.
- Enter PIN number.
- Remove the ATM Card.

Based on these activities, the system should either grant the access right to the account or reject the card. Next, we need to more explicitly define the system. With what are we interacting? We are interacting with an ATMMachine and the BankClient. So, the other objects of this use case are ATMMachine and BankClient.

Now that we have identified the objects involved in the use case, we need to list them in a line along the top of a page and drop dotted lines beneath each object (see Figure 7–4). The client in this case is whoever tries to access an account

FIGURE 7–4
The sequence diagram for the Invalid PIN use case.

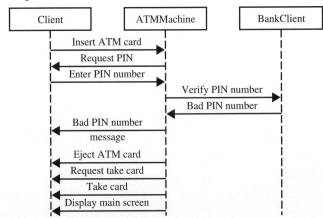

through the ATM, and may or may not have an account. The BankClient on the other hand has an account.

The dotted lines are the lifelines discussed in Chapter 5. The line on the right represents an actor, in this case the BankClient, or an event that is outside the system boundary. Recall from Chapter 5 that an event arrow connect objects. In effect, the event arrow suggests that a message is moving between those two objects. An example of an event message is the request for a PIN. An event line can pass over an object without stopping at that object. Each event must have a descriptive name. In some cases, several objects are active simultaneously, even if they are only waiting for another object to return information to them. In other cases, an object becomes active when it receives a message and then becomes inactive as soon as it responds [5]. Similarly, we can develop sequence diagrams for other use cases (as in Figures 7–5 and 7–7). Collaboration diagrams are just another view of the sequence diagrams and therefore can be created automatically; most UML modeling tools automatically create them (see Figures 7–6 and 7–8).

The following classes have been identified by modeling the UML sequence/ collaboration diagrams: Bank, BankClient, ATMMachine, Account, Checking Account, and Savings Account.

Similarly other classes can be identified by developing the remaining sequence/ collaboration diagrams. Developing the other sequence/collaboration diagrams has been left as an exercise; see problem 1–3.

FIGURE 7–5

Sequence diagram for the Withdraw Checking use case.

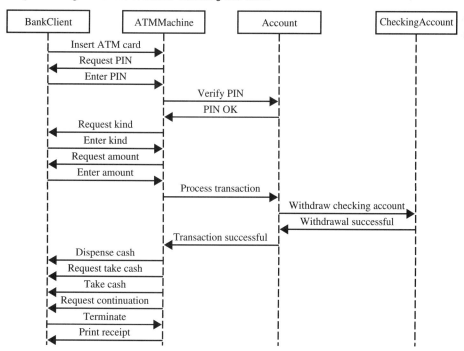

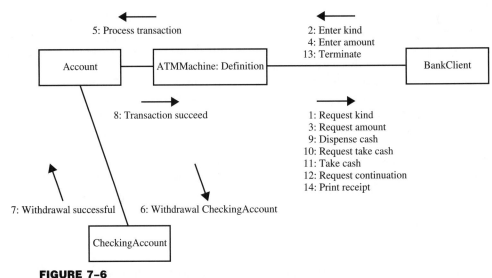

FIGURE 7–6
The collaboration diagram for the Withdraw Checking use case.

FIGURE 7–7
The sequence diagram for the Withdraw More from Checking use case.

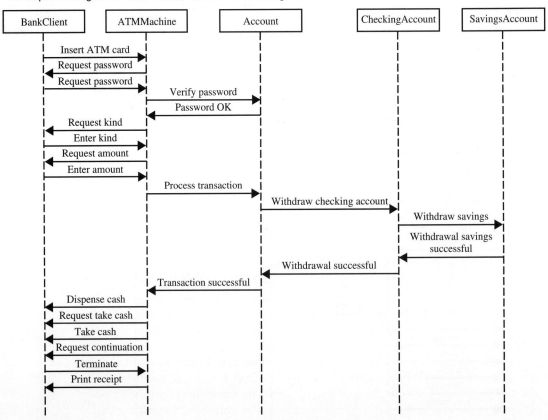

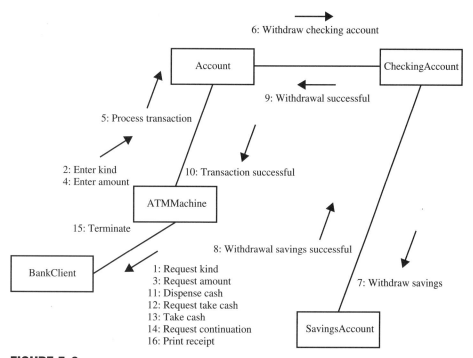

FIGURE 7–8
The collaboration diagram for the Withdraw More from Checking use case.

7.7 CLASSES, RESPONSIBILITIES, AND COLLABORATORS

Classes, responsibilities, and collaborators (CRC), developed by Cunningham, Wilkerson, and Beck, was first presented as a way of teaching the basic concepts of object-oriented development [12]. ***Classes, Responsibilities, and Collaborators*** is a technique used for identifying classes' responsibilities and therefore their attributes and methods. Furthermore, Classes, Responsibilities, and Collaborators can help us identify classes. Classes, Responsibilities, and Collaborators is more a teaching technique than a method for identifying classes. Classes, Responsibilities, and Collaborators is based on the idea that an object either can accomplish a certain responsibility itself or it may require the assistance of other objects. If it requires the assistance of other objects, it must collaborate with those objects to fulfill its responsibility [13]. By identifying an object's responsibilities and ***collaborators*** (cooperative objects with which it works) you can identify its attributes and methods.

Classes, Responsibilities, and Collaborators cards are 4″ × 6″ index cards. All the information for an object is written on a card, which is cheap, portable, readily available, and familiar. Figure 7–9 shows an idealized card. The class name should appear in the upper left-hand corner, a bulleted list of responsibilities should appear under it in the left two thirds of the card, and the list of collaborators should appear in the right third. However, rather than simply tracing the details of a collaboration in the form of message sending, Classes, Responsibilities, and Collaborators cards place the designer's focus on the motivation for collaboration by representing (potentially) many messages as phrases of English text.

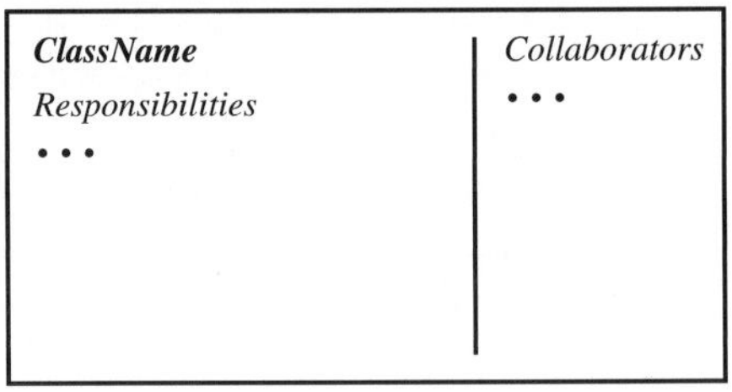

ClassName	*Collaborators*
Responsibilities	• • •
• • •	

FIGURE 7–9
A Classes, Responsibilities, and Collaborators (CRC) index card.

Classes, Responsibilities, and Collaborators stresses the importance of creating objects, not to meet mythical future needs, but only under the demands of the moment. This ensures that a design contains only as much information as the designer has directly experienced and avoids premature complexity. Working in teams helps here, because a concerned designer can influence team members by suggesting scenarios aimed specifically at suspected weaknesses or omissions.

7.7.1 Classes, Responsibilities, and Collaborators Process

The Classes, Responsibilities, and Collaborators process consists of three steps (see Figure 7–10) [1]:

1. Identify classes' responsibilities (and identify classes).
2. Assign responsibilities.
3. Identify collaborators.

Classes are identified and grouped by common attributes, which also provides candidates for superclasses. The class names then are written onto Classes, Responsibilities, and Collaborators cards. The card also notes sub- and superclasses to show the class structure. The application's requirements then are examined for actions and information associated with each class to find the responsibilities of each class.

Next, the responsibilities are distributed; they should be as general as possible and placed as high as possible in the inheritance hierarchy.

The idea in locating collaborators is to identify how classes interact. Classes (cards) that have a close collaboration are grouped together physically.

FIGURE 7–10
The Classes, Resposibilities, and Collaborators process.

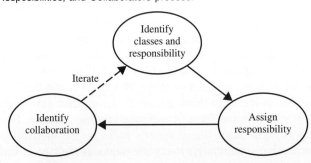

7.7.2 The ViaNet Bank ATM System: Identifying Classes by Using Classes, Responsibilities, and Collaborators[1]

We already identified the initial classes of the bank system. The objective of this example is to identify objects' responsibilities such as attributes and methods in that system.

Account and Transaction provide the banking model. Note that Transaction assumes an active role while money is being dispensed and a passive role thereafter.

The class Account is responsible mostly to the BankClient class and it collaborates with several objects to fulfill its responsibilities. Among the responsibilities of the Account class to the BankClient class is to keep track of the BankClient balance, account number, and other data that need to be remembered. These are the attributes of the Account class. Furthermore, the Account class provides certain services or methods, such as means for BankClient to deposit or withdraw an amount and display the account's Balance (see Figure 7–11).

Classes, Responsibilities, and Collaborators encourages team members to pick up the card and assume a role while "executing" a scenario. It is not unusual to see a designer with a card in each hand, waving them about, making a strong identification with the objects while describing their collaboration. Ward Cunningham writes:

Classes, Responsibilities, and Collaborators cards work by taking people through programming episodes together. As cards are written for familiar objects, all participants pick up the same context and ready themselves for decision making. Then, by waving cards and pointing fingers and yelling statements like, "no, this guy should do that," decisions are made. Finally, the group starts to relax as consensus has been reached and the issue becomes simply finding the right words to record a decision as a responsibility on a card.

In similar fashion other cards for the classes that have been identified earlier in this chapter must be created, with the list of their responsibilities and their collaborators. As you can see from Figure 7–10, this process is iterative.

Start with few cards (classes) then proceed to play "what if." If the situation calls for a responsibility not already covered by one of the objects, either add the responsibility to an object or create a new object to address that responsibility. If one of the objects becomes too cluttered during this process, copy the information on

FIGURE 7–11
Classes, Responsibilities, and Collaborators for the Account object.

Account	Checking Account
balance	(subclass)
number	Savings Account
-----	(subclass)
deposit	Transaction
withdraw	
getBalance	

---

[1]This section is adapted from "Laboratory for Teaching Object-Oriented Thinking" by Kent Beck and Ward Cunningham, with permission of the Association for Computing Machinery.

BOX 7.1

Real-World Issues on the Agenda
CRC: HOW DO TEAMS SHAPE OBJECTS? HOW DO OBJECTS SHAPE TEAMS?

Ward Cunningham

CRC stands for Classes, Responsibilities, and Collaborators. My colleague, Kent Beck, and I would struggle to coax a program into existence sitting side-by-side, sharing the controls of a then new Smalltalk workstation. We found repeatedly that our problems would yield when we could articulate the responsibilities of the objects we had made and the collaborations they would use to meet those responsibilities. I had many months' experience with such grappling before I ever tried to duplicate the sensation away from a computer. The first ever CRC Cards were written at 4:00 AM one morning on my dining room table. The first ever team development of CRC Cards took place around 9:00 AM that same day as Brian Wilkerson and I grappled with responsibilities at a cafeteria table 1000 feet from our machines. As with Kent many times before, here I was coaxing a program into existence. I'd like to leave CRC for the moment and instead focus on what I mean by coaxing a program into existence.

A program is decision made. Humans make those decisions and write them into programs. When I compare the research programming I did early on to the production programming I've done recently, I find that the activities differ only in the quantity of decisions made on a given day. In both cases decisions come in spurts. A period of investigation precedes a spurt of decisions. Likewise, a period of rather mechanical activity following through with consequences follows a decision spurt. The feeling one gets is of lifting a problem up into the mind, struggling with it until decisions come, then putting

those decisions down in place of the problem. Only then can one relax. This cycle repeats. It's what I call grappling. I feel it when I program, with cards or at a machine.

I now call these grapple cycles programming episodes. Episodic programming is most noticeable when decisions require judgment. Mechanical decisions, like looking something up in a book, don't feel particularly episodic. But, then, they aren't actually decisions. Designing framework software on the other hand does require judgment and progresses in distinct episodes.

CRC Cards work by taking people through programming episodes together. As cards are written for familiar objects, all participants pick up the same context and ready themselves for decision making. Then, by waving cards and pointing fingers and yelling statements like, "no, this guy should do that," decisions are made. Finally, the group starts to relax as consensus has been reached and the issue becomes simply finding the right words to record a decision as a responsibility on a card.

I've had people tell me about their struggles to make CRC Cards work. Often many none-too-fruitful sessions preceded an almost spiritual experience when the right people are finally assembled and they "come together" to break a logjam of indecision.

Such reports are, of course, satisfying. Even more satisfying is my more recent experience in front of the Smalltalk browsers. Having left research, I found myself swimming in a river of decisions. As I pointed out earlier, production programming re-

its card to a new card, searching for more concise ways of saying what the object does. If it is not possible to shrink the information further and the object is still too complex, create a new object to assume some of the responsibilities.

7.8 NAMING CLASSES

Naming a class is an important activity. Here are guidelines for naming classes:

- The class name should be singular. The class should describe a single object, so it should be the singular form of noun (it may be an adjective and a noun, such as YouthMember).

BOX 7.1 *(continued)*

quires many times more decisions per day than research. Production decisions are rarely as profound as those in research, but they are of equal or greater consequence and demand as much or more judgment. Our production team "came together" when we learned to work through episodes promptly and in synchronization so that our collective experience came to bear on all of our decision making.

We regularly worked two to a machine. This worked best when we had enough framework in place that our Smalltalk code read like specification. An episode would begin by poking around with "senders," "implementers," a few "inspectors" and an occasional "ctrl-c." We were lifting the problem into our collective consciousness. One would type, the other watch, then trade off. As we approached decisions, our attention would turn to each other. The communication would become complex as human communication often does. I won't attempt to analyze it except to say that it includes a lot of hand waving, body motion and statements like, "hey, that guy shouldn't do that." Finally, decisions would be made and the consequences followed through, not by writing on cards, but by adjusting the specification-like code. And, as with cards, we would search for just the right words to represent the decisions as they had come to us.

What I've just described, I'd felt in research. And, I thought of it as just a happy compatibility. In production, our machine sharing collaborations were more intentional, based on our need to work quickly and correctly. It was a practice that grew slowly in our core group of four implementers, individuals of only average compatibility. The practice spread by firsthand experience. First, others learned that I preferred collaborative episodes as a work style. Then, they chose to work that way, too. Ultimately, any possible pairing was likely in the office and a group of three would form when the problems required that much talent.

I'd like to point out again the unusually high capacity human-to-human communication path that is opened by two people sharing a machine. As the developers work through whole programming episodes together, the machine presents a broad range of situations to be dealt with, all, of course, relevant to the work at hand. In order to stay synchronized each programmer must at least follow the problem-solving strategies and techniques of the other. Things that worked were obvious. These spread quickly as did our general understanding of what worked well and what didn't in the program as a whole.

I now recognize the organization we built to be a High-Performance Team. Such teams are recognized by their ability to play to members' strengths while covering for each other's weaknesses. We were able to work at maximum productivity continuously and indefinitely. When an occasional crisis did occur, we simply pulled the most relevant people together and worked through the problem as another episode. We knew we were working on the most important thing in the most productive way. No further urgency was necessary.

In summary, Smalltalk's specification-like coding and incremental development environment permits a unique human-human-machine dialogue. CRC Cards allow larger groups to feel this dialogue which is based on repeated episodes of decision making. Finally, members of somewhat larger production development teams can exploit the human-human-machine dialogue on a pair-wise basis. The complex communication that then takes place will support a High-Performance organization with many benefits, a few of which I have mentioned.

- One general rule for naming classes is that you should use names with which the users or clients are comfortable. Choose the class name from standard vocabulary for the subject matter. Select the name with which the client is comfortable rather than semantically accurate terminology [3].
- The name of a class should reflect its intrinsic nature. Stick with the general terminology of the subject matter.
- Use readable names. Capitalize class names. By convention, the class name must begin with an upper-case letter. For compound words, capitalize the first letter of each word; for example, LoanWindow. While these conventions are not mandatory, they make the code consistent and easy to read. Do not add prefix

and suffix codes, they are a bother to read and troublesome when they need to be changed [3].

7.9 SUMMARY

Object analysis is a process by which we can identify the classes that play a role in achieving the system goals and requirements. The problem of classification may be regarded as one of discriminating *things*, not between the individual objects, but between classes via the search for features or invariant attributes (or behaviors) among members of a class.

Finding classes is one of the hardest activities in object-oriented analysis. Unfortunately classes are rarely just there for the picking. There is no such thing as the *perfect* class structure or the *right* set of objects. Nevertheless, several approaches—such as the use-case driven approach, the noun phrase, and the knowledge base of common class patterns, and Classes, Responsibilities, and Collaborators—can offer us guidelines and general rules for identifying the classes in the given problem domain. Furthermore, identifying classes is an iterative process, and as you gain more experience, you get better at identifying classes.

In this chapter, we studied four approaches for identifying classes: the noun phrase, common class patterns, use-case driven, and Classes, Responsibilities, and Collaborators. The process of identifying classes can improve gradually through the incremental process. Some classes will be missing in the first few cycles of identification, and others will be eliminated or refined later. Unless you are starting with a lot of domain knowledge, you probably will miss more classes than you will eliminate. Your design will go through many stages on its way to completion as you learn more about the problem.

To identify classes using the noun phrase approach, read through use cases, looking for noun phrases. Consider nouns in the textual description to be classes and verbs to be methods of the classes.

The second method for identifying classes is the common class patterns approach based on the knowledge base of the common classes proposed by various researchers. These researchers compiled and listed several categories for finding the candidate classes and objects.

The third method we studied was use-case driven. To identify objects of a system and their behaviors, the lowest level of executable use cases is further analyzed with a sequence and collaboration diagram pair. By walking through the steps, you can determine what objects are necessary for the steps to take place. Finally, we looked at the Classes, Responsibilities, and Collaborators, which is a useful tool for learning about class responsibilities and identifying classes. These approaches can be mixed for identifying the classes of a given problem.

Naming a class is an important activity, too. The class should describe a single object, so it should be a singular noun or an adjective and a noun. A general rule for naming classes is that you use names with which the users or clients are comfortable. Choose the class names from standard vocabulary for the subject matter.

KEY TERMS

Adjective class (p. 155)
Attribute class (p. 155)
Classes, Responsibilities, and Collaborators (CRC) (p. 169)
Classification (p. 152)
Collaborator (p. 169)
Common class patterns (p. 162)
Concepts class (p. 162)
Events class (p. 162)
Irrelevant class (p. 155)
Organization class (p. 162)
Places class (p. 162)
People (person) class (p. 162)
Redundant class (p. 155)
Tangible things and device class (p. 163)

REVIEW QUESTIONS

1. Where do objects come from?
2. Describe the noun phrase strategy for identifying tentative classes in a problem domain.
3. Describe relevant, fuzzy, and irrelevant classes.
4. How would you select candidate classes for the list of relevant and fuzzy classes?
5. What criteria would you use to eliminate a class?
6. What is the common class patterns strategy?
7. What clues would you use to identify classes?
8. How would you name classes?
9. What are the concepts classes?
10. What are the events classes?
11. What are the organization classes?
12. What are the other system classes?
13. What are the people (person) classes?
14. Explain the places class source.
15. What are the tangible things and devices classes?
16. Why is identifying classes an incremental process?
17. Why is developing a sequence/collaboration diagram a useful activity in identifying classes?
18. Why is Classes, Responsibilities, and Collaborators useful?

PROBLEMS

1. Develop sequence/collaboration diagrams for the Deposit Checking use case of the bank system.
2. Develop sequence/collaboration diagrams for the Deposit Savings use case of the bank system.
3. Develop sequence/collaboration diagrams for the Withdraw Savings Denied use case of the bank system.

4. Identify classes in the Grandma's Soup Unlimited problem (see Chapter 6) by using one (or a combination) of approaches you have learned in this chapter. Also, write a reason(s) for the approach that you have selected.

REFERENCES

1. Anderson, Michael; and Bergstrand, John. "Formalizing Use Cases with Message Sequence Charts." Master thesis, Department of Communication Systems, Lund Institute of Technology, 1995.
2. Booch, Grady. *Object-Oriented Analysis and Design with Applications*. Redwood, CA: Benjamin-Cummings, 1994.
3. Coad, Peter; and Yourdon, Edward. *Object-Oriented Analysis*, 2d ed. Englewood Cliffs, NJ: Yourdon Press, Prentice-Hall, 1991.
4. Gabriel, R.; White, J.; and Bobrow, D. "CLOS Integrating Object-Oriented and Functional Programming." *Communications of the ACM* 34, no. 9.
5. Harmon, P.; and Watson, M. *Understanding UML: The Developer's Guide with a Web-Based Application in Java*. San Mateo, CA: Morgan Kaufmann Publishers, 1998
6. Martin, James; and Odell, James. *Object-Oriented Analysis and Design*. Englewood Cliffs, NJ: Prentice-Hall, 1992.
7. *Object Modeling Quick Start*. Popkin Software & Systems, 1997.
8. Ross, R. *Entity Modeling: Techniques and Application*. Boston: Database Research Group, 1987.
9. Shaw, M. "Large Scale Systems Require Higher-Level Abstractions." *SIGSOFT Engineering Notes* 14, no. 3 (May 1989), p.143.
10. Shlaer, S.; and Mellor, S. *Object-Oriented System Analysis: Modeling the World in Data*. Englewood Cliffs, NJ: Yourdon Press, 1988.
11. Tou, J. T.; and Gonzalez, R. C. *Pattern Recognition Principles*. Reading, MA: Addison-Wesley, 1981.
12. Beck, Kent; and Cunningham, Ward. "A laboratory for teaching Object-Oriented Thinking," Object-Oriented Programming System Languages and Application OOP-SLA'89, October 1-6, 1989, New Orleans, LA.
13. Wirfs-Brock, Rebecca; Wilkerson, Brian; and Wiener, Lauren. *Designing Object-Oriented Software*. Englewood Cliffs, NJ: Prentice-Hall, 1992.

CHAPTER 8

Identifying Object Relationships, Attributes, and Methods

Objects contribute to the behavior of the system by collaborating with one another.

—Grady Booch [2]

Chapter Objectives

You should be able to define and understand

- Analyzing relationships among classes.
- Identifying association.
- Association patterns.
- Identifying super- and subclass hierarchies.
- Identifying aggregation or a-part-of compositions.
- Class responsibilities.
- Identifying attributes and methods by analyzing use cases and other UML diagrams.

8.1 INTRODUCTION

In an object-oriented environment, objects take on an active role in a system. Of course, objects do not exist in isolation but interact with each other. Indeed, these interactions and relationships are the application. All objects stand in relationship to others on whom they rely for services and control. The relationship among objects is based on the assumptions each makes about the other objects, including what operations can be performed and what behavior results [2]. Three types of relationships among objects are

- *Association*. How are objects associated? This information will guide us in designing classes.
- *Super-sub structure (also known as generalization hierarchy)*. How are objects organized into superclasses and subclasses? This information provides us the direction of inheritance.

- *Aggregation and a-part-of structure.* What is the composition of complex classes? This information guides us in defining mechanisms that properly manage object-within-object [6].

Generally speaking, the relationships among objects are known as *associations*. For example, a customer places an *order* for soup. The *order* is the association between the customer and soup objects. The hierarchical or super-sub relation allows the sharing of properties or inheritance. *A-part-of* structure is a familiar means of organizing components of a bigger object. For example, walls, windows, doors, and the like are part of a bigger object: a building.

In this chapter, we look at guidelines for identifying association, super-sub, and a-part-of relationships in the problem domain. We then proceed to identify attributes and methods. To do this we must first determine the responsibilities of the system. We saw that the system's responsibilities can be identified by analyzing use cases and their sequence and collaboration diagrams. Once you have identified the system's responsibilities and what information the system needs to remember, you can assign each responsibility to the class to which it logically belongs. This also aids in determining the purpose and role each class plays in the application.

8.2 ASSOCIATIONS

Association represents a physical or conceptual connection between two or more objects. For example, if an object has the responsibility for telling another object that a credit card number is valid or invalid, the two classes have an association. In Chapter 5, we learned that the binary associations are shown as lines connecting two class symbols. Ternary and higher-order associations are shown as diamonds connecting to a class symbol by lines, and the association name is written above or below the line. The association name can be omitted if the relationship is obvious. In some cases, you will want to provide names for the roles played by the individual classes making up the relationship. The role name on the side closest to each class describes the role that class plays relative to the class at the other end of the line, and vice versa [4] (see Figure 8–1).

FIGURE 8–1
Basic association. See Chapter 5 for a detailed discussion of association.

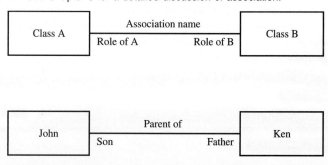

8.2.1 Identifying Associations

Identifying associations begins by analyzing the interactions between classes. After all, any dependency relationship between two or more classes is an association [7]. You must examine the responsibilities to determine dependencies. In other words, if an object is responsible for a specific task (behavior) and lacks all the necessary knowledge needed to perform the task, then the object must delegate the task to another object that possesses such knowledge. Wirfs-Brock, Wilkerson, and Wiener [8] provide the following questions that can help us to identify associations:

- Is the class capable of fulfilling the required task by itself?
- If not, what does it need?
- From what other class can it acquire what it needs?

Answering these questions helps us identify association. The approach you should take to identify association is flexibility. First, extract all candidates' associations from the problem statement and get them down on paper. You can refine them later. Notice that a-part-of structures (aggregation) and associations are very similar. So, how do you distinguish one from the other? It depends on the problem domain; after all, a-part-of structure is a special case of association. Simply pick the one most natural for the problem domain. If you can represent the problem more easily with association, then select it; otherwise, use a-part-of structure, which is described later in the chapter.

8.2.2 Guidelines for Identifying Association

The following are general guidelines for identifying the tentative associations:

- A dependency between two or more classes may be an association. Association often corresponds to a verb or prepositional phrase, such as part of, next to, works for, or contained in.
- A reference from one class to another is an association. Some associations are implicit or taken from general knowledge.

8.2.3 Common Association Patterns

The common association patterns are based on some of the common associations defined by researchers and practitioners: Rumbaugh et al. [7], Coad and Yourdon [3], and others. These include

- *Location association—next to, part of, contained in*. For example, consider a soup object, cheddar cheese is a-part-of soup. The a-part-of relation is a special type of association, discussed in more detail later in the chapter.
- *Communication association—talk to, order to*. For example, a customer places an order (communication association) with an operator person (see Figure 8–2).

These association patterns and similar ones can be stored in the repository and added to as more patterns are discovered. However, currently, this capability of the unified approach's repository is more conceptual than real, but it is my hope that CASE tool vendors in the near future will provide this capability.

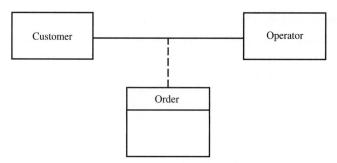

FIGURE 8–2
A customer places an order (communication association) with an operator person.

8.2.4 Eliminate Unnecessary Associations

- *Implementation association.* Defer implementation-specific associations to the design phase. Implementation associations are concerned with the implementation or design of the class within certain programming or development environments and not relationships among business objects (see Chapter 6 for a definition of business objects).
- *Ternary associations.* **Ternary** or n-ary **association** is an association among more than two classes (see Chapter 5). Ternary associations complicate the representation. When possible, restate ternary associations as binary associations.
- *Directed actions (or derived) association.* **Directed actions** (derived) **associations** can be defined in terms of other associations. Since they are redundant, avoid these types of association. For example, *Grandparent* of can be defined in terms of the parent of association (see Figure 8–3).

  Choose association names carefully. Do not say how or why a situation came about; say what it is. Add role names where appropriate, especially to distinguish multiple associations. These often are discovered by testing access paths to objects.

FIGURE 8–3
Grandparent of Ken can be defined in terms of the parent association.

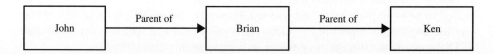

8.3 SUPER-SUB CLASS RELATIONSHIPS

The other aspect of classification (see Chapter 7) is identification of super-sub relations among classes. For the most part, a class is part of a hierarchy of classes, where the top class is the most general one and from it descend all other, more specialized classes. The super-sub class relationship represents the inheritance relationships between related classes, and the class hierarchy determines the lines of inheritance between classes. Class inheritance is useful for a number of reasons. For example, in some cases, you want to create a number of classes that are similar in all but a few characteristics. In other cases, someone already has developed a class that you can use, but you need to modify that class. Subclasses are more specialized versions of their superclasses. The classes are not ordered this way for convenience's sake.

Superclass-subclass relationships, also known as *generalization hierarchy*, allow objects to be built from other objects. Such relationships allow us to explicitly take advantage of the commonality of objects when constructing new classes. The super-sub class hierarchy is a relationship between classes, where one class is the parent class of another (derived) class. Recall from Chapter 2 that the parent class also is known as the *base* or *super class* or *ancestor*. The super-sub class hierarchy is based on inheritance, which is programming by extension as opposed to programming by reinvention [5]. The real advantage of using this technique is that we can build on what we already have and, more important, reuse what we already have. Inheritance allows classes to share and reuse behaviors and attributes. Where the behavior of a class instance is defined in that class's methods, a class also inherits the behaviors and attributes of all of its superclasses. Now let us take a look at guidelines for identifying classes.

8.3.1 Guidelines for Identifying Super-Sub Relationship, a Generalization

The following are guidelines for identifying super-sub relationships in the application:

- *Top-down*. Look for noun phrases composed of various adjectives in a class name. Often, you can discover additional special cases. Avoid excessive refinement. Specialize only when the subclasses have significant behavior. For example, a phone operator employee can be represented as a cook as well as a clerk or manager because they all have similar behaviors.
- *Bottom-up*. Look for classes with similar attributes or methods. In most cases, you can group them by moving the common attributes and methods to an abstract class. You may have to alter the definitions a bit; this is acceptable as long as generalization truly applies. However, do not force classes to fit a preconceived generalization structure.
- *Reusability*. Move attributes and behaviors (methods) as high as possible in the hierarchy. At the same time, do not create very specialized classes at the top of the hierarchy. This is easier said than done. The balancing act can be achieved through several iterations. This process ensures that you design objects that can be reused in another application.

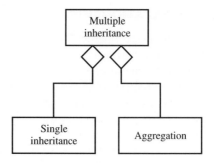

FIGURE 8–4
One way to achieve the benefits of multiple inheritance is to inherit from the most appropriate class and add an object of another class as an attribute. In essence, a multiple inheritance can be represented as an aggregation of a single inheritance and aggregation. This meta-model reflects this situation.

- *Multiple inheritance*. Avoid excessive use of multiple inheritance. Multiple inheritance brings with it complications such as how to determine which behavior to get from which class, particularly when several ancestors define the same method. It also is more difficult to understand programs written in a multiple inheritance system. One way of achieving the benefits of multiple inheritance is to inherit from the most appropriate class and add an object of another class as an attribute (see Figure 8–4, aggregation; we will look at this issue in Chapter 9). However, use multiple inheritance when it is appropriate. For example, if the owner of a restaurant prepares the soups, you can utilize multiple inheritance structure to define an OwnerOperator class that inherits its attributes and methods from both the Owner and Operator classes.

8.4 A-PART-OF RELATIONSHIPS—AGGREGATION

A-part-of relationship, also called *aggregation*, represents the situation where a class consists of several component classes. A class that is composed of other classes does not behave like its parts; actually, it behaves very differently. For example, a car consists of many other classes, one of which is a radio, but a car does not behave like a radio (see Figure 8–5).

Two major properties of a-part-of relationship are transitivity and antisymmetry [7]:

- *Transitivity*. The property where, if *A* is part of *B* and B is part of *C*, then *A* is part of *C*. For example, a carburetor is part of an engine and an engine is part of a car; therefore, a carburetor is part of a car. Figure 6–3 shows a-part-of structure.
- *Antisymmetry*. The property of a-part-of relation where, if *A* is part of *B*, then *B* is not part of *A*. For example, an engine is part of a car, but a car is not part of an engine.

A clear distinction between the part and the whole can help us determine where responsibilities for certain behavior must reside. This is done mainly by asking the following questions [3]:

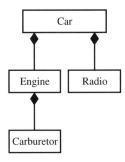

FIGURE 8–5

A-part-of composition. A carburetor is a part of an engine and an engine and a radio are parts of a car.

- Does the part class belong to a problem domain?
- Is the part class within the system's responsibilities?
- Does the part class capture more than a single value? (If it captures only a single value, then simply include it as an attribute with the whole class.)
- Does it provide a useful abstraction in dealing with the problem domain?

In Chapter 5, we saw that the UML uses hollow or filled diamonds to represent aggregations. A filled diamond signifies the strong form of aggregation, which is composition. For example, one might represent aggregation such as *container* and *collection* as hollow diamonds (see Figures 8–6 and 8–7) and use a solid diamond to represent composition, which is a strong form of aggregation (see Figure 8–5).

8.4.1 A-Part-of Relationship Patterns

To identify a-part-of structures, Coad and Yourdon [3] provide the following guidelines:

- *Assembly.* An assembly is constructed from its parts and an assembly-part situation physically exists; for example, a French onion soup is an assembly of onion, butter, flour, wine, French bread, cheddar cheese, and so on.
- *Container.* A physical whole encompasses but is not constructed from physical parts; for example, a house can be considered as a container for furniture and appliances (see Figure 8–6).

FIGURE 8–6

A house is a container.

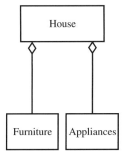

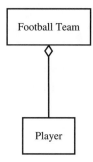

FIGURE 8–7
A football team is a collection of players.

- *Collection-member*. A conceptual whole encompasses parts that may be physical or conceptual; for example, a football team is a collection of players (see Figure 8–7).

8.5 CASE STUDY: RELATIONSHIP ANALYSIS FOR THE VIANET BANK ATM SYSTEM

To better gain experience in object relationship analysis, we use the familiar bank system case and apply the concepts in this chapter for identifying associations, super-sub relationships, and a-part-of relationships for the classes identified in Chapter 7.

As explained before, we must start by reading the requirement specification, which is presented here. Furthermore, object-oriented analysis and design are performed in an iterative process using class diagrams. Analysis is performed on a piece of the system, design details are added to this partial analysis model, and then the design is implemented. Changes can be made to the implementation and brought back into the analysis model to continue the cycle. This iterative process is unlike the traditional waterfall technique, in which all analysis is completed before design begins.

8.5.1 Identifying Classes' Relationships

One of the strengths of object-oriented analysis is the ability to model objects as they exist in the real world. To accurately do this, you must be able to model more than just an object's internal workings. You also must be able to model how objects relate to each other. Several different relationships exist in the ViaNet bank ATM system, so we need to define them.

8.5.2 Developing a UML Class Diagram Based on the Use-Case Analysis

The UML class diagram is the main static analysis and design diagram of a system. The analysis generally consists of the following class diagrams

- One class diagram for the system, which shows the identity and definition of classes in the system, their interrelationships, and various packages containing groupings of classes.

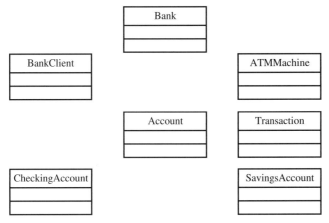

FIGURE 8–8
UML class diagram for the ViaNet bank ATM system. Some CASE tools such as the SA/Object Architect can automatically define classes and draw them from use cases or collaboration/ sequence diagrams. However, presently, it cannot identify all the classes. For this example, S/A Object was able to identify only the BankClient class.

- Multiple class diagrams that represent various pieces, or views, of the system class diagram.
- Multiple class diagrams, that show the specific static relationships between various classes.

First, we need to create the classes that have been identified in the previous chapter; we will add relationships later (see Figure 8–8).

8.5.3 Defining Association Relationships

Identifying association begins by analyzing the interactions of each class. Remember that any dependency between two or more classes is an association. The following are general guidelines for identifying the tentative associations, as explained in this chapter:

- Association often corresponds to verb or prepositional phrases, such as *part of, next to, works for*, or *contained in*.
- A reference from one class to another is an association. Some associations are implicit or taken from general knowledge.

Some common patterns of associations are these:

- *Location association*. For example, next to, part of, contained in (notice that a-part-of relation is a special type of association).
- *Directed actions association*.
- *Communication association*. For example, talk to, order from.

The first obvious relation is that each account belongs to a bank client since each BankClient has an account. Therefore, there is an association between the BankClient and Account classes. We need to establish cardinality among these

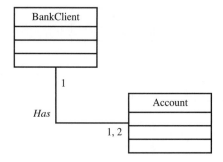

FIGURE 8–9
Defining the BankClient-Account association multiplicity. One Client can have one or more Accounts (checking and savings accounts).

classes. By default, in most CASE tools such as SA/Object Architect, all associations are considered one to one (one client can have only one account and vice versa). However, since each BankClient can have one or two accounts (see Chapter 6), we need to change the cardinality of the association (see Figure 8–9). Other associations and their cardinalities are defined in Table 8–1 and demonstrated in Figure 8–10.

8.5.4 Defining Super-Sub Relationships

Let us review the guidelines for identifying super-sub relationships:

• *Top-down*. Look for noun phrases composed of various adjectives in the class name.
• *Bottom-up*. Look for classes with similar attributes or methods. In most cases, you can group them by moving the common attributes and methods to an abstract class.
• *Reusability*. Move attributes and behaviors (methods) as high as possible in the hierarchy.
• *Multiple inheritance*. Avoid excessive use of multiple inheritance.

CheckingAccount and SavingsAccount both are types of accounts. They can be defined as *specializations* of the Account class. When implemented, the Account

TABLE 8–1			
SOME ASSOCIATIONS AND THEIR CARDINALITIES IN THE BANK SYSTEM			
Class	**Related class**	**Association name**	**Cardinality**
Account	BankClient	Has	One
BankClient	Account		One or two
SavingsAccount	CheckingAccount	Savings-Checking	One
CheckingAccount	SavingsAccount		Zero or one
Account	Transaction	Account-Transaction	Zero or more
Transaction	Account		One

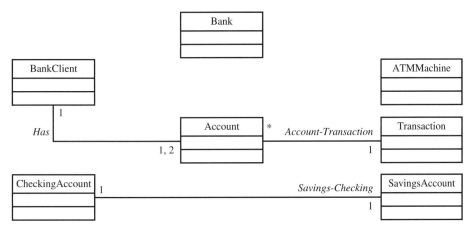

FIGURE 8–10
Associations among the ViaNet bank ATM system classes.

class will define attributes and services common to all kinds of accounts, with CheckingAccount and SavingsAccount each defining methods that make them more specialized. Figure 8–11 depicts the super-sub relationships among Accounts, SavingsAccount, and CheckingAccount.

8.5.5 Identifying the Aggregation/a-Part-of Relationship

To identify a-part-of structures, we look for the following clues:

- *Assembly*. A physical whole is constructed from physical parts.
- *Container*. A physical whole encompasses but is not constructed from physical parts.
- *Collection-Member*. A conceptual whole encompasses parts that may be physical or conceptual.

FIGURE 8–11
Super-sub relationships among the Account, SavingsAccount, and CheckingAccount classes.

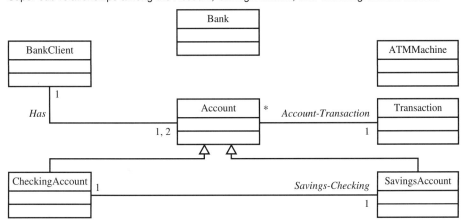

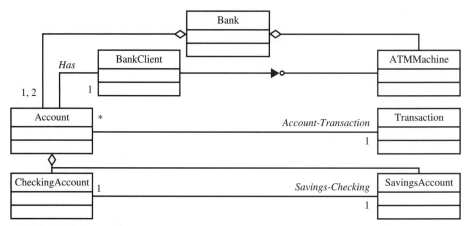

FIGURE 8–12
Association, generalization, and aggregation among the ViaNet bank classes. Notice that the super-sub arrows for CheckingAccount and SavingsAccount have merged. The relationship between BankClient and ATMMachine is an interface.

A bank consists of ATM machines, accounts, buildings, employees, and so forth. However, since buildings and employees are outside the domain of this application, we define the Bank class as an aggregation of ATMMachine and Account classes. Aggregation is a special type of association. Figure 8–12 depicts the association, generalization, and aggregation among the bank systems classes. If you are wondering what is the relationship between the BankClient and ATMMachine, it is an interface. Identifying a class interface is a design activity of object-oriented system development; we look at defining the interface relationship in Chapter 12.

8.6 CLASS RESPONSIBILITY: IDENTIFYING ATTRIBUTES AND METHODS

Identifying attributes and methods is like finding classes, still a difficult activity and an iterative process. Once again use cases and other UML diagrams will be our guide for identifying attributes, methods, and relationships among classes.

Responsibilities identify problems to be solved. Beck and Cunningham explain this point elegantly [1, p. 2], "A responsibility serves as a handle for discussing potential solutions. The responsibilities of an object are expressed by a handful of short verb phrases, each containing an active verb. The more that can be expressed by these phrases, the more powerful and concise the design."

Attributes are things an object must remember such as color, cost, and manufacturer. Identifying attributes of a system's classes starts with understanding the system's responsibilities. We saw that a system's responsibilities can be identified by developing use cases and the desired characteristics of the applications, such as determining what information users need from the system.

The following questions help in identifying the responsibilities of classes and deciding what data elements to keep track of [8]:

- What information about an object should we keep track of?
- What services must a class provide?

Answering the first question will help us identify attributes of a class. Answering the second question allows us to identify a class's methods. Wirfs-Brock, Wilkerson, and Wiener describe system responsibility thus:

> Responsibilities are meant to convey a sense of the purpose of an object and its place in the system. The responsibilities of an object are all the services it provides for all the contracts it supports. When you assign responsibilities to a class, you are stating that each and every instance of that class will have those responsibilities, whether there is just one instance or many. [8, p. 62]

In the following sections, we look at guidelines for identifying attributes and methods of classes in the problem domain by analyzing use cases. Furthermore, developing other UML diagrams such as UML activity and state diagrams also can assist in this process by helping us better understand classes' responsibilities.

8.7 CLASS RESPONSIBILITY: DEFINING ATTRIBUTES BY ANALYZING USE CASES AND OTHER UML DIAGRAMS

Attributes can be derived from scenario testing; therefore, by analyzing the use cases and sequence/collaboration, activity, and state diagrams, you can begin to understand classes' responsibilities and how they must interact to perform their tasks. The main goal here is to understand what the class is responsible for knowing. Responsibility is the key issue. Imagine yourself as an object in an object-oriented environment; what kind of questions would you like to ask [3]?

- How am I going to be used?
- How am I going to collaborate with other classes?
- How am I described in the context of this system's responsibility?
- What do I need to know?
- What state information do I need to remember over time?
- What states can I be in?

Using previous object-oriented analysis results or analysis patterns (if these are available) can be extremely useful in finding out what attributes can be reused directly and what lessons can be learned for defining attributes [3]. Furthermore, you can start to extrapolate which classes you will have to build and which existing classes you can reuse. As you do this, you also begin thinking about the inheritance structure. If you have several classes that seem related but have specific differences, you probably want to make them common subclasses of an existing class or one that you define. Often, bottom up, the superclasses are generated while coding, as you realize that common characteristics can be factored out or in.

8.7.1 Guidelines for Defining Attributes

Here are guidelines for identifying attributes of classes in use cases:

- Attributes usually correspond to nouns followed by prepositional phrases such as *cost of* the soup. Attributes also may correspond to adjectives or adverbs.

- Keep the class simple; state only enough attributes to define the object state.
- Attributes are less likely to be fully described in the problem statement. You must draw on your knowledge of the application domain and the real world to find them.
- Omit derived attributes. For example, do not use *time elapsed since order*. This can be derived from time of the order. Derived attributes should be expressed as a method.
- Do not carry discovery of attributes to excess. You can add more attributes in subsequent iterations.

Another point to remember is that you may think of many attributes that can be associated with a class. You must be careful to add only those attributes necessary to the design at hand. Let use cases guide you in this process. For example, your initial thought is that the library Member class may have attributes such as Name, Social Security Number, Age, and Weight. The attributes Age and Weight may be important to the class Member in a personal system, but it is not within the scope of the system since there is no scenario in Library Borrow Books that requires or needs to keep track of the Age and Weight of the member.

8.8 DEFINING ATTRIBUTES FOR VIANET BANK OBJECTS

In this section, we go through the bank system classes and define their attributes.

8.8.1 Defining Attributes for the BankClient Class

By analyzing the use cases, the sequence/collaboration diagrams (see Chapter 7) and the activity diagram (see Chapter 6), it is apparent that, for the BankClient class, the problem domain and system dictate certain attributes. In essence, what does the system need to know about the BankClient?

By looking at the activity diagram (see Figure 6–9) we notice that the BankClient must have a PIN number (or password) and Card number. Therefore, the PIN number and cardNumber are appropriate attributes for the BankClient. Let's now take a look at the use cases in Chapter 6 (Figures 6–9, 6–10, and 6–11) and Chapter 7, section 7.6. Other attributes of the BankClient class are drawn from our general knowledge of a BankClient. This usually is the case for defining attributes. The attributes of the BankClient are

firstName
lastName
pinNumber
cardNumber
account: Account

At this stage of the design we are concerned with the functionality of the BankClient object and not with implementation attributes.

8.8.2 Defining Attributes for the Account Class

Similarly, what information does the system need to know about an account? Based on the use cases in Chapter 6 (see Figures 6–9, 6–10, and 6–11) and the sequence/collaboration diagrams in Chapter 7 (see section 7.6 and Figures 7–4, 7–5, 7–6, 7–7, and 7–8), BankClient can interact with its account by entering the account number and then could deposit money, get an account history, or get the balance. Therefore, we have defined the following attributes for the Account class:

number

balance

8.8.3 Defining Attributes for the Transaction Class

The Transaction class, for the most part, must keep track of the time and amount of a transaction. Here are the attributes for the Transaction class:

transID

transDate

transTime

transType

amount

postBalance

8.8.4 Defining Attributes for the ATMMachine Class

Recall from Chapter 7 that the ATMMachine class was identified as part of the common class pattern (Tangible Things and Devices), which are physical objects or groups of objects that are tangible and with which the application interacts. Therefore, most attributes for this class describe its physical location and its state. The ATMMachine class could have the following attributes:

address

state

8.9 OBJECT RESPONSIBILITY: METHODS AND MESSAGES

Objects not only describe abstract data but also must provide some services. Methods and messages are the workhorses of object-oriented systems. In an object-oriented environment, every piece of data, or object, is surrounded by a rich set of routines called *methods*. These methods do everything from printing the object to initializing its variables.

Every class is responsible for storing certain information from the domain knowledge. It also is logical to assign the responsibility for performing any operation necessary on that information. By the same token, if an object requires certain information to perform some operation for which it is responsible, it is logical to assign it the responsibility for maintaining the information [8].

Operations (methods or behavior) in the object-oriented system usually correspond to queries about attributes (and sometimes association) of the objects [7]. In other words, methods are responsible for managing the value of attributes such as query, updating, reading, and writing; for example, an operation like getBalance, which can return the value of an account's balance. In the same fashion, we need a set of operations that can maintain or change values; for example, an operation like setBalance to set the value of the balance.

In this section, we learn how to define methods based on the UML diagrams, such as statechart, activity, and sequence/collaboration diagrams and use cases.

8.9.1 Defining Methods by Analyzing UML Diagrams and Use Cases

In Chapter 7, we learned that, in a sequence diagram, the objects involved are drawn on the diagram as vertical dashed lines. Furthermore, the events that occur between objects are drawn between the vertical object lines. An event is considered to be an action that transmits information. In other words, these actions are operations that the objects must perform and, as in the attributes, methods also can be derived from scenario testing.

For example, to define methods for the Account class, we look at sequence diagrams for the followings use cases (see Chapter 7):

Deposit Checking

Deposit Savings

Withdraw Checking

Withdraw More from Checking

Withdraw Savings

Withdraw Savings Denied

Checking Transaction History

Savings Transaction History

Sequence diagrams can assist us in defining the services the objects must provide. For example, by studying the sequence diagram for Withdraw Checking (see Figure 7–5), it is clear that the Account class (which is the superclass of CheckingAccount and SavingsAccount) must provide a service such as *withdrawal*. By analyzing the use cases, such as the one in Figure 6–11, it is apparent that Account class should provide the *deposit* operation. These behaviors are defined as services of the classes in the business model. Ultimately, these services are implemented as the methods for your objects.

8.10 DEFINING METHODS FOR VIANET BANK OBJECTS

Operations (methods or behavior) in the object-oriented system usually correspond to events or actions that transmit information in the sequence diagram or queries about attributes (and sometimes associations) of the objects [7]. In other words, methods are responsible for managing the value of attributes such as query, updating, reading, and writing.

8.10.1 Defining Account Class Operations

Deposit and withdrawal operations are available to the Client through the bank application, but they are provided as services by the Account class, since the account objects must be able to manipulate their internal attributes (that is, modify the bal-

ance based on the transaction). Account objects also must be able to create transaction records of any deposit or withdrawal they perform.

Here are the methods that we need to define for the Account class:

deposit

withdraw

createTransaction

The services added to the Account class are those that apply to all subclasses
of Account; namely, CheckingAccount and SavingsAccount. The subclass will either inherit these generic services without change or enhance them to suit their
own needs. For example, we will override the withdraw *method* of the CheckingAccount class.

8.10.2 Defining BankClient Class Operations

Analyzing the sequence diagram in Figure 7–4, it is apparent that the BankClient
requires a method to validate clients' passwords (see Figure 8–13).

8.10.3 Defining CheckingAccount Class Operations

The requirement specification states that, when a checking account has insufficient
funds to cover a withdrawal, it must try to withdraw the insufficient amount from

FIGURE 8–13

A more complete UML class diagram of the ViaNet bank ATM system.

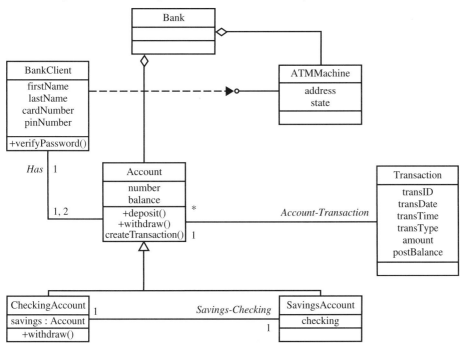

its related savings account. To provide the service, the CheckingAccount class needs a withdrawal service that enables the transfer. Similarly, we must add the withdrawal service to the CheckingAccount class. The withdrawal service appears in the CheckingAccount class symbol (see Figure 8–13).

8.11 SUMMARY

The chapter describes the guidelines for identifying object relationships, attributes, and methods. Identifying relationships among objects is important since these interactions and relationships become the application. We look at three types of relationships: association, super-sub structure (generalization hierarchy), and aggregation or a-part-of relations.

Association is a relationship among classes. The hierarchical relation allows the sharing of properties or inheritance. The a-part-of structure provides the means to organize components of a bigger object.

To identify associations, begin by analyzing the interactions of each class and responsibilities for dependencies. Look for a dependency between two or more classes; it is a hint that an association exists. Associations often correspond to verb or prepositional phrases, such as *part of*, *next to*, *works for*, or *contained in*. Furthermore, a reference from one class to another is an association. Some associations are implicit or taken from general knowledge. Some common associations patterns are *next to*, *part of*, and *contained in* a relation; directed actions and communication associations include *talk to* or *order from*.

To identify super-sub relationships in the application, look for noun phrases composed of various adjectives in the class name in top-down analysis. Specialize only when the subclasses have significant behavior. In bottom-up analysis, look for classes with similar attributes or methods. Group the classes by moving those classes with common attributes and methods as high as possible in the hierarchy. At the same time, do not create very specialized classes at the top of the hierarchy. This balancing act can be achieved through several iterations. The process ensures that you design objects that can be reused in another application. Finally, avoid excessive use of multiple inheritance. It is more difficult to understand programs written in a multiple inheritance system. One way of achieving the benefits of multiple inheritance is to inherit from the most appropriate class and add an object of another class as an attribute.

The a-part-of relationship, sometimes called *aggregation*, represents a situation where a class comprises several component classes. A class composed of other classes does not behave like its parts but very differently. For example, a car consists of many other classes, one of which is a radio, but a car does not behave like a radio. Some common aggregation/a-part-of patterns are assembly, container, and collection-member. The a-part-of structure is a special form of association, and similarly, association can be represented by the a-part-of relation.

Identifying attributes and methods is like finding classes, a difficult activity and an iterative process. Once again, the use cases and other UML diagrams will be a guide for identifying attributes, methods, and relationships among classes.

Methods and messages are the workhorses of object-oriented systems. The sequence diagrams can assist us in defining services that the objects must provide. An event is considered to be an action that transmits information; therefore, these actions are operations that the objects must perform. Additionally, operations (methods or behavior) in the object-oriented system usually correspond to queries about attributes and associations of the objects. Therefore, methods are responsible for managing the value of attributes such as query, updating, reading, and writing.

KEY TERMS

Aggregation (p. 182)
Antisymmetry (p. 182)
A-part-of relation (p. 182)
Assembly (p. 183)
Association (p. 178)
Collection-member (p. 184)
Container (p. 183)
Directed actions associations (p. 180)
Ternary association (p. 180)
Transitivity (p. 182)

REVIEW QUESTIONS

1. Why is identifying class hierarchy important in object-oriented analysis?
2. What is association?
3. What is generalization?
4. How would you identify a super-subclass structure?
5. What is an a-part-of structure? What are major properties of an a-part-of structure?
6. What guidelines would you use to identify a-part-of structures?
7. Is association different from an a-part-of relation?
8. What are some common associations?
9. What are unnecessary associations? How would you know?
10. Why do we need to identify the system's responsibilities?
11. How would you identify attributes?
12. How would you identify methods?
13. What are unnecessary attributes?
14. What does repeating attributes indicate?
15. Why do we need to justify classes with one attribute?

PROBLEMS

1. Do a literature search on object-oriented analysis patterns and write a report based on your findings.
2. See the details regarding Grandma's Soups Unlimited in Chapter 6.
   a. Identify a super-subclass relationship by following the guidelines for generalization.
   b. Identify an a-part-of structure by following the guidelines for an a-part-of structure.

c. Identify association for the classes in the problem by following the guidelines for identifying relationships and methods.

d. Identify attributes and attributes for the classes in the Grandma's Soups Unlimited problem, by following the guidelines for identifying methods and attributes.

3. Identify some of the attributes and methods in Grandma's Soups Unlimited (see Chapter 6).

REFERENCES

1. Beck, Kent; and Cunningham, Ward. "A Laboratory for Teaching Object-Oriented Thinking," Object-Oriented Programming System Languages and Application. OOPSLA'89, October 1-6, 1989, New Orleans, LA.
2. Booch, Grady. *Object-Oriented Analysis and Design with Applications*. Menlo Park, CA: Benjamin-Cummings, 1994.
3. Coad, P.; and Yourdon, E. *Object-Oriented Design*. Englewood Cliffs, NJ: Yourdon Press, 1991.
4. Harmon, P.; and Watson, M. *Understanding UML: The Developer's Guide with a Web-Based Application in Java*. Menlo Park, CA: Morgan Kaufmann Publishers, 1998.
5. LaLonde, Wilf; and Pugh, John. *SmallTalk V: Practice and Experience with a Disk*. Englewood Cliffs, NJ: Prentice-Hall, 1994.
6. Martin, James; and Odell, James. *Object-Oriented Analysis and Design*. Englewood Cliffs, NJ: Prentice-Hall, 1992.
7. Rumbaugh, James; Blaha, Michael; Premerlani, William; Eddy, Frederick; and Lorenson, William. *Object-Oriented Modeling and Design*. Englewood Cliffs, NJ: Prentice-Hall, 1991.
8. Wirfs-Brock, Rebecca; Wilkerson, Brian; and Wiener, Lauren. *Designing Object-Oriented Software*. Englewood Cliffs, NJ: Prentice-Hall, 1992.

PART FOUR

OBJECT-ORIENTED DESIGN

During the design phase, we must elevate the model into actual objects that can perform the required task. There is a shift in emphasis from the application domain to implementation. The classes identified during analysis provide us a framework for the design phase. In this part, we discuss business, view, and access layers classes. The part consists of Chapters 9, 10, 11, and 12.

CHAPTER 9

The Object-Oriented Design Process and Design Axioms

Chapter Objectives

You should be able to define and understand

- The object-oriented design process.
- Object-oriented design axioms and corollaries.
- Design patterns.

9.1 INTRODUCTION

It was explained in previous chapters that the main focus of the analysis phase of software development is on "what needs to be done." The objects discovered during analysis can serve as the framework for design [9]. The class's attributes, methods, and associations identified during analysis must be designed for implementation as a data type expressed in the implementation language. New classes must be introduced to store intermediate results during program execution. Emphasis shifts from the application domain to implementation and computer concepts such as user interfaces or view layer and access layer (see Figures 1–11 and 4–11).

During the analysis, we look at the physical entities or business objects in the system; that is, who the players are and how they cooperate to do the work of the application. These objects represent tangible elements of the business. As we saw in Chapter 7, these objects could be individuals, organizations, machines, or whatever else makes sense in the context of the real-world system. During the design phase, we elevate the model into logical entities, some of which might relate more to the computer domain (such as user interfaces or the access layer) than the real-world or the physical domain (such as people or employees). This is where we begin thinking about how to actually implement the problem in a program. The goal here is to design the classes that we need to implement the system. Fortunately, the design model does not look terribly different from the analysis model. The difference is that, at this level, we focus on the view and access classes, such as how to maintain information or the best way to interact with a user or present information. It also is useful, at this stage, to have a good understanding of the classes in a development environment that we are using to enforce reusability.

In software development, it is tempting not to be concerned with design. After all, you (the designer) are so involved with the system that it might be difficult to stop and think about the consequences of each design choice. However, the time spent on design has a great impact on the overall success of the software development project. A large payoff is associated with creating a good design "up front," before writing a single line of code. While this is true of all programming, classes and objects underscore the approach even more. Good design usually simplifies the implementation and maintenance of a project.

In this chapter, we look at the object-oriented design process and *axioms*. The basic goal of the axiomatic approach is to formalize the design process and assist in establishing a scientific foundation for the object-oriented design process, to provide a fundamental basis for the creation of systems. Without scientific principles, the design field never will be systematized and so will remain a subject difficult to comprehend, codify, teach, and practice [10].

9.2 THE OBJECT-ORIENTED DESIGN PROCESS

During the design phase the classes identified in object-oriented analysis must be revisited with a shift in focus to their implementation. New classes or attributes and methods must be added for implementation purposes and user interfaces.

The object-oriented design process consists of the following activities (see Figure 9–1):

1. Apply design axioms to design classes, their attributes, methods, associations, structures, and protocols (Chapter 10).
   1.1. Refine and complete the static UML class diagram by adding details to the UML class diagram. This step consists of the following activities:
      1.1.1. Refine attributes.
      1.1.2. Design methods and protocols by utilizing a UML activity diagram to represent the method's algorithm.
      1.1.3. Refine associations between classes (if required).
      1.1.4. Refine class hierarchy and design with inheritance (if required).
   1.2. Iterate and refine again.
2. Design the access layer (Chapter 11).
   2.1. *Create mirror classes.* For every business class identified and created, create one access class. For example, if there are three business classes (Class1, Class2, and Class3), create three access layer classes (Class1DB, Class2DB, and Class3DB).
   2.2. *Identify access layer class relationships.*

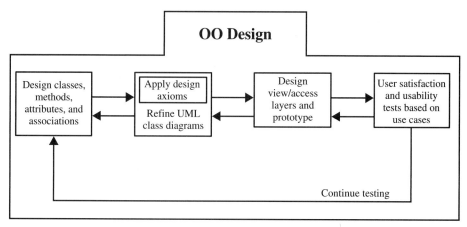

FIGURE 9–1
The object-oriented design process in the unified approach.

2.3. *Simplify classes and their relationships*. The main goal here is to eliminate redundant classes and structures.

    2.3.1. Redundant classes: Do not keep two classes that perform similar *translate request* and *translate results* activities. Simply select one and eliminate the other.

    2.3.2. Method classes: Revisit the classes that consist of only one or two methods to see if they can be eliminated or combined with existing classes.

2.4. Iterate and refine again.

3. Design the view layer classes (Chapter 12).

    3.1. Design the macro level user interface, identifying view layer objects.

    3.2. Design the micro level user interface, which includes these activities:

        3.2.1. Design the view layer objects by applying the design axioms and corollaries.

        3.2.2. Build a prototype of the view layer interface.

    3.3. Test usability and user satisfaction (Chapters 13 and 14).

    3.4. Iterate and refine.

4. Iterate and refine the whole design. Reapply the design axioms and, if needed, repeat the preceding steps.

Utilizing an incremental approach such as the UA, all stages of software development (analysis, modeling, designing, and implementation or programming) can be performed incrementally. Therefore, all the right decisions need not be made up front.

From the UML class diagram, you can begin to extrapolate which classes you will have to build and which existing classes you can reuse. As you do this, also begin thinking about the inheritance structure. If you have several classes that seem related but have specific differences, you probably will want to make them common subclasses of an existing class or one that you define. Often, superclasses are generated while coding, as you realize that common characteristics can be factored out or in. Good object-oriented design is very iterative. As long as you think in terms of class of objects, learn what already is there, and are willing to experiment, you soon will feel comfortable with the process.

Design also must be traceable across requirements, analysis, design, code, and testing. There must be a clear step-by-step approach to the design from the requirements model. All the designed components must directly trace back to the user requirements. Usage scenarios can serve as test cases to be used during system testing (see Figure 1–1).

9.3 OBJECT-ORIENTED DESIGN AXIOMS

By definition, an *axiom* is a fundamental truth that always is observed to be valid and for which there is no counterexample or exception. Suh explains that axioms may be hypothesized from a large number of observations by noting the common phenomena shared by all cases; they cannot be proven or derived, but they can be invalidated by counterexamples or exceptions. A *theorem* is a proposition that may not be self-evident but can be proven from accepted axioms. It, therefore, is equivalent to a law or principle. Consequently, a theorem is valid if its referent axioms and deductive steps are valid. A *corollary* is a proposition that follows from an axiom or another proposition that has been proven. Again, a corollary is shown to be valid or not valid in the same manner as a theorem [10].

The author has applied Suh's design axioms to object-oriented design. Axiom 1 deals with relationships between system components (such as classes, requirements, and software components), and Axiom 2 deals with the complexity of design.

- Axiom 1. *The independence axiom.* Maintain the independence of components.
- Axiom 2. *The information axiom.* Minimize the information content of the design.

Axiom 1 states that, during the design process, as we go from requirement and use case to a system component, each component must satisfy that requirement without affecting other requirements. To make this point clear, let's take a look at an example offered by Suh [10]. You been asked to design a refrigerator door, and there are two requirements: The door should provide access to food, and the energy lost should be minimal when the door is opened and closed. In other words, opening the door should be independent of losing energy. Is the vertically hung door a good design? We see that vertically hung door violates Axiom 1, because the two specific requirements (i.e., access to the food and minimal energy loss) are coupled and are not independent in the proposed design. When, for example, the door is opened to take out milk, cold air in the refrigerator escapes and warm air from the outside enters. What is an uncoupled design that somehow does not combine these two requirements? Once such uncoupled design of the refrigerator door is a horizontally hinged door, such as used in chest-type freezers. When the door is opened to take out milk, the cold air (since it is heavier than warm air) will sit at the bottom and not escape. Therefore, opening the door provides access to the food and is independent of energy loss. This type of design satisfies the first axiom.

Axiom 2 is concerned with simplicity. Scientific theoreticians often rely on a general rule known as *Occam's razor*, after William of Occam, a 14th century scholastic philosopher. Briefly put, Occam's razor says that, "The best theory explains the known facts with a minimum amount of complexity and maximum simplicity and straightforwardness."

Occam's razor has a very useful implication in approaching the design of an object-oriented application. Let us restate Occam's razor rule of simplicity in object-oriented terms:

> The best designs usually involve the least complex code but not necessarily the fewest number of classes or methods. Minimizing complexity should be the goal, because that produces the most easily maintained and enhanced application. In an object-oriented system, the best way to minimize complexity is to use inheritance and the system's built-in classes and to add as little as possible to what already is there.

9.4 COROLLARIES

From the two design axioms, many corollaries may be derived as a direct consequence of the axioms. These corollaries may be more useful in making specific design decisions, since they can be applied to actual situations more easily than the original axioms. They even may be called *design rules*, and all are derived from the two basic axioms [10] (see Figure 9–2):

• Corollary 1. *Uncoupled design with less information content.* Highly cohesive objects can improve coupling because only a minimal amount of essential information need be passed between objects.

FIGURE 9–2

The origin of corollaries. Corollaries 1, 2, and 3 are from both axioms, whereas corollary 4 is from axiom 1 and corollaries 5 and 6 are from axiom 2.

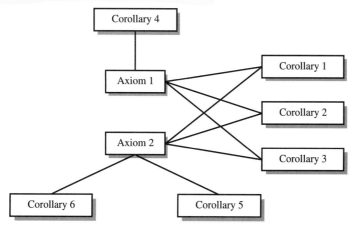

- Corollary 2. *Single purpose*. Each class must have a single, clearly defined purpose. When you document, you should be able to easily describe the purpose of a class in a few sentences.
- Corollary 3. *Large number of simple classes*. Keeping the classes simple allows reusability.
- Corollary 4. *Strong mapping*. There must be a strong association between the physical system (analysis's object) and logical design (design's object).
- Corollary 5. *Standardization*. Promote standardization by designing interchangeable components and reusing existing classes or components.
- Corollary 6. *Design with inheritance*. Common behavior (methods) must be moved to superclasses. The superclass-subclass structure must make logical sense.

9.4.1 Corollary 1. Uncoupled Design with Less Information Content

The main goal here is to maximize objects cohesiveness among objects and software components in order to improve coupling because only a minimal amount of essential information need be passed between components.

9.4.1.1 Coupling   *Coupling* is a measure of the strength of association established by a connection from one object or software component to another. Coupling is a binary relationship: A is coupled with B. Coupling is important when evaluating a design because it helps us focus on an important issue in design. For example, a change to one component of a system should have a minimal impact on other components [3]. Strong coupling among objects complicates a system, since the class is harder to understand or highly interrelated with other classes. The degree of coupling is a function of

1. How complicated the connection is.
2. Whether the connection refers to the object itself or something inside it.
3. What is being sent or received.

The degree, or strength, of coupling between two components is measured by the amount and complexity of information transmitted between them. Coupling increases (becomes stronger) with increasing complexity or obscurity of the interface. Coupling decreases (becomes lower) when the connection is to the component interface rather than to an internal component. Coupling also is lower for data connections than for control connections. Object-oriented design has two types of coupling: interaction coupling and inheritance coupling [3].

Interaction coupling involves the amount and complexity of messages between components. It is desirable to have little interaction. Coupling also applies to the complexity of the message. The general guideline is to keep the messages as simple and infrequent as possible. In general, if a message connection involves more than three parameters (e.g., in Method (X, Y, Z), the X, Y, and Z are parameters), examine it to see if it can be simplified. It has been documented that objects connected to many very complex messages are tightly coupled, meaning any change to one invariability leads to a ripple effect of changes in others (see Figure 9–3).

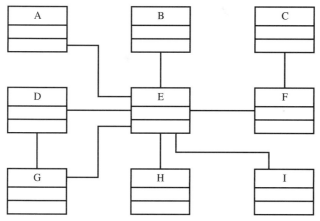

FIGURE 9–3
E is a tightly coupled object.

In addition to minimizing the complexity of message connections, also reduce the number of messages sent and received by an object [3]. Table 9–1 contains different types of interaction couplings.

Inheritance is a form of coupling between super- and subclasses. A subclass is coupled to its superclass in terms of attributes and methods. Unlike interaction coupling, high inheritance coupling is desirable. However, to achieve high inheritance

TABLE 9–1

TYPES OF COUPLING AMONG OBJECTS OR COMPONENTS (shown from highest to lowest)

Degree of coupling	Name	Description
Very high	Content coupling	The connection involves direct reference to attributes or methods of another object.
High	Common coupling	The connection involves two objects accessing a "global data space," for both to read and write.
Medium	Control coupling	The connection involves explicit control of the processing logic of one object by another.
Low	Stamp coupling	The connection involves passing an aggregate data structure to another object, which uses only a portion of the components of the data structure.
Very low	Data coupling	The connection involves either simple data items or aggregate structures all of whose elements are used by the receiving object. This should be the goal of an architectural design.

coupling in a system, each specialization class should not inherit lots of unrelated and unneeded methods and attributes. For example, if the subclass is overwriting most of the methods or not using them, this is an indication inheritance coupling is *low* and the designer should look for an alternative generalization-specialization structure (see Corollary 6).

9.4.1.2 Cohesion Coupling deals with interactions between objects or software components. We also need to consider interactions within a single object or software component, called *cohesion*. Cohesion reflects the "single-purposeness" of an object. Highly cohesive components can lower coupling because only a minimum of essential information need be passed between components. Cohesion also helps in designing classes that have very specific goals and clearly defined purposes (see Corollaries 2 and 3).

Method cohesion, like function cohesion, means that a method should carry only one function. A method that carries multiple functions is undesirable. Class cohesion means that all the class's methods and attributes must be highly cohesive, meaning to be used by internal methods or derived classes' methods. Inheritance cohesion is concerned with the following questions [3]:

- How interrelated are the classes?
- Does specialization really portray specialization or is it just something arbitrary?

See Corollary 6, which also addresses these questions.

9.4.2 Corollary 2. Single Purpose

Each class must have a purpose, as was explained in Chapter 7. Every class should be clearly defined and necessary in the context of achieving the system's goals. When you document a class, you should be able to easily explain its purpose in a sentence or two. If you cannot, then rethink the class and try to subdivide it into more independent pieces. In summary, keep it simple; to be more precise, each method must provide only one service. Each method should be of moderate size, no more than a page; half a page is better.

9.4.3 Corollary 3. Large Number of Simpler Classes, Reusability

A great benefit results from having a large number of simpler classes. You cannot possibly foresee all the future scenarios in which the classes you create will be reused. The less specialized the classes are, the more likely future problems can be solved by a recombination of existing classes, adding a minimal number of subclasses. A class that easily can be understood and reused (or inherited) contributes to the overall system, while a complex, poorly designed class is just so much dead weight and usually cannot be reused. Keep the following guideline in mind:

> The smaller are your classes, the better are your chances of reusing them in other projects. Large and complex classes are too specialized to be reused.

Object-oriented design offers a path for producing libraries of reusable parts [2]. The emphasis object-oriented design places on encapsulation, modularization, and polymorphism suggests reuse rather than building anew. Cox's description of a software IC library implies a similarity between object-oriented development and building hardware from a standard set of chips [5]. The software IC library is realized with the introduction of design patterns, discussed later in this chapter.

Coad and Yourdon argue that software reusability rarely is practiced effectively. But the organizations that will survive in the 21st century will be those that have achieved high levels of reusability—anywhere from 70–80 percent or more [3]. Griss [6] argues that, although reuse is widely desired and often the benefit of utilizing object technology, many object-oriented reuse efforts fail because of too narrow a focus on technology and not on the policies set forth by an organization. He recommended an institutionalized approach to software development, in which software assets intentionally are created or acquired to be reusable. These assets consistently are used and maintained to obtain high levels of reuse, thereby optimizing the organization's ability to produce high-quality software products rapidly and effectively [6].

Coad and Yourdon [3] describe four reasons why people are not utilizing this concept:

1. Software engineering textbooks teach new practitioners to build systems from "first principles"; reusability is not promoted or even discussed.

2. The "not invented here" syndrome and the intellectual challenge of solving an interesting software problem in one's own unique way mitigates against reusing someone else's software component.

3. Unsuccessful experiences with software reusability in the past have convinced many practitioners and development managers that the concept is not practical.

4. Most organizations provide no reward for reusability; sometimes productivity is measured in terms of new lines of code written plus a discounted credit (e.g., 50 percent less credit) for reused lines of code.

The primary benefit of software reusability is higher productivity. Roughly speaking, the software development team that achieves 80 percent reusability is four times as productive as the team that achieves only 20 percent reusability. Another form of reusability is using a design pattern, which will be explained in the next section.

9.4.4 Corollary 4. Strong Mapping

Object-oriented analysis and object-oriented design are based on the same model. As the model progresses from analysis to implementation, more detail is added, but it remains essentially the same. For example, during analysis we might identify a class Employee. During the design phase, we need to design this class—design its methods, its association with other objects, and its view and access classes. A strong mapping links classes identified during analysis and classes designed during the design phase (e.g., view and access classes). Martin and Odell describe this important issue very elegantly:

With OO techniques, the same paradigm is used for analysis, design, and implementation. The analyst identifies objects' types and inheritance, and thinks about events that change the state of objects. The designer adds detail to this model perhaps designing screens, user interaction, and client-server interaction. The thought process flows so naturally from analyst to design that it may be difficult to tell where analysis ends and design begins. [8, p. 100]

9.4.5 Corollary 5. Standardization

To reuse classes, you must have a good understanding of the classes in the object-oriented programming environment you are using. Most object-oriented systems, such as Smalltalk, Java, C++, or PowerBuilder, come with several built-in class libraries. Similarly, object-oriented systems are like organic systems, meaning that they grow as you create new applications. The knowledge of existing classes will help you determine what new classes are needed to accomplish the tasks and where you might inherit useful behavior rather than reinvent the wheel. However, class libraries are not always well documented or, worse yet, they are documented but not up to date. Furthermore, class libraries must be easily searched, based on users' criteria. For example, users should be able to search the class repository with commands like "show me all Facet classes." The concept of design patterns might provide a way to capture the design knowledge, document it, and store it in a repository that can be shared and reused in different applications.

9.4.6 Corollary 6. Designing with Inheritance

When you implement a class, you have to determine its ancestor, what attributes it will have, and what messages it will understand. Then, you have to construct its methods and protocols. Ideally, you will choose inheritance to minimize the amount of program instructions. Satisfying these constraints sometimes means that a class inherits from a superclass that may not be obvious at first glance.

For example, say, you are developing an application for the government that manages the licensing procedure for a variety of regulated entities. To simplify the example, focus on just two types of entities: motor vehicles and restaurants. Therefore, identifying classes is straightforward. All goes well as you begin to model these two portions of class hierarchy. Assuming that the system has no existing classes similar to a restaurant or a motor vehicle, you develop two classes, MotorVehicle and Restaurant.

Subclasses of the MotorVehicle class are PrivateVehicle and CommercialVehicle. These are further subdivided into whatever level of specificity seems appropriate (see Figure 9–4). Subclasses of Restaurant are designed to reflect their own licensing procedures. This is a simple, easy to understand design, although somewhat limited in the reusability of the classes. For example, if in another project you must build a system that models a vehicle assembly plant, the classes from the licensing application are not appropriate, since these classes have instructions and data that deal with the legal requirements of motor vehicle license acquisition and renewal.

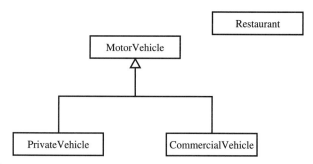

FIGURE 9–4
The initial single inheritance design.

In any case, the design is approved, implementation is accomplished, and the system goes into production. Now, here comes the event that every designer both knows well and dreads—when the nature of the real-world problem exceeds the bounds of the system, so far an elegant design. Say, six months later, while discussing some enhancements to the system with the right people (we learned how to identify right people in Chapter 6), one of them says, "What about coffee wagons, food trucks, and ice cream vendors? We're planning on licensing them as both restaurants and motor vehicles."

You know you need to redesign the application—but redesign how? The answer depends greatly on the inheritance mechanisms supported by the system's target language. If the language supports single inheritance exclusively, the choices are somewhat limited. You can choose to define a formal super class to both MotorVehicle and Restaurant, License, and move common methods and attributes from both classes into this License class (see Figure 9–5). However, the MotorVehicle and Restaurant classes have little in common, and for the most part, their attributes and methods are inappropriate for each other. For example, of what use is the gross weight of a diner or the address of a truck? This necessi-

FIGURE 9–5
The single inheritance design modified to allow licensing food trucks.

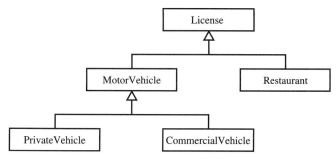

tates a very weak formal class (License) or numerous blocking behaviors in both MotorVehicle and Restaurant. This particular decision results in the least reusable classes and potentially extra code in several locations. So, let us try another approach.

Alternatively, you could preserve the original formal classes, MotorVehicle and Restaurant. Next, define a FoodTruck class to descend from CommercialVehicle and copy enough behavior into it from the Restaurant class to support the application's requirements (see Figure 9–6).

You can give FoodTruck copies of data and instructions from the Restaurant class that allow it to report on food type, health code categories, number of chefs and support staff, and the like. The class is not very reusable (Coad and Yourdon call it *cut-and-paste* reusability), but at least its extra code is localized, allowing simpler debugging and enhancement. Coad and Yourdon describe cut-and-paste type of reusability as follows [4, p. 138]:

> This is better than no reuse at all, but is the most primitive form of reuse. The clerical cost of transcribing the code has largely disappeared with today's cut-and-paste text editors; nevertheless, the software engineer runs the risk of introducing errors during the copying (and modifications) of the original code. Worse is the configuration management problem: it is almost impossible for the manager to keep track of the multiple mutated uses of the original "chunk" of code.

If, on the other hand, the intended language supports multiple inheritance, another route can be taken, one that more closely models the real-world situation. In this case, you design a specialized class, FoodTruck, and specify dual ancestry. Our new class alternative seems to preserve the integrity and code bulk of both ancestors and does nothing that appears to affect their reusability.

In actuality, since we never anticipated this problem in the original design, there probably are instance variables and methods in both ancestors that share the same names. Most languages that support multiple inheritance handle these "hits" by giving precedence to the first ancestor defined. Using this mechanism, reworking will be required in the FoodTruck descendant and, quite possibly, in both ancestors (see Figure 9–7). It easily can become difficult to determine which method,

FIGURE 9–6

Alternatively, you can modify the single inheritance design to allow licensing food trucks.

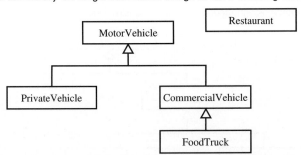

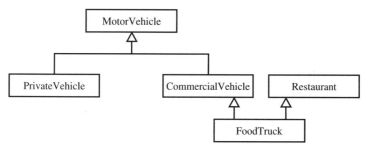

FIGURE 9–7
Multiple inheritance design of the system structure.

in which class, affected an erroneously updated variable in an instance of a new descendant. The difficulties in maintaining such a design increase geometrically with the number of ancestors assigned to a given class.

9.4.6.1 Achieving Multiple Inheritance in a Single Inheritance System *Single inheritance* means that each class has only a single superclass. This technique is used in Smalltalk and several other object-oriented systems. One result of using a single inheritance hierarchy is the absence of ambiguity as to how an object will respond to a given method; you simply trace up the class tree beginning with the object's class, looking for a method of the same name. However, languages like LISP or C++ have a multiple inheritance scheme whereby objects can inherit behavior from unrelated areas of the class tree. This could be desirable when you want a new class to behave similar to more than one existing class. However, multiple inheritance brings with it some complications, such as how to determine which behavior to get from which class, particularly when several ancestors define the same method. It also is more difficult to understand programs written in a multiple inheritance system.

One way of achieving the benefits of multiple inheritance in a language with single inheritance is to inherit from the most appropriate class and add an object of another class as an attribute or aggregation. Therefore, as class designer, you have two ways to borrow existing functionality in a class. One is to inherit it, and the other is to use the instance of the class (object) as an attribute. This approach is described in the next section.

9.4.6.2 Avoiding Inheriting Inappropriate Behaviors Beginners in an object-oriented system frequently err by designing subclasses that inherit from inappropriate superclasses. Before a class inherits, ask the following questions:

- Is the subclass fundamentally similar to its superclass (high inheritance coupling)?
- Is it an entirely new thing that simply wants to borrow some expertise from its superclass (low inheritance coupling)?

Often you will find that the latter is true, and if so, you should add an attribute that incorporates the proposed superclass's behavior rather than an inheritance from the superclass. This is because inheritors of a class must be intimate with all its implementation details, and if some implementation is inappropriate, the inheritor's proper functioning could be compromised. For example, if FoodTruck inherits from both Restaurant and CommercialVehicle classes, it might inherit a few inappropriate attributes and methods. A better approach would be to inherit only from CommercialVehicle and have an attribute of the type Restaurant (an instance of Restaurant class). In other words, Restaurant class becomes a-part-of FoodTruck class (see Figure 9–8).

9.5 DESIGN PATTERNS

In Chapter 4, we looked at the concept of patterns. A design pattern provides a scheme for refining the subsystems or components of a software system or the relationships among them [1]. In other words, *design patterns* are devices that allow systems to share knowledge about their design, by describing commonly recurring structures of communicating components that solve a general design problem within a particular context. For example, in programming, we have encountered many problems that occurred before and will occur again. The question we must ask ourselves is how we are going to solve it this time [7].

In Chapter 4, we learned that documenting patterns is one way that allows reuse and possibly sharing information learned about how it is best to solve a specific program design problem.

Essays usually are written by following a fairly well-defined form, and so is documenting design patterns (see Chapter 4 for the general form for documenting a pattern). Let us take a look at a design pattern example created by Kurotsuchi [7].

- *Pattern Name*: Facade
- *Rationale and Motivation*: The facade pattern can make the task of accessing a large number of modules much simpler by providing an additional interface layer. When designing good programs, programmers usually attempt to avoid excess coupling between modules/classes. Using this pattern helps to simplify

FIGURE 9–8
The FoodTruck class inherits from CommercialVehicle and has an attribute of the type Restaurant. The relationship between FoodTruck and Restaurant is a-part-of.

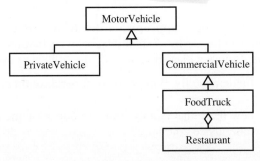

much of the interfacing that makes large amounts of coupling complex to use and difficult to understand. In a nutshell, this is accomplished by creating a small collection of classes that have a single class that is used to access them, the facade.

- *Classes*: There can be any number of classes involved in this "facade" system, but at least four or more classes are required: One client, the facade, and the classes underneath the facade. In a typical situation, the facade would have a limited amount of actual code, making calls to lower layers most of the time.
- *Advantages/Disadvantages*: As stated before, the primary advantage to using the facade is to make the interfacing between many modules or classes more manageable. One possible disadvantage to this pattern is that you may lose some functionality contained in the lower level of classes, but this depends on how the facade was designed.
- *Examples*: Imagine that you need to write a program that needs to represent a building as rooms that can be manipulated—manipulated as in interacting with objects in the room to change their state. The client that ordered this program has determined that there will be a need for only a finite number of objects (e.g., windows, screens, projectors, etc.) possible in each room and a finite number of operations that can be performed on each of them. You, as the program architect, have decided that the facade pattern will be an excellent way to keep the amount of interfacing low, considering the number of possible objects in each room, and the actions that the client has specified. A sample action for a room is to "prepare it for a presentation." You have decided that this will be part of your facade interface since it deals with a large number of classes but does not really need to bother the programmer with interacting with each of them when a room needs to be prepared. Here is how that facade might be organized (see Figure 9–9). Consider the sheer simplicity from the client's side of the problem.

FIGURE 9–9

Using a design pattern facade eliminates the need for the Client class to deal with a large number of classes.

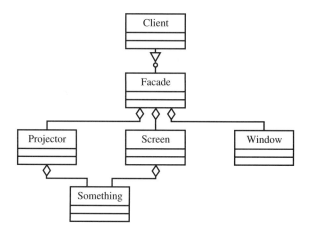

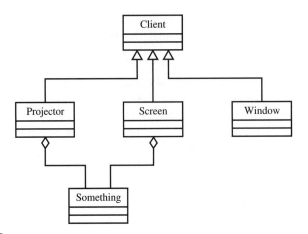

FIGURE 9–10
Not utilizing the design pattern facade, the Client class needs to deal with a large number of classes.

A less thought-out design may have looked like this, making lots of interaction by the client necessary (see Figure 9–10).

9.6 SUMMARY

In this chapter, we looked at the object-oriented design process and design axioms. Integrating design axioms and corollaries with incremental and evolutionary styles of software development will provide you a powerful way for designing systems.

During design, emphasis shifts from the application domain concept toward implementation, such as view (user interface) and access classes. The objects discovered during analysis serve as the framework for design.

The object-oriented design process consists of

- Designing classes (their attributes, methods, associations, structures, and protocols) and applying design axioms. If needed, this step is repeated.
- Designing the access layer.
- Designing the user interface.
- Testing user satisfaction and usability, based on the usage and use cases.
- Iterating and refining the design.

The two design axioms are

- Axiom 1. *The independence axiom.* Maintain the independence of components.
- Axiom 2. *The information axiom.* Minimize the information content of the design.

The six design corollaries are

- Corollary 1. Uncoupled design with less information content.

- Corollary 2. Single purpose.
- Corollary 3. Large number of simple classes.
- Corollary 4. Strong mapping.
- Corollary 5. Standardization.
- Corollary 6. Design with inheritance.

Finally, we looked at the concept of design patterns, which allow systems to share knowledge about their design. These describe commonly recurring problems. Rather than keep asking how to solve the problem this time, we could apply the design pattern (solution) in a previous problem.

KEY TERMS

Axiom (p. 202)
Cohesion (p. 206)
Corollary (p. 202)
Coupling (p. 204)
Design pattern (p. 212)
Theorem (p. 202)

REVIEW QUESTIONS

1. What is the task of design? Why do we need analysis?
2. What is the significance of Occam's razor?
3. How does Occam's razor relate to object-oriented design?
4. How would you differentiate good design from bad design?
5. What is the basic activity in designing an application?
6. Why is a large number of simple classes better than a small number of complex classes?
7. What is the significance of being able to describe in a few sentences what a class does?
8. What clues would you use to identify whether a class is in need of revision?
9. What is the common occurrence in the first attempt of designing classes with inheritance? How would you know? What should you do to fix it?
10. How can an object-oriented system be thought of as an organic system?
11. How can encapsulation, modularization, and polymorphism improve reusability? (Hint: Review Chapter 2.)
12. Why are people not utilizing reusability? List some reasons.
13. Why is it important to know about the classes in the object-oriented programming system you use?
14. How would you decide on subdividing your classes into a hierarchy of super- and subclasses?
15. What are the challenges in designing with inheritance?
16. Describe single and multiple inheritance.
17. What are the risks of a cut-and-paste type of reusability?
18. How can you achieve multiple inheritance in a single inheritance system?
19. How can you avoid a subclass inheriting inappropriate behavior?
20. List the object-oriented design axioms and corollaries.

21. What is the relationship between coupling and cohesion?

22. How would you further refine your design?

PROBLEMS

1. Consult the World Wide Web or the library to obtain an article on the Booch design method. Write a paper based on your findings.

2. Research the Web and write a report on the tools that support patterns-based design and development.

3. Revisit the classes that you identified in the object-oriented analysis for the Grandma's Soups application. What are some of the new classes or attributes and methods that must be added for implementation?

4. The compilers used every day to process computer code are a prime example of the facade pattern in action. What other examples are there?

REFERENCES

1. Appleton, Brad. "Patterns and Software: Essential Concepts and Terminology." http://www.enteract.com/~bradapp/docs/pattern-intro.html,1997.

2. Blum, Bruce I. *Software Engineering, a Holistic View.* New York: Oxford University Press, 1992.

3. Coad, P.; and Yourdon, E. *Object-Oriented Analysis.* Englewood Cliffs, NJ: Yourdon Press, 1991.

4. Coad, P.; and Yourdon, E. *Object-Oriented Design.* Englewood Cliffs, NJ: Yourdon Press, 1991.

5. Cox, B. J. *Object-Oriented Programming.* Reading, MA: Addison-Wesley, 1986.

6. Griss, M. L. "Software Reuse: Objects and Frameworks Are Not Enough." *Object Magazine* 4, no. 9 (February 1995).

7. Kurotsuchi, Brian T. "Design Patterns." http://www.csc.calpoly.edu/~dbutler/tutorials/winter96/patterns/.

8. Martin, James; and Odell, James. *Object-Oriented Analysis and Design.* Englewood Cliffs, NJ: Prentice-Hall, 1992.

9. Rumbaugh, James; Blaha, Michael; Premerlani, William; Eddy, Frederick; and Lorenson, William. *Object-Oriented Modeling and Design.* Englewood Cliffs, NJ: Prentice-Hall, 1991.

10. Suh, Nam. *The Principle of Design.* New York: Oxford University Press, 1990.

CHAPTER 10

Designing Classes

Chapter Objectives

You should be able to define and understand

- Designing classes.
- Designing protocols and class visibility.
- The UML object constraint language (OCL).
- Designing methods.

10.1 INTRODUCTION

Object-oriented design requires taking the objects identified during object-oriented analysis and designing classes to represent them. As a class designer, you have to know the specifics of the class you are designing and be aware of how that class interacts with other classes. Once you have identified your classes and their interactions, you are ready to design classes.

Underlying the functionality of any application is the quality of its design. In this chapter, we look at guidelines and approaches to use in designing classes and their methods. Although the design concepts to be discussed in this chapter are general, we will concentrate on designing the business classes (see Chapter 6). The access and view layer classes will be described in the subsequent chapters. However, the same concepts will apply to designing access and view layer classes.

10.2 THE OBJECT-ORIENTED DESIGN PHILOSOPHY

Object-oriented development requires that you think in terms of classes. A great benefit of the object-oriented approach is that classes organize related properties into units that stand on their own. We go through a similar process as we learn about the world around us. As new facts are acquired, we relate them to existing structures in our environment (model). After enough new facts are acquired about a certain area, we create new structures to accommodate the greater level of detail in our knowledge.

The single most important activity in designing an application is coming up with a set of classes that work together to provide the functionality you desire. A given problem always has many solutions. However, at this stage, you must translate the attributes and operations into system implementation. You need to decide where in the class tree your new classes will go. Many object-oriented programming languages and development environments, such as Smalltalk, C++, or PowerBuilder, come with several built-in class libraries. Your goal in using these systems should be to reuse rather than create anew. Similarly, if you design your classes with reusability in mind, you will gain a lot in productivity and reduce the time for developing new applications.

The first step in building an application, therefore, should be to design a set of classes, each of which has a specific expertise and all of which can work together in useful ways. Think of an object-oriented system as an organic system, one that evolves as you create each new application. Applying design axioms (see Chapter 9) and carefully designed classes can have a synergistic effect, not only on the current system but on its future evolution. If you exercise some discipline as you proceed, you will begin to see some extraordinary gains in your productivity compared to a conventional approach.

10.3 UML OBJECT CONSTRAINT LANGUAGE

In Chapter 5, we learned that the UML is a graphical language with a set of rules and semantics. The rules and semantics of the UML are expressed in English, in a form known as *object constraint language*. **Object constraint language** (OCL) is a specification language that uses simple logic for specifying the properties of a system.

Many UML modeling constructs require expression; for example, there are expressions for types, Boolean values, and numbers. Expressions are stated as strings in object constraint language. The syntax for some common navigational expressions is shown here. These forms can be chained together. The leftmost element must be an expression for an object or a set of objects. The expressions are meant to work on sets of values when applicable.

- *Item.selector.* The selector is the name of an attribute in the item. The result is the value of the attribute; for example, John.age (the age is an attribute of the object John, and John.age represents the value of the attribute).
- *Item.selector [qualifier-value].* The selector indicates a qualified association that qualifies the item. The result is the related object selected by the qualifier; for example, array indexing as a form of qualification; for example, John.Phone[2], assuming John has several phones.
- *Set -> select (boolean-expression).* The Boolean expression is written in terms

of objects within the set. The result is the subset of objects in the set for which the Boolean expression is true; for example, company.employee –> salary > 30000. This represents employees with salaries over $30,000.

Other expressions will be covered as we study their appropriate UML notations. However, for more details and syntax, see UML OCL documents.

10.4 DESIGNING CLASSES: THE PROCESS

In Chapter 9, we looked at the object-oriented design process. In this section, we concentrate on step 1 of the process, which consists of the followings activities:

1. Apply design axioms to design classes, their attributes, methods, associations, structures, and protocols.
   1.1. Refine and complete the static UML class diagram by adding details to that diagram.
      1.1.1. Refine attributes.
      1.1.2. Design methods and the protocols by utilizing a UML activity diagram to represent the method's algorithm.
      1.1.3. Refine the associations between classes (if required).
      1.1.4. Refine the class hierarchy and design with inheritance (if required).
   1.2. Iterate and refine.

Object-oriented design is an iterative process. After all, design is as much about discovery as construction. Do not be afraid to change your class design as you gain experience, and do not be afraid to change it a second, third, or fourth time. At each iteration, you can improve the design. However, the trick is to correct the design flaws as early as possible; redesigning late in the development cycle always is problematic and may be impossible.

10.5 CLASS VISIBILITY: DESIGNING WELL-DEFINED PUBLIC, PRIVATE, AND PROTECTED PROTOCOLS

In designing methods or attributes for classes, you are confronted with two problems. One is the ***protocol***, or interface to the class operations and its visibility; and the other is how it is implemented. Often the two have very little to do with each other. For example, you might have a class Bag for collecting various objects that counts multiple occurrences of its elements. One implementation decision might be that the Bag class uses another class, say, Dictionary (assuming that we have a class Dictionary), to actually hold its elements. Bags and dictionaries have very little in common, so this may seem curious to the outside world. Implementation, by definition, is hidden and off limits to other objects. The class's protocol, or the messages that a class understands, on the other hand, can be hidden from other objects (private protocol) or made available to other objects (public protocol). Public protocols define the functionality and external messages of an object; private protocols define the implementation of an object (see Figure 10–1).

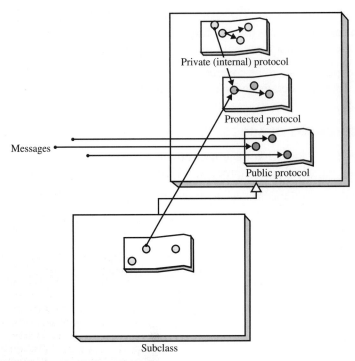

FIGURE 10-1
Public protocols define the functionality and external messages of an object, while private protocols define the implementation of an object.

It is important in object-oriented design to define the public protocol between the associated classes in the application. This is a set of messages that a class of a certain generic type must understand, although the interpretation and implementation of each message is up to the individual class.

A class also might have a set of methods that it uses only internally, messages to itself. This, the ***private protocol (visibility)*** of the class, includes messages that normally should not be sent from other objects; it is accessible only to operations of that class. In private protocol, only the class itself can use the method. The ***public protocol (visibility)*** defines the stated behavior of the class as a citizen in a population and is important information for users as well as future descendants, so it is accessible to all classes. If the methods or attributes can be used by the class itself or its subclasses, a protected protocol can be used. In a ***protected protocol (visibility)***, subclasses the can use the method in addition to the class itself.

Lack of a well-designed protocol can manifest itself as encapsulation leakage. The problem of ***encapsulation leakage*** occurs when details about a class's internal implementation are disclosed through the interface. As more internal details become visible, the flexibility to make changes in the future decreases. If an implementation is completely open, almost no flexibility is retained for future changes. It is fine to reveal implementation when that is intentional, necessary, and carefully controlled. However, do not make such a decision lightly because that could impact the flexibility and therefore the quality of the design.

For example, public or protected methods that can access private attributes can reveal an important aspect of your implementation. If anyone uses these functions and you change their location, the type of attribute, or the protocol of the method, this could make the client application inoperable.

Design the interface between a superclass and its subclasses just as carefully as the class's interface to clients; this is the contract between the super- and subclasses. If this interface is not designed properly, it can lead to violating the encapsulation of the superclass. The protected portion of the class interface can be accessed only by subclasses. This feature is helpful but cannot express the totality of the relationship between a class and its subclasses. Other important factors include which functions might or might not be overridden and how they must behave. It also is crucial to consider the relationship among methods. Some methods might need to be overridden in groups to preserve the class's semantics. The bottom line is this: Design your interface to subclasses so that a subclass that uses every supported aspect of that interface does not compromise the integrity of the public interface. The following paragraphs summarize the differences between these layers.

10.5.1 Private and Protected Protocol Layers: Internal

Items in these layers define the implementation of the object. Apply the design axioms and corollaries, especially Corollary 1 (uncoupled design with less information content, see Chapter 9) to decide what should be private: what attributes (instance variables)? What methods? Remember, highly cohesive objects can improve coupling because only a minimal amount of essential information need be passed between objects.

10.5.2 Public Protocol Layer: External

Items in this layer define the functionality of the object. Here are some things to keep in mind when designing class protocols:

- Good design allows for polymorphism.
- Not all protocol should be public; again apply design axioms and corollaries.

The following key questions must be answered:

- What are the class interfaces and protocols?
- What public (external) protocol will be used or what external messages must the system understand?
- What private or protected (internal) protocol will be used or what internal messages or messages from a subclass must the system understand?

10.6 DESIGNING CLASSES: REFINING ATTRIBUTES

Attributes identified in object-oriented analysis must be refined with an eye on implementation during this phase. In the analysis phase, the name of the attribute was sufficient. However, in the design phase, detailed information must be added to the model (especially, that defining the class attributes and operations). The main goal of this activity is to refine existing attributes (identified in analysis) or add attributes that can elevate the system into implementation.

10.6.1 Attribute Types

The three basic types of attributes are

1. Single-value attributes.
2. Multiplicity or multivalue attributes.
3. Reference to another object, or instance connection.

Attributes represent the state of an object. When the state of the object changes, these changes are reflected in the value of attributes. The single-value attribute is the most common attribute type. It has only one value or state. For example, attributes such as name, address, or salary are of the single-value type.

The multiplicity or multivalue attribute is the opposite of the single-value attribute since, as its name implies, it can have a collection of many values at any point in time [2]. For example, if we want to keep track of the names of people who have called a customer support line for help, we must use the multivalues attributes.

Instance connection attributes are required to provide the mapping needed by an object to fulfill its responsibilities, in other words, instance connection model association. For example, a person might have one or more bank accounts. A person has zero to many instance connections to Account(s). Similarly, an Account can be assigned to one or more persons (i.e., joint account). Therefore, an Account also has zero to many instance connections to Person(s).

10.6.2 UML Attribute Presentation

As discussed in Chapter 5, OCL can be used during the design phase to define the class attributes. The following is the attribute presentation suggested by UML:

visibility name : type-expression=initial-value

Where *visibility* is one of the following:

+ public visibility (accessibility to all classes).
# protected visibility (accessibility to subclasses and operations of the class).
− private visibility (accessibility only to operations of the class).

Type-expression is a language-dependent specification of the implementation type of an attribute.

Initial-value is a language-dependent expression for the initial value of a newly created object. The initial value is optional. For example, +size: length = 100

The UML style guidelines recommend beginning attribute names with a lower-case letter.

In the absence of a multiplicity indicator (array), an attribute holds exactly one value. Multiplicity may be indicated by placing a multiplicity indicator in brackets after attribute name; for example, names[10]: String

points[2..*]: Point

The multiplicity of 0..1 provides the possibility of null values: the absence of a value, as opposed to a particular value from the range. For example, the following declaration permits a distinction between the null value and an empty string: name[0..1]: String

10.7 REFINING ATTRIBUTES FOR THE VIANET BANK OBJECTS

In this section, we go through the ViaNet bank ATM system classes and refine the attributes identified during object-oriented analysis (see Chapter 8).

10.7.1 Refining Attributes for the BankClient Class

During object-oriented analysis, we identified the following attributes (see Chapter 8):

firstName

lastName

pinNumber

cardNumber

At this stage, we need to add more information to these attributes, such as visibility and implementation type. Furthermore, additional attributes can be identified during this phase to enable implementation of the class:

#firstName: String

#lastName: String

#pinNumber: String

#cardNumber: String

#account: Account (instance connection)

In Chapter 8, we identified an association between the BankClient and the Account classes (see Figure 8–9). To design this association, we need to add an *account* attribute of type Account, since the BankClient needs to know about his or her account and this attribute can provide such information for the BankClient class. This is an example of instance connection, where it represents the association between the BankClient and the Account objects. All the attributes have been given *protected visibility*.

10.7.2 Refining Attributes for the Account Class

Here is the refined list of attributes for the Account class:

#number: String

#balance: float

#transaction: Transaction (This attribute is needed for implementing the association between the Account and Transaction classes.)

#bankClient: BankClient (This attribute is needed for implementing the association between the Account and BankClient classes.)

At this point we must make the Account class very general, so that it can be reused by the checking and savings accounts.

10.7.3 Refining Attributes for the Transaction Class

The attributes for the Transaction class are these:

#transID: String
#transDate: Date
#transTime: Time
#transType: String
#amount: float
#postBalance: float

Problem 10.1

Why do we not need the account attribute for the Transaction class? Hint: Do transaction objects need to know about account objects?

10.7.4 Refining Attributes for the ATMMachine Class

The ATMMachine class could have the following attributes:

#address: String
#state: String

10.7.5 Refining Attributes for the CheckingAccount Class

Add the *savings* attribute to the class. The purpose of this attribute is to implement the association between the CheckingAccount and SavingsAccount classes.

10.7.6 Refining Attributes for the SavingsAccount Class

Add the *checking* attribute to the class. The purpose of this attribute is to implement the association between the SavingsAccount and CheckingAccount classes.

Figure 10–2 (see Chapter 8) shows a more complete UML class diagram for the bank system. At this stage, we also need to add a very short description of each attribute or certain attribute constraints. For example,

Class ATMMachine
#address: String (The address for this ATM machine.)
#state: String (The state of operation for this ATM machine, such as running, off, idle, out of money, security alarm.)

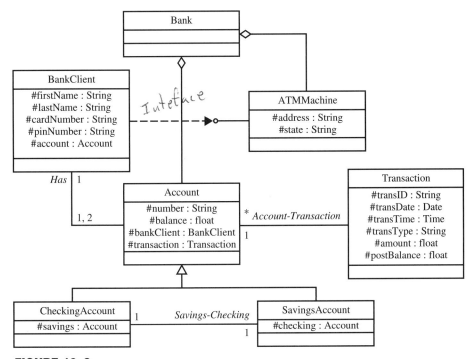

FIGURE 10–2
A more complete UML class diagram for the ViaNet bank system.

10.8 DESIGNING METHODS AND PROTOCOLS

The main goal of this activity is to specify the algorithm for methods identified so far. Once you have designed your methods in some formal structure such as UML activity diagrams with an OCL description, they can be converted to programming language manually or in automated fashion (i.e., using CASE tools). A class can provide several types of methods [3]:

- *Constructor*. Method that creates instances (objects) of the class.
- *Destructor*. The method that destroys instances.
- *Conversion method*. The method that converts a value from one unit of measure to another.
- *Copy method*. The method that copies the contents of one instance to another instance.
- *Attribute set*. The method that sets the values of one or more attributes.
- *Attribute get*. The method that returns the values of one or more attributes.
- *I/O methods*. The methods that provide or receive data to or from a device.
- *Domain specific*. The method specific to the application.

Recall from Chapter 9, Corollary 1, that in designing methods and protocols you must minimize the complexity of message connections and keep as low as possible the number of messages sent and received by an object. Your goal should be to maximize cohesiveness among objects and software components to improve coupling, because only a minimal amount of essential information should be passed between components. Abstraction leads to simplicity and straightforward-ness and, at the same time, increases class versatility. The requirement of simpli-fication, while retaining functionality, seems to lead to increased utility. Here are five rules [1]:

1. If it looks messy, then it's probably a bad design.
2. If it is too complex, then it's probably a bad design.
3. If it is too big, then it's probably a bad design.
4. If people don't like it, then it's probably a bad design.
5. If it doesn't work, then it's probably a bad design.

10.8.1 Design Issues: Avoiding Design Pitfalls

As described in Chapter 9, it is important to apply design axioms to avoid com-mon design problems and pitfalls. For example, we learned that it is much better to have a large set of simple classes than a few large, complex classes. A common occurrence is that, in your first attempt, your class might be too big and therefore more complex than it needs to be. Take the time to apply the design axioms and corollaries, then critique what you have proposed. You may find you can gather common pieces of expertise from several classes, which in itself becomes another "peer" class that the others consult; or you might be able to create a superclass for several classes that gathers in a single place very similar code. Your goal should be maximum reuse of what you have to avoid creating new classes as much as pos-sible. Take the time to think in this way—good news, this gets easier over time.

Lost object focus is another problem with class definitions. A meaningful class definition starts out simple and clean but, as time goes on and changes are made, becomes larger and larger, with the class identity becoming harder to state con-cisely (Corollary 2). This happens when you keep making incremental changes to an existing class. If the class does not quite handle a situation, someone adds a tweak to its description. When the next problem comes up, another tweak is added. Or, when a new feature is requested, another tweak is added, and so on. Apply the design axioms and corollaries, such as Corollary 2 (which states that each class must have a single, clearly defined purpose). When you document, you easily should be able to describe the purpose of a class in a few sentences.

These problems can be detected early on. Here are some of the warning signs that something is going amiss. There are bugs because the internal state of an ob-ject is too hard to track and solutions consist of adding patches. Patches are char-acterized by code that looks like this: "If this is the case, then force that to be true" or "Do this just in case we need to" or "Do this before calling that function, be-cause it expects this."

Some possible actions to solve this problem are these:

• Keep a careful eye on the class design and make sure that an object's role re-mains well defined. If an object loses focus, you need to modify the design. Ap-ply Corollary 2 (single purpose).

- Move some functions into new classes that the object would use. Apply Corollary 1 (uncoupled design with less information content).
- Break up the class into two or more classes. Apply Corollary 3 (large number of simple classes).
- Rethink the class definition based on experience gained.

10.8.2 UML Operation Presentation

The following operation presentation has been suggested by the UML. The operation syntax is this:

visibility name: (parameter-list): return-type-expression

Where *visibility* is one of:

+   public visibility (accessibility to all classes).

\#   protected visibility (accessibility to subclasses and operations of the class).

−   private visibility (accessibility only to operations of the class).

Here, *name* is the name of the operation.

Parameter-list: is a list of parameters, separated by commas, each specified by *name: type-expression = default value* (where name is the name of the parameter, type-expression is the language-dependent specification of an implementation type, and default-value is an optional value).

Return-type-expression: is a language-dependent specification of the implementation of the value returned by the method. If return-type is omitted, the operation does not return a value; for example,

+getName(): aName

+getAccountNumber (account: type): account Number

The UML guidelines recommend beginning operation names with a lowercase letter.

10.9 DESIGNING METHODS FOR THE VIANET BANK OBJECTS

At this point, the design of the bank business model is conceptually complete. You have identified the objects that make up your business layer, as well as what services they provide. All that remains is to design methods, the user interface, database access, and implement the methods using any object-oriented programming language. To keep the book language independent, we represent the methods' algorithms with UML activity diagrams, which very easily can be translated into any language. In essence, this phase prepares the system for the implementation. The actual coding and implementation (although they are beyond the scope of this book) should be relatively easy and, for the most part, can be automated by using CASE tools. This is because we know what we want to code. It is always difficult to code when we have no clear understanding of what we want to do.

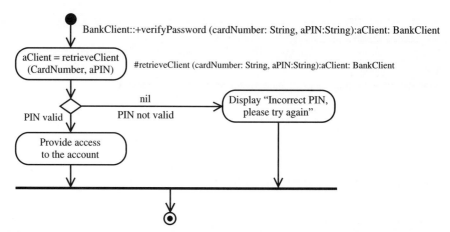

FIGURE 10–3

An activity diagram for the BankClient class verifyPassword method, using OCL to describe the diagram. The syntax for describing a class's method is Class name::methodName. We postpone design of the retrieveClient to Chapter 11, Section 11.10, Designing Access Layer Classes.

10.9.1 BankClient Class VerifyPassword Method

The following describes the verifyPassword service in greater detail. A client PIN code is sent from the ATMMachine object and used as an argument in the verify-Password method. The verifyPassword method retrieves the client record and checks the entered PIN number against the client's PIN number. If they match, it allows the user to proceed. Otherwise, a message sent to the ATMMachine displays "Incorrect PIN, please try again" (see Figure 10–3).

The verifyPassword methods performs first creates a bank client object and attempts to retrieve the client data based on the supplied card and PIN numbers. At this stage, we realize that we need to have another method, retrieveClient. The retrieveClient method takes two arguments, the card number and a PIN number, and returns the client object or "nil" if the password is not valid. We postpone design of the retrieveClient method to Chapter 11 (Section 11.10, designing the access layer classes).

10.9.2 Account Class Deposit Method

The following describes the deposit service in greater detail. An amount to be deposited is sent to an account object and used as an argument to the deposit service. The account adjusts its balance to its current balance plus the deposit amount. The account object records the deposit by creating a transaction object containing the date and time, posted balance, and transaction type and amount (see Figure 10–4).

Once again we have discovered another method, updateClient. This method, as the name suggests, updates client data. We postpone design of the updateClient method to the Chapter 11 (designing the access layer classes).

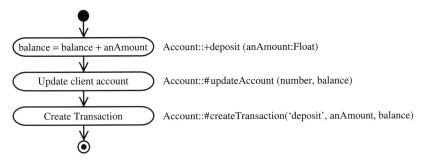

FIGURE 10–4
An activity diagram for the Account class deposit method.

10.9.3 Account Class Withdraw Method

This is the generic withdrawal method that simply withdraws funds if they are available. It is designed to be inherited by the CheckingAccount and SavingsAccount classes to implement automatic funds transfer. The following describes the withdraw method. An amount to be withdrawn is sent to an account object and used as the argument to the withdraw service. The account checks its balance for sufficient funds. If enough funds are available, the account makes the withdrawal and updates its balance; otherwise, it returns an error, saying "insufficient funds." If successful, the account records the withdrawal by creating a transaction object containing date and time, posted balance, and transaction type and amount (see Figure 10–5).

10.9.4 Account Class CreateTransaction Method

The createTransaction method generates a record of each transaction performed against it. The description is as follows. Each time a successful transaction is

FIGURE 10–5
An activity diagram for the Account class withdraw method.

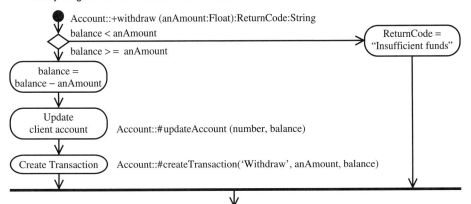

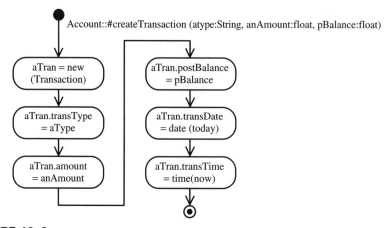

FIGURE 10–6
An activity diagram for the Account class createTransaction method.

performed against an account, the account object creates a transaction object to record it. Arguments into this service include transaction type (withdrawal or deposit), the transaction amount, and the balance after the transaction. The account creates a new transaction object and sets its attributes to the desired information. Add this description to the *createTransaction's* description field (see Figure 10–6).

10.9.5 Checking Account Class Withdraw Method

This is the checking account-specific version of the withdrawal service. It takes into consideration the possibility of withdrawing excess funds from a companion savings account. The description is as follows. An amount to be withdrawn is sent to a checking account and used as the argument to the withdrawal service. If the account has insufficient funds to cover the amount but has a companion savings account, it tries to withdraw the excess from there. If the companion account has insufficient funds, this method returns the appropriate error message. If the companion account has enough funds, the excess is withdrawn from there, and the checking account balance goes to zero (0). If successful, the account records the withdrawal by creating a transaction object containing the date and time, posted balance, and transaction type and amount (see Figure 10–7).

10.9.6 ATMMachine Class Operations

The ATMMachine class provides an interface (view) to the bank system. We postpone designing this class to Chapter 12.

10.10 PACKAGES AND MANAGING CLASSES

A package groups and manages the modeling elements, such as classes, their associations, and their structures. Packages themselves may be nested within other packages. A package may contain both other packages and ordinary model ele-

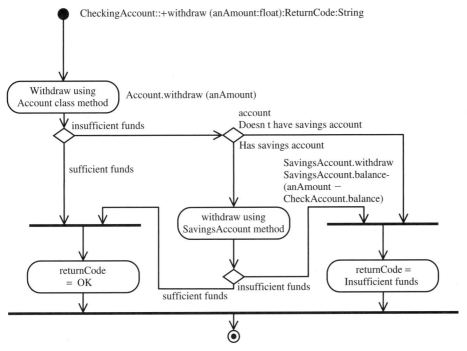

CheckingAccount::+withdraw (anAmount:float):ReturnCode:String

FIGURE 10-7
An activity diagram for the CheckingAccount class withdrawal method.

ments. The entire system description can be thought of as a single high-level sub-system package with everything else in it. All kinds of UML model elements and diagrams can be organized into packages. For example, some packages may contain groups of classes and their relationships, subsystems, or models. A package provides a hierarchy of different system components and can reference other packages. For example, the bank system can be viewed as a package that contains other packages, such as Account package, Client package, and so on. Classes can be packaged based on the services they provide or grouped into the business classes, access classes, and view classes (see Figure 10–8). Furthermore, since packages own model elements and model fragments, they can be used by CASE tools as the basic storage and access control.

In Chapter 5, we learned that a package is shown as a large rectangle with a small rectangular tab. If the contents of the package are shown, then the name of the package may be placed within the tab. A keyword string may be placed above the package name. The keywords *subsystem* and *model* indicate that the package is a meta-model subsystem or model. The visibility of a package element outside the package may be indicated by preceding the name of the element by a visibility symbol (+ for public, − for private, # for protected). If the element is in an inner package, its visibility as exported by the outer package is obtained by combining the visibility of an element within the package with the visibility of the package itself: The most restrictive visibility prevails.

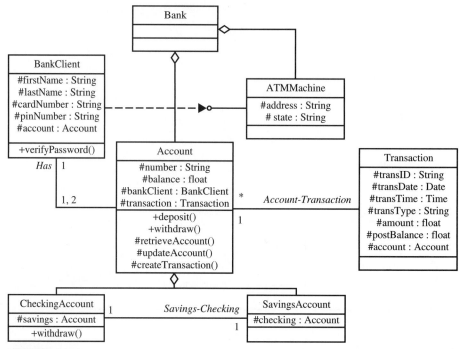

FIGURE 10–8
More complete UML class diagram for the ViaNet bank ATM system. Note that the method parameter list is not shown.

Relationships may be drawn between package symbols to show relationships between at least some of the elements in the packages. In particular, dependency between packages implies one or more dependencies among the elements. Figure 10–9 depicts an even more complete class diagram the ViaNet bank ATM system.

10.11 SUMMARY

The single most important activity in designing an application is coming up with a set of classes that work together to provide the needed functionality. After all, underlying the functionality of any application is the quality of its design.

This chapter concentrated on the first step of the object-oriented design process, which consists of applying the design axioms and corollaries to design classes, their attributes, methods, associations, structures, and protocols; then, iterating and refining.

During the analysis phase, the name of the attribute should be sufficient. However, during the design phase, detailed information must be added to the model (especially, definitions of the class attributes and operations). The UML provides a language to do just that. The rules and semantics of the UML can be expressed in English, in a form known as *object constraint language* (OCL). OCL is a specification language that uses simple logic for specifying the properties of a system.

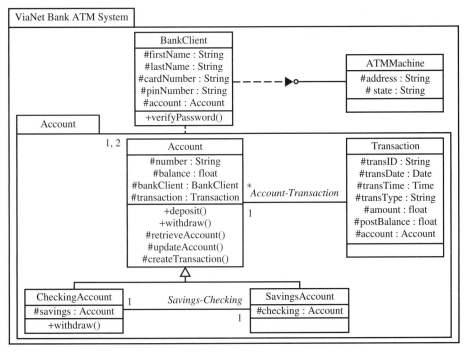

FIGURE 10–9
The ViaNet bank ATM system package and its subsystems.

Lack of a well-designed protocol can manifest itself as encapsulation leakage. This problem occurs when details about a class's internal implementation are disclosed through the interface. As more internal details become visible, the flexibility for making changes in the future is decreased. If an implementation is completely open, almost no flexibility is retained for future changes. Decide what attributes and methods should be private, protected, or public. Use private and protected protocols to define the implementation of the object; use public protocols to define the functionality of the object.

Remember five rules to avoid bad design:

1. If it looks messy, then it's probably a bad design.
2. If it is too complex, then it's probably a bad design.
3. If it is too big, then it's probably a bad design.
4. If people don't like it, then it's probably a bad design.
5. If it doesn't work, then it's probably a bad design.

The UML package is a grouping of model elements. It can organize the modeling elements including classes. Packages themselves may be nested within other packages. A package may contain both other packages and ordinary model elements. The entire system description can be thought of as a single, high-level subsystem package with everything else in it.

Object-oriented design is an iterative process. Designing is as much about discovery as construction. Do not be afraid to change a class design, based on experience gained, and do not be afraid to change it a second, third, or fourth time. At each iteration, you can improve the design. However, the trick is to fix the design as early as possible; redesigning late in the development cycle is problematic and may be impossible.

KEY TERMS

Encapsulation leakage (p. 220)
Object constraint language (OCL) (p. 218)
Private protocol (visibility) (p. 220)
Protocol (p. 219)
Protected protocol (visibility) (p. 220)
Public protocol (visibility) (p. 220)

REVIEW QUESTIONS

1. What are public and private protocols? What is the significance of separating these two protocols?
2. What are some characteristics of a *bad* design?
3. One of the most important skills you can develop is questioning your design, which causes you to think, "Wait a minute, this is starting to get messy." What are some other warning signs that things are about to go amiss?
4. How do design axioms help avoid design pitfalls?
5. Name some problems that come from the lack of a well-designed protocol; for example, giving every method and attribute public visibility.
6. We learned that, to design association, we need to add an instance connection attribute to a class. In a client-server association, does the server need to know about the client? In other words, must we add instance connection attributes of the client in the server class?

PROBLEMS

1. Which corollary (or corollaries) would you apply to design well-defined public, private, and protected protocols?
2. To solve some of the design pitfalls, we could apply the following corollaries. Please apply each corollary and explain how the design axioms and corollaries can help in avoiding design axioms:

- Keep a careful eye on the class design and make sure that an object's role remains well defined. If an object loses focus, you need to modify the design. Apply Corollary 2 (single purpose).
- Move some functions into new classes that the object would use. Apply Corollary 1 (uncoupled design with less information content).
- Break up the class into two or more classes. Apply Corollary 3 (large number of simple classes).

3. Design the queue, order queue, and inventory queue classes in the Grandma's Soups application (see Chapter 6).

REFERENCES

1. Gause, Donald G.; and Weinberg, G. M. *Exploring Requirements: Quality Before Design*. New York: Dorset House, 1989.
2. Norman, Ronald. *Object-Oriented Systems Analysis and Design*. Englewood Cliffs, NJ: Prentice-Hall, 1996.
3. Texel, Putnam; and Williams, Charles B. *Use Cases Combined with Booch OMT UML*. Englewood Cliffs, NJ: Prentice-Hall, 1997.

CHAPTER 11

Access Layer: Object Storage and Object Interoperability

Chapter Objectives

You should be able to define and understand

- Object storage and persistence.
- Database management systems and their technology.
- Client-server computing.
- Distributed databases.
- Distributed object computing.
- Object-oriented database management systems.
- Object-relational systems.
- Designing access layer objects.

11.1 INTRODUCTION

A *database management system* (DBMS) is a set of programs that enables the creation and maintenance of a collection of related data. A DBMS and associated programs access, manipulate, protect, and manage the data. The fundamental purpose of a DBMS is to provide a reliable, persistent data storage facility and the mechanisms for efficient, convenient data access and retrieval. A database is supposed to represent a real-world situation as completely and accurately as possible. The data model incorporated into a database system defines a framework of concepts that can be used to express an application [5].

Persistence refers to the ability of some objects to outlive the programs that created them. Object lifetimes can be short, as for local objects (these objects are transient), or long, as for objects stored indefinitely in a database (these objects are persistent). Most object-oriented languages do not support serialization or object

237

persistence, which is the process of writing or reading an object to and from a persistent storage medium, such as a disk file. Even though a reliable, persistent storage facility is the most important aspect of a database, there are many other aspects as well. Persistent object stores do not support query or interactive user interface facilities, as found in fully supported object-oriented database management systems. Furthermore, controlling concurrent access by users, providing ad-hoc query capability, and allowing independent control over the physical location of data are examples of features that differentiate a full database from simply a persistent store. This chapter introduces you to the issues regarding object storage, relational and object-oriented database management systems, object interoperability, and other technologies. We then look at current trends to combine object and relational systems to provide a very practical solution to object storage. We conclude the chapter with a discussion on how to design the access layer objects.

11.2 OBJECT STORE AND PERSISTENCE: AN OVERVIEW

A program will create a large amount of data throughout its execution. Each item of data will have a different lifetime. Atkinson et al. [1] describe six broad categories for the lifetime of data:

1. Transient results to the evaluation of expressions.
2. Variables involved in procedure activation (parameters and variables with a localized scope).
3. Global variables and variables that are dynamically allocated.
4. Data that exist between the executions of a program.
5. Data that exist between the versions of a program.
6. Data that outlive a program.

The first three categories are *transient data*, data that cease to exist beyond the lifetime of the creating process. The other three are nontransient, or *persistent,* data.

Typically, programming languages provide excellent, integrated support for the first three categories of transient data. The other three categories can be supported by a DBMS, or a file system.

The same issues also apply to objects; after all, objects have a lifetime, too. They are created explicitly and can exist for a period of time (during the application session). However, an object can persist beyond application session boundaries, during which the object is stored in a file or a database. A file or a database can provide a longer life for objects—longer than the duration of the process in which they were created. From a language perspective, this characteristic is called *persistence*. Essential elements in providing a persistent store are [4]:

- Identification of persistent objects or reachability (object ID).
- Properties of objects and their interconnections. The store must be able to coherently manage nonpointer and pointer data (i.e., interobject references).
- Scale of the object store. The object store should provide a conceptually infinite store.

- Stability. The system should be able to recover from unexpected failures and return the system to a recent self-consistent state. This is similar to the reliability requirements of a DBMS, object-oriented or not.

Having separate methods of manipulating the data presents many problems. Atkinson et al. [1] claim that typical programs devote significant amounts of code to transferring data to and from the file system or DBMS. Additionally, the use of these external storage mechanisms leads to a variety of technical issues, which will be examined in the following sections.

11.3 DATABASE MANAGEMENT SYSTEMS

Databases usually are large bodies of data seen as critical resources to a company. As mentioned earlier, a DBMS is a set of programs that enable the creation and maintenance of a collection of related data. DBMSs have a number of properties that distinguish them from the file-based data management approach. In traditional file processing, each application defines and implements the files it requires. Using a database approach, a single repository of data is maintained, which can be defined once and subsequently accessed by various users (see Figure 11–1).

A fundamental characteristic of the database approach is that the DBMS contains not only the data but a complete definition of the data formats it manages. This description is known as the *schema*, or *meta-data*, and contains a complete definition of the data formats, such as the data structures, types, and constraints.

In traditional file processing applications, such meta-data usually are encapsulated in the application programs themselves. In DBMS, the format of the meta-data is independent of any particular application data structure; therefore, it will

FIGURE 11–1

Database system vs. file system.

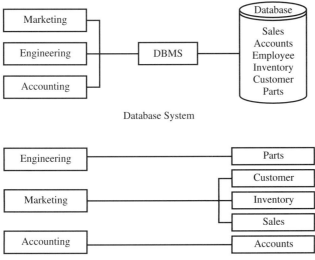

Database System

File System

provide a generic storage management mechanism. Another advantage of the database approach is program-data independence. By moving the meta-data into an external DBMS, a layer of insulation is created between the applications and the stored data structures. This allows any number of applications to access the data in a simplified and uniform manner.

11.3.1 Database Views

The DBMS provides the database users with a conceptual representation that is independent of the low-level details (physical view) of how the data are stored. The database can provide an abstract data model that uses logical concepts such as field, records, and tables and their interrelationships. Such a model is understood more easily by the user than the low-level storage concepts.

This abstract data model also can facilitate multiple views of the same underlying data. Many applications will use the same shared information but each will be interested in only a subset of the data. The DBMS can provide multiple virtual views of the data that are tailored to individual applications. This allows the convenience of a private data representation with the advantage of globally managed information.

11.3.2 Database Models

A database model is a collection of logical constructs used to represent the data structure and data relationships within the database. Basically, database models may be grouped into two categories: conceptual models and implementation models. The conceptual model focuses on the logical nature of that data presentation. Therefore, the conceptual model is concerned with *what* is represented in the database and the implementation model is concerned with *how* it is represented [12].

11.3.2.1 Hierarchical Model   The hierarchical model represents data as a single-rooted tree. Each node in the tree represents a data object and the connections represent a parent-child relationship. For example, a node might be a record containing information about Motor vehicle and its child nodes could contain a record about Bus parts (see Figure 11–2). Interestingly enough, a hierarchical model resembles super-sub relationship of objects.

FIGURE 11–2
A hierarchical model. The top layer, the root, is perceived as the parent of the segment directly below it. In this case motor vehicle is the parent of Bus, Truck, and Car. A segment also is called a node. The segments below another node are the children of the node above them. Bus, Truck, and Car are the children of Motor Vehicle.

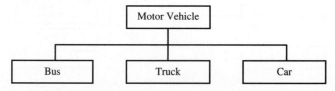

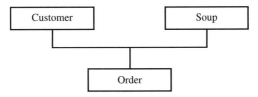

FIGURE 11–3
Network model. An Order contains data from both Customer and Soup.

11.3.2.2 Network Model A network database model is similar to a hierarchical database, with one distinction. Unlike the hierarchical model, a network model's record can have more than one parent. For example, in Figure 11–3, an Order contains data from the Soup and Customer nodes.

11.3.2.3 Relational Model Of all the database models, the relational model has the simplest, most uniform structure and is the most commercially widespread. The primary concept in this database model is the relation, which can be thought of as a table. The columns of each table are attributes that define the data or value domain for entries in that column. The rows of each table are **tuples** representing individual data objects being stored. A relational table should have only one primary key. A **primary key** is a combination of one or more attributes whose *value* unambiguously locates each row in the table. In Figure 11–4, Soup-ID, Cust-ID, and Order-ID are primary keys in Soup, Customer, and Order tables. A **foreign key** is a primary key of one table that is embedded in another table to link the tables. In Figure 11–4, Soup-ID and Cust-ID are foreign keys in the Order table.

FIGURE 11–4
The figure depicts primary and foreign keys in a relation database. Soup-ID is a primary key of the Soup table, Cust-ID is a primary key of the Customer table, and Order-ID is a primary key of the Order table. Soup-ID and Cust-ID are foreign keys in the Order table.

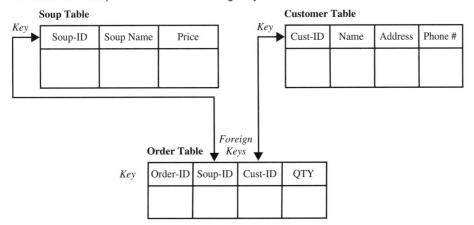

11.3.3 Database Interface

The interface on a database must include a data definition language (DDL), a query, and data manipulation language (DML). These languages must be designed to fully reflect the flexibility and constraints inherent in the data model. Database systems have adopted two approaches for interfaces with the system. One is to embed a database language, such as structured query language (SQL), in the host programming language. This approach is a very popular way of defining and designing a database and its schema, especially with the popularity of languages such as SQL, which has become an industry standard for defining databases. The problem with this approach is that application programmers have to learn and use two different languages. Furthermore, the application programmers have to negotiate the differences in the data models and data structures allowed in both languages [8].

Another approach is to extend the host programming language with database-related constructs. This is the major approach, since application programmers need to learn only a new construct of the same language rather than a completely new language. Many of the currently operational databases and object-oriented database systems have adopted this approach; a good example is GemStone from Servio Logic, which has extended the Smalltalk object-oriented programming.

11.3.3.1 Database Schema and Data Definition Language   To represent information in a database, a mechanism must exist to describe or specify to the database the entities of interest. A *data definition language* (DDL) is the language used to describe the structure of and relationships between objects stored in a database. This structure of information is termed the *database schema*. In traditional databases, the schema of a database is the collection of record types and set types or the collection of relationships, templates, and table records used to store information about entities of interest to the application.

For example, to create logical structure or schema, the following SQL command can be used:

```
CREATE SCHEMA AUTHORIZATION (creator)
CREATE DATABASE (database name)
```

For example,

```
CREATE TABLE INVENTORY (Inventory_Number CHAR(10)NOT NULL
DESCRIPTION CHAR(25) NOT NULL PRICE DECIMAL (9, 2));
```

where the boldface words are SQL keywords.

11.3.3.2 Data Manipulation Language and Query Capabilities   Any time data are collected on virtually any topic, someone will want to ask questions about it. Someone will want the answers to simple questions like "How many of them are there?" or more intricate questions like "What is the percentage of people between ages 21 and 45 who have been employed for five years and like playing tennis?"

Asking questions—more formally, making queries of the data—is a typical and common use of a database. A query usually is expressed through a query language. A *data manipulation language* (DML) is the language that allows users to access and manipulate (such as, create, save, or destroy) data organization. The *structured query language* (SQL) is the standard DML for relational DBMSs. SQL is widely used for its query capabilities. The query usually specifies

- The domain of the discourse over which to ask the query.
- The elements of general interest.
- The conditions or constraints that apply.
- The ordering, sorting, or grouping of elements and the constraints that apply to the ordering or grouping.

Query processes generally have sophisticated "engines" that determine the best way to approach the database and execute the query over it. They may use information in the database or knowledge of the whereabouts of particular data in the network to optimize the retrieval of a query.

Traditionally, DML are either procedural or nonprocedural. A procedural DML requires users to specify what data are desired and how to get the data. A nonprocedural DML, like most databases' fourth generation programming language (4GLs), requires users to specify what data are needed but not how to get the data. Object-oriented query and data manipulation languages, such as Object SQL, provide object management capabilities to the data manipulation language.

In a relational DBMS, the DML is independent of the host programming language. A host language such as C or COBOL would be used to write the body of the application. Typically, SQL statements then are embedded in C or COBOL applications to manipulate data. Once SQL is used to request and retrieve database data, the results of the SQL retrieval must be transformed into the data structures of the programming language. A disadvantage of this approach is that programmers code in two languages, SQL and the host language. Another is that the structural transformation is required in both database access directions, to and from the database.

For example, to check the table content, the SELECT command is used, followed by the desired attributes. Or, if you want to see all the attributes listed, use the (*) to indicate all the attributes: SELECT DESCRIPTION, PRICE FROM INVENTORY; where inventory is the name of a table.

11.4 LOGICAL AND PHYSICAL DATABASE ORGANIZATION AND ACCESS CONTROL

Logical database organization refers to the conceptual view of database structure and the relationships within the database. For example, object-oriented systems represent databases composed of objects, and many allow multiple databases to share information by defining the same object. Physical database organization refers to how the logical components of the database are represented in a physical form by operating system constructs (i.e., objects may be represented as files).

11.4.1 Shareability and Transactions

Data and objects in the database often need to be accessed and shared by different applications. With multiple applications having access to the object concurrently, it is likely that conflicts over object access will arise. The database then must detect and mediate these conflicts and promote the greatest amount of sharing possible without sacrificing the integrity of data. This mediation process is managed through concurrency control policies, implemented, in part, by transactions.

A *transaction* is a unit of change in which many individual modifications are aggregated into a single modification that occurs in its entirety or not at all. Thus, either all changes to objects within a given transaction are applied to the database or none of the changes. A transaction is said to *commit* if all changes can be made successfully to the database and to *abort* if canceled because all changes to the database cannot be made successfully. This ability of transactions ensures **atomicity** of change that maintain the database in a consistent state.

Many transaction systems are designed primarily for short transactions (lasting on the order of seconds or minutes). They are less suitable for long transactions, lasting hours or longer. Object databases typically are designed to support both short and long transactions. A concurrence control policy dictates what happens when conflicts arise between transactions that attempt access to the same object and how these conflicts are to be resolved.

11.4.2 Concurrency Policy

As you might expect, when several users (or applications) attempt to read and write the same object simultaneously, they create a contention for object. The concurrency control mechanism is established to mediate such conflicts by making policies that dictate how they will be handled.

A basic goal of the transaction is to provide each user with a consistent view of the database. This means that transactions must occur in serial order. In other words, a given user must see the database as it exists either before a given transaction occurs or after that transaction.

The most conservative way to enforce serialization is to allow a user to lock all objects or records when they are accessed and to release the locks only after a transaction commits. This approach, traditionally known as a *conservative* or *pessimistic policy*, provides exclusive access to the object, despite what is done to it. The policy is very conservative because no other user can view the data until the object is released. However, by distinguishing between querying (reading or getting data from) the object and writing to it (which is achieved by qualifying the type of lock placed in the object-read lock or -write lock), somewhat greater concurrency can be achieved. This policy allows many readers of an object but only one writer.

Under an optimistic policy, two conflicting transactions are compared in their entirety and then their serial ordering is determined. As long as the database is able to serialize them so that all the objects viewed by each transaction are from a consistent state of the database, both can continue even though they have read and write locks on a shared object. Thus, a process can be allowed to obtain a read lock on an object already write locked if its entire transaction can be serialized as if it occurred either entirely before or entirely after the conflicting transaction. The reverse also is true: A process may be allowed to obtain a write lock on an object that has a read lock if its entire transaction can be serialized as if it occurred after the conflicting transaction. In such cases, the optimistic policy allows more processes to operate concurrently than the conservative policy.

11.5 DISTRIBUTED DATABASES AND CLIENT-SERVER COMPUTING

Many modern databases are ***distributed databases***, which implies that portions of the database reside on different nodes (computers) and disk drives in the network. Usually, each portion of the database is managed by a server, a process responsible for controlling access and retrieval of data from the database portion. The server dispenses information to client applications and makes queries or data requests to these client applications or other servers. Clients generally reside on nodes in the network other than those on which the servers execute. However, both can reside on the same node, too.

11.5.1 What Is Client-Server Computing?

Client-server computing is the logical extension of modular programming. The fundamental assumption of modular programming is that separation of a large piece of software into its constituent parts ("modules") creates the possibility for easier development and better maintainability.

Client-server computing extends this theory a step further by recognizing that all those modules need not be executed within the same memory space or even on the same machine. With this architecture, the calling module becomes the "client" (that which requests a service) and the called module becomes the "server" (that which provides the service; see Figure 11–5). Another important component of client-server computing is connectivity, which allows applications to communicate transparently with other programs or processes, regardless of their locations. The key element of connectivity is the network operating system (NOS), also known as *middleware*. The NOS provides services such as routing, distribution, messages, filing and printing, and network management [6].

The client is a process (program) that sends a message to a server process (program) requesting that the server perform a task (service). Client programs usually manage the user interface portion of the application, validate data entered by the user, dispatch requests to server programs, and sometimes execute business logic. The business layer contains all the objects that represent the business (real objects),

FIGURE 11–5
Two-tier client-server system.

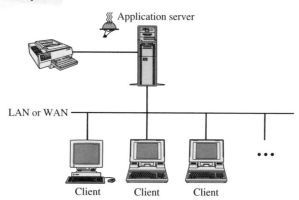

such as Order, Customer, Lineitem, Inventory. The client-based process is the front-end of the application, which the user sees and interacts with. The client process contains solution-specific logic and provides the interface between the user and the rest of the application system. It also manages the local resources with which the user interacts, such as the monitor, keyboard, workstation, CPU, and peripherals. A key component of a client workstation is the graphical user interface (GUI), which normally is a part of the operating system (i.e., the Windows manager). It is responsible for detecting user actions, managing the Windows on the display, and displaying the data in the Windows.

A server process (program) fulfills the client request by performing the task requested. Server programs generally receive requests from client programs, execute database retrieval and updates, manage data integrity, and dispatch responses to client requests. Sometimes, server programs execute common or complex business logic. The server-based process "may" run on another machine on the network. This server could be the host operating system or network file server; the server then is provided both file system services and application services. In some cases, another desktop machine provides the application services. The server process acts as a software engine that manages shared resources such as databases, printers, communication links, or high-powered processors. The server process performs the back-end tasks that are common to similar applications.

The server can take different forms. The simplest form of server is a file server. With a file server, the client passes requests for files or file records over a network to the file server. This form of data service requires large bandwidth (the range of data that can be sent over a given medium simultaneously) and can considerably slow down a network with many users. Traditional LAN computing allows users to share resources, such as data files and peripheral devices [6].

More advanced forms of servers are database servers, transaction servers, application servers, and more recently object servers. With database servers, clients pass SQL requests as messages to the server and the results of the query are returned over the network. Both the code that processes the SQL request and the data reside on the server, allowing it to use its own processing power to find the requested data. This is in contrast to the file server, which requires passing all the records back to the client and then letting the client find its own data.

With transaction servers, clients invoke remote procedures that reside on servers, which also contain an SQL database engine. The server has procedural statements to execute a group of SQL statements (transactions), which either all succeed or fail as a unit.

The applications based on transaction servers, handled by on-line transaction processing (OLTP), tend to be mission-critical applications that always require a 1–3 second response time and tight control over the security and the integrity of the database. The communication overhead in this approach is kept to a minimum, since the exchange typically consists of a single request and reply (as opposed to multiple SQL statements in database servers).

Application servers are not necessarily database centered but are used to serve user needs, such as downloading capabilities from Dow Jones or regulating an electronic mail process. Basing resources on a server allows users to share data, while security and management services, also based on the server, ensure data in-

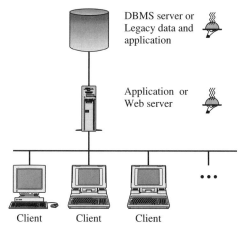

DBMS server or
Legacy data and
application

Application or
Web server

Client   Client   Client

FIGURE 11–6
Three-tiered architecture.

tegrity and security [6]. The logical extension of this is to have clients and servers running on the appropriate hardware and software platforms for their functions. For example, database management system servers should run on platforms specially designed and configured to perform queries, and file servers should run on platforms with special elements for managing files.

In a *two-tier* architecture, a client talks directly to a server, with no intervening server. This type of architecture typically is used in small environments with less than 50[1] users (see Figure 11–5). A common error in client-server development is to prepare a prototype of an application in a small, two-tier environment then scale up by simply adding more users to the server. This approach usually will result in an ineffective system, as the server becomes overwhelmed. To properly scale up to hundreds or thousands of users, it usually is necessary to move to a three-tier architecture [14].

A *three-tier* architecture introduces a server (application or Web server) between the client and the server. The role of the application or Web server is manifold. It can provide translation services (as in adapting a legacy application on a mainframe to a client-server environment), metering services (as in acting as a transaction monitor to limit the number of simultaneous requests to a given server), or intelligent agent services (as in mapping a request to a number of different servers, collating the results, and returning a single response to the client) [14] (see Figure 11–6).

Ravi Kalakota describes the basic characteristics of client-server architectures as follows [6]:

1. A combination of a client or front-end portion that interacts with the user and a server or backend portion that interacts with the shared resource. The client process contains solution-specific logic and provides the interface between the user and the rest

---

[1]Please note that this number depends on many other factors, such as number of transactions per second, as well as the size of the server, the capacity of the network, and so forth.

of the application system. The server process acts as a software engine that manages shared resources such as databases, printers, modems, or high-powered processors.

2. The front-end task and back-end task have fundamentally different requirements for computing resources such as processor speeds, memory, disk speeds and capacities, and input/output devices.

3. The environment is typically heterogeneous and multivendor. The hardware platform and operating system of client and server are not usually the same. Client and server processes communicate through a well-defined set of standard application program interfaces (APIs) . . .

4. An important characteristic of client-server systems is scalability. They can be scaled horizontally or vertically. Horizontal scaling means adding or removing client workstations with only a slight performance impact. Vertical scaling means migrating to a larger and faster server machine or multiservers.

Client-server and distributed computing have arisen because of a change in business needs. Unfortunately, most businesses have existing systems, based on older technology, that must be incorporated into the new, integrated environment; that is, mainframes with a great deal of legacy (older application) software.

Robertson-Dunn [13] answers the question "why build client-server applications?" by pointing out that "business demands the increased benefits." The distinguishing characteristic of a client-server application is the high degree of interaction among various application components [3]. These are the interactions between the client's requests and the server's reactions to those requests. To understand these interactions, we look at the client-server application's components. A typical client-server application consists of the following components:

1. *User interface.* This major component of the client-server application interacts with users, screens, Windows, Windows management, keyboard, and mouse handling.

2. *Business processing.* This part of the application uses the user interface data to perform business tasks. In this book, we look at how to develop this component by utilizing an object-oriented technology.

3. *Database processing.* This part of the application code manipulates data within the application. The data are managed by a database management system, object oriented or not. Data manipulation is done using a data manipulation language, such as SQL or a dialect of SQL (perhaps, an object-oriented query language). Ideally, the DBMS processing is transparent to the business processing layer of the application.

The development and implementation of client-server computing is more complex, more difficult, and more expensive than traditional, single process applications. However, utilizing an object-oriented methodology, we can manage the complexity of client-server applications.

11.5.2 Distributed and Cooperative Processing

The distributed processing means distribution of applications and business logic across multiple processing platforms. Distributed processing implies that processing will occur on more than one processor in order for a transaction to be com-

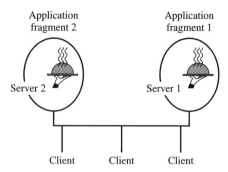

FIGURE 11-7
Distributed processing.

pleted. In other words, processing is distributed across two or more machines, where each process performs part of an application in a sequence. These processes may not run at the same time (see Figure 11–7). For example, in processing an order from a client, the client information may process at one machine and the account information then may process on a different machine. Often, the object used in a distributed processing environment also is distributed across platforms [6].

Cooperative processing is computing that requires two or more distinct processors to complete a single transaction. Cooperative processing is related to both distributed and client-server processing. Cooperative processing is a form of distributed computing in which two or more distinct processes are required to complete a single business transaction. Usually, these programs interact and execute concurrently on different processors (see Figure 11–8). Cooperative processing also can be considered to be a style of distributed processing, if communication between processors is performed through a message-passing architecture [6].

FIGURE 11-8
Cooperative processing.

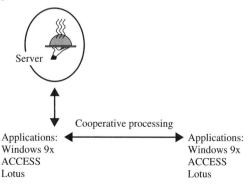

11.6 DISTRIBUTED OBJECTS COMPUTING: THE NEXT GENERATION OF CLIENT-SERVER COMPUTING

In the preceding section, we looked at what is now considered the first generation of client-server computing. Eventually, the server code in your client-server system will give way to collections of distributed objects. Since all of them will need to talk to each other, the second generation of client-server computing is based on distributed object computing, which will be covered in the next section.

Software technology is in the midst of a major computational shift toward distributed object computing (DOC). Distributed computing is poised for a second client-server revolution, a transition from first generation client-server era to a next generation client-server era. In this new client-server model, servers are plentiful instead of scarce (because every client can be a server) and proximity no longer matters. This immensely expanded client-server model is made possible by the recent exponential network growth and the progress in network-aware multithreaded desktop operating systems.

In the first generation client-server era, which still is very much in progress, SQL databases, transaction processing (TP) monitors, and groupware have begun to displace file servers as client-server application models. In the new client-server era, distributed object technology is expected to dominate other client-server application models.

Distributed object computing promises the most flexible client-server systems, because it utilizes reusable software components that can roam anywhere on networks, run on different platforms, communicate with legacy applications by means of object wrappers,[2] and manage themselves and the resources they control. Objects can help break monolithic applications into more manageable components that coexist on the expanded bus.

Distributed objects are reusable software components that can be distributed and accessed by users across the network. These objects can be assembled into distributed applications [9]. Distributed object computing introduces a higher level of abstraction into the world of distributed applications. Applications no longer consist of clients and servers but users, objects, and methods. The user no longer needs to know which server process performs a given function. All information about the function is hidden inside the encapsulated object. A message requesting an operation is sent to the object, and the appropriate method is invoked.

Distributed object computing will be the key part of tomorrow's information systems. DOC resulted from the need to integrate mission-critical applications and data residing on systems that are geographically remote, sometimes from users and often from each other, and running on many different hardware platforms. Furthermore, the information systems must link applications developed in different languages, use data from object and relational databases and from mainframe systems, and be optimized for use across the Internet and through departmental intranets. Historically, businesses have had to integrate applications and data by writing custom interfaces between systems, forcing developers to spend their time

---

[2] Conceptually, an object wrapper is very similar to an access layer, discussed later in this chapter.

building and maintaining an infrastructure rather than adding new business functionality.

Distributed object technology has been tied to standards from the early stage. Since 1989, the ***Object Management Group*** (OMG), with over 500 member companies, has been specifying the architecture for an open software bus on which object components written by different vendors can operate across networks and operating systems. The OMG and the object bus are well on their way to becoming the universal client-server middleware.

Currently, there are several competing DOC standards, including the Object Management Group's CORBA, OpenDoc, and Microsoft's ActiveX/DCOM. Although DOC technology offers unprecedented computing power, few organizations have been able to harness it as yet. The main reasons commonly cited for slow adoption of DOC include closed legacy architecture, incompatible protocols, inadequate network bandwidths, and security issues. In the next subsections, we look at Microsoft's DCOM and OMG's CORBA.

11.6.1 Common Object Request Broker Architecture

Many organizations are now adopting the Object Management Group's ***common object request broker architecture*** (CORBA), a standard proposed as a means to integrate distributed, heterogeneous business applications and data. The CORBA interface definition language (IDL) allows developers to specify language-neutral, object-oriented interfaces for application and system components. IDL definitions are stored in an interface repository, a sort of phone book that offers object interfaces and services. For distributed enterprise computing, the interface repository is central to communication among objects located on different systems.

CORBA ***object request brokers*** (ORBs) implement a communication channel through which applications can access object interfaces and request data and services (see Figure 11–9). The CORBA common object environment (COE) provides system-

FIGURE 11–9
The Common Object Request Broker Architecture (CORBA).

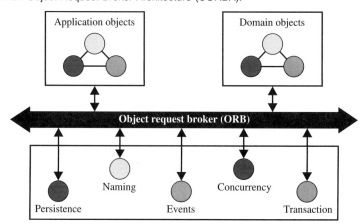

level services such as life cycle management for objects accessed through CORBA, event notification between objects, and transaction and concurrency control.

11.6.2 Microsoft's ActiveX/DCOM

Microsoft's component object model (COM) and its successor the distributed component object model (DCOM) are Microsoft's alternatives to OMG's distributed object architecture CORBA. Microsoft and the OMG are competitors, and few can say for sure which technology will win the challenge. Although CORBA benefits from wide industry support, DCOM is supported mostly by one enterprise, Microsoft. However, Microsoft is no small business concern and holds firmly a huge part of the microcomputer population, so DCOM has appeared a very serious competitor to CORBA. DCOM was bundled with Windows NT 4.0 and there is a good chance to see DCOM in all forthcoming Microsoft products.

The *distributed component object model*, Microsoft's alternative to OMG's CORBA, is an Internet and component strategy where ActiveX (formerly known as object linking and embedding, or OLE) plays the role of DCOM object. DCOM also is backed by a very efficient Web browser, the Microsoft Internet Explorer.

11.7 OBJECT-ORIENTED DATABASE MANAGEMENT SYSTEMS: THE PURE WORLD

Database management systems have progressed from indexed files to network and hierarchical database systems to relational systems. The requirements of traditional business data processing applications are well met in functionality and performance by relational database systems focused on the needs of business data processing applications. However, as many researchers observed, they are inadequate for a broader class of applications with unconventional and complex data type requirements. These requirements along with the popularity of object-oriented programming have resulted in great demand for an object-oriented DBMS (OODBMS). Therefore, the interest in OODBMS initially stemmed from the data storage requirements of design support applications (e.g., CAD, CASE, office information systems).

The *object-oriented database management system* is a marriage of object-oriented programming and database technology (see Figure 11–10) to provide what we now call *object-oriented databases*. Additionally, object-oriented databases allow all the benefits of an object orientation as well as the ability to have a strong equivalence with object-oriented programs, an equivalence that would be lost if an alternative were chosen, as with a purely relational database. By combining object-oriented programming with database technology, we have an integrated application development system, a significant characteristic of object-oriented database technology. Many advantages accrue from including the definition of operations with the definition of data. First, the defined operations apply universally and are not dependent on the particular database application running at the moment. Second, the data types can be extended to support complex data such as multimedia by defining new object classes that have operations to support the new kinds of information.

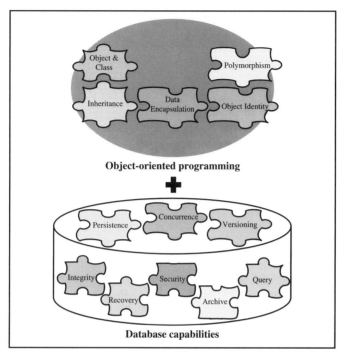

FIGURE 11–10

The object-oriented database management system is a marriage of object-oriented program-ming and database technology.

The "Object-Oriented Database System Manifesto" by Malcom Atkinson et al. [2] described the necessary characteristics that a system must satisfy to be con-sidered an object-oriented database. These categories can be broadly divided into *object-oriented* language properties and *database* requirements.

First, the rules that make it an object-oriented system are as follows:

1. *The system must support complex objects.* A system must provide simple ***atomic types of objects*** (integers, characters, etc.) from which complex objects can be built by applying constructors to atomic objects or other complex objects or both.
2. *Object identity must be supported.* A data object must have an identity and ex-istence independent of its values.
3. *Objects must be encapsulated.* An object must encapsulate both a program and its data. Encapsulation embodies the separation of interface and implementa-tion and the need for modularity.
4. *The system must support types or classes.* The system must support either the type concept (embodied by C++) or the class concept (embodied by Smalltalk).
5. *The system must support inheritance.* Classes and types can participate in a class hierarchy. The primary advantage of inheritance is that it factors out shared code and interfaces.

6. *The system must avoid premature binding.* This feature also is known as *late binding* or *dynamic binding* (see Chapter 2, which shows that the same method name can be used in different classes). Since classes and types support encapsulation and inheritance, the system must resolve conflicts in operation names at run time.

7. *The system must be computationally complete.* Any computable function should be expressible in the data manipulation language (DML) of the system, thereby allowing expression of any type of operation.

8. *The system must be extensible.* The user of the system should be able to create new types that have equal status to the system's predefined types.

These requirements are met by most modern object-oriented programming languages such as Smalltalk and C++. Also, clearly, these requirements are *not* met *directly* (more on this in the next section) by traditional relational, hierarchical, or network database systems.

Second, these rules make it a DBMS:

9. *It must be persistent, able to remember an object state.* The system must allow the programmer to have data survive beyond the execution of the creating process for it to be reused in another process.

10. *It must be able to manage very large databases.* The system must efficiently manage access to the secondary storage and provide performance features, such as indexing, clustering, buffering, and query optimization.

11. *It must accept concurrent users.* The system must allow multiple concurrent users and support the notions of atomic, serializable transactions.

12. *It must be able to recover from hardware and software failures.* The system must be able to recover from software and hardware failures and return to a coherent state.

13. *Data query must be simple.* The system must provide some high-level mechanism for ad-hoc browsing of the contents of the database. A graphical browser might fulfill this requirement sufficiently.

These database requirements are met by the majority of existing database systems. From these two sets of definitions it can be argued that an OODBMS is a DBMS with an underlying object-oriented model.

11.7.1 Object-Oriented Databases versus Traditional Databases

The scope of the responsibility of an OODBMS includes definition of the object structures, object manipulation, and recovery, which is the ability to maintain data integrity regardless of system, network, or media failure. Furthermore, OODBMSs like DBMSs must allow for sharing; secure, concurrent multiuser access; and efficient, reliable system performance.

One obvious difference between the traditional and object-oriented databases is derived from the object's ability to interact with other objects and with itself. The objects are an "active" component in an object-oriented database, in contrast to conventional database systems, where records play a passive role. Yet another distinguishing feature of object-oriented database is inheritance. Relational database systems do not explicitly provide inheritance of attributes and methods. Object-oriented databases, on the other hand, represent relationships explicitly, supporting both navigational and associative access to information. As the complexity of interrelationships between information within the database increases, so do the advantages of representing relationships explicitly. Another benefit of using explicit relationships is the improvement in data access performance over relational value-based relationships.

Object-oriented databases also differ from the more traditional relational databases in that they allow representation and storage of data in the form of objects. Each object has its own identity, or *object-ID* (as opposed to the purely value-oriented approach of traditional databases). The object identity is independent of the state of the object. For example, if one has a car object and we remodel the car and change its appearance, the engine, the transmission, and the tires so that it looks entirely different, it would still be recognized as the same object we had originally. Within an object-oriented database, one always can ask whether this is the same object I had previously, assuming one remembers the object's identity. Object identity allows objects to be related as well as shared within a distributed computing network.

All these advantages point to the application of object-oriented databases to information management problems that are characterized by the need to manage

- A large number of different data types.
- A large number of relationships between the objects.
- Objects with complex behaviors.

Application areas where this kind of complexity exists include engineering, manufacturing, simulations, office automation, and large information systems ("No More Fishing for Data" is a real-world example of this).

11.8 OBJECT-RELATIONAL SYSTEMS: THE PRACTICAL WORLD

In practice, even though many applications increasingly are developed in an object-oriented programming technology, chances are good that the data those applications need to access live in a very different universe—a relational database. In such an environment, the introduction of object-oriented development creates a fundamental mismatch between the programming model (objects) and the way in which existing data are stored (relational tables) [9].

To resolve the mismatch, a mapping tool between the application objects and the relational data must be established. Creating an object model from an existing relational database layout (schema) often is referred to as ***reverse engineering***. Conversely, creating a relational schema from an existing object model often is referred to as ***forward engineering***. In practice, over the life cycle of an application, forward and reverse engineering need to be combined in an iterative process to maintain the relationship between the object and relational data representations.

Tools that can be used to establish the object-relational mapping processes have begun to emerge. The main process in relational and object integration is defining the relationships between the table structures (represented as schemata) in the relational database with classes (representing classes) in the object model. Sun's Java

Real-World Issues on the Agenda
NO MORE FISHING FOR DATA

Client/Server: With the help of a three-tier decision support system, a Canadian department baits salmon spawning

Esther Shein

Tracking the spawning habits of salmon using high technology may sound like fishy business, but it's more important than you'd think—especially when you're up against the whims of Mother Nature.

The huge amount of data that needed to be tracked was daunting, according to Ian Williams, a senior biologist and head of the Fresh Water Habitats Science Group for the Department of Fisheries (DOF), in Nanaimo, British Columbia. To make matters worse, different groups within the DFO had been creating independent databases focusing on their area of interest. It was time for some serious streamlining.

THREE-TIER TO RESCUE

The consolidation came in the form of the decision support system, dubbed The Integrated Fraser Salmon model, which was built using Facet Decision Systems Inc.'s development environment. Facet's tool comprises middleware for links to third-party databases; an object-oriented spreadsheet-like development environment; and 3-D visualization tools. Facet's object-oriented capabilities and capacity to accommodate ever-changing business rules make it applicable for any industry—for example, finance—that needs to construct and analyze large data models.

The Fraser Salmon model was built in three layers: one for data access, one for data integration and one to parlay the biologist's rules which produces the technical results. DFO officials wanted all the miscellaneous databases linked so employees would have access to the same information—for example, the number of fish caught in oceans and rivers over a particular period, the estimated space still available for spawning and where forest fires occur. The top layer of the system contains policy analysis, which are tools to create and compare scenarios "to see technical impacts and translate them into the information you need to make decisions," explains Scott Akenhead, vice president of Business Development at Facet.

The model, which Akenhead likens to a spreadsheet, has cells that are object-oriented in nature, in the form of graphics, maps or the links to the Oracle data and rules written by a biologist.

The model differs from the typical data warehouse, because of the use of advanced object-oriented technology, which allows Facet to build a much larger model. "We didn't just assemble the data and drop it in their laps. The data was analyzed by the Facet system using rules the biologist provided," he explains.

"We found a way to make new object-oriented technology available to people who are not programmers," Akenhead says.

Today, using map as the user interface, the DFO has moved from raw digital map data (a representation of a paper map on-screen) to 3-D maps that can be analyzed to compare policy suggestions. "We created river networks and drainage surfaces from raw data, which are more useful to the biologist" because they do things the raw maps couldn't do, such as simulate the fish swimming up the streams, Akenhead says.

By Esther Shein, PC Week, September 23, 1996, Vol. 13, Number 38.

Blend is an example of such a tool. Java Blend allows the developer access to relational data as Java objects, thus avoiding the mismatch between the relational and object data models. Java Blend also has mapping capabilities to define Java classes from relational tables or relational tables from the Java classes [15].

11.8.1 Object-Relation Mapping

In a relational database, the schema is made up of tables, consisting of rows and columns, where each column has a name and a simple data type. In an object model, the counterpart to a table is a class (or classes), which has a set of attributes (properties or data members). Object classes describe behavior with methods.

A tuple (row) of a table contains data for a single entity that correlates to an object (instance of a class) in an object-oriented system. In addition, a stored procedure in a relational database may correlate to a method in an object-oriented architecture. A *stored procedure* is a module of precompiled SQL code maintained within the database that executes on the server to enforce rules the business has set about the data. Therefore, the mappings essential to object and relational integration are between a table and a class, between columns and attributes, between a row and an object, and between a stored procedure and a method.

For a tool to be able to define how relational data maps to and from application objects, it must have at least the following mapping capabilities (note all these are two-way mappings, meaning they map from the relational system to the object and from the object back to the relational system):

- Table-class mapping.
- Table-multiple classes mapping.
- Table-inherited classes mapping.
- Tables-inherited classes mapping.

Furthermore, in addition to mapping column values, the tool must be capable of interpretation of relational foreign keys. The tool must describe both how the foreign key can be used to navigate among classes and instances in the mapped object model and how referential integrity is maintained. *Referential integrity* means making sure that a dependent table's foreign key contains a value that refers to an existing valid tuple in another relation.

11.8.2 Table-Class Mapping

Table-class mapping is a simple one-to-one mapping of a table to a class and the mapping of columns in a table to properties in a class. In this mapping, a single table is mapped to a single class, as shown in Figure 11–11.

In such mapping, it is common to map all the columns to properties. However, this is not required, and it may be more efficient to map only those columns for which an object model is required by the application(s). With the table-class ap-

FIGURE 11–11

Table-class mapping. Each row in the table represents an object instance and each column in the table corresponds to an object attribute.

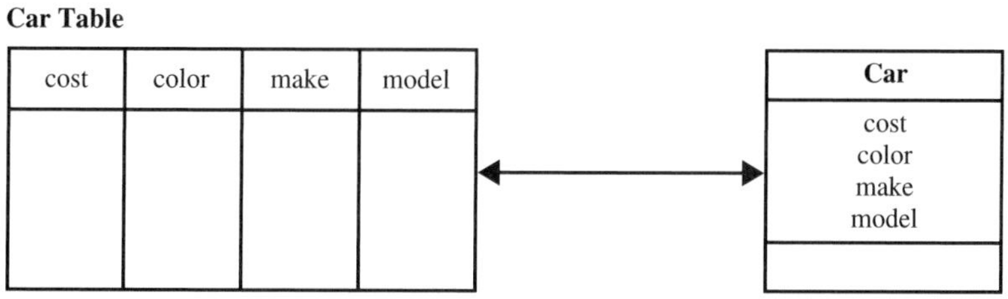

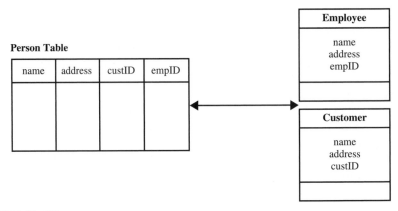

FIGURE 11–12
Table-multiple classes mapping. The custID column provides the discriminant. If the value for custID is null, an Employee instance is created at run time; otherwise, a Customer instance is created.

proach, each row in the table represents an object instance and each column in the table corresponds to an object attribute. This one-to-one mapping of the table-class approach provides a literal translation between a relational data representation and an application object. It is appealing in its simplicity but offers little flexibility.

11.8.3 Table-Multiple Classes Mapping

In the table-multiple classes mapping, a single table maps to multiple noninheriting classes. Two or more distinct, noninheriting classes have properties that are mapped to columns in a single table. At run time, a mapped table row is accessed as an instance of one of the classes, based on a column value in the table [11].

In Figure 11–12, the custID column provides the discriminant. If the value for custID is null, an Employee instance is created at run time; otherwise, a Customer instance is created.

11.8.4 Table-Inherited Classes Mapping

In table-inherited classes mapping, a single table maps to many classes that have a common superclass. This mapping allows the user to specify the columns to be shared among the related classes. The superclass may be either abstract or instantiated. In Figure 11–13, instances of salariedEmployee can be created for any row in the Person table that has a non null value for the Salary column. If Salary is null, the row is represented by an hourlyEmployee instance.

11.8.5 Tables-Inherited Classes Mapping

Another approach here is tables-inherited classes mapping, which allows the translation of *is-a* relationships that exist among tables in the relational schema into class inheritance relationships in the object model. In a relational database, an is-a relationship often is modeled by a primary key that acts as a foreign key to another table. In the object model, *is-a* is another term for an inheritance relation-

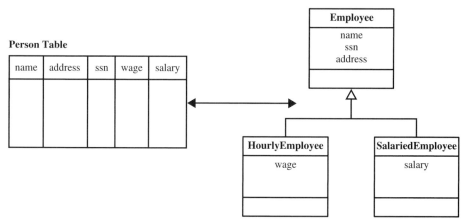

FIGURE 11-13

Table-inherited classes mapping. Instances of SalariedEmployee can be created for any row in the Person table that has a non null value for the salary column. If salary is null, the row is represented by an HourlyEmployee instance.

ship. By using the inheritance relationship in the object model, the mapping can express a richer and clearer definition of the relationships than is possible in the relational schema.

Figure 11–14 shows an example that maps a Person table to class Person and then maps a related Employee table to class Employee, which is a subclass of class Person. In this example, instances of Person are mapped directly from the Person table. However, instances of Employee can be created only for the rows in the Employee table (the joining of the Employee and Person tables on the SSN key). Furthermore, SSN is used both as a primary key on the Person table for activating instances of Person and as a foreign key on the Person table and a primary key on the Employee table for activating instances of type Employee.

11.8.6 Keys for Instance Navigation

In mapping columns to properties, the simplest approach is to translate a column's value into the corresponding class property value. There are two interpretations of this mapping: Either the column is a data value or it defines a navigable relationship between instances (i.e., a foreign key). The mapping also should specify how to convert each data value into a property value on an instance.

In addition to simple data conversion, mapping of column values defines the interpretation of relational foreign keys. The mapping describes both how the foreign key can be used to navigate among classes and instances in the mapped object model and how referential integrity is maintained. A foreign key defines a relationship between tables in a relational database. In an object model, this association is where objects can have references to other objects that enable instance-to-instance navigation.

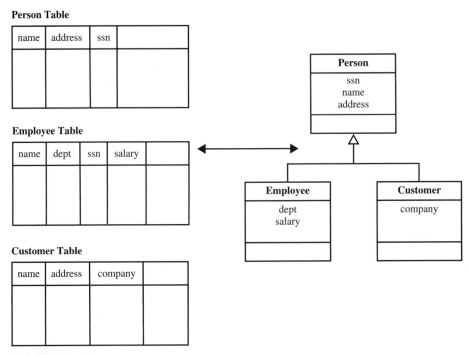

FIGURE 11–14

Tables-inherited classes mapping. Instances of Person are mapped directly from the Person table. However, instances of Employee can be created only for the rows in the Employee table (the joining of the Employee and Person tables on the ssn key). The ssn is used both as a primary key on the Person table and as a foreign key on the Person table and a primary key on the Employee table for activating instances of type Employee.

In Figure 11–15, the departmentID property of Employee uses the foreign key in column Employee.departmentID. Each Employee instance has a direct reference of class Department (association) to the department object to which it belongs.

A popular mechanism in relational databases is the use of stored procedures. As mentioned earlier, stored procedures are modules of precompiled SQL code stored in the database that execute on the server to enforce rules the business has set about the data. Mapping should support the use of stored procedures by allowing mapping of existing stored procedures to object methods.

11.9 MULTIDATABASE SYSTEMS

A different approach for integrating object-oriented applications with relational data environments is multidatabase systems or heterogeneous database systems, which facilitate the integration of heterogeneous databases and other information sources.

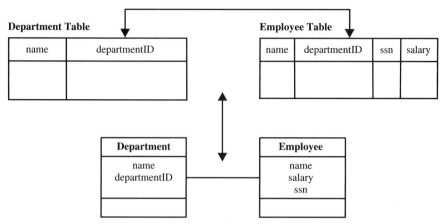

FIGURE 11–15
Class instance relationship.

Heterogeneous information systems facilitate the integration of heterogeneous information sources, where they can be structured (having regular schema), semi-structured, and sometimes even unstructured. Some heterogeneous information systems are constructed on a global schema over several databases. This way users can have the benefits of a database with a schema (i.e., uniform interfaces, such as an SQL-style interface) to access data stored in different databases and cross-database functionality. Such heterogeneous information systems are referred to as *federated multidatabase systems* [9].

Federated multidatabase systems, as a general solution to the problem of inter-operating heterogeneous data systems, provide uniform access to data stored in multiple databases that involve several different data models. A ***multidatabase system*** (MDBS) is a database system that resides unobtrusively on top of, say, existing relational and object databases and file systems (called *local database systems*) and presents a single database illusion to its users (see Figure 11–16). In particular, an MDBS maintains a single global database schema against which its users will issue queries and updates; an MDBS maintains only the global schema, and the local database systems actually maintain all user data. The global schema is constructed by consolidating (integrating) the schemata of the local databases; the schematic differences (conflicts) among them are handled by ***neutralization (homogenization)***, the process of consolidating the local schemata.

The MDBS translates the global queries and updates for dispatch to the appropriate local database system for actual processing, merges the results from them, and generates the final result for the user. Further, the MDBS coordinates the committing and aborting of global transactions by the local database systems that processed them to maintain the consistency of the data within the local databases. An MDBS actually controls multiple gateways (or drivers). It manages local databases through the gateways, one gateway for each local database.

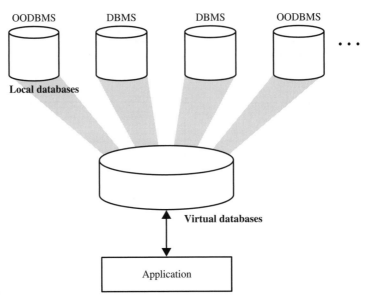

FIGURE 11–16
A multidatabase system (MDBS) is a database system that resides on top of, say existing relational and object databases and file systems (called local database systems) and presents a single database illusion to its users. In other words, users are under an impression that they are working with a single database.

To summarize the distinctive characteristics of multidatabase systems,

- Automatic generation of a unified global database schema from local databases, in addition to schema capturing and mapping for local databases.
- Provision of cross-database functionality (global queries, updates, and transactions) by using unified schemata.
- Integration of heterogeneous database systems with multiple databases.
- Integration of data types other than relational data through the use of such tools as driver generators.
- Provision of a uniform but diverse set of interfaces (e.g., an SQL-style interface, browsing tools, and C++) to access and manipulate data stored in local databases [9].

11.9.1 Open Database Connectivity: Multidatabase Application Programming Interfaces

The benefits of being able to port database applications by writing to an application programming interface (API) for a virtual DBMS are so appealing to software developers that the computer industry recently introduced several multidatabase APIs. Developers use these call-level interfaces for applications that access multiple databases using a single set of function calls, minimizing differences in application source code [10]. Open database connectivity (ODBC) is an application programming interface that provides solutions to the multidatabase programming problem. Initially proposed by Microsoft, ODBC provides a vendor-neutral mechanism for independently accessing multiple database hosts.

ODBC and the other APIs provide standard database access through a common client-side interface. It thus allows software developers to write desktop applications without the burden of learning multiple database APIs. Another ODBC advantage is the ability to store data for various applications or data from different sources in any database and transparently access or combine the data on an as-needed basis. Details of the back-end data structure are hidden from the user.

As a standard, ODBC has strong industry support. Currently, a majority of software and hardware vendors, including both Microsoft and Apple, have endorsed ODBC as the database interoperability standard. In addition, most database vendors either provide or will soon provide ODBC-compliant interfaces.

ODBC is conceptually similar to the Windows print model, where the application developer writes to a generic printer interface and a loadable driver maps that logic to hardware-specific commands. This approach virtualizes the target printer or DBMS because the person with the specialized knowledge to make the application logic work with the printer or database is the driver developer and not the application programmer. The application interacts with the ODBC driver manager, which sends the application calls (such as SQL statements) to the database. The driver manager loads and unloads drivers, performs status checks, and manages multiple connections between applications and data sources (see Figure 11–17).

FIGURE 11–17

Open database connectivity (ODBC) provides a mechanism for creating a virtual DBMS.

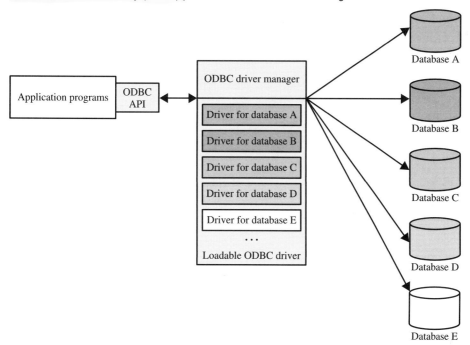

11.10 DESIGNING ACCESS LAYER CLASSES

Now that we studied DBMS, client-server, distributed objects, OODBMS relational-object systems, multidatabases, and other related technologies, we have a better appreciation for why we need an access layer.

The main idea behind creating an access layer is to create a set of classes that know how to communicate with the place(s) where the data actually reside. Regardless of where the data actually reside, whether it be a file, relational database, mainframe, Internet, DCOM, or via ORB, the access classes must be able to translate any data-related requests from the business layer into the appropriate protocol for data access. Furthermore, these classes also must be able to translate the data retrieved back into the appropriate business objects. The access layer's main responsibility is to provide a link between business or view objects and data storage. Three-layer architecture, in essence, is similar to three-tier architecture. For example, the view layer corresponds to the client tier, the business layer to the application server tier, and the access layer to the database tier of three-tier architecture (see Figure 11–18).

The access layer performs two major tasks:

1. *Translate the request.* The access layer must be able to translate any data-related requests from the business layer into the appropriate protocol for data

FIGURE 11–18

The business layer objects and view layer objects should not directly access the database. Instead, they should consult with the access layer for all external system connectivity.

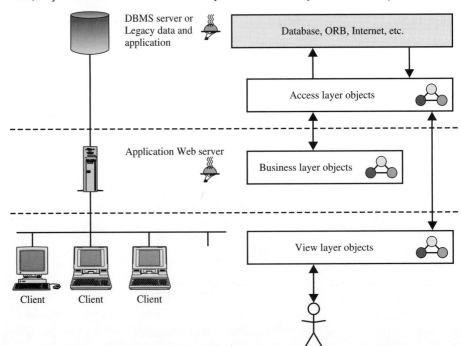

access. (For example, if customer number 55552 needs to be retrieved, the access layer must be able to create the correct SQL statement and execute it.)

2. *Translate the results.*The access layer also must be able to translate the data retrieved back into the appropriate business objects and pass those objects back into the business layer.

The main advantage of this approach is that the design is not tied to any database engine or distributed object technology, such as CORBA or DCOM. With this approach, we very easily can switch from one database to another with no major changes to the user interface or business layer objects. All we need to change are the access classes' methods. Other benefits of access layer classes are these:

- Access layer classes provide easy migration to emerging distributed object technology, such as CORBA and DCOM.
- These classes should be able to address the (relatively) modest needs of two-tier client-server architectures as well as the difficult demands of fine-grained, peer-to-peer distributed object architectures.

Designing the access layer object is the same as for business layer objects and the same guidelines apply to access layer classes, so we do not repeat them here (see Chapter 10). However, we need to deal with the following fundamental questions:

- How do we decide what access layer objects to include?
- How do access layer objects fit with business layer (or view layer) objects? Or, what is the relationship between a business class and its associated access class?

11.10.1 The Process

The access layer design process consists of the following activities (see Figures 11–19 and 11–20). If a class interacts with a *nonhuman actor*, such as another system, database, or the Web, then the class automatically should become an access class. The process of creating an access class for the business classes we identified so far follows:

1. For every business class identified, *mirror the business class package*. For every business class that has been identified and created, create one access class in the access layer package. For example, if there are three business classes (Class1, Class2, and Class3), create three access layer classes (Class1DB, Class2DB, and Class3DB).

2. *Define relationships.* The same rule as applies among business class objects also applies among access classes (see Chapter 8).

3. *Simplify classes and relationships.* The main goal here is to eliminate redundant or unnecessary classes or structures. In most cases, you can combine simple access classes and simplify the super- and subclass structures.

    3.1. *Redundant classes.* If you have more than one class that provides similar services (e.g., similar *Translate request* and *Translate results*), simply select one and eliminate the other(s).

    3.2. *Method classes.* Revisit the classes that consist of only one or two methods to see if they can be eliminated or combined with existing classes. If

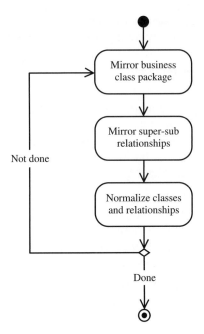

FIGURE 11–19
The process of creating access layer classes.

you can find no class from the access layer package, select its associated class from the business package and add the method(s) as a private method(s) to it. In this case, we have created an *access method*.

4. Iterate and refine.

In this process, the access layer classes are assumed to store not only the attributes but also the methods. This can done by utilizing an OODBMS or a relational database (as described in section 11.8.1).

Another approach is to let the methods be stored in a program (e.g., a compiled C++ program stored on a file) and store only the *persistent attributes*. Here is the modified process:

1. For every business class identified (see Figure 11–21), *determine if the class has persistent data*. An attribute can be either transient or persistent (nontransient). An attribute is *transient* if the following condition exists: Temporary storage for an expression evaluation or its value can be dynamically allocated. An attribute is *persistent* if the following condition exists: Data must exist between executions of a program or outlive the program. If the method has any persistent attributes, go to the next step (mirror the business class package); otherwise, the class needs no associated access layer class.

2. *Mirror the business class package.* For every business class identified and created, create one access class in the access layer package. For example, if there are three business classes (Class1, Class2, and Class3), create three access layer classes (Class1DB, Class2DB, and Class3DB).

Step 1. Mirror business class package

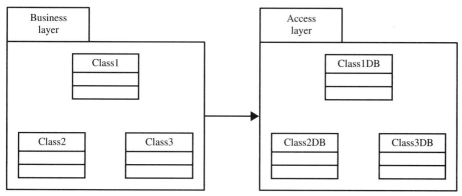

Step 2. Define relationships among access layer class

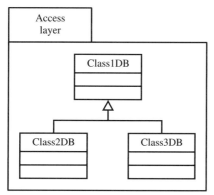

Step 3. Simplify classes and relationships

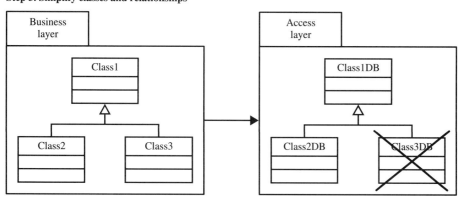

FIGURE 11–20

The process of creating access layer classes.

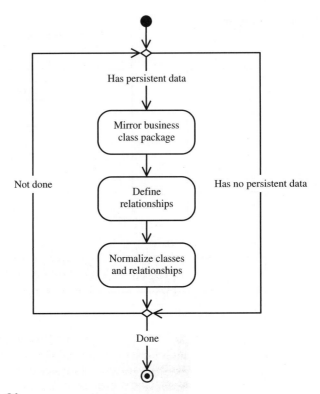

FIGURE 11–21
The process of creating access layer classes. Storing only the persistent attributes.

3. *Define relationships.* The same rule as applies among business class objects also applies among access classes (see Chapter 8).
4. *Simplify classes and relationships.* The main goal here is to eliminate redundant or unnecessary classes and structures. In most cases, you can combine simple access classes and simplify the super- and subclass structures.
   4.1. *Redundant classes.* If you have more than one class that provides similar services (e.g., similar *Translate request* and *Translate results*), simply select one and eliminate the other(s).
   4.2. *Method classes.* Revisit the classes that consist of only one or two methods to see if they can be eliminated or combined with existing classes.
5. Iterate and refine.

In either case, once an access class has been defined, all you need do is make it a-part-of its business class (see Figure 11–22).

Next, we apply this process to design the access layer classes for our bank system application. To make the problem more interesting, we use a relational database for storing the objects and the second approach in designing its access layer classes, assuming the methods will be stored in the program.

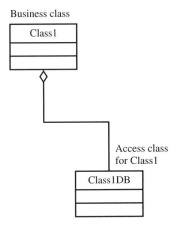

FIGURE 11–22
The relation between a business class and its associated access class.

11.11 CASE STUDY: DESIGNING THE ACCESS LAYER FOR THE VIANET BANK ATM

We are ready to develop the access layer for the ViaNet bank ATM. Remember that the main idea behind an access layer is to create a set of classes that know how to communicate with the data source. They are simply *mediators* between business or view classes and storage places or they communicate with other objects over a network through the ORB/DCOM, in the case of distributed objects.

11.11.1 Creating an Access Class for the BankClient Class

Here, we apply the access layer design process to identify the access classes.

Step 1. *Determine if a class has persistent data.*
Step 2. *Mirror the business class package.* Since the BankClient has persistent attributes, we need to create an access class for it.
Step 3. *Define relationships.*

TheBankClient class has the following attributes (see Chapter 10):

firstName
lastName
cardNumber
pinNumber
account

The firstName, lastName, cardNumber, and pinNumber are persistent attributes, and account is used to link (or implement the association among) the BankClient and Account classes. To link the BankClient table to the Account table we need to use the card number (cardNumber) as a primary key in both tables (see Figure 11–23).

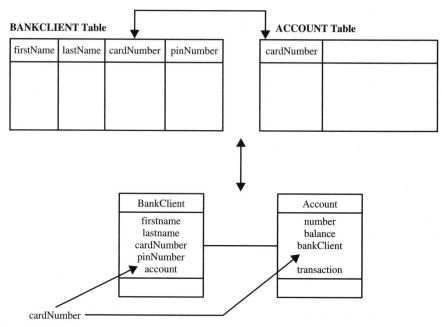

FIGURE 11–23

The cardNumber column facilitates the link between the BANKCLIENT and ACCOUNT tables. It also implements the association among the BankClient and Account classes. Note that the card-Number is a primary key for the ACCOUNT and BANKCLIENT tables.

Here we decided to create an access class instead of creating access method within the BankClient class. Let us call our access class BankDB. The purpose of this class is to save the state of the BankClient objects. In other words, it must update and retrieve the BankClient attributes by translating any data-related requests from the BankClient class into the appropriate protocol for data access.

Notice that *retrieveClient* method of BankClient object simply sends a message to the BankDB object to get the client information:

Listing 1.

```
BankClient::+retrieveClient (aCardNumber, aPIN): BankClient
     aBankDB : BankDB
     aBankDB.retrieveClient (aCardNumber, aPIN)
```

In here, all we need to do is to create an instance of the access class BankDB and then send a message to it to get information on the client object. The *retrieveClient* of the BankDB class will do the actual work of getting the information from the database. Let us assume our database is relational and we are using SQL:

Listing 2.

```
BankDB::+retrieveClient (aCardNumber, aPIN): BankClient
SELECT firstName, lastName
    FROM BANKCLIENT
        WHERE cardNumber = aCardnumber and pinNumber = aPin)
```

The *retrieveClient* return type is defined as BankClient to return the attributes of the BankClient. Access class methods (as you might guess) are highly language dependent. Remember that in actuality, during design, you have to select your implementation language. Since implementation is beyond the scope of this book and to keep the description language independent, the implementation details have been skipped for the most part. A return of null means that the supplied PIN number is not valid.

The *updateClient* method updates or changes attributes such as pinNumber, firstName, or lastName. Here again, just like the *retrieveClient* method, the BankClient::updateClient sends a message to the access class BankDB::update-Client to update client information:

Listing 3.

```
BankDB::+updateClient (aClient: BankClient, aCardNumber: String)
UPDATE BANKCLIENT
    SET firstName = aClient.firstName
    SET lastName = aClient.lastName
    SET pinNumber = aClient.pinNumber
            WHERE cardNumber = aCardnumber)
```

The Account class has the following attributes (see Chapter 10):

number

balance

bankClient

transaction

Attributes such as number and balance are persistent. The bankClient attribute is transient and is used for implementing the association between the Account and BankClient classes. We already have taken care of this link by adding *cardNumber* to the Account table. However, to link the Account table to the Transaction table, we need to add the *transID* as a foreign key to the Account table (see Figure 11–24).

Figure 11–25 shows how generalization relationships among the Account, CheckingAccount, and SavingsAccount classes have been represented in our relational database. Here, since we are using a relational database that provides no inheritance or super-sub generalization, we added four columns to the Account table: one for the savings account number (*sNumber*), one for the checking account number (*cNumber*), one for the savings balance (*sBalance*), and finally one for the checking balance (*cBalance*).

According to step 2, we need to add three more access classes: one for the Account class (AccountDB), one for the CheckingAccount class (CheckingAccountDB), and one for the SavingsAccount class (SavingsAccountDB). However, at this point, we realize that we need an access class with only four methods, two

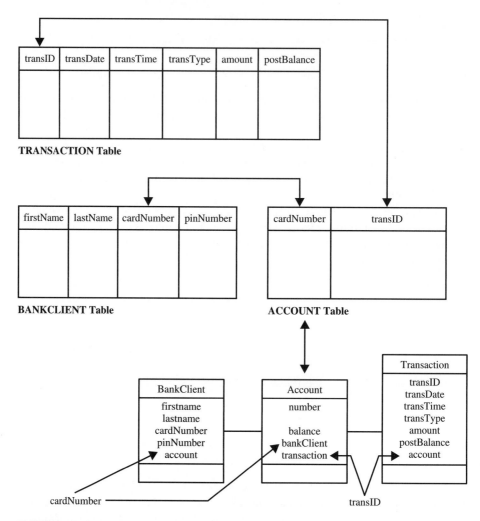

FIGURE 11–24

To represent the association between the ACCOUNT and TRANSACTION tables, we need to add transID to the ACCOUNT table as a foreign key.

methods for SavingsAccount (update and retrieve) and two methods for CheckingAccount. The Account class is an abstract class (has no instances since the accounts are either savings or checking accounts) and therefore needs no additional methods. The methods are

updateSavingsAccount
retrieveSavingsAccount
updateCheckingAccount
retrieveCheckingAccount

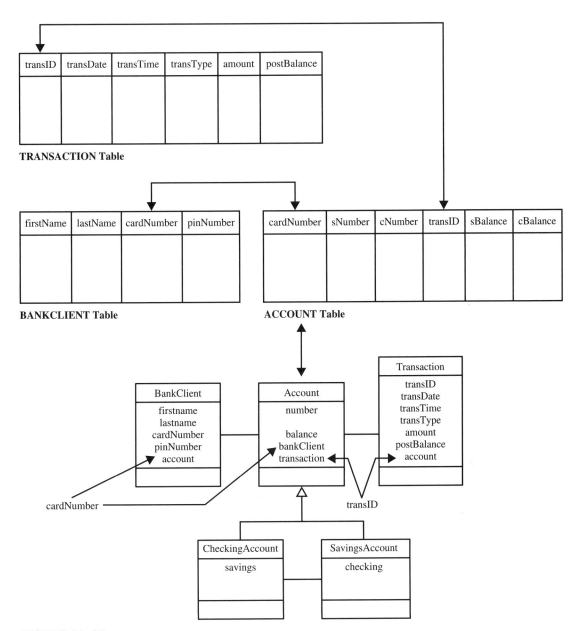

FIGURE 11–25

Four columns are added to the ACCOUNT table: one for the savings account number *(sNumber)*, one for the checking account number *(cNumber)*, one for the savings balance *(sBalance)*, and one for the checking balance *(cBalance)*. Instances of SavingsAccount and CheckingAccount can be created for any row in the ACCOUNT table that has a non null value for *sNumber* or *cNumber*.

The previous section explained that *method classes* are classes that consist of only one or two methods, and it is a good idea to combine method classes with existing access classes if it makes sense to do so. If you can find no class from the access layer package, select its associated class from the business package and create a private method(s) and add the methods to it. However, here, we add the methods to the BankDB class. After all, an Account is associated with a BankClient class and most times account and client information need to be accessed at the same time. Here *SavingsAccount::retrieveAccount* and *SavingsAccount::updateAccount* methods send messages to the access class *BankDB::retrieveSavingsAccount* and *BankDB::updateSavingsAccount* methods to perform the job. The CheckingAccount is similar (see Listings 6 and 10).

You might be wondering why *SavingsAccount::retrieveAccount* needs to use the *BankDB::retrieveSavingsAccount* to perform the job. Why does it not do the job itself? Well, *SavingsAccount::retrieveAccount* can perform this operation without calling the access class. However, if you need to switch to a different database, you must modify the method. Therefore, if you want to create an access method, make sure to make its protocol private so the impact on other classes will be minimal. For most cases, it is possible to use the access class instead of creating private access methods.

The following listing depicts the implementations of these methods:

Listing 4.

```
SavingsAccount::-retrieveAccount (): Account
bankDB.retrieveSavingsAccount (bankClient.cardNumber, number)
```

The *retrieveAccount* is an example of polymorphism (in which the same operation may behave differently on different classes), where it is overloading its superclass method by sending a message to the access class BankDB object to retrieve the savings account information. The same mechanism has been used to invoke other access class methods:

Listing 5.

```
BankDB::+retrieveSavingsAccount (aCardNumber: String, savingsNumber:
String): Account
SELECT sBalance, transID,
    FROM ACCOUNT
        WHERE cardNumber = aCardNumber and sNumber = savingsNumber)
```

Listing 6.

```
CheckingAccount::-retrieveAccount (): Account
bankDB.retrieveCheckingAccount (bankClient.cardNumber, number)
```

Listing 7.

```
BankDB::+retrieveCheckingAccount (aCardNumber: String, checkingNumber:
String): Account
SELECT cBalance, transID,
    FROM ACCOUNT
        WHERE cardNumber = aCardNumber and cNumber = checkingNumber)
```

Listing 8.

```
SavingsAccount::−updateAccount ():Account
bankDB.updateSavingsAccount (bankClient.cardNumber, number, balance)
```

Listing 9.

```
BankDB::+updateSavingsAccount (aCardPinNumber: String, aNumber: String
newBalance: float)
UPDATE ACCOUNT
    Set  sBalance = newBalance
        WHERE cardNumber = aCardNumber and sNumber = aNumber)
```

Listing 10.

```
CheckingAccount::−updateAccount ():Account
bankDB.updateCheckingAccount (bankClient.cardNumber, number, balance)
```

Listing 11.

```
BankDB::+updateCheckingAccount (aCardPinNumber: String, aNumber:
String newBalance: float)
UPDATE ACCOUNT
    Set cBalance = newBalance
        WHERE cardNumber = aCardNumber and  cNumber = aNumber)
```

Figure 11–26 depicts the relationships among the classes we have designed so far, especially the relationships among the access class and other business classes. Designing an access class for the Transaction class is left as an exercise; see problem 1.

11.12 SUMMARY

A database management system (DBMS) is a collection of related data and associated programs that access, manipulate, protect, and manage data. The fundamental purpose of a DBMS is to provide a reliable persistent data storage facility and the mechanisms for efficient, convenient data access and retrieval.

Many modern databases are distributed databases. This implies that portions of the database reside on different nodes (computers) and disk drives in the network. Usually, each portion of the database is managed by a server, a process responsible for controlling access and retrieval of data from the database portion. The server dispenses information to client applications and makes queries or data requests to the servers. Clients generally reside on nodes in the network other than those on which the servers execute.

Client-server computing is the logical extension of modular programming. The fundamental assumption of modular programming is that separation of a large piece of software into its constituent parts ("modules") creates the possibility for easier development and better maintainability.

Distributed computing is poised for a second client-server revolution, a transition to an immensely expanded client-server era. In this new client-server model, servers are plentiful instead of scarce (because every client can be a server) and

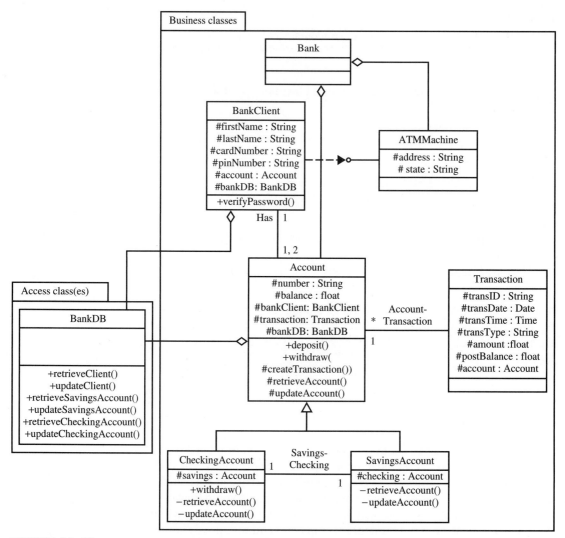

FIGURE 11–26

A still more complete UML class diagram of the ViaNet Bank ATM system. It shows the relationship of the new access class (BankDB) with the Account and BankClient business classes. Note the addition of the bankDB attributes to the Account and BankClient classes and addition of four new private methods to checkingAccount and SavingsAccount classes.

proximity no longer matters. The new generation of the client-server model is made possible by the recent exponential network growth and the progress in network-aware multithreaded desktop operating systems.

The object-oriented database technology is a marriage of object-oriented programming and database technology. The programming and database come together to provide what we call *object-oriented databases*. By combining object-oriented programming with database technology, we have an integrated application development system, a significant characteristic of object-oriented database technology. "The Object-Oriented Database System Manifesto" by Malcom Atkinson et al. describes the necessary characteristics a system must satisfy to be considered an object-oriented database. These categories can be broadly divided into object-oriented language properties and database requirements.

In practice, even though many applications increasingly are developed using object-oriented programming technology, chances are good that the data those applications need to access live in a very different universe—a relational database. To resolve such a mismatch, the application objects and the relational data must be mapped. Tools that can be used to establish the object-relational mapping processes have begun to emerge. The main process in relational-object integration is defining the relationships between the table structures (represented as schemata) in the relational database with classes (representing classes) in the object model.

A different approach for integrating object-oriented applications with relational data environments involves multidatabase systems or heterogeneous database systems, which facilitate the integration of heterogeneous databases and other information sources.

The main idea behind an access layer is to create a set of classes that know how to communicate with a data source. Regardless of whether the data actually are in a file, relational database, mainframe, or Internet, the access classes must be able to translate data-related requests from the business layer into the appropriate protocol for data access. Access layer classes provide easy migration to emerging distributed object technology, such as CORBA and DCOM. Furthermore, they should be able to address the (relatively) modest needs of two-tier client-server architectures as well as the difficult demands of fine-grained, peer-to-peer distributed object architectures.

KEY TERMS

Abort (p. 244)
Atomic type of objects (p. 253)
Atomicity (p. 244)
Commit (p. 244)
Common object request broker architecture (CORBA) (p. 251)
Data definition language (DDL) (p. 242)
Data manipulation language (DML) (p. 242)
Database management system (DBMS) (p. 237)
Distributed component object model (DCOM) (p. 252)
Distributed database (p. 245)
Distributed object computing (DOC) (p. 250)
Foreign key (p. 241)
Forward engineering (p. 255)
Homogenization (p. 261)
Meta-data (p. 239)

Multidatabase system (MDBS) (p. 261)
Neutralization (p. 261)
Object management group (OMG) (p. 251)
Object-oriented database management system (OODBMS) (p. 252)
Object request broker (ORB) (p. 251)
Persistence (p. 237)
Primary key (p. 241)
Referential integrity (p. 257)
Reverse engineering (p. 255)
Schema (p. 239)
Stored procedure (p. 257)
Structured query language (SQL) (p. 243)
Transaction (p. 244)
Tuples (p. 241)

REVIEW QUESTIONS

1. How do you distinguish transient data from persistent data?
2. What is a DBMS?
3. Is a persistent object the same as a DBMS? What are the differences?
4. What is a relational database? Explain tuple, primary key, and foreign key.
5. What is a database schema? What is the difference between a schema and meta-data?
6. What is a DDL?
7. What a distributed database?
8. What is concurrency control?
9. What is shareability?
10. What is a transaction?
11. What is a concurrency policy?
12. What is a query?
13. Describe client-server computing.
14. What are different types of servers? Briefly describe each.
15. Why do you think DOC is so important in the computing world?
16. Describe CORBA, ORB, and DCOM.
17. What is an OODBMS? Describe the differences between an OODBMS and object-oriented programming.
18. Describe the necessary characteristics that a system must satisfy to be considered an object-oriented database.
19. Describe reverse and forward engineering.
20. Describe a federated multidatabase system.
21. Describe the process of creating the access layer classes.

PROBLEMS

1. Design an access class for the Transaction class of the bank system. Try both alternatives and write a paragraph pro or con for each design. (Design it once as an access class, the second time as access methods. Compare these approaches and report on their similarities and differences.)

2. Consult the WWW to obtain information on DOC, especially comparing CORBA with DCOM. Write a research paper based on your findings.

3. Consult the WWW to obtain information on the object-relational systems and tools. Select one of the development tools, and write on your rationale for selecting that tool.

4. Consult the WWW to obtain information on OODBMS vendors. Select one of the development tools and write on your rationale for selecting that tool.

5. Consult the WWW or the library to obtain an article on objected-oriented DML and query languages. Write a paper based on your findings.

6. Consult the WWW or the library to obtain an article on the Web objects. Write a paper based on your findings.

7. Consult the WWW or the library to obtain an article on ActiveX. Write a paper based on your findings.

8. Some developments in SQL technology involve the integration of object-oriented features into mainstream commercial databases. Despite the growing number of object databases available today, there is no commercial SQL standard to create and access objects stored in such databases. OQL (object query language) and SQL3 are two separate but overlapping efforts to merge object database technology with standardized, next-generation query languages. Do research to find out more about SQL3 and OQL.

9. The ViaNet bank system wants to go on-line and create on-line banking, where customers can be connected electronically to the bank through the Internet and should be able to conduct almost the same banking transactions as they would with a regular ATM machine. The only variation from previous requirements is that they cannot withdraw cash from the ATM machine, but instead they can write electronic checks to a payee. Design the architecture for the on-line banking of the ViaNet bank.

REFERENCES

1. Atkinson, M. P.; Bailey, P. J.; Chrisholm, K. J.; Cockshott, W. P.; and Morrison, R. "An Approach to Persistent Programming." *Computer Journal* 26, no. 4 (1983), pp. 360–65.

2. Atkinson, M.; Bancilhon, F.; DeWilt, D; Dittrich, K; Maier, D.; and Zdonik. "The Object-Oriented Database System Manifesto." In *Proceedings of the First International Conference on Deductive and Object-Oriented Databases*, Kyoto, Japan, December 1989, pp. 223–40.

3. Berson, Alex. *Client/Server Architecture*. New York: McGraw-Hill, 1992.

4. Brown, A. L.; and Morrison, R. "A Generic Persistent Object Store." *Software Engineering Journal* 7, no. 2 (1992), pp. 161–68.

5. Dittrich, Klaus R. "Object-Oriented Database Systems: The Notion and Issues." Proceedings of the 1986 IEEE International Workshop on Object-Oriented Database Systems.

6. Kalakota, Ravi. comp.client-server FAQ, 1996.

7. Kalakota, Ravi; and Whinston, Andrew. *The Frontiers of Electronic Commerce*. Reading, MA: Addison-Wesley, 1995.

8. Kim, Won. *Object-Oriented Database*. Cambridge, MA: Massachusetts Institute of Technology Press, 1990.

9. Lee, Juhnyoung; and Forslund, David. "Coexistence of Relations and Objects in Distributed Object Computing." White paper, Sunrise (July 26, 1995).

10. North, Ken. "Understanding Multidatabase APIs and ODBC." *DBMS* (June 1994).

11. ONTOS, Inc. "Object/Relational Integration: How to Use Objects to Enhance Your Relational Data." White paper, 1998.

12. Rob, Peter; and Coronel, Carlos. *Database Systems—Design, Implementation, and Management*, 2d ed. Belmont, CA: Wadsworth Publishing Company, 1997.

13. Robertson-Dunn, Bernard. comp.client-server FAQ, 1996.

14. Taylor, Lloyd. comp.client-server FAQ, 1996.

15. White, Set; Cattell, Rick; and Finkelstein, Shel. "Enterprise Java Platform Data Access." *Proceedings of ACM SIGMOD International Conference on Management of Data* 27, no. 2 (June 1998).

CHAPTER 12

View Layer: Designing Interface Objects

Chapter Objectives

You should be able to define and understand

- Identifying view classes.
- Designing interface objects.

12.1 INTRODUCTION

Once the analysis is complete (and sometimes concurrently), we can start designing the user interfaces for the objects and determining how these objects are to be presented. The main goal of a user interface (UI) is to display and obtain needed information in an accessible, efficient manner. The design of the software's interface, more than anything else, affects how a user interacts and therefore experiences an application [5]. It is important for a design to provide users the information they need and clearly tell them how to successfully complete a task. A well-designed UI has visual appeal that motivates users to use your application. In addition, it should use the limited screen space efficiently.

In this chapter, we learn how to design the view layer by mapping the UI objects to the view layer objects, we look at UI design rules based on the design corollaries, and finally, we look at the guidelines for developing a graphical user interface. A *graphical user interface* (GUI) uses icons to represent objects, a pointing device to select operations, and graphic imagery to represent relationships. See Appendix B for a review of Windows and graphical user interface basics and treatments.

12.2 USER INTERFACE DESIGN AS A CREATIVE PROCESS

Creative thinking is not confined to a particular field or a few individuals but is possessed in varying degrees by people in many occupations: The artist sketches, the journalist promotes an idea, the teacher encourages student development, the

BOX 12.1

Real-World Issues on Agenda

TOWARD AN OBJECT-ORIENTED USER INTERFACE

In the mid-1980s, mainstream PC software developers started making the move from character-based user interfaces such as DOS to graphical user interfaces (GUIs). We now face the next major shift in UI design, from GUI to OOUI (object-oriented user interface).[1] Like the last software design transition, the move to OOUI requires some rethinking about how to design software, not only from the development side but also from the human computer interface side.

Why objects? Tandy Trower, director of the Advanced User Interface group at Microsoft explains that using objects to express an interface is a natural choice because we interact with our environment largely through the manipulation of objects. Objects also allow the definition of a simple, common set of interactive conventions that can be applied consistently across the interface. For example, an object has properties, characteristics, or attributes that define its appearance or state, such as its color or size. Because objects, as large as a file or as small as a single character, can have properties, viewing and editing those properties can be generalized across the interface [5].

An *object-oriented user interface* focuses on objects, the "things" people use to accomplish their work. Users see and manipulate object representations of their information. Each different kind of object supports actions appropriate for the information it represents. Typical users need not be aware of computer programs and underlying computer technology [2].

While many of the concepts are similar, object-oriented programming (OOP) and object-oriented user interfaces are not the same thing. Simply us-

ing an object-oriented language does not guarantee an OOUI; as a matter of fact, you need not use an object-oriented language to create an OOUI, but it helps. Because the concepts involved are similar, the two disciplines can be used in a complementary relationship. The primary distinction to keep in mind is that OOUI design concentrates on the objects perceived by users, and object-oriented programming focuses on implementation details, which often need to be hidden from the user.

An OOUI allows a user to focus on objects and work with them directly, which more closely reflects the user's view of doing work. This is in contrast to the traditional application-oriented or current graphical user interfaces, where users must find a program appropriate for both the task they want to perform and the type of information they want to use, start the program, then use some mechanism provided by the program, such as an Open dialog, to locate their information and use it.

OOUI UNDER THE MICROSCOPE

An object-oriented user interface allows organizing objects in the computer environment similarly to how we organize objects in the real world. We can keep objects used in many tasks in a common, convenient place and objects used for specific tasks in more specific places.

UI objects typically are represented on a user's screen as icons. Icons are small graphic images that help a user identify an object. They typically consist of a picture that conveys the object's class and a text title that identifies the specific object. Icons are intended to provide a concise, easy-to-manipulate representation of an object regardless

scientist develops a theory, the manager implements a new strategy, and the programmer develops a new software system or improves an existing system to create a better one.

Creativity implies newness, but often it is concerned with the improvement of old products as much as with the creation of a new one. For example, newly created software must be useful, it should be of benefit to people, yet should not be so much of an innovation that others will not use it. A "how to make something better" attitude, tempered with good judgment, is an essential characteristic of an effective, creative process.

BOX 12.1 (CONTINUED)

of how much additional information the object may contain. If desired, we can "open" an icon to see another view with this additional information. We can perform actions on icons using various techniques, such as point selecting, choosing an action from a menu, or dragging and dropping. Icons help depict the class of an object by providing a pictorial representation. For example, consider Windows 98 or its predecessor Windows 95, where you can click the right mouse button while selecting any object (icon) on the desktop, which will result in a menu popping up that gives access to the icon's properties and the operations possible on the icon.

Although we create and manipulate objects, many people never need to be consciously aware of the class to which an object belongs. For example, a person approaching a recliner need not stop and think, "This is a sofa, which belongs to the class chair. Therefore, I can sit on it." Likewise, a user can work with charts and come to expect that all charts will behave in the same way without caring that the charts are a subclass of the data object class.

UI classes also are very useful to you when designing an interface, because they force us to think about making clear distinctions among the classes of objects that should be provided the user. Classes must be carefully defined with respect to tasks and distinctions that users currently understand and that are useful. When the UI classes are carefully defined, these distinctions make it easy for users to learn the role of an object in performing their tasks and to predict how an object will behave.

In Chapter 2, we saw that most objects—except the most basic ones—are composed of and may contain other objects. For example, a spreadsheet is an object composed of cells, and cells are objects that may contain text, mathematical formulas, video, and so forth. Breaking down such objects into the objects from which they are composed is decomposition. The depth to which object decomposition should be supported in the interface depends entirely on what a user finds useful in performing a particular task. A user writing a report, for example, probably would not be interested in dealing with objects smaller than characters, so in this task characters would be elemental objects. However, a user creating or editing a character font might need to manipulate individual pixels or strokes. In this task, characters would be composed of pixels or strokes, and therefore a character would not be an elemental object.

WHY OOUI?

An OOUI lessens the need for users to be aware of the programming providing the functions they employ. Instead, they can concentrate on locating the objects needed to accomplish their task and on performing actions on those objects. The aspects of starting and running programs are hidden to all but those users who want to be aware of them. A user should need to know only which objects are required to complete the task and how to use those objects to achieve the desired result [2]. The learning process is further simplified because the user has to deal with only one process, viewing an object, as opposed to starting an application, then finding and opening or creating a file. Although this is the main objective of OOUI, we are a few years away from completely achieving the goal. However, a computer is a tool, and as with any other tool, it has to be learned to be used effectively. Therefore, when you can help a user by simplifying the process of learning to use a tool, you should do so.

_____

[1] However, currently we are in a transition phase between GUI and OOUI.

By bringing together, in the mind, various combinations of known objects or situations, we are using inventive imagination to develop new products, systems, or designs. It is not necessary to visualize absolutely new objects or to go beyond the bounds of our own experience. Inventive imagination can take place simply by putting together known materials (objects) in a new way. Therefore, a developer might conceive new software by using inventive imagination to combine objects already in his or her mind to satisfy user needs and requirements. As an example of this, see the Real-World Issues on Agenda "Toward an Object-Oriented User Interface."

Is creative ability born in an individual or can someone develop this ability? Both parts of this question can be answered in the affirmative. Certainly, some people are born with more creativity than others, just as certain people are born with better skills (athletes, artists, etc.) in some areas, than others. Just as it is possible to develop mental and physical skills through study and practice, it is possible to develop and improve one's creative ability.

To view user interface design as a creative process, it is necessary to understand what the creative process really involves. The creative process, in part, is a combination of the following:

1. A curious and imaginative mind.
2. A broad background and fundamental knowledge of existing tools and methods.
3. An enthusiastic desire to do a complete and thorough job of discovering solutions once a problem has been defined.
4. Being able to deal with uncertainty and ambiguity and to defer premature closure.

One aid to development or restoration of curiosity is to train yourself to be observant. You must be observant of any software that you are using. You must ask how or from what objects or components the user interface is made, how satisfied the users are with the UI, why it was designed using particular controls, why and how it was developed as it was, and how much it costs. These observations lead the creative thinker to see ways in which software can be improved or to devise a better component to take its place.

12.3 DESIGNING VIEW LAYER CLASSES

An implicit benefit of three-layer architecture and separation of the view layer from the business and access layers is that, when you design the UI objects, you have to think more explicitly about distinctions between objects that are useful to users. A distinguishing characteristic of view layer objects or interface objects is that they are the only exposed objects of an application with which users can interact. After all, view layer classes or interface objects are objects that represent the set of operations in the business that users must perform to complete their tasks, ideally in a way they find natural, easy to remember, and useful. Any objects that have direct contact with the outside world are visible in interface objects, whereas business or access objects are more independent of their environment.

As explained in Chapter 4, the view layer objects are responsible for two major aspects of the applications:

1. *Input—responding to user interaction.* The user interface must be designed to translate an action by the user, such as clicking on a button or selecting from a menu, into an appropriate response. That response may be to open or close another interface or to send a message down into the business layer to start some business process. Remember, the business logic does not exist here, just the knowledge of which message to send to which business object.
2. *Output—displaying or printing business objects.* This layer must paint the best picture possible of the business objects for the user. In one interface, this may

mean entry fields and list boxes to display an order and its items. In another, it may be a graph of the total price of a customer's orders.

The process of designing view layer classes is divided into four major activities:

1. *The macro level UI design process—identifying view layer objects.* This activity, for the most part, takes place during the analysis phase of system development. The main objective of the macro process is to identify classes that interact with human actors by analyzing the use cases developed in the analysis phase. As described in previous chapters, each use case involves actors and the task they want the system to do. These use cases should capture a complete, unambiguous, and consistent picture of the interface requirements of the system. After all, use cases concentrate on describing what the system does rather than how it does it by separating the behavior of a system from the way it is implemented, which requires viewing the system from the user's perspective rather than that of the machine. However, in this phase, we also need to address the issue of how the interface must be implemented. Sequence or collaboration diagrams can help by allowing us to zoom in on the actor-system interaction and extrapolate interface classes that interact with human actors; thus, assisting us in identifying and gathering the requirements for the view layer objects and designing them.

2. *Micro level UI design activities:*

    2.1 *Designing the view layer objects by applying design axioms and corollaries.* In designing view layer objects, decide how to use and extend the components so they best support application-specific functions and provide the most usable interface.

    2.2 *Prototyping the view layer interface.* After defining a design model, prepare a prototype of some of the basic aspects of the design. Prototyping is particularly useful early in the design process.

3. *Testing usability and user satisfaction.* "We must test the application to make sure it meets the audience requirements. To ensure user satisfaction, we must measure user satisfaction and its usability along the way as the UI design takes form. Usability experts agree that usability evaluation should be part of the development process rather than a post-mortem or forensic activity. Despite the importance of usability and user satisfaction, many system developers still fail to pay adequate attention to usability, focusing primarily on functionality" [4, pp. 61–62]. In too many cases, usability still is not given adequate consideration. Adoption of usability in the later stages of the life cycle will not produce sufficient improvement of overall quality. We will study how to develop user satisfaction and usability in Chapter 14.

4. *Refining and iterating the design.*

12.4 MACRO-LEVEL PROCESS: IDENTIFYING VIEW CLASSES BY ANALYZING USE CASES

The interface object handles all communication with the actor but processes no business rules or object storage activities. In essence, the interface object will operate as a buffer between the user and the rest of the business objects [3]. The interface object is responsible for behavior related directly to the tasks involving contact with actors. Interface objects are unlike business objects, which lie inside the business layer and involve no interaction with actors. For example, computing employee overtime is an example of a business object service. However, the data entry for the employee overtime is an interface object.

Jacobson, Ericsson, and Jacobson explain that an interface object can participate in several use cases. Often, the interface object has a coordinating responsibility in the process, at least responsibility for those tasks that come into direct contact with the user. As explained in earlier chapters, the first step here is to begin with the use cases, which help us to understand the users' objectives and tasks. Different users have different needs; for example, advanced, or "power," users want efficiency whereas other users may want ease of use. Similarly, users with disabilities or in an international market have still different requirements. The challenge is to provide efficiency for advanced users without introducing complexity for less-experienced users. However, developing use cases for advanced as well as less-experienced users might lead you to solutions such as shortcuts to support more advanced users.

The view layer macro process consists of two steps:

1. For every class identified (see Figure 12–1), *determine if the class interacts with a human actor*. If so, perform the following; otherwise, move to the next class.
   1.1 *Identify the view (interface) objects for the class*. Zoom in on the view objects by utilizing sequence or collaboration diagrams to identify the interface objects, their responsibilities, and the requirements for this class.
   1.2 *Define the relationships among the view (interface) objects*. The interface objects, like access classes, for the most part, are associated with the business classes. Therefore, you can let business classes guide you in defining the relationships among the view classes. Furthermore, the same rule as applies in identifying relationships among business class objects also applies among interface objects (see Chapter 8).
2. Iterate and refine.

The advantage of utilizing use cases in identifying and designing view layer objects is that the focus centers on the user, and including users as part of the planning and design is the best way to ensure accommodating them. Once the interface objects have been identified, we must identify the basic components or objects used in the user tasks and the behavior and the characteristics that differentiate each kind of object, including the relationships of interface objects to each other and to the user. Also identify the actions performed, the objects to which they apply, and the state information or attributes that each object in the task must preserve, display, and allow to be edited. Figure 12–2 shows the relationships among business, access, and view layer objects. The relationships among view class and business class objects is opposite of that among business class and access class objects. After all, the interface object handles all communication with the user but does not process any business rules; that will be done by the business objects.

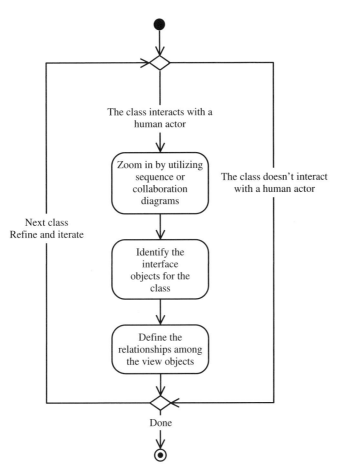

FIGURE 12–1
The macro-level design process.

Effective interface design is more than just following a set of rules. It also involves early planning of the interface and continued work through the software development process. The process of designing the user interface involves clarifying the specific needs of the application, identifying the use cases and interface objects, and then devising a design that best meets users' needs. The remainder of this chapter describes the micro-level UI design process and the issues involved.

12.5 MICRO-LEVEL PROCESS

To be successful, the design of the view layer objects must be user driven or user centered. A *user-centered interface* replicates the user's view of doing things by providing the outcomes users expect for any action. For example, if the goal of an

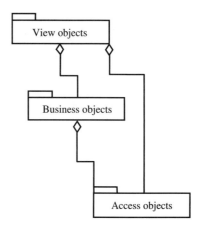

FIGURE 12–2
The relationships among business, access, and view objects. In some situations the view class can become a direct aggregate of the access object, as when designing a Web interface that must communicate with an application/Web server through access objects. See also Figure 11–18.

application is to automate what was a paper process, then the tool should be simple and natural. Design your application so it allows users to apply their previous real-world knowledge of the paper process to the application interface. Your design then can support this work environment and goal. After all, the main goal of view layer design is to address users' needs.

The following is the process of designing view (interface) objects:

1. For every interface object identified in the macro UI design process (see Figure 12–3), *apply micro-level UI design rules and corollaries to develop the UI.* Apply design rules and GUI guidelines to design the UI for the interface objects identified.
2. Iterate and refine.

In the following sections, we look at the three UI design rules based on the design axioms and corollaries of Chapter 9.

12.5.1 UI Design Rule 1. Making the Interface Simple (Application of Corollary 2)

First and foremost, your user interface should be so simple that users are unaware of the tools and mechanisms that make the application work. As applications become more complicated, users must have an even simpler interface, so they can learn new applications more easily. Today's car engines are so complex that they have onboard computers and sophisticated electronics. However, the driver interface remains simple: The driver needs only a steering wheel and the gas and brake pedals to operate a car. Drivers do not have to understand what is under the hood or even be aware of it to drive a car, because the driver interface remains simple. The UI should provide the same simplicity for users.

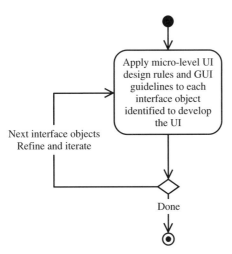

FIGURE 12–3
The micro-level design process.

This rule is an application of Corollary 2 (single purpose, see Chapter 9) in UI design. Here, it means that each UI class must have a single, clearly defined purpose. Similarly, when you document, you should be able easily to describe the purpose of the UI class with a few sentences. Furthermore, we have all heard the acronym KISS (Keep It Simple, Stupid). Maria Capucciati, an expert in user interface design and standards, has a better acronym for KISS—Keep It Simple and Straightforward. She says that, once you know what fields or choices to include in your application, ask yourself if they really are necessary. Labels, static text, check boxes, group boxes, and option buttons often clutter the interface and take up twice the room mandated by the actual data. If a user cannot sit before one of your screens and figure out what to do without asking a multitude of questions, your interface is not simple enough; ideally, in the final product, all the problems will have been solved.

A number of additional factors may affect the design of your application. For example, deadlines may require you to deliver a product to market with a minimal design process, or comparative evaluations may force you to consider additional features. Remember that additional features and shortcuts can affect the product. There is no simple equation to determine when a design trade-off is appropriate. So, in evaluating the impact, consider the following:

- Every additional feature potentially affects the performance, complexity, stability, maintenance, and support costs of an application.
- It is harder to fix a design problem after the release of a product because users may adapt, or even become dependent on, a peculiarity in the design.
- Simplicity is different from being simplistic. Making something simple to use often requires a good deal of work and code.
- Features implemented by a small extension in the application code do not necessarily have a proportional effect in a user interface. For example, if the primary

task is selecting a single object, extending it to support selection of multiple objects could make the frequent, simple task more difficult to carry out. Designing a UI based on its purpose will be explained in the next section.

12.5.2 UI Design Rule 2. Making the Interface Transparent and Natural (Application of Corollary 4)

The user interface should be so intuitive and natural that users can anticipate what to do next by applying their previous knowledge of doing tasks without a computer. An application, therefore, should reflect a real-world model of the users' goals and the tasks necessary to reach those goals.

The second UI rule is an application of Corollary 4 (strong mapping) in UI design. Here, this corollary implies that there should be strong mapping between the user's view of doing things and UI classes. A *metaphor*, or analogy, relates two otherwise unrelated things by using one to denote the other (such as a question mark to label a Help button). For example, writers use metaphors to help readers understand a conceptual image or model of the subject. This principle also applies to UI design. Using metaphors is a way to develop the users' conceptual model of an application. Familiar metaphors can assist the users to transfer their previous knowledge from their work environment to the application interface and create a strong mapping between the users' view and the UI objects. You must be careful in choosing a metaphor to make sure it meets the expectations users have because of their real-world experience. Often an application design is based on a single metaphor. For example, billing, insurance, inventory, and banking applications can represent forms that are visually equivalent to the paper forms users are accustomed to seeing.

The UI should not make users focus on the mechanics of an application. A good user interface does not bother the user with mechanics. Computers should be viewed as a tool for completing tasks, as a car is a tool for getting from one place to another. Users should not have to know how an application works to get a task done, as they should not have to know how a car engine works to get from one place to another. A goal of user interface design is to make the user interaction with the computer as simple and natural as possible.

12.5.3 UI Design Rule 3. Allowing Users to Be in Control of the Software (Application of Corollary 1)

The third UI design rule states that the users always should feel in control of the software, rather than feeling controlled by the software. This concept has a number of implications. The first implication is the operational assumption that actions are started by the user rather than the computer or software, that the user plays an active rather than reactive role. Task automation and constraints still are possible, but you should implement them in a balanced way that allows the user freedom of choice.

The second implication is that users, because of their widely varying skills and preferences, must be able to customize aspects of the interface. The system software provides user access to many of these aspects. The software should reflect user settings for different system properties such as color, fonts, or other options.

The final implication is that the software should be as interactive and responsive as possible. Avoid modes whenever possible. A *mode* is a state that excludes general interaction or otherwise limits the user to specific interactions. Users are in control when they are able to switch from one activity to another, change their minds easily, and stop activities they no longer want to continue. Users should be able to cancel or suspend any time-consuming activity without causing disastrous results. There are situations in which modes are useful; for example, selecting a file name before opening it. The dialog that gets me the file name must be modal (more on this later in the section).

This rule is a subtle but important application of Corollary 1 (uncoupled design with less information content) in UI design. It implies that the UI object should represent, at most, one business object, perhaps just some services of that business object. The main idea here is to avoid creating a single UI class for several business objects, since it makes the UI less flexible and forces the user to perform tasks in a monolithic way. Some of the ways to put users in control are these:

- Make the interface forgiving.
- Make the interface visual.
- Provide immediate feedback.
- Avoid modes.
- Make the interface consistent.

12.5.3.1 Make the Interface Forgiving The users' actions should be easily reversed. When users are in control, they should be able to explore without fear of causing an irreversible mistake. Users like to explore an interface and often learn by trial and error. They should be able to back up or undo previous actions. An effective interface allows for interactive discovery. Actions that are destructive and may cause the unexpected loss of data should require a confirmation or, better, should be reversible or recoverable. Even within the best designed interface, users can make mistakes. These mistakes can be both physical (accidentally pointing to the wrong command or data) and mental (making a wrong decision about which command or data to select). An effective design avoids situations that are likely to result in errors. It also accommodates potential user errors and makes it easy for the user to recover. Users feel more comfortable with a system when their mistakes do not cause serious or irreversible results.

12.5.3.2 Make the Interface Visual Design the interface so users can see, rather than recall, how to proceed. Whenever possible, provide users a list of items from which to choose, instead of making them remember valid choices.

12.5.3.3 Provide Immediate Feedback Users should never press a key or select an action without receiving immediate visual or audible feedback or both. When the cursor is on a choice, for example, the color, emphasis, and selection indicators show users they can select that choice. After users select a choice, the color, emphasis, and selection indicators change to show users their choice is selected.

12.5.3.4 Avoid Modes   Users are in a mode whenever they must cancel what they are doing before they can do something else or when the same action has different results in different situations. Modes force users to focus on the way an application works, instead of on the task they want to complete. Modes, therefore, interfere with users' ability to use their conceptual model of how the application should work. It is not always possible to design a modeless application; however, you should make modes an exception and limit them to the smallest possible scope. Whenever users are in a mode, you should make it obvious by providing good visual cues. The method for ending the mode should be easy to learn and remember. These are some of the modes that can be used in the user interface:

- *Modal dialog.* Sometimes an application needs information to continue, such as the name of a file into which users want to save something. When an error occurs, users may be required to perform an action before they continue their task. The visual cue for modal dialog is a color boundary for the dialog box that contains the modal dialog.
- *Spring-loaded modes.* Users are in a **spring-loaded mode** when they continually must take some action to remain in that mode; for example, dragging the mouse with a mouse button pressed to highlight a portion of text. In this case, the visual cue for the mode is the highlighting, and the text should stay highlighted for other operations such as Cut and Paste.
- *Tool-driven modes.* If you are in a drawing application, you may be able to choose a tool, such as a pencil or a paintbrush, for drawing. After you select the tool, the mouse pointer shape changes to match the selected tool. You are in a mode, but you are not likely to be confused because the changed mouse pointer is a constant reminder you are in a mode.

12.5.3.5 Make the Interface Consistent   Consistency is one way to develop and reinforce the user's conceptual model of applications and give the user the feeling that he or she is in control, since the user can predict the behavior of the system. User interfaces should be consistent throughout the applications; for example, using a consistent user interface for the inventory application.

12.6 THE PURPOSE OF A VIEW LAYER INTERFACE

Your user interface can employ one or more windows. Each window should serve a clear, specific purpose. Windows commonly are used for the following purposes:

- *Forms and data entry windows.* **Data entry windows** provide access to data that users can retrieve, display, and change in the application.
- *Dialog boxes.* Dialog boxes display status information or ask users to supply information or make a decision before continuing with a task. A typical feature of a dialog box is the OK button that a user clicks with a mouse to process the selected choices.
- *Application windows (main windows).* An **application window** is a container of application objects or icons. In other words, it contains an entire application with which users can interact.

You should be able to explain the purpose of a window in the application in a single sentence. If a window serves multiple purposes, consider creating a separate one for each.

12.6.1 Guidelines for Designing Forms and Data Entry Windows

When designing a data entry window or forms (or Web forms), identify the information you want to display or change. Consider the following issues:

- In general, what kind of information will users work with and why? For example, a user might want to change inventory information, enter orders, or maintain prices for stock items.
- Do users need access to all the information in a table or just some information? When working with a portion of the information in a table, use a query that selects the rows and columns users want.
- In what order do users want rows to appear? For example, users might want to change inventory information stored alphabetically, chronologically, or by inventory number. You have to provide a mechanism for the user so that the order can be modified.

Next, identify the tasks that users need to work with data on the form or data entry window. Typical data entry tasks include the following:

- Navigating rows in a table, such as moving forward and backward, and going to the first and last record.
- Adding and deleting rows.
- Changing data in rows.
- Saving and abandoning changes.

You can provide menus, push buttons, and speed bar buttons that users choose to initiate tasks. You can put controls anywhere on a window. However, the layout you choose determines how successfully users can enter data using the form. Here are some guidelines to consider:

- You can use an existing paper form, such as a printed invoice, as the starting point for your design.
- If the printed form contains too much information to fit on a screen, consider using a main window with optional smaller windows that users can display on demand or using a window with multiple pages (see Figure 12–4). Users typically are more productive when a screen is not cluttered.
- Users scan a screen in the same way they read a page of a book, from left to right and top to bottom. In general, put required or frequently entered information toward the top and left side of the form, entering optional or seldom-entered information toward the bottom and right side. For example, on a window for entering inventory data, the inventory number and item name might best be placed in the upper-left corner, while the signature could appear lower and to the right (see Figure 12–5).
- When information is positioned vertically, align fields at their left edges (in Western countries). This usually makes it easier for the user to scan the information.

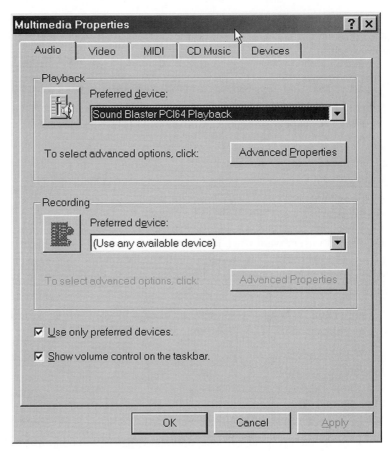

FIGURE 12–4
An example of a dialog box with multiple pages in the Microsoft multimedia setup.

Text labels usually are left aligned and placed above or to the left of the areas to which they apply. When placing text labels to the left of text box controls, align the height of the text with text displayed in the text box (see Figure 12–6).

- When entering data, users expect to type information from left to right and top to bottom, as if they were using a typewriter (usually the Tab key moves the focus from one control to another). Arrange controls in the sequence users expect to enter data. However, you may want the users to be able to jump from one group of controls to the beginning of another group, skipping over individual controls. For example, when entering address information, users expect to enter the Address, City, State, and Zip Code (see Figure 12–7).

- Put similar or related information together, and use visual effects to emphasize the grouping. For example, you might want to put a company's billing and shipping address information in separate groups. To emphasize a group, you can enclose its controls in a distinct visual area using a rectangle, lines, alignment, or colors (see Figure 12–4).

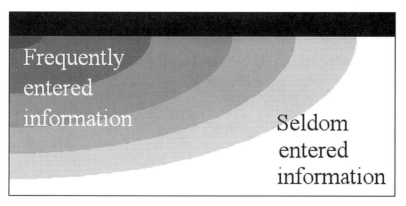

FIGURE 12–5

Required information should be put toward the top and left side of the form, entering optional or seldom entered information toward the bottom.

FIGURE 12–6

Place text labels to the left of text box controls, align the height of the text with text displayed in the text box.

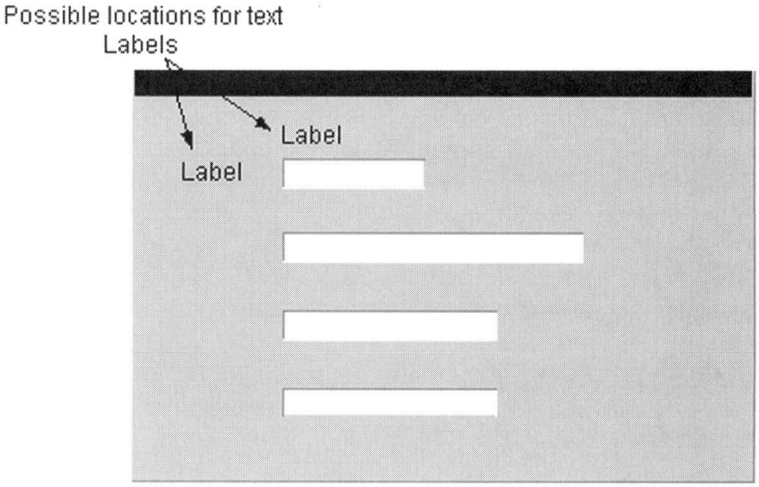

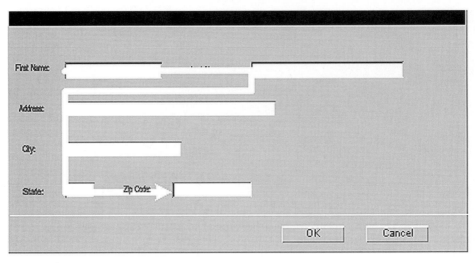

FIGURE 12–7
Arrange controls left to right and top to bottom.

The Real-World Issues on Agenda "Future of the GUI Landscape" examines window presentations for the future.

12.6.2 Guidelines for Designing Dialog Boxes and Error Messages

A dialog box provides an exchange of information or a dialog between the user and the application. Because dialog boxes generally appear after a particular menu item (including pop-up or cascading menu items) or a command button, define the title text to be the name of the associated command from the menu item or command button. However, do not include ellipses and avoid including the command's menu title unless necessary to compose a reasonable title for the dialog box. For example, for a Print command on the File Menu, define the dialog box window's title text as Print, Not Print . . ., or File Print.

If the dialog box is for an error message, use the following guidelines:

- Your error message should be positive. For example instead of displaying "You have typed an illegal date format," display the message "Enter date format mm/dd/yyyy."[2]
- Your error message should be constructive. For example, avoid messages such as "You should know better! Use the OK button"; instead display "Press the Undo button and try again." The users should feel as if they are controlling the system rather than the software is controlling them.

---

[2] Note: Sometimes, an innocent design decision (such as representing date as mm/dd/yy) can have immense implications. The case in point is the Y2K (year 2000) problem, where for many computer and software systems, the year 2000 will bring a host of problems related to software programs that were designed to record the year using only the last two digits.

BOX 12.2

Real-World Issues on Agenda

FUTURE OF THE GUI LANDSCAPE: 3-D OR FLATLAND?

Stephanie Wilkinson

Not so long ago, using icons, windows and drop-down menus to navigate applications was a radical idea for corporate systems builders. Today, that GUI is all but ubiquitous. But what will the GUI of tomorrow look like?

If the visionaries had their way, corporate PC users would interact with their computers in a wholly naturalistic way. They'd never need help screens to explain an icon or find a file or launch an application. Everything would appear "virtually real." Everything would be three-dimensional.

"The GUI interface of today is a vast two-dimensional flatland," says John Latta, president of 4th Wave Inc., an Alexandria, Va., research firm. "3-D is a portal to the next generation."

3-D isn't just for games anymore. Corporate IT departments are awakening to the power of data visualization, next-generation GUIs and of course, the lure of the Web. Here's the business justification for going 3-D:

Because 3-D environments are more like real life, workers can perform tasks more easily and with less training. 3-D interfaces trade cognitive effort for simple perception: instead of having to mull over how to attach a document to a memo using commands or icons, the user chooses a stapler on the desktop.

More information can be presented—and understood—in a 3-D format than in 2-D. Example: An 80-page organizational chart can be represented in 3-D on a single screen. The hierarchical and lateral relationships between departments and employees are also instantly apparent.

3-D ratchets up the power of data mining a full notch. By using 3-D, commonplace data matrix—national widget sales in seven regions over the last three quarters, for instance—can be transformed into a full-color, animated map that allows hidden trends to emerge.

"The average office worker has to deal with vast amounts of information, most of which is not well-organized," says Robertson. A 3-D interface not only allows users to see more on screen at once, "they also see the structure of that information," he notes. For instance, the contents of a user's hard drive could appear in 3-D space, allowing the user to locate files and launch applications by zooming in on—or "foregrounding"—a particular part of the scene.

Of course, analysts such as Latta say there is no guarantee that what comes from Microsoft will become the next GUI standard. Xerox PARC itself is working on a 3-D interface technology that will eventually result in a commercial version called WebForager. And Intel Corp., which has a vision of how the task of graphics processing should take place inside the box, is readying its own set of APIs.

So there's no need to worry quite yet about choosing the next corporate GUI and making the transition to 3-D on every desktop. Says Latta: "That's probably still a few years away."

_____

By Stephanie Wilkinson, *PC Week*, September 23, 1996, Vol. 13, Number 38.

• Your error message should be brief and meaningful. For example, "*ERROR*: type check *Offending Command . . .*" Although this message might be useful for the programmer during the testing and debugging phase, it is not a useful message for the user of your system.

• Orient the controls in the dialog box in the direction people read. This usually means left to right and top to bottom. Locate the primary field with which the user interacts as close to the upper-left corner as possible. Follow similar guidelines for orienting controls within a group in the dialog box.

12.6.3 Guidelines for the Command Buttons Layout

Lay out the major command buttons either stacked along the upper-right border of the dialog box or lined up across the bottom of the dialog box (see Figure 12–8). Positioning buttons on the left border is very popular in Web interfaces (see Figure 12–9). Position the most important button, typically the default command, as the first button in the set. If you use the OK and Cancel buttons, group them together. If you include a Help command button, make it the last button in the set.

You can use other arrangements if there is a compelling reason, such as a natural mapping relationship. For example, it makes sense to place buttons labeled North, South, East, and West in a compasslike layout. Similarly, a command button that modifies or provides direct support for another control may be grouped or placed next to that control. However, avoid making this button the default button because the user will expect the default button to be in the conventional location. Once again, let consistency guide you through the design.

For easy readability, make buttons a consistent length. Consistent visual and operational styles will allow users to transfer their knowledge and skills more easily. However, if maintaining this consistency greatly expands the space required by a set of buttons, it may be reasonable to have one button larger than the rest. Placement of command buttons (or other controls) within a tabbed page implies the application of only the transactions on that page. If command buttons are placed within the window but not on the tabbed page, they apply to the entire window (see Figure 12–4).

FIGURE 12–8
Arrange the command buttons either along the upper-right border of the form or dialog box or lined up across the bottom.

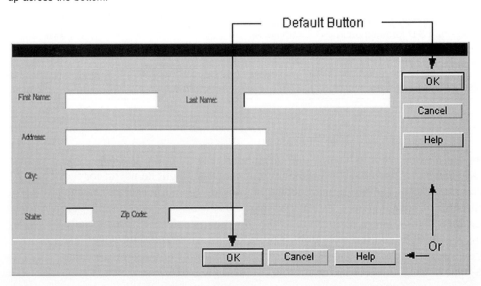

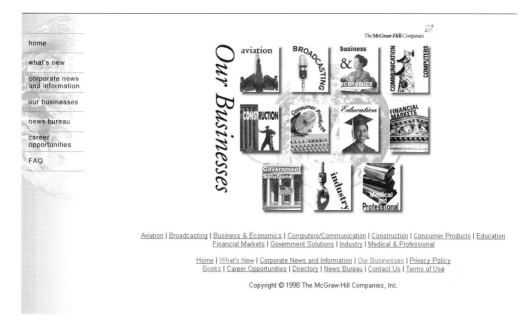

FIGURE 12–9
Positioning buttons on the left is popular in Web interfaces.

12.6.4 Guidelines for Designing Application Windows

A typical application window consists of a frame (or border) that defines its extent and a title bar that identifies what is being viewed in the window. If the viewable content of the window exceeds the current size of the window, scroll bars are used. The window also can include other components like menu bars, toolbars, and status bars.

An application window usually contains common drop-down menus. While a command drop-down menu is not required for all applications, apply these guidelines when including such menus in your software's interface:

- *The File menu.* The File menu provides an interface for the primary operations that apply to a file. Your application should include commands such as Open, Save, Save As . . ., and Print. Place the Exit command at the bottom of the File menu preceded by a menu separator. When the user chooses the Exit command, close any open windows and files and stop any further processing. If the object remains active even when its window is closed, such as a folder or printer, then include the Close command instead of Exit.
- *The Edit menu.* Include general purpose editing commands on the Edit menu. These commands include the Cut, Copy, and Paste commands. Depending on your application, you might include the Undo, Find, and Delete commands.

- *The View menu and other command menus.* Commands on the View menu should change the user's view of data in the window. On this menu, include commands that affect the view and not the data itself; for example, Zoom or Outline. Also include commands for controlling the display of particular interface elements in the view; for example, Show Ruler. These commands should be placed on the pop-up menu of the window.
- *The Window menu.* Use the Window menu in multiple document, interface-style applications for managing the windows within the main workspace.
- *The Help menu.* The Help menu contains commands that provide access to Help information. Include a Help Topics command. This command provides access to the Help Topics browser, which displays topics included in the application's Help file. Alternatively, provide individual commands that access specific pages of the Help Topics browser, such as Contents, Index, and Find Topic. Also include other user assistance commands or wizards that can guide the users and show them how to use the system. It is conventional to provide access to copyright and version information for the application, which should be included in the About Application name command on this menu. Other command menus can be added, depending on your application's needs.
- *Toolbars and status bars.* Like menu bars, toolbars and status bars are special interface constructs for managing sets of controls. A toolbar is a panel that contains a set of controls, as shown in Figure 12–10, designed to provide quick access to specific commands or options. Some specialized toolbars are called *ribbons*, *toolboxes*, and *palettes*. A status bar, shown in Figure 12–11, is a special area within a window, typically at the bottom, that displays information such as the current state of what is being viewed in the window or any other contextual information, such as keyboard state. You also can use the status bar to provide descriptive messages about a selected menu or toolbar button, and it provides excellent feedback to the users. Like a toolbar, a status bar can contain controls; however, typically, it includes read-only or noninteractive information.

12.6.5 Guidelines for Using Colors

For all objects on a window, you can use colors to add visual appeal to the form. However, consider the hardware. Your Windows-based application may end up being run on just about any sort of monitor. Do not choose colors exclusive to a particular configuration, unless you know your application will be run on that specific hardware. In fact, do not dismiss the possibility that a user will run your application with no color support at all.

Figure out a color scheme. If you use multiple colors, do not mix them indiscriminately. Nothing looks worse than a circus interface [1]. Do you have a good color sense? If you cannot make everyday color decisions, ask an artist or a designer to review your color scheme. Use color as a highlight to get attention. If there is one field you want the user to fill first, color it in such a way that it will stand out from the other fields.

FIGURE 12–10
Toolbar.

FIGURE 12–11
Status bar.

How long will users be sitting in front of your application? If it is eight hours a day, this is not the place for screaming red text on a sunny yellow background. Use common sense and consideration. Go for soothing, cool, and neutral colors such as blues or other neutral colors. Text must be readable at all times; black is the standard color, but blue and dark gray also can work.

Associate meanings to the colors of your interface. For example, use blue for all the uneditable fields, green to indicate fields that will update dynamically, and red to indicate error conditions. If you choose to do this, ensure color consistency from screen to screen and make sure the users know what these various colors indicate. Do not use light gray for any text except to indicate an unavailable condition.

Remember that a certain percentage of the population is color blind. Do not let color be your only visual cue. Use an animated button, a sound package, or a message box. Finally, color will not hide poor functionality.

The following guidelines can help you use colors in the most effective manner:

- You can use identical or similar colors to indicate related information. For example, savings account fields might appear in one color. Use different or contrasting colors to distinguish groups of information from each other. For example, checking and savings accounts could appear in different colors.
- For an object background, use a contrasting but complementary color. For example, in an entry field, make sure that the background color contrasts with the data color so that the user can easily read data in the field.
- You can use bright colors to call attention to certain elements on the screen, and you can use dim colors to make other elements less noticeable. For example, you might want to display the required field in a brighter color than optional fields.
- Use colors consistently within each window and among all windows in your application. For example, the colors for push buttons should be the same throughout.
- Using too many colors can be visually distracting and will make your application less interesting.
- Allow the user to modify the color configuration of your application.

12.6.6 Guidelines for Using Fonts

Consistency is the key to an effective use of fonts and color in your interface. Most commercial applications use 12-point System font for menus and 10-point System font in dialog boxes. These are fairly safe choices for most purposes. If System is too boring for you, any other sans serif font is easy to read (such as Arial or Helvetica). The most practical serif font is Times New Roman.

Avoid Courier unless you deliberately want something to look like it came from a typewriter. Other fonts may be appropriate for word processing or desktop publishing purposes but do not really belong on Windows-based application screens. Avoid using all uppercase text in labels or any other text on your screens: It is harder to read and feels like you are shouting at the users. The only exception is the OK command button. Also avoid mixing more than two fonts, point sizes, or styles, so your screens have a cohesive look. The following guidelines can help you use fonts to best convey information:

- Use commonly installed fonts, not specialized fonts that users might not have on their machines.
- Use bold for control labels, so they will remain legible when the object is dimmed.
- Use fonts consistently within each form and among all forms in your application. For example, the fonts for check box controls should be the same throughout. Consistency is reassuring to users, and psychologically makes users feel in control.
- Using too many font styles, sizes, and colors can be visually distracting and should be avoided. Too many font styles are confusing and make users feel less in control.
- To emphasize text, increase its font size relative to other words on the form or use a contrasting color. Avoid underlines; they can be confusing and difficult to read on the screen.

12.7 PROTOTYPING THE USER INTERFACE

Rapid prototyping encourages the incremental development approach, "grow, don't build." Prototyping involves a number of iterations. Through each iteration, we add a little more to the application, and as we understand the problem a little better, we can make more improvements. This, in turn, makes the debugging task easier.

It is highly desirable to prepare a prototype of the user interface during the analysis to better understand the system requirements. This can be done with most CASE tools,[3] operational software using visual prototyping, or normal development tools. Visual and rapid prototyping is a valuable asset in many ways. First, it provides an effective tool for communicating the design. Second, it can help you define task flow and better visualize the design. Finally, it provides a low-cost ve-

---

[3] System Architect Screen Painter can be used to prototype Windows screens and menus.

hicle for getting user input on a design. This is particularly useful early in the design process.

Creating a user interface generally consists of three steps (see Figure 12–12):

1. Create the user interface objects (such as buttons, data entry fields).
2. Link or assign the appropriate behaviors or actions to these user interface objects and their events.
3. Test, debug, then add more by going back to step 1.

FIGURE 12–12
Prototyping user interface consists of three steps.

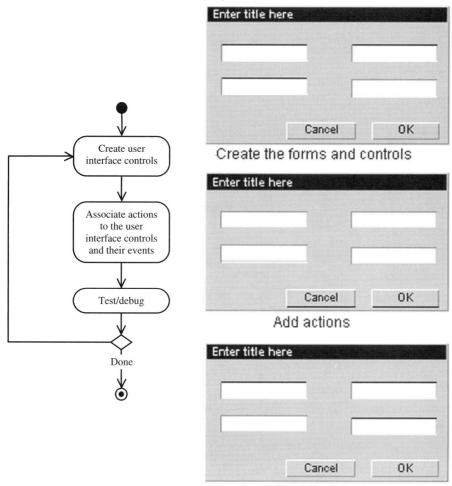

When you complete the first prototype, meet with the user for an exchange of ideas about how the system would go together. When approaching the user, describe your prototype briefly. The main purpose should be to spark ideas. The user should not feel that you are imposing or even suggesting this design. You should be very positive about the user's system and wishes. Instead of using leading phrases like "we could do this . . ." or "It would be easier if we . . .," choose phrases that give the user the feeling that he or she is in charge. Some example phrases are [5]:

"Do you think that if we did . . . it would make it easier for the users?"

"Do users ever complain about . . .? We could add . . . to make it easier."

This cooperative approach usually results in more of your ideas being used in the end.

12.8 CASE STUDY: DESIGNING USER INTERFACE FOR THE VIANET BANK ATM

Here we are designing a GUI interface for the ViaNet bank ATM for two reasons. First, the ViaNet bank wants to deploy touch-screen kiosks instead of conventional ATM machines (see Figure 12–13). The second reason is that, in the near future, the ViaNet wants to create "on-line banking," where customers can be connected electronically to the bank via the Internet and conduct most of their banking needs. Therefore, ViaNet would like to experiment with GUI interface and perhaps reuse some of the UI design concept for the on-line banking project (see Figure 12–14).

FIGURE 12–13
Touch screen kiosk.

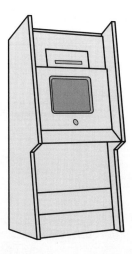

FIGURE 12–14
An example of an on-line banking project.

12.8.1 THE VIEW LAYER MACRO PROCESS

The first step here is to identify the interface objects, their requirements, and their responsibilities by applying the macro process to identify the view classes. When creating user interfaces for a business model, it is important to remember the role that view objects play in an application. The interface should be designed to give the user access to the business process modeled in the business layer. It is not designed to perform the business processing itself.

For every class identified (so far we have identified the following classes: Account, ATMMachine, Bank, BankDB, CheckingAccount, SavingsAccount, and Transaction),

- *Determine if the class interacts with a human actor.* The only class that interacts with a human actor is ATMMachine.
- *Identify the interface objects for the class.* The next step is to go through the sequence and collaboration diagrams to identify the interface objects, their responsibilities, and the requirements for this class.

In Chapter 6, we identified the scenarios or use cases for the ViaNet bank. The various scenarios involve Checking Account, Savings Account, and general bank Transaction (see Figures 6–9, 6–10, and 6–11). These use cases interact directly with actors:

1. Bank transaction (see Figure 6–9).
2. Checking transaction history (see Figure 6–9).

3. Deposit checking (see Figure 6–10).
4. Deposit savings (see Figure 6–11).
5. Savings transaction history (see Figure 6–9).
6. Withdraw checking (see Figure 6–10).
7. Withdraw savings (see Figure 6–11).
8. Valid/invalid PIN (see Figure 7–4, we have only a sequence diagram for this one).

Based on these use cases, we have identified eight view or interface objects. The sequence and collaboration diagrams can be very useful here to help us better understand the responsibility of the view layers objects. To understand the responsibilities of the interface objects, we need to look at the sequence and collaboration diagrams and study the events that these interface objects must process or generate. Such events will tell us the makeup of these objects. For example, the PIN validation user interface must be able to get a user's PIN number and check whether it is valid (see Figures 7–4 through 7–8).

Furthermore, by walking through the steps of sequence diagrams for each scenario (such as withdraw, deposit, or an account information), you can determine what view objects are necessary for the steps to take place. Therefore, the process of creating sequence diagrams also assists in identifying view layer classes and even understanding their relationships.

- *Define relationships among the view (interface) objects.* Next, we need to identify the relationships among these view objects and their associated business classes.

So far, we have identified eight view classes:

AccountTransactionUI(for a bank transaction)

CheckingTransactionHistoryUI

SavingsTransactionHistoryUI

BankClientAccessUI (for validating a PIN code)

DepositCheckingUI

DepositSavingsUI

WithdrawCheckingUI

WithdrawSavingsUI

The three transaction view objects—AccountTransactionUI, CheckingTransactionHistoryUI, and SavingsTransactionHistoryUI—basically do the same thing, display the transaction history on either a checking or savings account. (To refresh your memory, look at Figures 11–23 through 11–25 to see how we implemented this for object storage and the access class). Therefore, we need only one view class for displaying transaction history, and let us call it *AccountTransactionUI*.

The AccountTransactionUI view class is the account transaction interface that displays the transaction history for both savings and checking accounts. Figure 12–15 depicts the relation among the AccountTransactionUI and the account class. The relationship between the view class and business object is opposite of that between business class and access class. As said earlier, the interface object handles all communication with the user but processes no business rules and lets that work

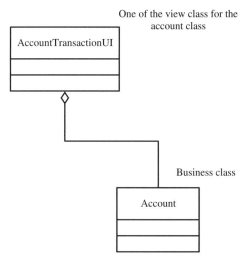

FIGURE 12–15
Relation between the view class AccountTransactionUI and its associated business class (Account).

be done by the business objects themselves. In this case, the account class provides the information to AccountTransactionUI for display to the users.

The BankClientAccessUI view class provides access control and PIN code validation for a bank client (see Figure 12–16).

The four remaining view objects are the DepositCheckingUI view class (interface for deposit to checking accounts), DepositSavingsUI view class (interface for deposit to savings accounts), WithdrawSavingsUI view class (interface for with-

FIGURE 12–16
Relation between the view class (BankClientAccessUI) and its associated business class (BankClient).

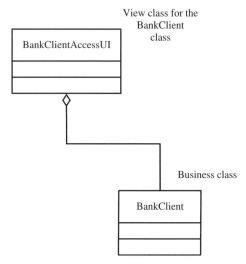

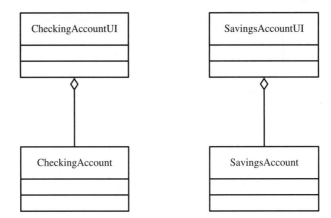

FIGURE 12–17
The view classes for checking and savings accounts.

drawal from savings accounts), and WithdrawCheckingUI view class (interface for withdrawal from savings accounts).

- *Iterate and refine.* This is the final step. Through the iteration and refinement process, we notice that the four classes DepositCheckingUI, DepositSavingsUI, WithdrawSavingsUI, and WithdrawCheckingUI basically provide a single service, which is getting the amount of the transaction (whether user wants to withdraw or deposit) and sending appropriate messages to SavingsAccount or CheckingAccount business classes. Therefore, they are good candidates to be combined into two view classes, one for CheckingAccount and one for SavingsAccount (by following UI rule 3). The CheckingAccountUI and SavingsAccountUI allow users to deposit money to or withdraw money from checking and savings accounts.

The CheckingAccountUI view class provides the interface for a checking account deposit or withdrawal (see Figure 12–17).

The SavingsAccountUI view class provides the interface for a savings account deposit or withdrawal (see Figure 12–17).

Finally, we need to create one more view class that provides the main control or the main UI to the ViaNet bank system. The MainUI view class provides the main control interface for the ViaNet bank system.

12.8.2 The View Layer Micro Process

Based on the outcome of the macro process, we have the following view classes:

BankClientAccessUI
MainUI
AccountTransactionUI
CheckingAccountUI
SavingsAccountUI

For every interface object identified in the macro UI design process,

- *Apply micro-level UI design rules and corollaries to develop the UI.* We need to go through each identified interface object and apply design rules (such as making the UI simple, transparent, and controlled by the user) and GUI guidelines to design them.
- *Iterate and refine.*

12.8.3 The BankClientAccessUI Interface Object

The BankClientAccessUI provides clients access to the system by allowing them to enter their PIN code for validation. The BankClientAccessUI is designed to work with a card reader device, where the user can insert the card and the card number should be displayed automatically in the card number field. In a situation where there is no card reader, such as on-line banking (e.g., user wants to log onto the system from home), the user must enter his or her card number (see Figure 12–18).

12.8.4 The MainUI Interface Object

The MainUI provides the main control to the ATM services. Users can select to deposit money to savings or checking, withdraw money from savings or checking, inquire as to a balance or transaction history, or quit the session (see Figure 12–19).

12.8.5 The AccountTransactionUI Interface Object

The AccountTransactionUI interface object will display the transaction history of either a savings or checking account. The user must select the account type by pressing the radio buttons. Figure 12–20 displays the account balance inquiry and transaction history interface.

FIGURE 12–18

The BankClientAccessUI interface. The buttons are enlarged to make it easier for touch screen users. The numeric keypad on the right side of the dialog box is for data entry and is not a component of the BankClientAccessUI.

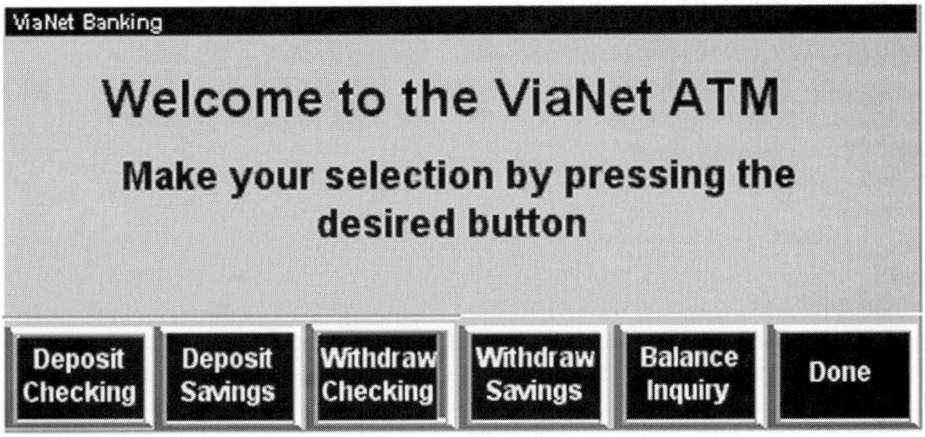

FIGURE 12–19
The MainUI interface.

FIGURE 12–20
The AccountTransactionUI interface.

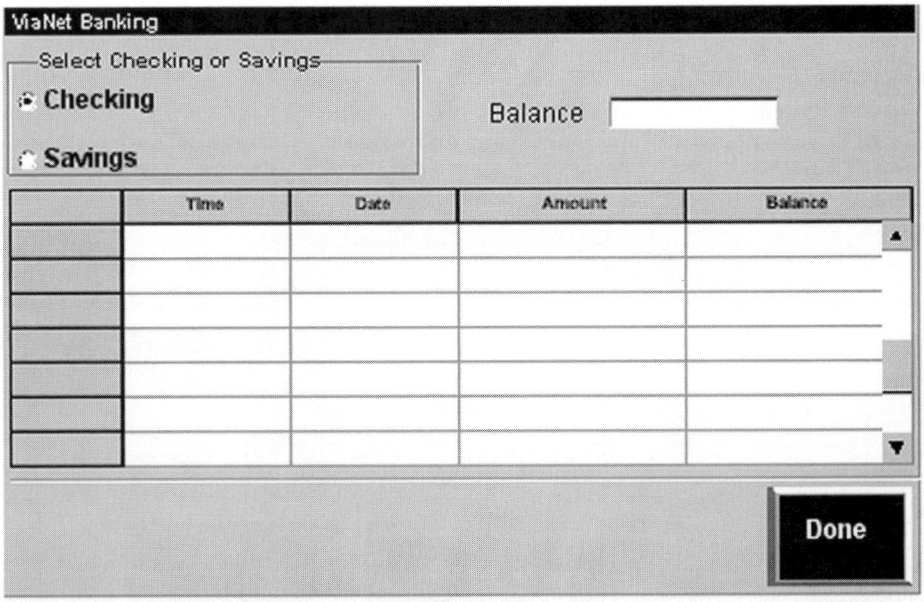

12.8.6 The CheckingAccountUI and SavingsAccountUI Interface Objects

The CheckingAccountUI and SavingsAccountUI interface objects allow users to deposit to and withdraw from checking and savings accounts. These two interfaces are designed with two tabs, one for deposit and one for withdrawal. When users press one of the MainUI's buttons, say, Deposit Savings, the SavingsAccountUI will be activated and the system should go automatically to the Deposit Savings window. Figure 12–21 displays the SavingsAccountUI and CheckingAccountUI interfaces.

See problem 8 for an alternative design for SavingsAccountUI and CheckingAccountUI classes. It always is a good idea to create an alternative design and select the one that best satisfies the requirements.

12.8.7 Defining the Interface Behavior

The role of a view layer object is to allow the users to manipulate the business model. The actions a user takes on a screen (for example, pressing the Done button) should be translated into a request to the business object for some kind of processing. When the processing is completed, the interface can update itself by displaying new information, opening a new window, or the like.

Defining behavior for an interface consists of identifying the *events* to which you want the system to respond and the *actions* to be taken when the event occurs. Both GUI and business objects can generate events when something happens to them (for example, a button is pushed or a client's name changes). In response to these events, you define actions to take. An action is a combination of an object and a message sent to it.

FIGURE 12–21

The CheckingAccountUI and SavingsAccountUI interface objects.

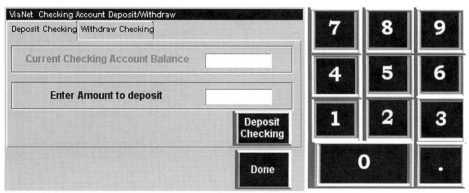

FIGURE 12-21
Continued.

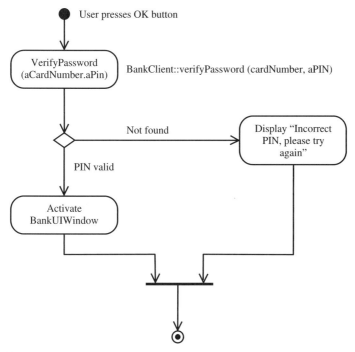

FIGURE 12–22
An activity diagram for the BankClientAccessUI.

12.8.7.1 Identifying Events and Actions for the BankClientAccessUI Interface Object When the user inserts his or her card, types in a PIN code, and presses the OK button, the interface should send the message **BankClient::verifyPassword** (see Chapter 10) to the object to identify the client. If the password is found correct, the MainUI should be displayed and provide users with the ATM services; otherwise, an error message should be displayed. Figure 12–22 is the UML activity diagram of BankClientAccessUI events and actions.

12.8.7.2 Identifying Events and Actions for the MainUI Interface Object
From this interface, the user should be able to do the following:

- Deposit into the checking account by pressing the Deposit Checking button.
- Deposit into the savings account by pressing the Deposit Savings button.
- Withdraw from the savings account by pressing the Withdraw Savings button.
- Withdraw from the checking account by pressing the Withdraw Checking button.
- View balance and transaction history by pressing the Balance Inquiry button.
- Exit the ATM by pressing Done.

Figure 12–23 is the UML activity diagram of MainUI events and actions.

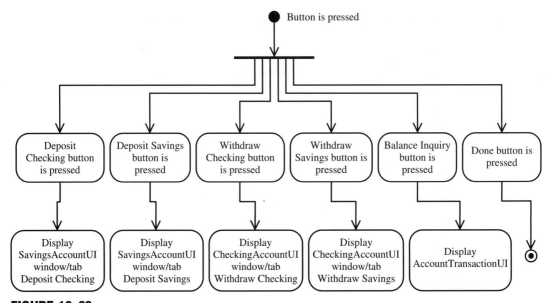

FIGURE 12–23
An activity diagram for the MainUI.

12.8.7.3 Identifying Events and Actions for the SavingsAccountUI Interface Object
The SavingsAccountUI has two tabs. First, the SavingsAccountUI opens the appropriate tab. For example, if the user selects the Deposit Savings from the MainUI, the SavingsAccountUI will display the Deposit Savings tab. Figure 12–24 shows the activity diagram for the Deposit Savings. A withdrawal is similar to Deposit Savings and has been left as an exercise; see problem 6.

FIGURE 12–24
Activity diagram for processing a deposit to a savings account.

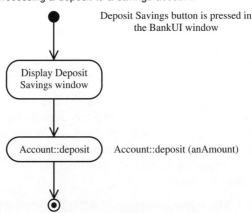

Identifying events and actions for the CheckingAccountUI interface object is left as an exercise; see problem 7.

12.8.7.4 Identifying Events and Actions for the AccountTransactionUI Interface Object

A user can select either savings or checking account by pressing on the Savings or Checking radio button. The system then will display the balance and transaction history for the selected account type. The default is the checking account, so when the AccountTransactionUI window is opened for the first time, it will show the checking account history. Pressing on the savings account radio button will cause it to display the savings account balance and history. To close the display and get back to MainUI, the user presses the Done button (see Figure 12–25). Notice that here we assume that the account has a method called displayTrans, which takes a string parameter for type of account (Savings or Checking) and retrieves the appropriate transaction. Since we did not identify or design it, we need to develop it here. This occurs quite often during software development, which is why the process is iterative.

Figure 12–26 shows the relationships among the classes we have designed so far, especially the relationship among the view classes and other business classes.

FIGURE 12–25
Activity diagram for displaying the account transaction.

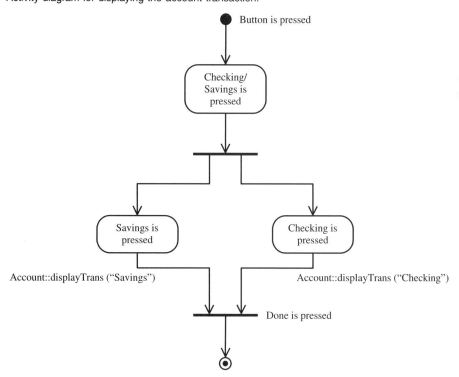

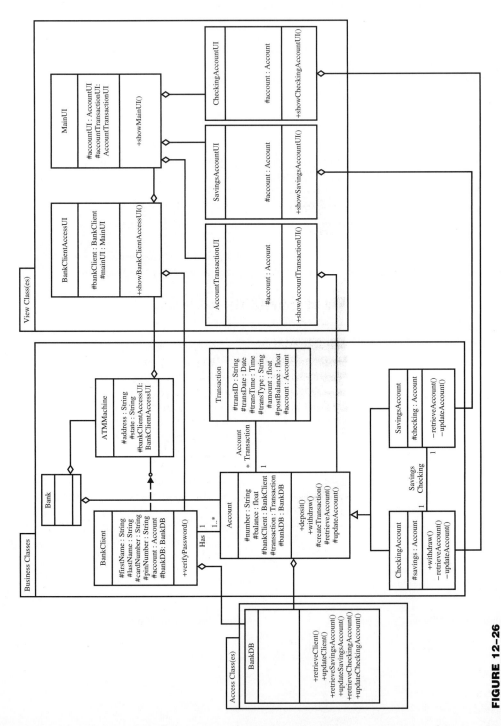

FIGURE 12–26
UML class diagram of the ViaNet ATM system, showing the relationship of the new view classes with the business and access classes.

12.9 SUMMARY

The main goal of a user interface is to display and obtain information needed in an accessible, efficient manner. The design of a software's interface, more than anything else, affects how the user interacts and, therefore, experiences the application. It is important for the design to provide users the information they need and clearly tell them how to complete a task successfully. A well-designed UI has visual appeal that motivates users to use the application. In addition, it should use the limited screen space efficiently.

In this chapter, we learned that the process of designing view layer classes consists of the following steps:

1. Macro-level UI design process: identify view layer objects.
2. Micro-level UI design activities:
    2.1. Design the view layer objects by applying the design axioms and corollaries.
    2.2. Prepare a prototype of the view layer interface.
3. Test usability and user satisfaction.
4. Refine and iterate.

The first step of the process concerns identifying the view classes and their responsibilities by utilizing the view layer macro-level process. The second step is to design these classes by utilizing view layer micro-level processes. User satisfaction and usability testing will be studied in the next chapter. Furthermore, we looked at UI design rules, which are based on the design corollaries; and finally we studied the guidelines for developing a graphical user interface (GUI).

The guidelines are not a substitution for effective evaluation and iterative refinement within a design. However, they can provide helpful advice during the design process. Guidelines emphasize the need to understand the intended audience and the tasks to be carried out, the need to adopt an iterative design process and identify use cases, and the need to consider carefully how the guidelines can be applied in specific situations. Nevertheless, the benefits gained from following design guidelines should not be underestimated. They provide valuable reference material to help with difficult decisions that crop up during the design process, and they are a springboard for ideas and a checklist for omissions. Used with the proper respect and in context, they are a valuable adjunct to relying on designer intuition alone to solve interface problems.

KEY TERMS

Application window (p. 292)
Data entry window (p. 292)
Graphical user interface (GUI) (p. 281)
Metaphor (p. 290)
Mode (p. 291)
Object-oriented user interface (OOUI) (p. 282)
Spring-loaded mode (p. 292)
User-centered interface (p. 287)

REVIEW QUESTIONS

1. Why is user interface one of the most important components of any software?
2. How can we develop or improve our creativity?
3. Perform a research on GUI and OOUI and write a short paper comparing them.
4. Why do users find OOUI easier to use?
5. How can use cases help us design the view layer objects?
6. Describe the macro and micro processes of view layer design.
7. How can metaphors be used in the design of a user interface?
8. Under what circumstances can you use modes in your user interface?
9. Describe the UI design rules.
10. What is KISS?
11. How would you achieve consistency in your user interface?
12. How can you make your UI forgiving?
13. Describe some of the ways that you can provide the user feedback.

PROBLEMS

1. A touch screen is one way to interact with the ViaNet kiosk. What are some other ways to interact with ViaNet kiosk? Use your imagination to design an interface. Also, design it for people with disability challenges.
2. Research the WWW or your local library on OOUI tools on the market and write a paper of your findings.
3. Please describe problems with the design of the window in Figure 12–27.
4. How can you improve the design of the interface in Figure 12–28?
5. The window in Figure 12–29 suffers from an overkill of radio buttons. Improve the interface by redesigning it.

FIGURE 12–27
Problem 3.

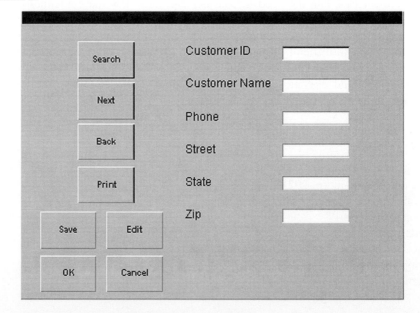

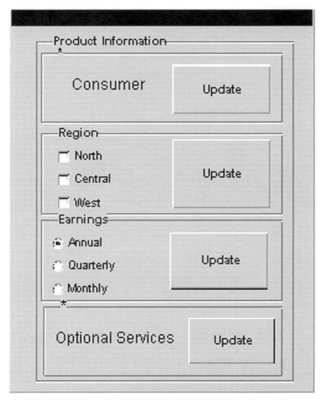

FIGURE 12–28
Problem 4.

FIGURE 12–29
Problem 5.

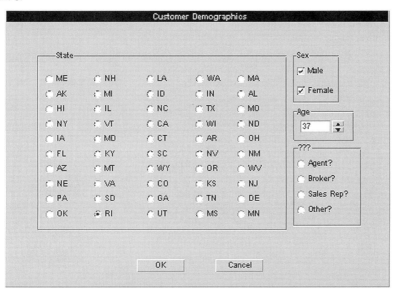

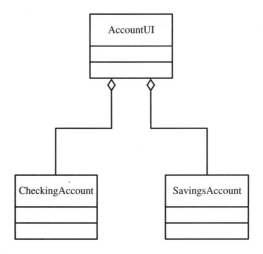

FIGURE 12–30
The AccountUI view class for both CheckingAccount and SavingsAccount classes.

6. Develop an activity diagram for Withdraw Savings.

7. Identify events and actions for the CheckingAccountUI interface object.

8. An alternative design to the ViaNet bank UI would be to create one view class (say, AccountUI) instead of separate view classes for CheckingAccount and SavingsAccount (see Figure 12–30). Figure 12–31 shows an alternative design for the AccountUI. Compare this design to the one in the text and point out advantages and disadvantages to each design.

FIGURE 12–31
An alternative design for the AccountUI interface object.

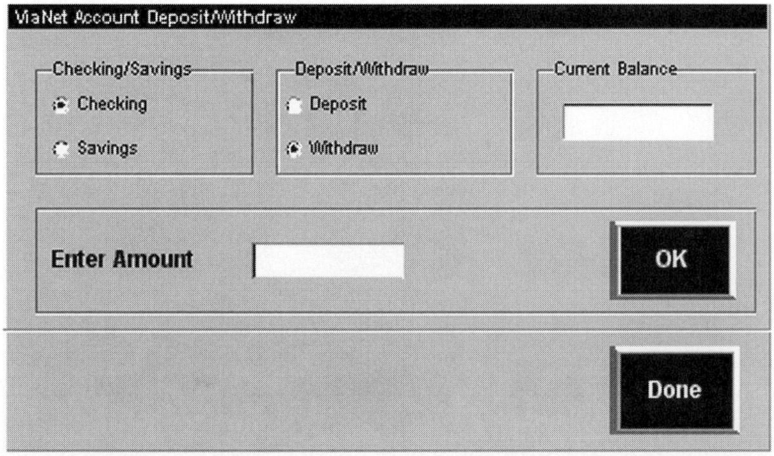

REFERENCES

1. Capucciati, Maria R. *Putting Your Best Face Forward: Designing an Effective User Interface*. Redmond, WA: Microsoft Press, 1991.
2. IBM. Human-user interaction, object-oriented user interface, http://www.ibm.com/ibm/hci, 1997.
3. Jacobson, Ivar; Ericsson, Maria; and Jacobson, Agneta. *The Object Advantage Business Process, Reengineering with Object Technology*. Reading, MA: Addison-Wesley, 1995.
4. Sulaiman, Suziah. "Usability and the Software Production Life Cycle." *Proceedings of the CHI '96, Conference Companion on Human Factors in Computing Systems: Common Ground*, Vancouver, British Columbia, 1996, pp. 61–62.
5. Trower, Tandy. *Creating a Well-Designed User Interface*. Stanford, CA: University Video Communication, 1994.

PART FIVE

SOFTWARE QUALITY

Producing high-quality software means providing users with products that meet their needs and expectations. The essence of quality is customer satisfaction. In this part, different dimensions of software quality and testing are discussed. Testing may be conducted for different reasons. Quality assurance testing looks for potential problems in a proposed design. Usability testing, on the other hand, tests how well the interface fits user needs and expectations. To ensure user satisfaction with the finished product, user satisfaction must be measured along the way as the design takes form. In this part, we also study how to develop test plans for quality assurance, user satisfaction, and software usability. Part V consists of Chapters 13 and 14.

CHAPTER 13

Software Quality Assurance

Chapter Objectives

You should be able to define and understand

- Testing strategies.
- The impact of an object orientation on testing.
- How to develop test cases.
- How to develop test plans.

13.1 INTRODUCTION

To develop and deliver robust systems, we need a high level of confidence that [2]

- Each component will behave correctly.
- Collective behavior is correct.
- No incorrect collective behavior will be produced.

Not only do we need to test components or the individual objects, we also must examine collective behaviors to ensure maximum operational reliability. Verifying components in isolation is necessary but not sufficient to meet this end [2].

In the early history of computers, live bugs could be a problem (see Bugs and Debugging). Moths and other forms of natural insect life no longer trouble digital computers. However, bugs and the need to debug programs remain.

In a 1966 article in *Scientific American*, computer scientist Christopher Strachey wrote,

Although programming techniques have improved immensely since the early years, the process of finding and correcting errors in programming—"debugging" still remains a most difficult, confused and unsatisfactory operation. The chief impact of this state of affairs is psychological. Although we are happy to pay lip service to the adage that to err is human, most of us like to make a small private reservation about our own perfor-

Bugs and Debugging

The use of the term *bug* in computing has been traced to Grace Murray Hopper during the final days of World War II. On September 9, 1945, she was part of a team at Harvard University, working to build the Mark II, a large relay computer (actually a room-size electronic calculator). It was a hot summer evening and the Mark II's developers had the window open. Suddenly, the device stopped its calculations. The trouble turned out to involve a flip-flop switch (a relay). When the defective relay was located, the team found a moth in it (the first case of a "bug"). "We got a pair of tweezers," wrote programmer Hopper. "Very carefully we took the moth out of the relay, and put it in the logbook, and put scotch tape over it."

After that, whenever Howard Aiken asked if a team was "making any numbers," negative responses were given with explanation "we are debugging the computer."

mance on special occasions when we really try. It is somewhat deflating to be shown publicly and incontrovertibly by a machine that even when we do try, we in fact make just as many mistakes as other people. If your pride cannot recover from this blow, you will never make a programmer.

Although three decades have elapsed since these lines were written, they still capture the essence and mystique of debugging.

Precisely speaking, the elimination of the syntactical bug is the process of debugging, whereas the detection and elimination of the logical bug is the process of testing. Gruenberger writes,

The logical bugs can be extremely subtle and may need a great deal of effort to eliminate them. It is commonly accepted that all large software systems (operating or application) have bugs remaining in them. The number of possible paths through a large computer program is enormous, and it is physically impossible to explore all of them. The single path containing a bug may not be followed in actual production runs for a long time (if ever) after the program has been certified as correct by its author or others. [10]

In this chapter, we look at the testing strategies, the impact of an object orientation on software quality, and some guidelines for developing comprehensive test cases and plans that can detect and identify potential problems before delivering the software to its users. After all, defects can affect how well the software satisfies the users' requirements. Chapter 14 addresses usability and user satisfaction tests.

13.2 QUALITY ASSURANCE TESTS

One reason why quality assurance is needed is because computers are infamous for doing what you tell them to do, not necessarily what you want them to do. To close this gap, the code must be free of errors or bugs that cause unexpected results, a process called *debugging*. **Debugging** is the process of finding out where something went wrong and correcting the code to eliminate the errors or bugs that cause unexpected results. For example, if an incorrect result was produced at the end of a long series of computations, perhaps you forgot to assign the correct value to a variable, chose the wrong operator, or used an incorrect formula.

Testing and searching for bugs is a balance of science, art, and luck. Sometimes, the error is obvious: The bug shows its hideous head the first time you run the application. Other bugs are stealthy and might not surface until a method receives a certain value or until you take a closer look at the output and find out that the results are off by a factor of a certain fraction or the middle initials in a list of names are wrong. There are no magic tricks to debugging; however, by selecting appropriate testing strategies and a sound test plan, you can locate the errors in your system and fix them using readily available debugging tools. A software debugging system can provide tools for finding errors in programs and correcting them. Let us take a look at the kinds of errors you might encounter when you run your program:

- *Language* (syntax) *errors* result from incorrectly constructed code, such as an incorrectly typed keyword or some necessary punctuation omitted. These are the easiest types of errors to detect; for the most part, you need no debugging tools to detect them. The very first time you run your program the system will report the existence of these errors.
- *Run-time errors* occur and are detected as the program is running, when a statement attempts an operation that is impossible to carry out. For example, if the program tries to access a nonexistent object (say, a file), a run-time error will occur.
- *Logic errors* occur when code does not perform the way you intended. The code might be syntactically valid and run without performing any invalid operations and yet produce incorrect results. Only by testing the code and analyzing the results can you verify that the code performs as intended. Logic errors also can produce run-time errors.

The elimination of the syntactical bug is the process of debugging, whereas the detection and elimination of the logical bug is the process of testing. As you might have experienced by now, logical errors are the hardest type of error to find.

Quality assurance testing can be divided into two major categories: error-based testing and scenario-based testing. **Error-based testing** techniques search a given class's method for particular clues of interests, then describe how these clues should be tested. For example, say we want to test the payrollComputation method of an Employee class: *anEmployee.computePayroll (hours)*. To test this method, we must try different values for *hours* (say, 40, 0, 100, and −10) to see if the program can handle them (this also is known as *testing the boundary conditions*). The method should be able to handle any value; if not, the error must be recorded and reported. Similarly, the technique can be used to perform integration testing by testing the object that processes a message and not the object that sends the message.

Scenario-based testing, also called *usage-based testing*, concentrates on what the user does, not what the product does. This means capturing use cases and the tasks users perform, then performing them and their variants as tests. These scenarios also can identify interaction bugs. They often are more complex and realistic than error-based tests. Scenario-based tests tend to exercise multiple subsystems in a single test, because that is what users do. The tests will not find everything, but they will cover at least the higher visibility system interaction bugs [12].

13.3 TESTING STRATEGIES

The extent of testing a system is controlled by many factors, such as the risks involved, limitations on resources, and deadlines. In light of these issues, we must deploy a testing strategy that does the "best" job of finding defects in a product within the given constraints. There are many testing strategies, but most testing uses a combination of these: black box testing, white box testing, top-down testing, and bottom-up testing. However, no strategy or combination of strategies truly can prove the correctness of a system; it can establish only its "acceptability."

13.3.1 Black Box Testing

The concept of the black box is used to represent a system whose inside workings are not available for inspection [16]. In a black box, the test item is treated as "black," since its logic is unknown; all that is known is what goes in and what comes out, or the input and output (see Figure 13–1). Weinberg describes writing a user manual as an example of a black box approach to requirements. The user manual does not show the internal logic, because the users of the system do not care about what is inside the system.

In *black box testing*, you try various inputs and examine the resulting output; you can learn what the box does but nothing about how this conversion is implemented [15]. Black box testing works very nicely in testing objects in an object-oriented environment. The black box testing technique also can be used for scenario-based tests, where the system's inside may not be available for inspection but the input and output are defined through use cases or other analysis information.

FIGURE 13–1
The black box is an imaginary box that hides its internal workings.

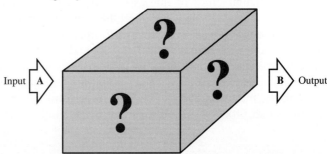

13.3.2 White Box Testing

White box testing assumes that the specific logic is important and must be tested to guarantee the system's proper functioning. The main use of the white box is in error-based testing, when you already have tested all objects of an application and all external or *public methods* of an object that you believe to be of greater importance (see Figure 13–2). In white box testing, you are looking for bugs that have a low probability of execution, have been carelessly implemented, or were overlooked previously [3].

One form of white box testing, called *path testing*, makes certain that each path in a object's method is executed at least once during testing. Two types of path testing are statement testing coverage and branch testing coverage [3]:

- *Statement testing coverage*. The main idea of statement testing coverage is to test every statement in the object's method by executing it at least once. Murray states, "Testing less than this for new software is unconscionable and should be criminalized" [quoted in 2]. However, realistically, it is impossible to test a program on every single input, so you never can be sure that a program will not fail on some input.
- *Branch testing coverage*. The main idea behind branch testing coverage is to perform enough tests to ensure that every branch alternative has been executed at least once under some test [3]. As in statement testing coverage, it is unfeasible to fully test any program of considerable size.

Most debugging tools are excellent in statement and branch testing coverage. White box testing is useful for error-based testing.

13.3.3 Top-Down Testing

Top-down testing assumes that the main logic or object interactions and systems messages of the application need more testing than an individual object's methods or supporting logic. A top-down strategy can detect the serious design flaws early in the implementation.

In theory, top-down testing should find critical design errors early in the testing process and significantly improve the quality of the delivered software because of

FIGURE 13–2

In a white-box testing strategy, the internal workings are known.

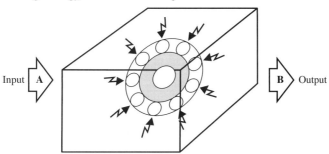

the iterative nature of the test [6]. A top-down strategy supports testing the user interface and event-driven systems.

Testing the user interface using a top-down approach means testing interface navigation. This serves two purposes, according to Conger. First, the top-down approach can test the navigation through screens and verify that it matches the requirements. Second, users can see, at an early stage, how the final application will look and feel [6]. This approach also is useful for scenario-based testing. Top-down testing is useful to test subsystem and system integration.

13.3.4 Bottom-Up Testing

Bottom-up testing starts with the details of the system and proceeds to higher levels by a progressive aggregation of details until they collectively fit the requirements for the system. This approach is more appropriate for testing the individual objects in a system. Here, you test each object, then combine them and test their interaction and the messages passed among objects by utilizing the top-down approach.

In bottom-up testing, you start with the methods and classes that call or rely on no others. You test them thoroughly. Then you progress to the next level up: those methods and classes that use only the bottom level ones already tested. Next, you test combinations of the bottom two layers. Proceed until you are testing the entire program. This strategy makes sense because you are checking the behavior of a piece of code before it is used by another. Bottom-up testing leads to integration testing, which leads to systems testing.

13.4 IMPACT OF OBJECT ORIENTATION ON TESTING

The impact of an object orientation on testing is summarized by the following [12]:

- Some types of errors could become less plausible (not worth testing for).
- Some types of errors could become more plausible (worth testing for now).
- Some new types of errors might appear.

For example, when you invoke a method, it may be hard to tell exactly which method gets executed. The method may belong to one of many classes. It can be hard to tell the exact class of the method. When the code accesses it, it may get an unexpected value. In a non-object-oriented system, when you looked at

$$x = \text{computePayroll}();$$

you had to think about the behaviors of a single function. In an object-oriented environment, you may have to think about the behaviors of *base::computePayroll()*, of *derived::computePayroll*, and so on. For a single message, you need to explore (or at least think about) the union of all distinct behaviors. The problem can be complicated if you have multiple inheritance. However, by applying the design axioms and corollaries of object-oriented design (OOD; see Chapter 9), you can limit the differences in behavior between base and derived classes.

The testing approach is essentially the same in both environments. The problem of testing messages in an object orientation is the same as testing code that takes a function as a parameter and then invokes it. Marick argues that the process of testing variable uses in OOD essentially does not change, but you have to look in more places to decide what needs testing. Has the plausibility of faults changed? Are some types of fault now more plausible or less plausible? Since object-oriented methods generally are smaller, these are easier to test. At the same time, there are more opportunities for integration faults. They become more likely, more plausible.

13.4.1 Impact of Inheritance in Testing

Suppose you have this situation [12]: The base class contains methods inherited() and redefined() and the derived class redefines the redefined() method.

The derived::redefined has to be tested afresh since it is a new code. Does derived::inherited() have to be retested? If it uses redefined() and the redefined() has changed, the derived::inherited() may mishandle the new behavior. So, it needs new tests even though the derived::inherited() itself has not changed.

If the base::inherited has been changed, the derived::inherited() may not have to be completely tested. Whether it does depends on the base methods; otherwise, it must be tested again. The point here is that, if you do not follow the OOD guidelines, especially if you don't test incrementally, you will end up with objects that are extremely hard to debug and maintain.

13.4.2 Reusability of Tests

If base::redefined() and derived::redefined() are two different methods with different protocols and implementations, each needs a different set of test requirements derived from the use cases, analysis, design, or implementation. But the methods are likely to be similar. Their sets of test requirements will overlap. The better the OOD, the greater is the overlap. You need to write new tests only for those derived::redefined requirements not satisfied by the base::redefined tests. If you have to apply the base::redefined tests to objects of the class "derived," the test inputs may be appropriate for both classes but the expected results might differ in the derived class [12].

Marick argues that the simpler is a test, the more likely it is to be reusable in subclasses. But simple tests tend to find only the faults you specifically target; complex tests are better at both finding those faults and stumbling across others by sheer luck. There is a trade-off here, one of many between simple and complex tests.

The models developed for analysis and design should be used for testing as well. For example, the class diagram describes relationships between objects; that is, an object of one class may use or contain an object of another class, which is useful information for testing. Furthermore, the use-case diagram and the highest level class diagrams can benefit the scenario-based testing. Since a class diagram shows the inheritance structure, which is important information for error-based testing, it can be used not only during analysis but also during testing.

13.5 TEST CASES

To have a comprehensive testing scheme, the test must cover all methods or a good majority of them. All the services of your system must be checked by at least one test. To test a system, you must construct some test input cases, then describe how the output will look. Next, perform the tests and compare the outcome with the expected output. The good news is that the use cases developed during analysis can be used to describe the usage test cases. After all, tests always should be designed from specifications and not by looking at the product! Myers describes the objective of testing as follows [13]:

- Testing is the process of executing a program with the intent of finding errors.
- A good test case is the one that has a high probability of detecting an as-yet undiscovered error.
- A successful test case is the one that detects an as-yet undiscovered error.

13.5.1 Guidelines for Developing Quality Assurance Test Cases

Gause and Weinberg provide a wonderful example to highlight the essence of a test case. Say, we want to test our new and improved "Superchalk":

> Writing a geometry lesson on a blackboard is clearly normal use for Superchalk. Drawing on clothing is not normal, but is quite reasonable to expect. Eating Superchalk may be unreasonable, but the design will have to deal with this issue in some way, in order to prevent lawsuits. No single failure of requirements work leads to more lawsuits than the confident declaration. [8, p. 252]

Basically, a test case is a set of what-if questions. Freedman [Weinberg][7] and Thomas [14] have developed guidelines that have been adapted for the UA:

- Describe which feature or service (external or internal) your test attempts to cover.
- If the test case is based on a use case (i.e., this is a usage test), it is a good idea to refer to the use-case name. Remember that the use cases are the source of test cases. In theory, the software is supposed to match the use cases, not the reverse. As soon as you have enough of use cases, go ahead and write the test plan for that piece.
- Specify what you are testing and which particular feature (methods). Then, specify what you are going to do to test the feature and what you expect to happen.
- Test the normal use of the object's methods.
- Test the abnormal but reasonable use of the object's methods.
- Test the abnormal and unreasonable use of the object's methods.
- Test the boundary conditions. For example, if an edit control accepts 32 characters, try 33, then try 40. Also specify when you expect error dialog boxes, when you expect some default event, and when functionality still is being defined.
- Test objects' interactions and the messages sent among them. If you have developed sequence diagrams, they can assist you in this process.
- When the revisions have been made, document the cases so they become the starting basis for the follow-up test.
- Attempting to reach agreement on answers generally will raise other what-if questions. Add these to the list and answer them, repeat the process until the list is stabilized, then you need not add any more questions.

- The internal quality of the software, such as its reusability and extendability, should be assessed as well. Although the reusability and extendability are more difficult to test, nevertheless they are extremely important. Software reusability rarely is practiced effectively. The organizations that will survive in the 21st century will be those that have achieved high levels of reusability—anywhere from 70–80 percent or more [5]. Griss [9] argues that, although reuse is widely desired and often the benefit of utilizing object technology, many object-oriented reuse efforts fail because of too narrow a focus on technology rather than the policies set forth by an organization. He recommends an institutionalized approach to software development, in which software assets intentionally are created or acquired to be reusable. These assets then are consistently used and maintained to obtain high levels of reuse, thereby optimizing the organization's ability to produce high-quality software products rapidly and effectively. Your test case may measure what percentage of the system has been reused, say, measured in terms of reused lines of code as opposed to new lines of code written.

Specifying results is crucial in developing test cases. You should test cases that are supposed to fail. During such tests, it is a good idea to alert the person running them that failure is expected. Say, we are testing a File Open feature. We need to specify the result as follows:

1. Drop down the File menu and select Open.
2. Try opening the following types of files:
   - A file that is there (should work).
   - A file that is not there (should get an *Error* message).
   - A file name with international characters (should work).
   - A file type that the program does not open (should get a message or conversion dialog box).

13.6 TEST PLAN

On paper, it may seem that everything will fall into place with no preparation and a bug-free product will be shipped. However, in the real world, it may be a good idea to use a test plan to find bugs and remove them. A dreaded and frequently overlooked activity in software development is writing the test plan. A ***test plan*** is developed to detect and identify potential problems before delivering the software to its users. Your users might demand a test plan as one item delivered with the program. In other cases, no test plan is required, but that does not mean you should not have one. A test plan offers a road map for testing activities, whether usability, user satisfaction, or quality assurance tests. It should state the test objectives and how to meet them.

The test plan need not be very large; in fact, devoting too much time to the plan can be counterproductive. The following steps are needed to create a test plan:

1. *Objectives of the test*. Create the objectives and describe how to achieve them. For example, if the objective is usability of the system, that must be stated and also how to realize it. (Usability testing will be covered in Chapter 14.)

2. *Development of a test case*. Develop test data, both input and expected output, based on the domain of the data and the expected behaviors that must be tested (more on this in the next section).
3. *Test analysis*. This step involves the examination of the test output and the documentation of the test results. If bugs are detected, then this is reported and the activity centers on debugging. After debugging, steps 1 through 3 must be repeated until no bugs can be detected.

All passed tests should be repeated with the revised program, called ***regression testing***, which can discover errors introduced during the debugging process. When sufficient testing is believed to have been conducted, this fact should be reported, and testing for this specific product is complete [3].

According to Tamara Thomas [14], the test planner at Microsoft, a good test plan is one of the strongest tools you might have. It gives you the chance to be clear with other groups or departments about what will be tested, how it will be tested, and the intended schedule. Thomas explains that, with a good, clear test plan, you can assign testing features to other people in an efficient manner. You then can use the plan to track what has been tested, who did the testing, and how the testing was done. You also can use your plan as a checklist, to make sure that you do not forget to test any features.

Who should do the testing? For a small application, the designer or the design team usually will develop the test plan and test cases and, in some situations, actually will perform the tests. However, many organizations have a separate team, such as a quality assurance group, that works closely with the design team and is responsible for these activities (such as developing the test plans and actually performing the tests). Most software companies also use ***beta testing***, a popular, inexpensive, and effective way to test software on a select group of the actual users of the system. This is in contrast to ***alpha testing***, where testing is done by in-house testers, such as programmers, software engineers, and internal users. If you are going to perform beta testing, make sure to include it in your plan, since it needs to be communicated to your users well in advance of the availability of your application in a beta version.

13.6.1 Guidelines for Developing Test Plans

As software gains complexity and interaction among programs is more tightly coupled, planning becomes essential. A good test plan not only prevents overlooking a feature (or features), it also helps divide the work load among other people, explains Thomas.

The following guidelines have been developed by Thomas for writing test plans [14]:

- You may have requirements that dictate a specific appearance or format for your test plan. These requirements may be generated by the users. Whatever the appearance of your test plan, try to include as much detail as possible about the tests.
- The test plan should contain a schedule and a list of required resources. List how many people will be needed, when the testing will be done, and what equipment will be required.

- After you have determined what types of testing are necessary (such as black box, white box, top-down, or bottom-up testing), you need to document specifically what you are going to do. Document every type of test you plan to complete. The level of detail in your plan may be driven by several factors, such as the following: How much test time do you have? Will you use the test plan as a training tool for newer team members?
- A *configuration control system* provides a way of tracking the changes to the code. At a minimum, every time the code changes, a record should be kept that tracks which module has been changed, who changed it, and when it was altered, with a comment about why the change was made. Without configuration control, you may have difficulty keeping the testing in line with the changes, since frequent changes may occur without being communicated to the testers.
- A well-thought-out design tends to produce better code and result in more complete testing, so it is a good idea to try to keep the plan up to date. Generally, the older a plan gets, the less useful it becomes. If a test plan is so old that it has become part of the fossil record, it is not terribly useful. As you approach the end of a project, you will have less time to create plans. If you do not take the time to document the work that needs to be done, you risk forgetting something in the mad dash to the finish line. Try to develop a habit of routinely bringing the test plan in sync with the product or product specification.
- At the end of each month or as you reach each milestone, take time to complete routine updates. This will help you avoid being overwhelmed by being so out-of-date that you need to rewrite the whole plan. Keep configuration information on your plan, too. Notes about who made which updates and when can be very helpful down the road.

13.7 CONTINUOUS TESTING

Software is tested to determine whether it conforms to the specifications of requirements. Software is maintained when errors are found and corrected, and software is extended when new functionality is added to an already existing program. There can be different reasons for testing, such as to test for potential problems in a proposed design or to compare two or more designs to determine which is better, given a specific task or set of tasks.

A common practice among developers is to turn over applications to a quality assurance (QA) group for testing only after development is completed. Since it is not involved in the initial plan, the testing team usually has no clear picture of the system and therefore cannot develop an effective test plan. Furthermore, testing the whole system and detecting bugs is more difficult than testing smaller pieces of the application as it is being developed. The practice of waiting until after the development to test an application for bugs and performance could waste thousands of dollars and hours of time.

Testing often uncovers design weaknesses or, at least, provides information you will want to use. Then, you can repeat the entire process, taking what you have learned and reworking your design, or move onto reprototyping and retesting. Testing must take place on a continuous basis, and this refining cycle must continue

BOX 3.2

Real-World Issues on the Agenda
CONTINUOUS TESTING CURES THE LAST-MINUTE CRUNCH

Erin Callaway

Remember cramming for exams in college? As the clock ticked to 4 A.M. and the coffee ran cold, a nagging voice inside your head jeered, "If you studied each day, you'd be asleep right now."

Well, the same is true for testing applications. If you wait until after development to test an application for bugs and performance, you could be wasting thousands of dollars and hours of time. Fortunately, more corporate developers are starting to pay attention to that little voice that's telling them after-the-fact testing just doesn't make sense.

That's what happened at Bankers Trust in 1992. "Our testing was very complete and good, but it was costing a lot of money and would add months onto a project," says Glenn Shimamoto, vice president of technology and strategic planning at the New York bank. In one case, testing added nearly six months to the development of a funds transfer application. The problem: Developers would turn applications over to a quality assurance group for testing only after development was completed. Since the QA group wasn't included in the initial plan, it didn't have a clear picture of its rules until it came time to test.

Software Quality Engineering Corp., a training and consulting company in Jacksonville, Fla., helped Bankers adopt better testing practices. Now, all of Bankers' in-house application-development efforts integrate sophisticated testing plans from day one of the project. They also use automated testing tools.

Why don't more companies incorporate continuous testing in their application development? At Bankers, it was simply the fact that the accounting frameworks did not separate testing from total development costs. Neglect, oversight, and pressure to deliver a product while the business need is hot are some of the other culprits. But, says Ed Weller, a fellow of software processes at Bull HN Information Systems Inc., in Phoenix, "It comes down to a reluctance on the part of a lot of people [and organizations] to take a hard look at failure data."

Weller, a software and hardware process improvement veteran, emphasizes the benefits of formally applying lessons learned from past development mistakes to future projects.

At Bankers, one clear benefit is improved customer satisfaction: Users now say application roll out is "quiet" because the quality of the product is so much better.

But like digging for gold, improving the testing process requires hard work. And results won't be obvious overnight. In fact, it may take two, even three development cycles before the payback really becomes clear.

So if you decide to tackle testing yourself, be prepared to make a long-term commitment. Says Bull's Weller: "This is something you commit to for the rest of your life."

By Erin Callaway, *PC Week*, March 25, 1995, Vol. 13, Number 12.

throughout the development process until you are satisfied with the results. During this iterative process, your prototypes will be transformed incrementally into the actual application. The use cases and usage scenarios can become test scenarios and, therefore, will drive the test plans. Here are the steps to successful testing:

- *Understand and communicate the business case* for improved testing.
- *Develop an internal infrastructure* to support continuous testing.
- *Look for leaders* who will commit to and own the process.
- *Measure* and document your findings in a defect recording system.
- *Publicize improvements* as they are made and let people know what they are doing better.

13.8 MYERS'S DEBUGGING PRINCIPLES

I conclude this discussion with the Myers's bug location and debugging principles [13]:

1. Bug Locating Principles
   - Think.
   - If you reach an impasse, sleep on it.
   - If the impasse remains, describe the problem to someone else.
   - Use debugging tools (this is slightly different from Myers's suggestion).
   - Experimentation should be done as a last resort (this is slightly different from Myers's suggestion).
2. Debugging Principles
   - Where there is one bug, there is likely to be another.
   - Fix the error, not just the symptom of it.
   - The probability of the solution being correct drops as the size of the program increases.
   - Beware of the possibility that an error correction will create a new error (this is less of a problem in an object-oriented environment).

13.9 CASE STUDY: DEVELOPING TEST CASES FOR THE VIANET BANK ATM SYSTEM

In Chapter 6, we identified the scenarios or use cases for the ViaNet bank ATM system. The ViaNet bank ATM system has scenarios involving Checking Account, Savings Account, and general Bank Transaction (see Figures 6–9, 6–10, and 6–11). Here again is a list of the use cases that drive many object-oriented activities, including the usability testing:

- Bank Transaction (see Figure 6–9).
- Checking Transaction History (see Figure 6–9).
- Deposit Checking (see Figure 6–10).
- Deposit Savings (see Figure 6–11).
- Savings Transaction History (see Figure 6–9).
- Withdraw Checking (see Figure 6–10).
- Withdraw Savings (see Figure 6–11).
- Valid/Invalid PIN (see Figure 7–4).

The activity diagrams and sequence/collaboration diagrams created for these use cases are used to develop the usability test cases. For example, you can draw activity and sequence diagrams to model each scenario that exists when a bank client withdraws, deposits, or needs information on an account. Walking through the steps can assist you in developing a usage test case.

Let us develop a test case for the activities involved in the ATM transaction based on the use cases identified so far. (See the activity diagram in Figure 6–8 and the sequence diagram of Figure 7–4 to refresh your memory.)

A test case general format is this: *If it receives certain* input, *it produces certain* output.

1. If a bank client inserts his or her card, the system will respond by requesting the password.
2. If the password is incorrect the system must display the bad password message, eject the card, and request the client to take the card.
3. After the transaction is completed, the system should show the main screen.
4. If a bank client selected an incorrect command when entering the transaction, the system will respond immediately by indicating that some error has been made. The system should allow the customer to correct the mistake and not force him or her to make a withdrawal if the intention was to make a deposit.
5. If an unauthorized customer attempts access to someone else's account, the system should record the time, date, and if possible the identity of the person (not based on the original use cases).
6. If the cash is low, the system will notify the bank for additional money (not based on the original use cases).
7. If an act of vandalism is committed, the system will sound an alarm and call security (not based on the original use cases).
8. If the customer enters a wrong PIN number, the system will give the customer three more chances to correct it; otherwise, it will abort the operation.

And so on.

This is an iterative process; at every iteration, a new issue will be exposed that will help you refine the system. A positive side effect of a test plan is that it might raise some new questions. As the test cases are performed, new test cases will come up, and you should repeat the test. Gause and Weinberg argue that, even if you never attempt to answer the test plans, just developing them might lead you to other, overlooked issues.

13.10 SUMMARY

Testing may be conducted for different reasons. Quality assurance testing looks for potential problems in a proposed design. In this chapter, we looked at guidelines and the basic concept of test plans and saw that, for the most part, use cases can be used to describe the usage test cases. Also, some of the techniques, strategies, and approaches for quality assurance testing and the impact of object orientation on testing are discussed.

Testing is a balance of art, science, and luck. It may seem that everything will fall into place without any preparation and a bug-free product will be shipped. However, in the real world, we must develop a test plan for locating and removing bugs. A test plan offers a road map for testing activity; it should state test objectives and how to meet them. The plan need not be very large; in fact, devoting too much time to the plan can be counterproductive.

There are no magic tricks to debugging; however, by selecting appropriate testing strategies and a sound test plan, you can locate the errors in your system and fix them by utilizing debugging tools.

Once you have created fully tested and debugged classes of objects, you can put them into a library for use or reuse. The essence of an object-oriented system is that you can take for granted that these fully tested objects will perform their desired functions and seal them off in your mind like black boxes.

Testing must take place on a continuous basis, and this refining cycle must continue throughout the development process until you are satisfied with the results.

KEY TERMS

Alpha testing (p. 334)
Beta testing (p. 334)
Black box testing (p. 328)
Bottom-up testing (p. 330)
Branch testing coverage (p. 329)
Configuration control system (p. 335)
Debugging (p. 327)
Error-based testing (p. 327)
Language errors (p. 327)
Path testing (p. 329)
Regression testing (p. 334)
Scenario-based testing (p. 328)
Statement testing coverage (p. 329)
Test plan (p. 333)
Top-down testing (p. 329)
Usage-based testing (p. 328)
White box testing (p. 329)

REVIEW QUESTIONS

1. What is a successful test when you are looking for bugs?
2. Describe the different testing strategies.
3. What is black box testing?
4. When would you use white box testing?
5. If you do not know what is inside the box, how would you test it?
6. In black box testing, you have to test the normal use of functions, the abnormal but reasonable use of functions, and the abnormal and unreasonable use of functions—why?
7. What is the importance of developing a test case?
8. What is white box testing?
9. What is path testing?
10. What is statement testing coverage?
11. What is branch testing coverage?
12. Describe top-down and bottom-up strategies. Which do you prefer and why?
13. What is regression testing?
14. What is a test plan? What steps are followed in developing a test plan?
15. Why are debugging tools important?
16. What basic activities are performed in using debugging tools?

PROBLEMS

1. How would you decide whether a product you are buying is bug free?

2. Research on the WWW or your local library to write a paper on when software must be tested; make sure to include some real-world examples in your report.

3. Consult the WWW or the library to obtain an article that describes beta testing. What are the advantages and disadvantages of this form of testing? Write a paper based on your findings.

4. Do research on the McCabe theory of software complexity and also the McCabe test tool.

REFERENCES

1. Beizer, Boris. *Software Testing Techniques*, 2d ed. New York: Van Nostrand-Reinhold, 1990.

2. Binder, Robert V. "The FREE Approach for System Testing: Use-Cases, Threads, and Relations." *Object* 6, no. 2 (February 1996).

3. Blum, Bruce I. *Software Engineering: A Holistic View*. New York: Oxford University Press, 1992.

4. Chow, Tsun S. "Testing Software Design Modeled by Finite State Machines." *IEEE Transactions on Software Engineering* SE-4, no. 3 (January 1978), pp. 178–86.

5. Coad, P.; and Yourdon, E. *Object-Oriented Design*. Englewood Cliffs, NJ: Yourdon Press, 1991.

6. Conger, Sue. *The New Software Engineering*. Belmont, CA: Wadsworth Publishing Company, 1994.

7. Freedman, Daniel P.; and Weinberg, Gerald M. *Handbook of Walkthroughs, Inspections, and Technical Reviews*, 3d ed. Glenview, IL: Scott, Foresman and Co., 1983.

8. Gause, Donald C.; and Weinberg, Gerald M. *Exploring Requirements Quality Before Design*. New York: Dorset House, 1989.

9. Griss, M. L. "Software Reuse: Objects and Frameworks Are Not Enough." *Object* 4, no. 9 (February 1995).

10. Gruenberger, F. "Bug." In Ralston, Anthony; and Reilly, Edwin D., Jr., eds. *Encyclopedia of Computer Science and Engineering*, 2d ed., p. 189. New York: Van Nostrand-Reinhold Company, 1983.

11. Hopcroft, John E.; and Ullman, Jeffrey D. *An Introduction to Automata Theory, Languages, and Computation*. Reading, MA: Addison-Wesley, 1987.

12. Marick, Brian. *The Craft of Software Testing: Subsystems Testing Including Object-Based and Object-Oriented Testing*. Englewood Cliffs, NJ: Prentice-Hall, 1995.

13. Myers, G. J. *The Art of Software Testing*. New York: John Wiley & Sons, 1979.

14. Thomas, Tamara. *The Benefits of Writing a Good Test Plan, the Windows Interface Guidelines, a Guide for Designing Software*. Redmond, WA: Microsoft Press, 1994.

15. Weinberg, Gerald M. *The Psychology of Computer Programming*. New York: Van Nostrand-Reinhold, 1971.

16. Weinberg, Gerald M. *Rethinking Systems Analysis and Design*. New York: Dorset House, 1988.

CHAPTER 14

System Usability and Measuring User Satisfaction

Ninety percent of product development efforts fail. About thirty percent fail to produce anything at all, but most of the failures don't have that problem. They do produce a product, but people don't like it. They do not use it at all, or if they do, they may grumble endlessly.
—Donald C. Gause and Gerald Weinberg

Chapter Objectives

You should be able to define and understand

- Usability testing.
- User satisfaction testing.

14.1 INTRODUCTION

Quality refers to the ability of products to meet the users' needs and expectations. The task of satisfying user requirements is the basic motivation for quality. Quality also means striving to do the things right the first time, while always looking to improve how things are being done. Sometimes, this even means spending more time in the initial phases of a project—such as analysis and design—making sure that you are doing the right things. Having to correct fewer problems means significantly less wasted time and capital. When all the losses caused by poor quality are considered, high quality usually costs less than poor quality.

Two main issues in software quality are *validation* or user satisfaction and *verification* or quality assurance (see Chapter 3). There are different reasons for testing. You can use testing to look for potential problems in a proposed design. You can focus on comparing two or more designs to determine which is better, given a specific task or set of tasks. Usability testing is different from quality assurance testing in that, rather than finding programming defects, you assess how well the interface or the software fits the use cases, which are the reflections of users' needs and expectations. To ensure user satisfaction, we must measure it throughout the system development with user satisfaction tests. Furthermore, these tests can be used as a communication vehicle between designers and end users [3]. In the next section, we look at user satisfaction tests that can be invaluable in developing high-

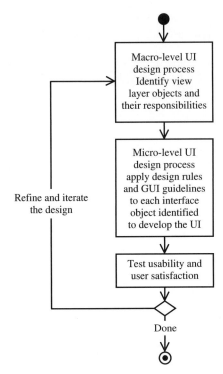

FIGURE 14-1
The process of designing view layer classes.

quality software. In Chapter 12, we learned that the process of designing view layer classes consists of the following steps (see Figure 14–1):

1. Macro-level UI Design Process—Identifying view layer objects.
2. Micro-level UI Design Activities.
3. Testing usability and user satisfaction.
4. Refining and iterating the design.

In spite of the great effort involved in developing user interfaces and the potential costs of bad ones, many user interfaces are not evaluated for their usability or acceptability to users, risking failure in the field. Bad user interfaces can contribute to human error, possibly resulting in personal and financial damages [2]. Usability should be a subset of software quality characteristics. This means that usability must be placed at the same level as other characteristics, such as reliability, correctness, and maintainability [1]. Usability is an important characteristic in determining the quality of the product. In this chapter, we look at usability testing and issues regarding user satisfaction and its measurement. We study how to develop user satisfaction and usability tests that are based on the use cases. The use cases identified during the analysis phase can be used in testing the design.

Once the design is complete, you can walk users through the steps of the scenarios to determine if the design enables the scenarios to occur as planned.

14.2 USABILITY TESTING

The International Organization for Standardization (ISO) defines *usability* as the effectiveness, efficiency, and satisfaction with which a specified set of users can achieve a specified set of tasks in particular environments. The ISO definition requires

- *Defining tasks.* What are the tasks?
- *Defining users.* Who are the users?
- *A means for measuring effectiveness, efficiency, and satisfaction.* How do we measure usability?

The phrase *two sides of the same coin* is helpful for describing the relationship between the usability and functionality of a system. Both are essential for the development of high-quality software [4]. ***Usability testing*** measures the ease of use as well as the degree of comfort and satisfaction users have with the software. Products with poor usability can be difficult to learn, complicated to operate, and misused or not used at all. Therefore, low product usability leads to high costs for users and a bad reputation for the developers.

Usability is one of the most crucial factors in the design and development of a product, especially the user interface. Therefore, usability testing must be a key part of the UI design process. Usability testing should begin in the early stages of product development; for example, it can be used to gather information about how users do their work and find out their tasks, which can complement use cases. You can incorporate your findings into the usability test plan and test cases. As the design progresses, usability testing continues to provide valuable input for analyzing initial design concepts and, in the later stages of product development, can be used to test specific product tasks, especially the UI.

Usability test cases begin with the identification of use cases that can specify the target audience, tasks, and test goals. When designing a test, focus on use cases or tasks, not features. Even if your goal is testing specific features, remember that your users will use them within the context of particular tasks. It also is a good idea to run a pilot test to work the bugs out of the tasks to be tested and make certain the task scenarios, prototype, and test equipment work smoothly.

Test cases must include all use cases identified so far. Recall from Chapter 4 that the use case can be used through most activities of software development. Furthermore, by following Jacobson's life cycle model, you can produce designs that are traceable across requirements, analysis, design, implementation, and testing. The main advantage is that all design traces directly back to the user requirements. Use cases and usage scenarios can become test scenarios; and therefore, the use case will drive the usability, user satisfaction, and quality assurance test cases (see Figure 14–2).

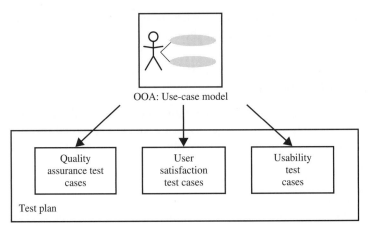

FIGURE 14–2
The use cases identified during analysis can be used in testing the design. Once the design is complete, walk users through the steps of the scenarios to determine if the design enables the scenarios to occur as planned.

14.2.1 Guidelines for Developing Usability Testing

Many techniques can be used to gather usability information. In addition to use cases, focus groups can be helpful for generating initial ideas or trying out new ideas. A focus group requires a moderator who directs the discussion about aspects of a task or design but allows participants to freely express their opinions.

Usability tests can be conducted in a one-on-one fashion, as a demonstration, or as a "walk through," in which you take the users through a set of sample scenarios and ask about their impressions along the way. In a technique called the *Wizard of Oz,* a testing specialist simulates the interaction of an interface. Although these latter techniques can be valuable, they often require a trained, experienced test coordinator [5]. Let us take a look at some guidelines for developing usability testing:

- The usability testing should include all of a software's components.
- Usability testing need not be very expensive or elaborate, such as including trained specialists working in a soundproof lab with one-way mirrors and sophisticated recording equipment. Even the small investment of tape recorder, stopwatch, and notepad in an office or conference room can produce excellent results.
- Similarly, all tests need not involve many subjects. More typically, quick, iterative tests with a small, well-targeted sample of 6 to 10 participants can identify 80–90 percent of most design problems.
- Consider the user's experience as part of your software usability. You can study 80–90 percent of most design problems with as few as three or four users if you target only a single skill level of users, such as novices or intermediate level users.
- Apply usability testing early and often.

14.2.2 Recording the Usability Test

When conducting the usability test, provide an environment comparable to the target setting; usually a quiet location, free from distractions is best. Make participants feel comfortable. It often helps to emphasize that you are testing the software, not the participants. If the participants become confused or frustrated, it is no reflection on them. Unless you have participated yourself, you may be surprised by the pressure many test participants feel. You can alleviate some of the pressure by explaining the testing process and equipment.

Tandy Trower, director of the Advanced User Interface group at Microsoft, explains that the users must have reasonable time to try to work through any difficult situation they encounter. Although it generally is best not to interrupt participants during a test, they may get stuck or end up in situations that require intervention. This need not disqualify the test data, as long as the test coordinator carefully guides or hints around a problem. Begin with general hints before moving to specific advice. For more difficult situations, you may need to stop the test and make adjustments. Keep in mind that less intervention usually yields better results. Always record the techniques and search patterns users employ when attempting to work through a difficulty and the number and type of hints you have to provide them.

Ask subjects to think aloud as they work, so you can hear what assumptions and inferences they are making. As the participants work, record the time they take to perform a task as well as any problems they encounter. You may want to follow up the session with the *user satisfaction* test (more on this in the next section) and a questionnaire that asks the participants to evaluate the product or tasks they performed.

Record the test results using a portable tape recorder or, better, a video camera. Since even the best observer can miss details, reviewing the data later will prove invaluable. Recorded data also allows more direct comparison among multiple participants. It usually is risky to base conclusions on observing a single subject. Recorded data allows the design team to review and evaluate the results.

Whenever possible, involve all members of the design team in observing the test and reviewing the results. This ensures a common reference point and better design solutions as team members apply their own insights to what they observe. If direct observation is not possible, make the recorded results available to the entire team.

To ensure user satisfaction and therefore high-quality software, measure user satisfaction along the way as the design takes form [3]. In the next section, we look at the user satisfaction test, which can be an invaluable tool in developing high-quality software.

14.3 USER SATISFACTION TEST

User satisfaction testing is the process of quantifying the usability test with some measurable attributes of the test, such as functionality, cost, or ease of use. Usability can be assessed by defining measurable goals, such as

- 95 percent of users should be able to find how to withdraw money from the ATM machine without error and with no formal training.

- 70 percent of all users should experience the new function as "a clear improvement over the previous one."
- 90 percent of consumers should be able to operate the VCR within 30 minutes.

Furthermore, if the product is being built incrementally, the best measure of user satisfaction is the product itself, since you can observe how users are using it—or avoiding it [3]. A positive side effect of testing with a prototype is that you can observe how people actually use the software. In addition to prototyping and usability testing, another tool that can assist us in developing high-quality software is measuring and monitoring user satisfaction during software development, especially during the design and development of the user interface. Gause and Weinberg have developed a user satisfaction test that can be used along with usability testing. Here are the principal objectives of the user satisfaction test [3]:

- As a communication vehicle between designers, as well as between users and designers.
- To detect and evaluate changes during the design process.
- To provide a periodic indication of divergence of opinion about the current design.
- To enable pinpointing specific areas of dissatisfaction for remedy.
- To provide a clear understanding of just how the completed design is to be evaluated.

Even if the results are never summarized and no one fills out a questionnaire, the process of creating the test itself will provide useful information. Additionally, the test is inexpensive, easy to use, and it is educational to both those who administer it and those who take it.

14.3.1 Guidelines for Developing a User Satisfaction Test

The format of every user satisfaction test is basically the same, but its content is different for each project. Once again, the use cases can provide you with an excellent source of information throughout this process. Furthermore, you must work with the users or clients to find out what attributes should be included in the test. Ask the users to select a limited number (5 to 10) of attributes by which the final product can be evaluated. For example, the user might select the following attributes for a customer tracking system: ease of use, functionality, cost, intuitiveness of user interface, and reliability.

A test based on these attributes is shown in Figure 14–3. Once these attributes have been identified, they can play a crucial role in the evaluation of the final product. Keep these attributes in the foreground, rather than make assumptions about how the design will be evaluated [3]. The user must use his or her judgment to answer each question by selecting a number between 1 and 10, with 10 as the most favorable and 1 as the least. Comments often are the most significant part of the test. Gause and Weinberg raise the following important point in conducting a user satisfaction test [3, p. 239]: "When the design of the test has been drafted, show it to the clients and ask, 'If you fill this out monthly (or at whatever interval), will it enable you to express what you like and don't like?' If they answer negatively then find out what attributes would enable them to express themselves and revise the test."

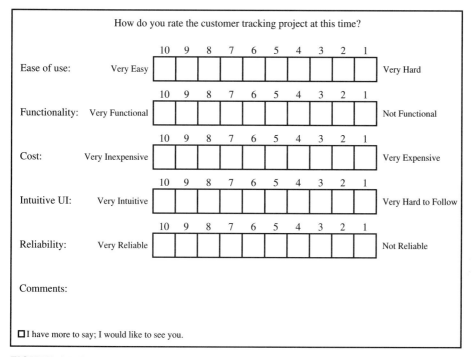

FIGURE 14–3
A custom form for user satisfaction test.

14.4 A TOOL FOR ANALYZING USER SATISFACTION: THE USER SATISFACTION TEST TEMPLATE

Commercial off-the-shelf (COTS) *software* tools are already written and a few are available for analyzing and conducting user satisfaction tests. However, here, I have selected an electronic spreadsheet to demonstrate how it can be used to record and analyze the user satisfaction test. The user satisfaction test spreadsheet (USTS) automates many bookkeeping tasks and can assist in analyzing the user satisfaction test results. Furthermore, it offers a quick start for creating a user satisfaction test for a particular project.

Recall from the previous section that the tests need not involve many subjects. More typically, quick, iterative tests with a small, well-targeted sample of 6 to 10 participants can identify 80–90 percent of most design problems. The spreadsheet should be designed to record responses from up to 10 users. However, if there are inputs from more than 10 users, it must allow for that (see Figures 14–4 and 14–5).

One use of a tool like this is that it shows patterns in user satisfaction level. For example, a shift in the user satisfaction rating indicates that something is happening (see Figure 14–6). Gause and Weinberg explain that this shift is sufficient cause to follow up with an interview. The user satisfaction test can be a tool for

Information | Zoom | Print | Tips

Measuring User Satisfaction

Project Name: **Customer Tracking System**

User	1	2	3	4	5	6	7	8	9	##	1	2	3	4	5	6	7	8	9	##	1	2	3	4	5	6	7	8	9	##	1	2	3	4
Ease of Use	1	7									4	2									4	2									5	2		
Functionality	4	4									6	8									8	7									2	2		
Intuitiveness of U	4	6									5	8									8	8									5	5		
Cost	1	1									5	5									5	5									6	6		
Reliability	3	4									6	8									8	7									7	7		
Comments																																		

General Comments:

Contents | UST | Summary | Chart | Information | CHART1

FIGURE 14–4
A user satisfaction test for a customer tracking system.

FIGURE 14–5
A user satisfaction summary sheet. The main thing to look for in the responses is changes over time. A shift in the user satisfaction rating indicates that something is happening.

Measuring User Satisfaction

Project Name: Customer Tracking System

	Test #1 Period 1	Test #2 Period 2	Test #3 Period 3	Test #4 Period 4	Test #5 Period 5	Test #6 Period 6
Overall Average	4	6	6	5	6	7
Overall High	7	8	8	7	8	9
Overall Low	1	2	2	2	2	4

Changes		Improvemen	mprovemen	Problem	mprovemen	mprovement
Comments						

Contents | UST | Summary | Chart | Information | CHART1

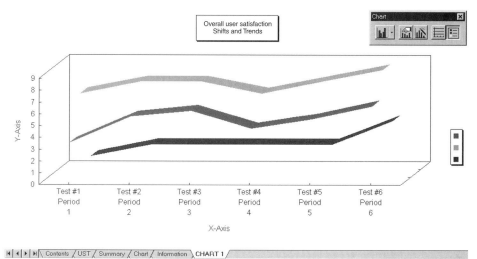

FIGURE 14–6
Periodical plotting can reveal shifts in user satisfaction, which can pinpoint a problem. Plotting the high and low responses indicates where to go for maximum information (Gause and Weinberg (3).

finding out what attributes are important or unimportant. An interesting side effect of developing a user satisfaction test is that you benefit from it even if the test is never administered to anyone; it still provides useful information. However, performing the test regularly helps to keep the user involved in the system. It also helps you focus on user wishes. Here is the user satisfaction cycle that has been suggested by Gause and Weinberg:

1. Create a user satisfaction test for your own project. Create a custom form that fits the project's needs and the culture of your organization. Use cases are a great source of information; however, make sure to involve the user in creation of the test.
2. Conduct the test regularly and frequently.
3. Read the comments very carefully, especially if they express a strong feeling. Never forget that feelings are facts, the most important facts you have about the users of the system.
4. Use the information from user satisfaction test, usability test, reactions to prototypes, interviews recorded, and other comments to improve the product.

Another benefit of the user satisfaction test is that you can continue using it even after the product is delivered. The results then become a measure of how well users are learning to use the product and how well it is being maintained. They also provide a starting point for initiating follow-up projects [3].

14.5 CASE STUDY: DEVELOPING USABILITY TEST PLANS AND TEST CASES FOR THE VIANET BANK ATM SYSTEM

In Chapter 13, we learned that test plans need not be very large; in fact, devoting too much time to the plans can be counterproductive. Having this in mind let us develop a usability test plan for the ViaNet ATM kiosk by going through the followings steps (see Chapter 13).

14.5.1 Develop Test Objectives

The first step is to develop objectives for the test plan. Generally, test objectives are based on the requirements, use cases, or current or desired system usage. In this case, ease of use is the most important requirement, since the ViaNet bank customers should be able to perform their tasks with basically no training and are not expected to read a user manual before withdrawing money from their checking accounts.

Here are the objectives to test the usability of the ViaNet bank ATM kiosk and its user interface:

- 95 percent of users should be able to find out how to withdraw money from the ATM machine without error or any formal training.
- 90 percent of consumers should be able to operate the ATM within 90 seconds.

14.5.2 Develop Test Cases

Test cases for usability testing are slightly different from test cases for quality assurance. Basically, here, we are not testing the input and expected output but how users interact with the system. Once again, the use cases created during analysis can be used to develop scenarios for the usability test. The usability test scenarios are based on the following use cases:

Deposit Checking (see Figure 6–10).
Withdraw Checking (see Figure 6–10).
Deposit Savings (see Figure 6–11).
Withdraw Savings (see Figure 6–11).
Savings Transaction History (see Figure 6–9).
Checking Transaction History (see Figure 6–9).

Next we need to select a small number of test participants (6 to 10) who have never before used the kiosk and ask them to perform the following scenarios based on the use case:

1. Deposit $1056.65 to your checking account.
2. Withdraw $40 from your checking account.
3. Deposit $200 to your savings account.
4. Withdraw $55 from savings account.
5. Get your savings account transaction history.
6. Get your checking account transaction history.

Start by explaining the testing process and equipment to the participants to ease the pressure. Remember to make participants feel comfortable by emphasizing that you are testing the software, not them. If they become confused or frustrated, it is no reflection on them but the poor usability of the system. Make sure to ask them to think aloud as they work, so you can hear what assumptions and inferences they are making. After all, if they cannot perform these tasks with ease, then the system is not useful.

As the participants work, record the time they take to perform a task as well as any problems they encounter. In this case, we used the kiosk video camera to record the test results along with a tape recorder. This allowed the design team to review and evaluate how the participants interacted with the user interface, like those developed in Chapter 12 (see Chapter 12, Figures 12–18 to 12–21). For example, look for things such as whether they are finding the appropriate buttons easily and the buttons are the right size.

Once the test subjects complete their tasks, conduct a user satisfaction test to measure their level of satisfaction with the kiosk. The format of the user satisfaction test is basically the same as the one we studied earlier in this chapter (see Figure 14–3), but its content is different for the ViaNet bank. The users, uses cases, and test objects should provide the attributes to be included in the test. Here, the following attributes have been selected, since the ease of use is the main issue of the user interface:

- Is easy to operate.
- Buttons are the right size and easily located.
- Is efficient to use.
- Is fun to use.
- Is visually pleasing.
- Provides easy recovery from errors.

Based on these attributes, the test shown in Figure 14–7 can be performed. Remember, as explained earlier, these attributes can play a crucial role in the evaluation of the final product.

14.5.3 Analyze the Tests

The final step is to analyze the tests and document the test results. Here, we need to answer questions such as these: What percentage were able to operate the ATM within 90 seconds or without error? Were the participants able to find out how to withdraw money from the ATM machine with no help? The results of the analysis must be examined.

We also need to analyze the results of user satisfaction tests. The USTS described earlier or a tool similar to it can be used to record and graph the results of user satisfaction tests. As we learned earlier, a shift in user satisfaction pattern indicates that something is happening and a follow-up interview is needed to find out the reasons for the changes. The user satisfaction test can be used as a tool for finding out what attributes are important or unimportant. For example, based on the user satisfaction test, we might find that the users do not agree that the system "is efficient to use," and it got a low score. After the follow-up interviews, it became apparent that participants wanted, in addition to entering the amount for withdrawal, to be able to select from a list with predefined values (say, $20, $40,

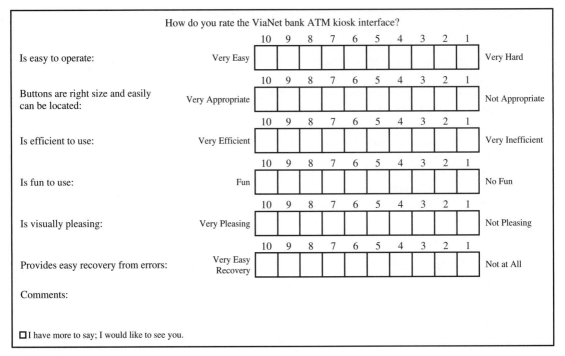

FIGURE 14–7
A form for the ViaNet bank ATM kiosk user satisfaction test.

$60, $80, $100, and $200). This would speed up the process at the ATM kiosk. Based on the result of the test, the UI was modified to reflect the wishes of the users (see Figure 14–8).

You need also to pay close attention to comments, especially if they express a strong feeling. Remember, feelings are facts, the most important facts you have about the users of the system.

14.6 SUMMARY

In this chapter, we looked at different dimensions of quality in software development. We discussed the importance of the usability and user satisfaction tests. The main point here is that you must focus on the users' perception. Many systems that are adequate technically have failed because of poor user perception. This can be prevented, or at least minimized, by utilizing usability and user satisfaction tests as part of your UI design process.

Usability testing begins with defining the target audience and test goals. When designing a test, focus on tasks, not features. Even if your goal is testing specific features, remember that your customers will use them within the context of particular tasks. The use cases identified during analysis can be used in testing your

FIGURE 14-8

The CheckingAccountUI and SavingsAccountUI interface objects for withdrawal modified based on the usability and user satisfaction tests. The users have the option of selecting quick withdrawal or selecting *other option* and then entering the amount they want to withdraw.

design. Once the design is complete, you can walk users through the steps of the scenarios to determine if the design enables the scenarios to occur as planned.

An interesting side effect of developing user satisfaction tests is that you benefit from it even if the test is never administered to anyone; it still provides useful information. However, performing the test regularly helps keep the user actively involved in the system development. It also helps us stay focused on the users' wishes.

KEY TERMS

Commercial off-the-shelf software (p. 347)
Usability testing (p. 343)
User satisfaction testing (p. 345)

REVIEW QUESTIONS

1. What is validation?
2. What is verification?
3. What is quality?
4. Why do we need usability testing? When do we use usability testing?
5. Why do we need to apply usability testing early on? Why should we apply it often?
6. Why should usability testing include all components of the software?
7. What are some other techniques to gather usability information?
8. Describe the "Wizard of Oz" technique.
9. What is a user satisfaction test?
10. Why do we need to measure user satisfaction?
11. How do you develop a custom form for a user satisfaction test?
12. What is the significance of comments in a user satisfaction form?

PROBLEMS

1. Create a user satisfaction test for a bank system application.
2. Following an elaborate effort on your part to do things right the first time, you decide to develop the world's best user satisfaction test form (in your opinion!). After testing the forms with the users, you come across the following response, "This form stinks!" What should you do at this point?

REFERENCES

1. Boehm, B.W.; Brown, J. R.; Kaspar, H.; Lipow, M.; Macleod, G.; and Merrit, M. *Characteristics of Software Quality*. Amsterdam: TRW Series of Software Technology, North-Holland, 1978.
2. Chin, J. P.; Diehl, V. A.; and Norman, K. L. "Development of an Instrument Measuring User Satisfaction of the Human-Computer Interface." *Proceedings of the Computer-Human Interaction* CHI'88, pp. 213–18. Washington, DC.
3. Gause, Donald; and Weinberg, Gerald. *Exploring Requirements Quality Before Design*. New York: Dorset House, 1989.
4. Sulaiman, Suziah. "Usability and the Software Production Life Cycle." *Proceedings of the Computer-Human Interaction* CHI'96, pp. 61–2, (October, 1996). British Columbia, Canada.
5. Thomas, Tamara. *The Benefits of Writing a Good Test Plan, the Windows Interface Guidelines, a Guide for Designing Software*. Redmond, WA: Microsoft Press, 1994.
6. Weinberg, Gerald M. *Rethinking System Analysis and Design*. New York: Dorset House Publishing, 1988.

Document Template

This appendix contains a template and a sample system document of the ViaNet bank ATM system to demonstrate use of the template. The template originally was developed by Bell and Evans [1] for documenting a system requirement and has been modified here to incorporate the unified approach and unified modeling language. Most CASE tools provide documentation capability. For example, SA/Object Architecture provides the ability to customize reports and documentation. The template in this appendix is not expected to replace the documentation capability of a CASE tool but to be used as an example and guideline for developing comprehensive documentation of the system development.

We begin with a rough outline of what to expect and follow with the ViaNet bank ATM system example.

1. *Scope*. The following subsections describe the scope of the [application name] in terms of its audience, organization, and applicable documents.
   1.1. *Audience*. The intended users are [user title] (with [prerequisite knowledge]).
   1.2. *Organization*. This document describes the [application name] system requirements in terms of [documentation organization headings].
   1.3. *Applicable documents*. The following documents provide information necessary to understand this document. [List of applicable documents]
2. *System requirements specification*. The following subsection describes the [application name] system requirements specification in terms of the problem statements and feasibility studies. [The problem statement goes here.]
3. *Activity diagram of business process*. An activity diagram of the as-is processes goes here.
4. *UML use-case model*. The use-case model goes here. Describe the use cases and actors. The [application] consists of the following use cases:

   [List of actors]
   [List of use cases and use-case description]

[Use-case name]

[Use-case description]

5. *UML interaction diagrams.* Include the interaction (sequence and collaboration) diagrams here.
6. *UML class diagrams.* The class diagrams go here.
   6.1. *List business, access, and view classes.* The [application] consists of the following classes [list of classes].
   6.2. *Description of the business layer classes.* The business layer contains all of the objects that represent the business and how they interact to accomplish the business processes. Business objects have no special knowledge of how they are being displayed. They are designed to be independent of any particular interface. Furthermore, business objects have no special knowledge of "where they come from." They need to know only who to talk to about being stored or retrieved. The following subsections describe business classes in terms of purpose, superclass-subclass hierarchy, a-part-of structure, structure diagram, attributes, methods, and associations.

   [Class name] serves the following purpose:

   [Purpose of the class]

   6.2.1. *Superclass(es).* [Class name] is a subclass of the following class(es) [list of superclass(es)].
   6.2.2. *Subclass(es).* The [class name] has the following subclass(es) [list of subclass(es)].
   6.2.3. *A-part-of structures or aggregation.* The [class name] is a-part-of [whole class name].
   6.2.4. *Association.* The following table lists all associations of [class name] and describes the association along with the name of the associated class.
   6.2.5. *Methods.* The following activity diagrams describe the methods of the [class name].
   6.3. *Description of the access layer classes.* The access layer contains objects that know how to communicate with the data source, whether in a relational database, mainframe, Internet, or file. The following subsections describe access classes in terms of purpose, superclass-subclass hierarchy, a-part-of structure, structure diagram, attributes, methods, and associations. [Class name] serves the following purpose [purpose of the class].
   6.3.1. *Superclass(es).* [Class name] is a subclass of the following class(es) [list of superclass(es)].
   6.3.2. *Subclass(es).* The [class name] has the following subclass(es) [list of subclass(es)].
   6.3.3 *A-part-of structures and aggregation.* The [class name] is a-part-of [whole class name].
   6.3.4. *Association.* The following table lists all associations of [class name] and describes the association along with the name of the associated class.

6.3.5. *Methods*. The following activity diagrams describe the methods of the [class name].

6.4. *Description of the user interface (view layer) classes*. The user interface layer objects translate an action by the user, such as clicking on a button or selecting from a menu, into an appropriate response. That response may be to open or close another interface or to send a message to the business layer to start some business process, Remember, the business logic does not exist here, just the knowledge of which message to send to which business object. The following subsections describe interface classes in terms of purpose, superclass-subclass hierarchy, a-part-of structure, structure diagram, attributes, methods, and associations. [Class name] serves the following purpose [purpose of the class].

6.4.1. *Superclass(es)*. [Class name] is subclass of the following class(es) [list of superclass(es)].

6.4.2. *Subclass(es)*. The [class name] has the following subclass(es) [list of subclass(es)].

6.4.3. *A-part-of structures and aggregation*. The [class name] is a-part-of [whole class name].

6.4.4. *Association*. The following table lists all associations of [class name] and describes the association along with the name of the associated class.

6.4.5. *Screen*. The following screen is the snapshot of [class name] class [show a snapshot of the screen].

6.4.6. *The interface behavior: events and actions*. The following activity diagrams describe the methods of the [class name].

6.5. *Packages*. The [application] consists of the following subjects [list of packages].

7. *Testing*

7.1. *Test plan and test cases*. The test plan and test cases go here.

7.1.1. *Usability testing*. The usability testing scenarios go here.

7.1.2. *User satisfaction testing*. The user satisfaction test goes here.

7.1.3 *Other testing results*. Other testing results go here.

Now that we know what to expect, we can begin the ViaNet bank ATM system example. Figure A–2 shows the title page.

A.1 SCOPE

The following subsections describe the scope of the ViaNet bank ATM system in terms of its audience, organization, and applicable documents.

A.1.1 Audience

The intended users are the people responsible for implementing the ViaNet bank ATM system.

A.1.2 Organization

This document describes the ViaNet bank ATM system requirements in terms of system requirements, executive summary, analysis, and design diagrams.

A.1.3 Applicable Documents

The following documents provide information necessary to understand this document:

   None [this part can be skipped; it is included for completeness].

A.2 SYSTEM REQUIREMENTS SPECIFICATION

The following subsection describes the ViaNet bank ATM system requirements specification in terms of the problem statements and feasibility studies.

Problem Statement

The ViaNet bank client must be able to deposit an amount to and withdraw an amount from his or her accounts using the bank application. Each transaction must be recorded, and the client must have the ability to review all transactions performed against a given account. Recorded transactions must include the date, time, transaction type, amount, and account balance after the transaction.

   A ViaNet bank client can have two types of accounts: a checking account and a savings account. For each checking account, one related savings account can exist.

   The application must verify that a client can gain access to his or her account by identification via a personal identification number (PIN) code.

   Neither a checking nor a savings account can have a negative balance. The application should automatically withdraw funds from a related savings account if the requested withdrawal amount on the checking account is more than its current balance.

   If the savings account balance is insufficient to cover the requested withdrawal amount, the application should inform the user and terminate the transaction.

Assumptions   The assumptions for the bank application are as follows:

- Access to the ViaNet bank accounts is provided by a PIN code consisting of four integer digits between 0 and 9.
- One PIN code allows access to all accounts held by a bank client.
- No receipts will be provided for any account transactions.
- The bank application operates for a single banking institution only.
- There is no automatic transfer from a related checking account to a savings account. If the balance on a savings account is less than the withdrawal amount requested, the transaction will stop and the bank client will be notified.

A.3 ACTIVITY DIAGRAM OF A BUSINESS PROCESS

Figure A–1 is an activity diagram of ATM activities.

A.4 UML USE CASE MODEL

Figures A–2, A–3, and A–4 show the checking account, savings account, and systems transaction packages.

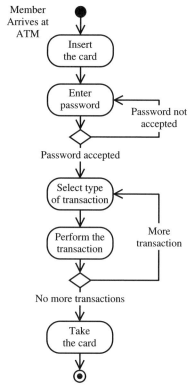

FIGURE A–1
Activities involved in an ATM transaction.

Description of the Use Cases and Actors

[The bank application will be used by one category of users: bank clients. Notice that identifying the actors of the system is an iterative process and can be modified as you learn more about the system.] The actor in the bank system is

- Actor Name: Bank Client
  Description: The bank client must be able to deposit an amount to and withdraw an amount from his or her accounts using the bank application.
- Use-Case Name: Bank ATM Transaction
  Description: The bank clients interact with the bank system by going through the approval process. After the approval process, the bank client can perform the transaction. Here are the steps, which have been shown in the activity diagram (Figure A–1):
  1. Bank client inserts ATM card.
  2. Perform the approval process.
  3. Ask type of transaction.
  4. Enter type of transaction.
  5. Perform transaction.

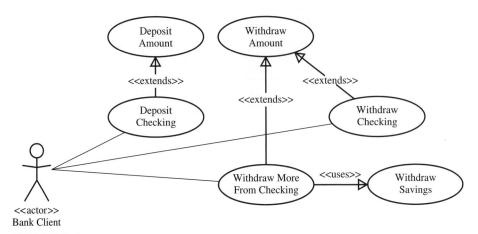

FIGURE A–2
The checking account package.

6. Eject card.
7. Request bank client take card.
8. Bank client takes card.

- Use-Case Name: Approval Process
   Description: The client enters a PIN code that consists of four digits. If the PIN code is valid, the client's accounts become available. These are the steps:
   1. Request password.

FIGURE A–3
The savings account package.

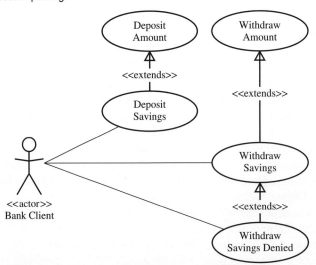

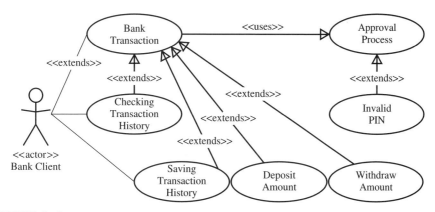

FIGURE A–4
The system transaction package.

2. Bank client enters password.
3. Verify password.
* Use-Case Name: Invalid PIN
  Description: The PIN code is not valid; an appropriate message is displayed to the client. This use case extends the approval process.
* Use-Case Name: Deposit Amount
  Description: The bank clients interact with the bank system after passing the approval process by requesting to deposit money into an account. The client selects the account to which a deposit is going to be made and enters an amount in dollar currency. The system creates a record of the transaction. This use case extends the bank transaction use case. Here are the steps:
  1. Request account type.
  2. Request deposit amount.
  3. Bank client enters deposit amount.
  4. Bank client puts the check or cash in the envelope and inserts it into the ATM machine.
* Use-Case Name: Deposit Savings
  Description: The client selects the savings account to which a deposit is going to be made. Other steps are similar to the deposit amount use case. The system creates a record of the transaction. This use case extends the deposit amount use case.
* Use-Case Name: Deposit Checking
  Description: The client selects the checking account to which a deposit is going to be made. Other steps are similar to the deposit amount use case. The system creates a record of the transaction. This use case extends the deposit amount use case.
* Use-Case Name: Withdraw Amount
  Description: The bank client interacts with the bank system after the approval process by requesting to withdraw money from a checking account. After

verifying that sufficient funds are in the account, the transaction is performed. This use case extends the bank transaction use case. Here are the steps:

1. Request account type.

2. Request withdrawal amount.

3. Bank client enters withdrawal amount.

4. Verify sufficient funds.

5. Eject cash.

- Use-Case Name: Withdraw Checking

  Description: The client tries to withdraw an amount from a checking account. The amount is less than or equal to the checking account's balance; and the transaction is performed. This use case extends the withdraw amount use case.

- Use-Case Name: Withdraw More from Checking

  Description: The client tries to withdraw an amount from a checking account. The amount is more than the checking account's balance; the insufficient amount is withdrawn from the client's related savings account. The system creates a record of the transaction, and the withdrawal is successful. This use case extends the withdraw checking use case and uses the withdraw savings use case.

- Use-Case Name: Withdraw Savings

  Description: The client tries to withdraw an amount from a savings account. The amount is less than or equal to the balance, and the transaction is performed on the savings account. The system creates a record of the transaction because the withdrawal is successful. This use case extends the withdraw amount use case.

- Use-Case Name: Withdraw Savings Denied

  Description: The client tries to withdraw an amount from a savings account. If the amount is more than the balance, the transaction is halted and a message is displayed. This use case extends the withdraw savings use case.

- Use-Case Name: Checking Transaction History

  Description: The bank client requests a history of transactions for his or her checking account. The system displays the transaction history for the checking account. This use case extends the bank transaction use case.

- Use-Case Name: Savings Transaction History

  Description: The bank client requests a history of transactions for his or her savings account. The system displays the transaction history for the savings account. This use case extends the bank transaction use case.

A.5 UML INTERACTION DIAGRAMS

Figures A–5 through A–9 show sequence and collaboration diagrams for some of the preceding use cases.

A.6 UML CLASS DIAGRAMS

Figure A–10 shows a class diagram of the ViaNet ATM system.

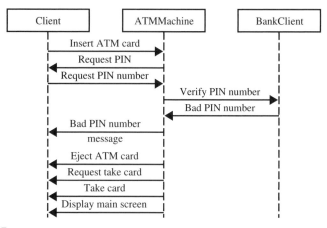

FIGURE A-5

The sequence diagram for the invalid PIN use case.

FIGURE A-6

The sequence diagram for the withdraw checking use case.

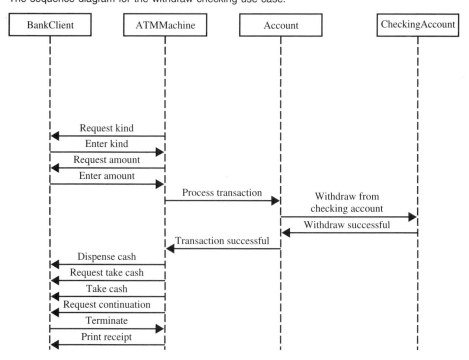

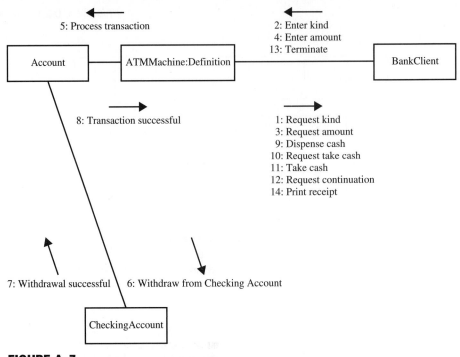

FIGURE A–7
Collaboration diagram for the withdraw checking use case.

FIGURE A–8
Sequence diagram for the withdraw more from checking use case.

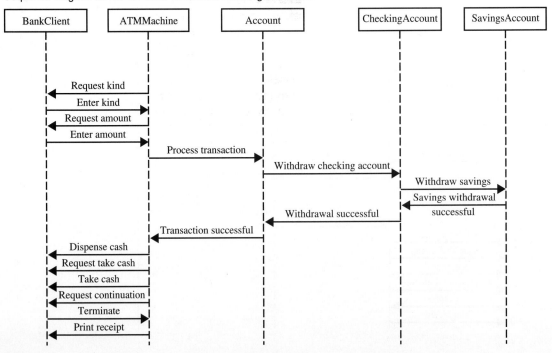

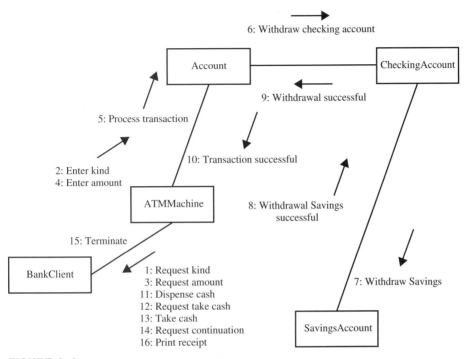

FIGURE A-9
Collaboration diagram for the withdraw more from checking use case.

A.6.1 List of Business, Access, and View Classes

Business classes:

ATMMachine
Bank
BankClient
Account
CheckingAccount
SavingsAccount
Transaction

Access Classes:

BankDB

View Classes:

BankClientAccessUI
MainUI
AccountTransactionUI
SavingsAccountUI
CheckingAccountUI

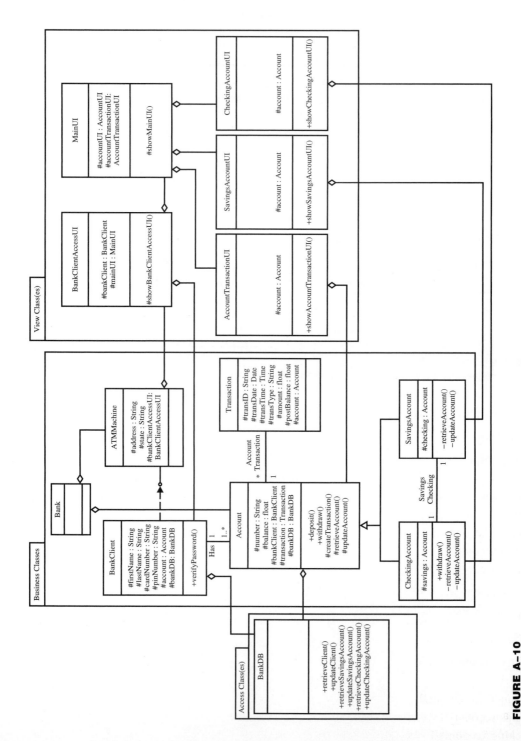

FIGURE A–10

UML class diagram of the ViaNet ATM system, showing the relationship of the view classes to the business and access classes.

A.6.2 Description of the Business Layer Classes

The business layer contains all the objects that represent the business and how they interact to accomplish the business processes. Business objects have no special knowledge of how they are being displayed. They are designed to be independent of any particular interface. Furthermore, business objects have no special knowledge of "where they come from." They need to know only who to talk to about being stored or retrieved.

The following subsections describe business classes in terms of purpose, superclass-subclass hierarchy, a-part-of structure, structure diagram, attributes, methods, and associations.

- ATMMachine class
  Purpose: ATMMachine class provides the interface or access to the bank system.
- Bank class
  Purpose: Bank clients belong to the Bank class. It is a repository of accounts and it processes the accounts' transactions.
- BankClient class
  Purpose: A client is an individual that has a checking account and possibly a savings account.
- Account class
  Purpose: An account class is a *formal* (or abstract) class; it defines the common behaviors that can be inherited by more specific classes such as CheckingAccount or SavingsAccount.
- CheckingAccount class
  Purpose: This class models a client's checking account and provides more specialized withdrawal services.
- SavingsAccount class
  Purpose: This class models a client's savings account.
- Transaction class
  Purpose: This class keeps track of transactions—time, date, type, amount, and balance.

A.6.2.1 Superclass(es)   The Account class is the superclass of the Checking account and Savings account classes.

A.6.2.2 Subclass(es)   The following classes are subclasses of the account class:

Checking account.
Savings account.

A.6.2.3 A-Part-of Structures and Aggregation   [This is not applicable for business classes.]

A.6.2.4 Association   The following classes are associated:

The bank client and account classes.
The account classes and transaction classes.

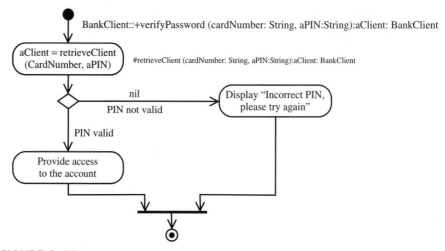

FIGURE A–11
Activity diagram for the BankClient class verifyPassword method.

A.6.2.5 Methods Figures A–11 through A–15 show activity diagrams for the preceding classes and their actions.

A.6.3 Description of the Access Layer Classes

The access layer contains objects that know how to reach the place where the data actually reside, whether in a relational database, mainframe, Internet, or file.

The following subsections describe access classes in terms of purpose, superclass-subclass hierarchy, a-part-of structure, structure diagram, attributes, methods, and associations.

FIGURE A–12
Activity diagram for the account class deposit method.

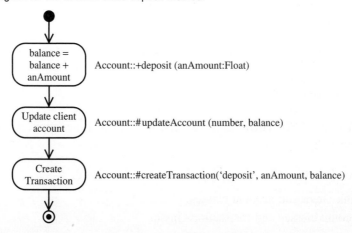

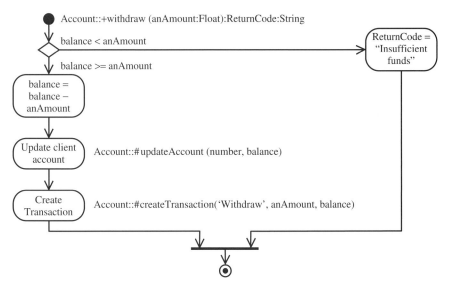

FIGURE A–13
Activity diagram for the Account class withdraw method.

FIGURE A–14
Activity diagram for the Account class createTransaction method.

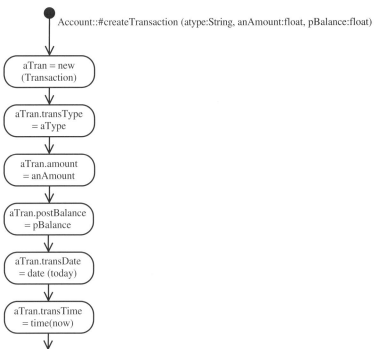

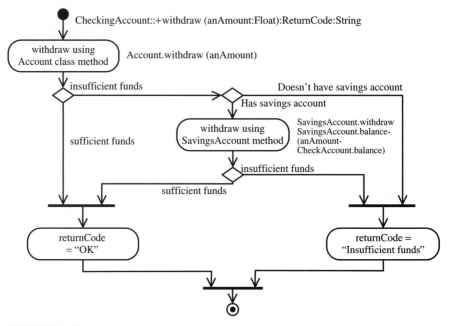

FIGURE A–15
Activity diagram for the CheckingAccount class withdraw method.

- BankDB Class
  Purpose: This is the only access class for the system. It performs the actual work of getting the information from the database or storing it on the database.

A.6.3.1 Superclass(es)   None.

A.6.3.2 Subclass(es)   None.

A.6.3.3 A-Part-of Structures and Aggregation   The BankDB class is a-part-of the Bank Client and Account classes.

A.6.3.4 Association   None.

A.6.3.5 Methods

Listing 1.
```
BankClient::+retrieveClient (aCardNumber, aPIN): BankClient
    aBankDB : BankDB
    aBankDB.retrieveClient (aCardNumber, aPIN)
```

Listing 2.
```
BankDB::+retrieveClient (aCardNumber, aPIN): BankClient
SELECT firstName, lastName
    FROM BANKCLIENT
        WHERE cardNumber = aCardnumber and pinNumber = aPin)
```

Listing 3.

```
BankDB::+updateClient (aClient: BankClient, aCardNumber: String)
UPDATE BANKCLIENT
    SET firstName = aClient.firstName
    SET lastName = aClient.lastName
    SET pinNumber = aClient.pinNumber
        WHERE cardNumber = aCardnumber)
```

Listing 4.

```
SavingsAccount::-retrieveAccount (): Account
bankDB.retrieveSavingsAccount (bankClient.cardNumber, number)
```

Listing 5.

```
BankDB::+retrieveSavingsAccount (aCardNumber: String, savingsNum-
ber: String): Account
SELECT sBalance, transID,
    FROM ACCOUNT
        WHERE cardNumber = aCardNumber and sNumber = savingsNumber)
```

Listing 6.

```
CheckingAccount::-retrieveAccount (): Account
bankDB.retrieveCheckingAccount (bankClient.cardNumber, number)
```

Listing 7.

```
BankDB::+retrieveCheckingAccount (aCardNumber: String, check-
ingNumber: String): Account
SELECT cBalance, transID,
    FROM ACCOUNT
        WHERE cardNumber = aCardNumber and cNumber = checkingNum-
        ber)
```

Listing 8.

```
SavingsAccount::-updateAccount (): Account
bankDB.updateSavingsAccount (bankClient.cardNumber, number, bal-
ance)
```

Listing 9.

```
BankDB::+updateSavingsAccount (aCardPinNumber: String, aNumber:
String newBalance: float)
UPDATE ACCOUNT
    Set sBalance = newBalance
        WHERE cardNumber = aCardNumber and sNumber = aNumber)
```

Listing 10.

```
CheckingAccount::-updateAccount (): Account
bankDB.updateCheckingAccount (bankClient.cardNumber, number, bal-
ance)
```

Listing 11.

```
BankDB::+updateCheckingAccount (aCardPinNumber: String, aNumber:
String newBalance: float)
UPDATE ACCOUNT
    Set cBalance = newBalance
        WHERE cardNumber = aCardNumber and cNumber = aNumber)
```

A.6.4 Description of the User Interface (View Layer) Classes

The user interface layer objects translate an action by the user, such as clicking on a button or selecting from a menu, into an appropriate response. That response may be to open or close another interface or to send a message to the business layer to start some business process. Remember, the business logic does not exist here, just the knowledge of which message to send to which business object.

The following subsections describe interface classes in terms of purpose, superclass-subclass hierarchy, a-part-of structure, structure diagram, attributes, methods, and associations:

- *AccountTransactionUI view class.* This is the account transaction interface that displays the transaction history for both savings and checking accounts.
- *BankClientAccessUI class.* This class provides the access control and PIN code validation for a bank client.
- *WithdrawSavingsUI class.* This class provides the interface for withdrawal from savings accounts.
- *WithdrawCheckingUI class.* This class provides the interface for withdrawal from checking accounts.
- *CheckingAccountUI class.* This view class provides the interface for deposit to or withdrawal from checking accounts.
- *SavingsAccountUI class.* This view class provides the interface for deposit to or withdrawal from savings accounts.
- *MainUI class.* This view class provides the main control interface for the ViaNet bank system.

A.6.4.1 Superclass(es)   None.

A.6.4.2 Subclass(es)   None.

A.6.4.3 A-Part-of Structures and Aggregation   See Figure A–10.

A.6.4.4 Association   None.

A.6.4.5 Screen   Figures A–16 through A–19 show snapshots of the screens bank clients see in their interface with the ViaNet bank ATM system.

A.6.4.6 The Interface Behavior: Events and Actions   Figures A–20 through A–23 are activity diagrams detailing the systems actions when bank clients initiate various processes.

A.6.5 Packages
See Figure A–10.

A.7 TESTING

A.7.1 Test Cases

1. If a bank client inserts his or her card, the system will respond by requesting the password (PIN number).
2. If the password is incorrect the system must display the bad password message, eject the card, and request the client to take the card.

FIGURE A–16
The BankClientAccessUI interface. The buttons are a little oversize to make it easier for touch screen users. The numeric keypad on the right is for data entry and is not a component of the BankClientAccessUI.

3. After the transaction is completed, the system should show the main screen.
4. If a bank client selects an incorrect command when entering the transaction, the system will respond immediately by indicating that some errors have been made. The system should allow the customer to correct the mistake and not force the client to make a withdrawal if his or her intention is to make a deposit.

FIGURE A–17
The MainUI interface.

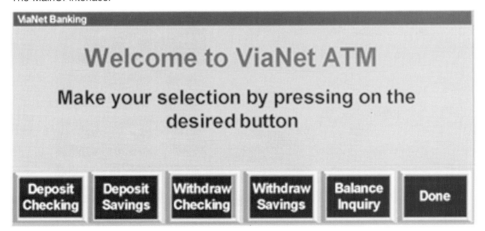

FIGURE A–18
The AccountTransactionUI interface.

FIGURE A–19
The CheckingAccountUI and SavingsAccountUI interface objects.

FIGURE A–19
Continued.

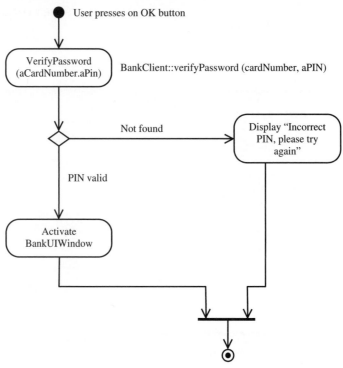

FIGURE A–20
An Activity diagram for the BankClientAccessUI.

FIGURE A–21
Activity diagram for the MainUI.

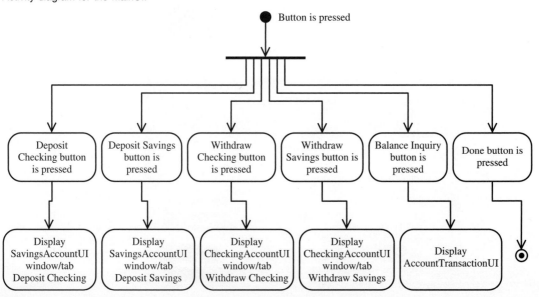

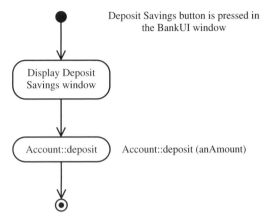

FIGURE A–22
Activity diagram for processing a deposit to a savings account.

FIGURE A–23
Activity diagram for displaying the account transaction.

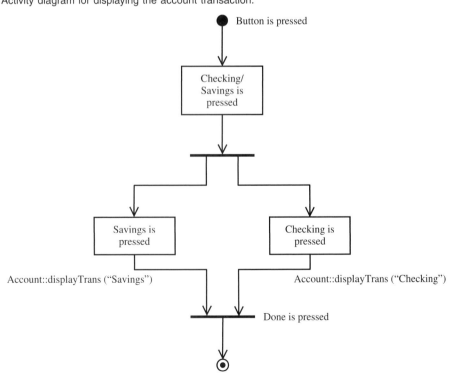

5. If an unauthorized customer attempts access to an account, the system should record the time, date, and if possible, the identity of the person (not based on the original use cases).
6. If the cash is low, the system will notify the bank for additional money (not based on the original use cases).
7. If an act of vandalism occurs, the system will sound an alarm and call security (not based on the original use cases).
8. If the customer enters a wrong PIN number, the system will give the customer three more chances to correct it; otherwise, the system will abort the operation.

A.7.1.1 Usability Testing Scenarios

Scenario 1. Deposit $1056.65 to a checking account.
Scenario 2. Withdraw $40 from a checking account.
Scenario 3. Deposit $200 to a savings account.
Scenario 4. Withdraw $55 from a savings account.
Scenario 5. Get a savings account transaction history.
Scenario 6. Get a checking account transaction history.

FIGURE A–24
A form for the ViaNet bank ATM Kiosk user satisfaction.

A.7.1.2 User Satisfaction Testing   The following attributes have been selected for measuring user satisfaction (see Figure A–24).

- Easy to operate.
- Buttons are the right size and located easily.
- Efficient to use.
- Fun to use.
- Visually pleasing.
- Provides easy recovery from errors.

REFERENCES

1. Bell, Paula; and Evans, Charlotte. *Mastering Documentation*. New York: John Wiley and Sons, 1989.

Introduction to Graphical User Interface

B.1 GRAPHICAL OPERATING SYSTEM

A graphical user interface (GUI) consists of the windows or dialog boxes and GUI controls, with which users interact, as well as the objects needed to manage or control the interfaces. In an event-driven environment like Windows, an application performs processing in response to an event. For example, selecting from a menu, clicking on the OK button with mouse pointer, and clicking on or uncovering a window are events that can trigger a response from the application, whether it is to resize the window, update a record, or display a dialog box. Furthermore, in an event-driven application, you simply assign event-handling procedures to events; then the procedures execute whenever the event takes place. The procedure should be truly generic and not depend on lots of assumptions about the values of memory variables.

B.2 HOW WINDOWS WORKS

Windows is an event-driven system, meaning that it responds to events from the user, like mouse movements, clicks, and menu selections, or from other sources, like other programs. Windows must interpret these events into messages called *Windows messages*. These messages are sent to the appropriate window of the application that is running.

One of the biggest differences between graphical operating systems and applications (such as Windows and Windows-based applications) and command-based or character-based (such as DOS or DOS-based applications) operating systems and applications is the way they receive user input. In a DOS environment, a program reads from the keyboard by making an explicit call to a function. The function typically waits until the user presses a key before returning a character code to the program. In contrast, in the Windows environment, Windows receives all input from the keyboard and mouse, then places the input in the appropriate application's

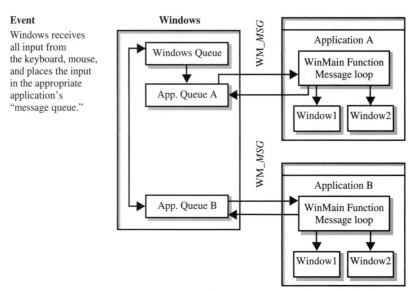

FIGURE B–1

When the application is ready to retrieve input, it simply reads the next input message from its message queue. When a user presses and releases a mouse button, Windows dispatches the mouse messages to the application queue. Next, the application has the responsibility to process these messages.

"message queue." When the application is ready to retrieve input, it simply reads the input message from its message queue. For example, when you press and release a mouse button, Windows dispatches the mouse messages to the application's message queue. Next, the application has the responsibility to process these messages. Applications, therefore, must be programmed to respond to Windows messages and alter the Windows system as a result, such as by displaying a customer signature bitmap graphic or dialog box. An application controls the Windows session by calling Windows functions. Therefore, a two-way communication travels between applications and Windows. Windows sends a Windows message to the application, and the application calls Window functions (see Figure B–1).

For example, assume you have created a dialog box with one button, which closes the dialog box when a user clicks on it. Windows then sends a Windows message to the application telling it that the button is clicked. After all, Windows owns the dialog box. The application knows to respond to the *Click On* message.

This process continues throughout the operation of a program. However, the issue is complicated by the possibility that many applications may run at the same time. Therefore, Windows messages must be funneled to the correct applications, and each application may control only its own portion of the screen. Normally, this would hopelessly complicate the program

However, most new object-oriented development tools for Windows, such as Visual Basic, PowerBuilder, or Visual C++, and many CASE tools contain classes that greatly simplify the process. This is mainly because Windows messages sent by Windows to, say, a PowerBuilder's application are received directly by the appropriate PowerBuilder's objects. For example, if the user clicks on a button, the Power-Builder button object gets a message that it has been clicked. These objects know how to handle many Windows events, which greatly simplifies application developments.

B.3 EVENT-DRIVEN USER INTERFACE DESIGN

A major source of confusion for programmers who are new to Windows programming is the event-driven design. Traditionally, programs were written in a top-down, procedural style. Quite often, execution of the program was determined in the highest level "main" procedure, where step by step, as subroutine calls were being made, the programmer was able to follow through the code.

The event-driven approach is fundamentally different. An event-driven system factors out the user interface, such as the keyboard or mouse. The system then sends messages to the program, telling it what "events" have occurred. For example, the user may have selected a particular menu item or typed in some text. The program therefore has its execution path determined by the way it interacts with the system. In an event-driven system, it no longer is easy to see which path a program will take. The program, in essence, becomes a program with no program-defined "main" procedure. In the event-driven environment, not all events require a response. In fact, a typical Windows application responds to only a fraction of events that take place in the application. For example, if you do not want a Windows application to respond to a right mouse click, you simply can have the application ignore the event when it takes place. No special action is required to ignore an event. You simply associate no method to that event. The main advantages of an event-driven system are the modularity of its design and the ability to easily develop the user interface apart from the internal workings of the program.

B.4 GRAPHICAL USER INTERFACE OBJECTS

A Windows application consists of graphical objects and the instructions that give them functionality. A GUI object is a small window that has very simple input or output functions. For example, an "edit object" is a simple window that lets the user enter and edit text. Some of the GUI objects include

- *Menus*. Menus are the principal means of user input in a Windows application. A menu is a list of commands that users can view and choose from.
- *Dialog boxes*. A dialog box is a temporary window displayed to let the user supply more information for a command. A dialog box contains one or more GUI objects.
- *Icons*. Icons are small bitmap graphics, generally 32×32 or 16×32 pixels in size, used to represent minimized windows. Icons can represent an individual application or groups of applications.
- *Cursor*. A cursor is a visual cue or small bitmap graphic, 32×32 pixels in size, that represents to users the current position of the mouse on the screen. Windows programs use customized cursors to show what type of task the user currently is performing.
- *Bitmap*. A bitmap is a binary representation of a graphic image in a program. Windows itself uses lots of bitmap graphics; for example, the images representing

various controls on a typical window, such as scroll bar arrows. The control menu and the minimize symbols also are bitmap graphics. Each bit, or group of bits, in the bitmap represents one pixel of the image.

- *Strings*. Strings contain text, such as descriptions, prompts, and error messages, that is displayed as a part of the Windows program. Because these text strings are Windows resources separate from the program, you can edit or translate messages displayed by a program to another language without having to make any changes to the program's source code.
- *Accelerators*. Accelerators are keyboard combinations (or hot keys) that a user presses to perform a task in an application. For example, a Windows program can include the accelerator Ctrl + V, which the user presses to paste text or images from the clipboard into a file the program has open.
- *Fonts*. Windows programs use fonts to define the typeface, size, and style of text. For example, a particular character that a program can display on screen or print on a printer might be 10-point Times Roman bold. In this case, the typeface is Times Roman, the size is 10 points, and the style is bold.

The following sections describe edit boxes, check boxes, combo boxes, list boxes, push buttons, scroll bars, spin boxes, and text objects in more detail.

B.4.1 Edit Boxes

Edit boxes (or entry fields) are rectangular areas used to enter or modify a single field. They are most useful when used for entering data during program operation. For example, multiple edit controls could be used to collect information on a data entry screen. Figure B–2 shows an example of an edit box.

FIGURE B–2
An example of the Edit box.

B.4.2 Push Buttons

A task is performed when the push button is selected or clicked on. Because they perform a task, push buttons are commonly referred to as *command buttons*.

Typically a window that uses push buttons designates one button in the window as the default push button. Default push buttons behave the same as push buttons, except that the default push button is activated if you press Enter; thus, the default push button indicates the window's default action. A default push button is displayed with a bold border to distinguish it from a standard push button (see Figure B–3).

B.4.3 Check Boxes

Check boxes generally are used to present a two-state option; basically, they let you enable or disable an option. A check box is a small square frame; an X in the frame indicates the option is enabled and the absence of the X indicates it is disabled. When multiple check boxes are displayed together, each is independent of the others. Check boxes might be used to present a set of fonts, for example, that can be loaded into an application. You check each font you want to load; those you do not check will not be loaded (see Figure B–4).

B.4.4 Radio Buttons

A radio button is a small round frame; when selected, a dot appears within the button. Multiple buttons are used to present mutually exclusive options, like selecting a radio station on older car radios. Typically multiple radio buttons are defined as a logical group, permitting only one to be selected. For example, radio buttons might be used to let you select a font for a character; although several fonts might be available, only one could be selected (see Figure B–5).

FIGURE B–3
An example of the default button.

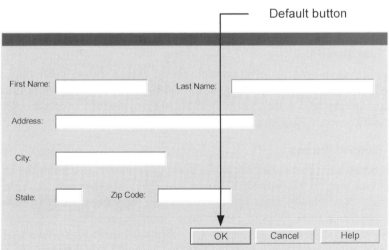

FIGURE B–4
An example of the use of the check box.

B.4.5 List Boxes

You can activate a list box, scroll through the list, then click or double-click on an item. When any of these events occurs, the list box receives an event notification. For example, say, you want to display file names so that the user can select one from the list to open (see Figure B–6).

B.4.6 Combo Boxes

Combo boxes are a particular type of list box. A combo box combines the features of a list box with an entry field. A combo box lets you select a value from a list by entering characters in a text box or by selecting the value directly from the list.

You can create three types of combo boxes: simple drop-down box, drop-down combo box, and drop-down list. Figure B–7 illustrates these three styles. A *simple combo box* appears with a text box and drop-down list. This is the most appropriate

Radio buttons →

FIGURE B–5
An example of radio buttons.

box for a list with a limited number of items. A *drop-down combo box* appears with a text box only. To display the drop-down list, you have to click on the arrow button. These types of combo boxes are most appropriate for forms with many items in a limited amount of space. A *drop-down list* is similar to the drop-down combo box, except you are restricted to items on the list.

FIGURE B–6
An example of list boxes.

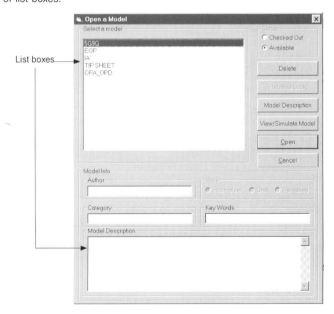

List boxes →

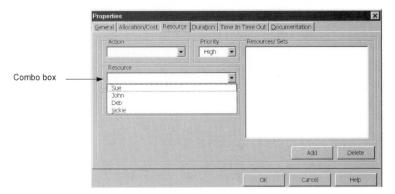

FIGURE B–7
An example of a combo box.

B.4.7 Spin Boxes

Spin box control allows you to enter values by either typing them in the text box or by increasing or decreasing the current value using the up and down arrow buttons (see Figure B–8).

B.4.8 Scroll Bars and Slider Buttons

Scroll bars (vertical and horizontal) are the primary mechanism for changing the view in an application window, a list box, or a combo box. However, you can use a scroll bar to increase or decrease a value by moving a slider button. Unlike spin boxes, scroll bars do not accept keyboard input. Instead, to increase or decrease the value, you simply drag the slider button. As you move the slider button, the value continually is updated to reflect the position of the button. For example, a scroll bar that varies a numeric value between 1 and 20 sets the value to 10 when the slider button is at the center of the scroll bar (see Figure B–9).

B.4.9 Text

Text objects most commonly are used as a prompt, heading, label, or reminder. Since text objects are read-only, they do not accept keyboard input and they cannot be linked to data. For example, a text object can prompt the user to enter values in an entry field or give brief instructions on using a scroll bar.

FIGURE B–8
An example of a spin box, where you can enter values by either typing them in the text box or by increasing or decreasing the current value using the up and down arrow buttons.

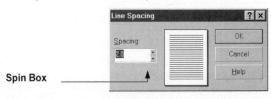

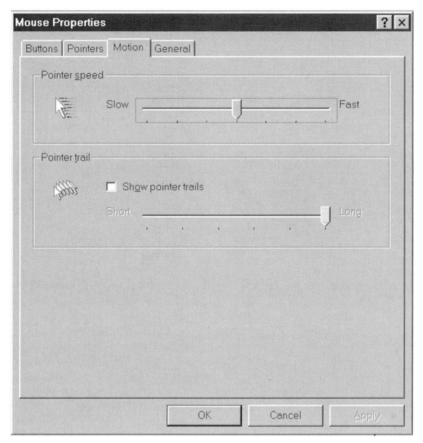

FIGURE B–9
An example of slider buttons.

Glossary

abort   Cancel a transaction because all changes to a database cannot be made successfully.

abstract (or *formal*) **classes**   Classes that have no instances but define the common behaviors that can be inherited by more specific classes.

abstract use case   One that has no initiating actors but is used by other use cases.

activity diagram   A variation or special case of a state machine in which the states are activities representing the performance of operations and the transitions are triggered by the completion of the operations.

actors   External factors that interact with the system.

adjective class   An adjective can suggest a different kind of class, different use of the same class, or it could be a completely irrelevant class.

aggregation   The ability of an attribute to be an object itself. See also *a-part-of*.

algorithm-centric methodology   Development of an algorithm that can accomplish a specified task, then building data structures for that algorithm to use.

alpha testing   Testing done by in-house testers, such as programmers, software engineers, and internal users.

analysis prototype   An aid for exploring the problem domain, used for informing the user and demonstrating the proof of a concept.

antisymmetry   A property of a-part-of relation where, if *A* is part of *B*, then *B* is not part of *A*.

a-part-of   Also called *aggregation*, this represents the situation where a class consists of several component classes. A-part-of is a special case of association.

application window   Container of application objects or icons. In other words, it contains an entire application with which users can interact.

assembly   An a-part-of association that represents a physical whole constructed from physical parts.

association class   An association that also has class properties.

atomic type of objects   Simple objects such as integers, characters, and the like.

atomicity   Requires that—unless all operations of a transaction are completed—the transaction is aborted.

attribute class   Objects used only as values and so must be defined or restated as attributes and not as a class.

attributes (or *properties*)   These represent the state of an object.

axiom   A fundamental truth that always is observed to be valid and for which there is no counterexample or exception.

base class   See *subclass*.

beta testing   A popular, inexpensive, and effective way to test software on a select group of actual users, who perform tests on the software as they would use it in their normal environment.

black box testing   Testing by trying various inputs and examining the resulting output without knowing how the conversion is implemented.

bottom-up testing   Starting with the details of the system and proceeding to higher levels by a progressive aggregation of details until they collectively fit the requirements for the system.

branch testing coverage   Performing enough tests to ensure that every branch alternative has been executed at least once under some test.

cardinality   The (often nonspecific) number of instances of one class that may relate to a single instance of an associated class.

class   A mechanism used to distinguish one type of object from another.

class diagram   The main static structure analysis diagram for the system, it represents the class structure of a system including the relationships between classes and the inheritance structure.

class hierarchy   An ordering of properties and behaviors used as the basis for making distinctions between classes and subclasses.

class protocol   A generic grouping that defines the properties and methods (procedures) of the objects within it.

class responsibilities and collaboration (CRC)   A technique for identifying classes' responsibilities and, therefore, their attributes and methods.

classification   The process of checking to see if an object belongs to a category or a class.

client-server association   See *consumer-producer relationship*.

cohesion   Interaction within a single object software component; it reflects "single-purposeness" of an object.

collaboration   Interactions between objects.

collaboration diagram   Represents a collaboration, which is a set of objects related in a particular context, and interaction, which is a set of messages exchanged among the objects within collaboration to achieve a desired outcome.

collaborator   Cooperative object with which an object works.

collection-member   An a-part-of association that represents a conceptual whole that encompasses but is not constructed from its parts, which may be conceptual or physical.

commercial off-the-shelf software (COTS)   Software that is already written and commercially available to implement a part of the required software functionality.

commit   Allow a transaction because all changes to a database can be made successfully.

common class patterns   A classification approach based on a knowledge base of the common classes or patterns.

common object request broker architecture (CORBA)   A standard proposed as a means to integrate distributed, heterogeneous business applications and data.

component-based development   An industrialized approach to software development.

component diagram   Models the physical components (such as source code, executable program, user interface) in a design.

concepts class   Principles or ideas; not tangible things but things used to organize or keep track of business activities or communications.

concrete use case   A use case that interacts with actor(s).

configuration control system   A way of tracking the changes to the code. At a minimum, every time the code changes, a record should be kept that tracks which module has been changed, who changed it, and when it was altered, with a comment about why the change was made.

consumer-producer relationship (or *client-server association*, *use relationship*)   One-way interaction in which one object requests the service of another object. The object that makes the request is the consumer, and the other object that receives the request and provides the service is the producer.

container   An a-part-of association that represents a physical whole that encompasses but is not constructed from its parts, which also are physical.

corollary   A proposition that follows from an axiom or another proposition that has been proven. A corollary is shown to be valid or not valid in the same manner as a theorem.

correctness   Measures the consistency of the product requirements with respect to the design specification.

correspondence   Measures how well the delivered system matches the needs of the operational environment, as described in the original requirements statement.

coupling   A measure of the strength of association established by a connection from one object or software component to another.

data-centric methodology   Determining how to structure the data, then building the algorithm around that structure.

data entry window   Provides access to data that users can retrieve, display, and change in the application.

data manipulation language (DML)   The language that allows users to access and manipulate (such as create, save, or destroy) data organization.

database definition language (DDL)   The language used to describe the structure of and relationships between objects stored in a database.

database management system (DBMS)   A set of programs that enables the creation and maintenance of a collection of related data.

debugging   The process of determining where something went wrong and correcting the code to eliminate errors or bugs that cause unexpected results.

deployment diagram   Shows the configuration of run-time processing elements and the software components, processes, and objects that live in them.

derived class   See *subclass*.

design pattern   A device that allows systems to share knowledge about their design by describing commonly recurring structures of communicating components that solve a general design problem within a particular context.

directed actions (derived) **association**   An association that can be defined in terms of other associations.

distributed component object model (DCOM)   Microsoft's alternative to OMG's CORBA, an Internet and component strategy where ActiveX (formerly known as object linking and embedding, or OLE) plays the role of the DCOM object.

distributed database   Different portions of the database reside on different nodes (computers) and disk drives in the network. Usually, each portion of the database is managed by a server, a process responsible for controlling access and retrieval of data from the database portion.

distributed object computing (DOC)   Utilizes reusable software components that can be distributed across the network and can be accessed by users across the network. These objects can be assembled into distributed applications.

domain prototype   An aid for the incremental development of the ultimate software solution.

dynamic binding   The process of determining at run time which function to invoke.

dynamic inheritance   The ability of objects to change and evolve over time.

dynamic model   Represents a system's procedures or behaviors that, taken together, reflect its behavior over time.

encapsulation   Containment of the object inside a "capsule." The user cannot see inside the capsule but can use the object by calling the program part of it.

encapsulation leakage   Occurs when details about a class's internal implementation are disclosed through the interface.

error-based testing   Testing involves searching a given class's method for particular clues of interest, then describing how these clues should be tested.

events class   Points in time that must be recorded.

extends association   Used when one use case is similar to another use case but does a bit more or is more specialized; in essence, it is like a subclass.

foreign key   A primary key of one relational table that is embedded in another table.

formal classes   See *abstract classes*.

forward engineering   Creating a relational schema from an existing object model.

framework   A reusable design expressed as a set of abstract classes and the way their instances collaborate.

graphical user interface (GUI)   User interface using icons to represent objects, a pointing device to select operations, and graphical imagery to represent relationships.

homogenization   See *neutralization*.

horizontal prototype   A simulation of the interface (that is, it has the entire user interface that will be in the full-featured system) but contains no functionality, used to provide a good, overall feel of the system.

implementation diagram   Shows the implementation phase of a system's development, such as the source code and run-time implementation structures.

inheritance   The property of object-oriented systems that allows use of the commonality of objects when constructing new classes. In inheritance, one class is the parent (or ancestor) of another derived (descendant) class.

instance   Each object is an instance of a class.

instance variable   An object's data.

interaction diagram   Uses collaboration and sequence diagrams to capture the action of a single use case.

irrelevant class   Identified classes that either have no purpose or will be unnecessary .

language (syntax) **errors**   These result from incorrectly constructed code, such as an incorrectly typed keyword or omitted punctuation.

layered architecture   An approach to software development that allows us to separate business objects that represent tangible elements of the business from how they are represented to the user through an interface or physically stored in a database. The layered approach consists of the view or user interface, business, and access layers.

lifeline   Represents the existence of an object at a particular time.

message   Nonspecific function calls for objects to perform operations; in other words, to perform an operation in an object-oriented environment, a message is sent to an object.

meta-class   A class of classes.

meta-data   See *schema*.

meta-model   A model of modeling elements; a language for specifying a model, in this case an object model.

metaphor (analogy)   Relating two otherwise unrelated things by using one to denote the other (such as a question mark to label a Help button).

method   That which implements the behavior of an object.

mode   A state that excludes general interaction or otherwise limits the user to specific interactions.

model   An abstract representation of a system constructed to understand the system prior to building or modifying it.

model dependency   Represents a situation in which a change to the target element may require a change to the source element in the dependency, thus indicating the relationship between two or more model elements.

multidatabase system (MDBS)   A database system that resides unobtrusively on top of, say, existing relational and object databases and file systems (called *local database systems*) and presents a single database illusion to its users.

multiple inheritance   The inheritance, in some object-oriented systems, that permits a class to inherit its attributes and methods from more than one superclass.

multiplicity   Specifies the range of allowable associated classes.

n-ary association   An association among more than two classes.

neutralization   The process of consolidating the local schemata and resolving the schematic differences and conflicts among them.

note   A graphic symbol containing textual information; it also could contain embedded images.

object   A combination of "data" and "logic"; the representation of some real-world entity.

object constraint language (OCL)   A specification language that uses simple logic for specifying properties of a system.

object identifier (OID)   In an object system, object identity often is implemented as some kind of object identifier or *unique identifier (UID)*.

Object Management Group (OMG)   An organization of over 500 companies that, since 1989, has been specifying the architecture for an open software bus on which object components written by different vendors can communicate across various networks and operating systems.

object-oriented analysis   Concerns determining the system requirements and identifying classes and their relationship to other objects in a given application.

object-oriented database management system (OODBMS)   A marriage of object-oriented programming and database technology.

object-oriented design (OOD)   The goal of object-oriented design is to design the classes identified during the analysis phase and the user interface.

object-oriented programming   A method of writing programs that allows the base concepts of the language to be extended to include ideas and terms closer to those of its applications.

object-oriented user interface (OOUI).   A user interface in which users see and manipulate object representations of their information and need not be aware of the computer programs and underlying technology.

object persistence   The ability of an object to endure beyond application session boundaries, by storing the object in a file or a database.

object references   These directly denote the object to which they refer, often by using the OID of the object as the reference.

object request broker (ORB)   Middleware that implements a communication channel through which applications can access object interfaces and request data and services.

OR association   Indicates a situation in which only one of several potential associations may be initiated at one time for any single object.

organization class   The organizational units to which people belong. For example, an accounting department might be considered a potential class.

package   A group of model elements, used to designate not only logical and physical groupings but also use-case groups.

pattern   Represents the "essential structure and insight of a successful family of proven solutions to a recurring problem that arises within a certain context and system of forces."

pattern mining   The process of looking for patterns to document.

pattern thumbnail   An abstract, overview, or short summary of a pattern.

path testing   Makes certain that each path in a object's method is executed at least once during testing.

people (person) **class**   Represents the roles people play and the people who perform some function. People can be divided into two types: those representing the users of the system, such as an operator or a clerk who interacts with systems, and those who do not use the system but about whom information is kept by the system.

per-class protection   In its most common (e.g., Ada, C++, Eiffel) form, this allows class methods to access any object of that class and not just the receiver.

per-object protection   Allows methods to access only the receiver.

persistence   The ability of some objects to outlive the programs that created them.

polymorphism   The ability of the same operation to behave differently on different classes.

primary key   A combination of one or more attributes whose value unambiguously locates each row in a relational table.

private protocol (visibility)   Accessibility only to operations of the class itself; this includes methods the class uses only internally.

properties   See *attributes*.

protected protocol (visibility)   Accessibility only to subclasses and operations of the class.

protocol   Interface to the class operations and their visibility; messages that a class understands.

proto-pattern   A pattern that has not yet been proven to recur.

public protocol (visibility)   Accessibility to all classes; it defines the stated behavior of the class.

qualifier   An association attribute.

rapid application development (RAD)   A set of tools and techniques that can be used to build an application faster than typically possible with traditional methods.

redundant class   If more than one class is being used to describe the same idea, select the one that is the most meaningful in the context of the system and discard the other (redundant) class(es).

referential integrity   Making sure that a dependent table's foreign key contains a value that refers to an existing valid tuple in another relation.

regression testing   All passed tests are repeated with the revised program.

reverse engineering   Creating an object model from an existing relational database layout (schema).

role   A set of responsibilities for an actor in a software system. An actor may play several roles or the same role may be played by several actors.

scenario-based (usage-based) **testing**   Testing that concentrates on what the user does, not what the product does.

schema (or meta-data)   A complete definition of the data formats, such as the data structures, types, and constraints.

sequence diagram   An easy and intuitive way of describing the behaviors of a system by viewing the interaction between the system and its environment.

software components   Functional units of a program, building blocks offering a collection of reusable services.

software development life cycle (SDLC)   Consists of three macro processes: analysis, design, and implementation.

software development methodology   A series of processes that, if followed, can lead to development of an application.

software development process   The transformation of users' needs through the application domain to a software solution that satisfies those needs.

spring-loaded mode   A mode that requires users to continually take some action to remain in that mode.

statechart diagram   Shows the sequence of states that an object goes through during its life in response to outside stimuli and messages.

statement testing coverage   Ensuring every statement in the object's method is executed at least once.

static binding   The determination at compile time of which process to invoke.

static model   Provides a snapshot of a system's parameters at rest or at a specific point in time.

stereotype   A built-in extensibility mechanism of the UML, allowing the user, during modeling, to define a subclass of existing modeling elements with the same form but a different intent.

stored procedure   A module of precompiled SQL code maintained within the database that executes on the server to enforce rules the business has set about the data.

structured query language (SQL)   The standard DML for relational and object-oriented DBMSs, SQL is used widely for its query capabilities.

subclass (or *base class, derived class, descendant class*)   Groupings of objects that inherit all of the properties and methods (procedures) defined in their *superclass.*

swimlane   Represents responsibility for part of the overall activity and may be implemented by one or more objects.

tangible things and device class   Physical objects or groups of objects that are tangible and devices with which the application interacts.

ternary association   An association among more than two classes. Ternary associations can complicate the representation.

test plan   A plan developed to detect and identify potential problems before delivering the software to its users.

theorem   A proposition that may not be self-evident but can be proven from accepted axioms. It therefore is equivalent to a law or principle.

top-down testing   Assumes that the main logic or object interactions and system messages of the application need more testing than an individual object's methods or supporting logic. A top-down strategy can detect the serious design flaws early in the implementation.

transaction   A unit of change in which many individual modifications are aggregated into a single modification that occurs in its entirety or not at all.

transitivity   A property of a-part-of relationship where if *A* is part of *B* and *B* is part of *C*, then *A* is part of *C*.

tuples   The rows of each table in the relational database, representing the individual data objects being stored.

two-three rule   To identify actors, start with naming at least two, preferably three, people who could serve as the actor in the system.

unified approach (UA)   A methodology for software development, based on methodologies by Booch, Rumbaugh, Jacobson, and others, that tries to combine the best practices, processes, and guidelines along with the Object Management Group's unified modeling language for a better understanding of object-oriented concepts and system development.

unified modeling language (UML)   A set of notations and conventions and diagrams to describe and model an application.

unique identifier (UID)   See *object identifier (OID)*.

usability testing   Measures the ease of use as well as the comfort and satisfaction users have with the system.

usage-based testing   See *scenario-based testing*.

use case   Scenarios of typical interactions between a user and a computer system that captures users' goals and needs.

use-case diagram   A graph of actors, a set of use cases enclosed by a system boundary, communication (participation) associations between the actors and the use cases, and generalization among the use cases.

use-case model   A representation of the interaction between users and a system. It captures the goal of the users and the responsibility of the system to its users.

use relationship   See *consumer-producer relationship*.

user–centered interface   One that replicates the user's view of doing things by providing the outcome users expect for any action.

user satisfaction testing   The process of quantifying the usability test with some measurable attributes of the test, such as functionality, cost, or ease of use.

uses association   Extracting common sequences into a new, shared use case.

validation   The task of predicting correspondence: "Am I building the right product?" True correspondence cannot be determined until the system is in place.

verification   The task of determining correctness: "Am I building the product right?"

vertical prototype   A subset of the system features with complete functionality, used to test the few implemented functions in great depth.

waterfall approach   An approach to software development that starts with deciding what to do and how to do it, then doing it, testing, and using the application.

white box testing   Assumes that the specific logic is important and must be tested to guarantee the system's proper functioning.

Name Index

Subject Index